D1106197

BENJAMIN FRANKLIN BUTLER

CIVIL WAR AMERICA

Peter S. Carmichael, Caroline E. Janney,
and Aaron Sheehan-Dean, editors

This landmark series interprets broadly the history and culture of the Civil War era through the long nineteenth century and beyond. Drawing on diverse approaches and methods, the series publishes historical works that explore all aspects of the war, biographies of leading commanders, and tactical and campaign studies, along with select editions of primary sources. Together, these books shed new light on an era that remains central to our understanding of American and world history.

BENJAMIN FRANKLIN BUTLER

A NOISY, FEARLESS LIFE

Elizabeth D. Leonard

THE UNIVERSITY OF NORTH CAROLINA PRESS

Chapel Hill

Manufactured in the United States of America
Designed by Kristina Kachele Design, llc
Set in Chaparral Pro with Publica Slab display
by Kristina Kachele Design, llc
The University of North Carolina Press has been a member
of the Green Press Initiative since 2003.
Jacket illustrations: (front) courtesy of Special Collections & Archives,
Colby College Libraries, Waterville, Maine; (back) courtesy of Prints and
Photographs Division, Library of Congress, Washington, D.C.

Library of Congress Cataloging-in-Publication Data
Names: Leonard, Elizabeth D., author.
Title: Benjamin Franklin Butler : a noisy, fearless life / Elizabeth D. Leonard.
Other titles: Civil War America (Series)
Description: Chapel Hill : The University of North Carolina Press, [2022] |
Series: Civil War America | Includes bibliographical references and index.
Identifiers: LCCN 2021049407 | ISBN 9781469668048 (cloth) |
ISBN 9781469668055 (ebook)
Subjects: LCSH: Butler, Benjamin F. (Benjamin Franklin), 1818–1893. |
Generals—United States—Biography. | Statesmen—
United States—Biography. | United States—History—
Civil War, 1861–1865—Biography. | LCGFT: Biographies.
Classification: LCC E467.1.B87 L46 2022 |
DDC 355.0092 [B]—dc23/eng/20211020
LC record available at https://lccn.loc.gov/2021049407

To the memory of my esteemed predecessor as
Colby College's Civil War historian,
Harold B. Raymond (1919–2008).
Hal's decency, kindness, generosity, scholarly excellence,
and brilliance as a teacher shaped and enriched the
department of history where I had the privilege of
spending the bulk of my professional career.
Thank you, Hal, for helping us all be better historians,
both inside the classroom and out,
and for the guidance you offered in your wise
and judicious assessment of the college's
most famous Civil War alumnus,
Benjamin Franklin Butler.
You led the way.

Contents

Illustrations

He was a noisy and fearless advocate of radical causes including the rights of organized labor, woman suffrage, greenback currency, and public ownership of railroads. In the Civil War he was an enthusiastic supporter of arming Blacks and in Reconstruction he fought for their civil rights long after other politicians had given up. He was usually the champion of the underprivileged and managed to offend almost every established interest in nineteenth-century America.
—HISTORIAN HAROLD B. RAYMOND, "THE 'BEAST'
AT THE TOP OF THE STAIRS," APRIL 1977

Preface

MEMORY

Benjamin Franklin
Butler
Jurist Soldier Statesman
Patriot
His talents were devoted to
the service of his country
and the advancement of his
fellow men

So begins the epitaph on the massive headstone that marks Benjamin Franklin Butler's grave at the Hildreth Family Cemetery in Lowell, Massachusetts. Next come details about his birth, marriage, and death, and then these words: "The true touchstone of civil liberty is not that all men are equal but that every man has the right to be the equal of every other man if he can."[1]

It is not known who devised this weighty affirmation, but it seems likely that Butler crafted it himself. Certainly he would have endorsed the statement as a clear expression of what became the guiding principle of his life and work, namely, that regardless of class or race or other defining characteristic at birth, all "men" (and today Butler surely would have included "and women") deserve a level playing field on which to strive for success. The epitaph as a whole also encapsulates Butler's commitment to the idea that performing one's civic duty means helping ensure equal opportunity for all, as he had tried to do . . . unless, of course (a point left implicit), those seeking help were—like Confederates during the Civil War—guilty of trying to destroy the United States.

How accurately the sentiments expressed in this epitaph reflect the *reality* of Butler's life, work, and purpose has long been a matter of debate. Even during his lifetime, Butler was a highly controversial figure "who made a very great impression on the public interest," and not always in a positive sense. Maine Republican James Blaine reportedly once described Butler as an "original" and "picturesque" individual with "a talent for turbulence." And in the century and more since his death in January 1893, the "memory" of what kind of person Butler really was, and what motivations truly underlay his actions as a lawyer, politician, and soldier—even as a husband and father—has taken various forms. In 1918, in response to the recent publication of his *Private and Official Correspondence*, one journalist observed wryly that the late general "has not had the best of reputations among us." No man of his era, wrote another reviewer, "has been more 'cussed' and discussed" than Butler, who, a third reviewer declared, had a "natural propensity to make the form and manner of his actions as offensive as possible." He was "a general without capacity, a man without character," sneered the industrialist, self-professed wartime copperhead, one-time president of the American Historical Association, and author of a multivolume history of the United States, James Ford Rhodes, during the Massachusetts state legislature's 1914 hearings regarding the possible erection of a statue to Butler in Boston. Such harsh depictions of Butler have been both abundant and persistent; enduring caricatures have attacked him as mercurial, arrogant, tyrannical, incompetent, duplicitous, and/or driven purely by greed and ego. Indeed, down to the present some of the nicknames that have dogged him most tenaciously are "Beast," "Damnedest Yankee," "Devil," "Spoons," and "Stormy Petrel."[2]

Among those who began the process of memorializing Butler was, perhaps not surprisingly, the man himself, whose massive and, it must be said, largely (but not exclusively) self-congratulatory 1,100-page-long *Autobiography and Personal Reminiscences* (colloquially known as *Butler's Book*) appeared in 1892. Butler's passing the following year yielded widely ranging assessments from those who knew (or claimed to have known) him in various settings. "Gen. Butler had a stormy career," one journalist wrote simply, upon learning of the former general's death. Another quoted one of Butler's former congressional colleagues as saying, colorfully, "He was like a volcano with the smoke just curling out of the top, but which might break forth in a seething torrent of fire and smoke at any moment." "He was a man of most contradictory qualities," remarked the Rev. Dr. William H. Thomas in the eulogy he gave at Lowell's St. Paul's Methodist Episcopal Church on the evening before Butler's public funeral. "To say that he was not always great nor great in everything is to say that he never attained what never has been attained." Rather, Thomas continued, Butler was full of "weaknesses and inconsistencies," a "man of like infirmities with other men," whose friends, even, would never assert that "in his headlong pursuit of success he was always scrupulous to use only such means as would be approved by the accepted standards of ethics." Indeed, Thomas added, Butler "would not claim so himself."[3] Butler's ego was certainly robust, but so was his sense of humor, and he often demonstrated a striking and, among major historical figures, refreshing capacity for candid and critical self-reflection.

Butler was and remains a controversial individual. At the time of his death, however, it bears noting how many observers offered a more appreciative picture of the man than simplistic nicknames like "Beast"—devised by opponents during the Civil War and perpetuated by Lost Cause apologists later—allow. "He was always arrayed against an army of enemies and was always supported by an army of friends," wrote one journalist. "He scorned sham and empty profession," Dr. Thomas told his gathered mourners; "as he found the cup of life so he openly drank it" and, for better or worse, "whatever he did he did it with his might," deploying "all his tremendous energies" and "his exhaustless resources." "His ready wit, his fearlessness, his picturesque personality, his large participation in all public affairs, his interest . . . in the under dog in every fight, and especially the charm and loyalty of his personal friendships gave him a hold that will last as long as he is remembered," said Butler's predecessor as governor of Massachusetts, John Davis Long. "His opinions were never disguised nor withheld," commented a New York newspaper. "He was no pretender and no hypocrite." Indeed, upon his death the *Boston Globe* observed an outpouring of profound grief among "people of every walk in life" who acknowledged Butler's pricklier qualities but loved and revered him just the same. These included people of high station and low, "the members of the legal profession, with whom he had often metaphorically crossed swords, politicians with whom he was seldom in agreement," his "old comrades in arms," as well as individuals who passed their lives "in the humbler walks of life."[4]

Significantly, African Americans were among those *most* eager to display their respect and appreciation for Butler—as well as their grief—both at the time of his demise and after. Evidence of this appears clearly in the visible bereavement of his valet and "bodyman" of more than fifteen years, Albert

West, the magnificent floral tribute Frederick Douglass, the great political activist and orator, sent for his funeral, and the participation of Charles Remond Douglass, Christian A. Fleetwood, and dozens of other US Colored Troops (USCT) veterans and other Black Americans in activities associated with Butler's death and burial. And there is more. "The news of the death of Gen. Butler has caused sadness among the colored people of this city," reported the *Boston Globe*, noting that Boston's Black citizens hoped to present a bronze bust of the deceased, "to be placed in one of the new public buildings" in Lowell, his longtime home, as a "token of gratitude" for the many ways Butler had supported the Black community and advanced Black Americans' rights of citizenship during and since the Civil War. At a special Lowell city council meeting on January 12, 1893, numerous comments echoed this reaction. A Mr. Donovan of Ward 8 praised Butler's "unflinching devotion to the rights of the poor and oppressed of every race, creed, and color." A Mr. Banks of Ward 9 commended Butler for being an advocate for Black Americans, insisting that "no man whom Massachusetts has given to the country is dearer to us," and that "to him we owe as much as to any other one man." A month after the funeral, the *Echo*—the student newspaper of Butler's alma mater in Maine, Colby College—reported that a "mass meeting" of Blacks in faraway Denver, Colorado, had taken place specifically in order to give participants "an opportunity of paying a tribute to the memory of the late Benjamin F. Butler" as a "far-sighted statesman, a brave soldier and a loyal citizen" who had done much more than most "for the negro during the storm and stress of the war period and in the after days of trial whenever they need[ed] a friend." These Black Coloradans pledged "to ever revere his memory as a true friend and benefactor," to "do what in us lies toward the perpetuation of his great deeds," and to "hand his name down to our posterity as the name of one who was the embodiment of all that was brave, true and noble, and as one of the most consistent champions of human liberty that the age has seen."[5]

REAPPRAISAL

Seven decades after Butler's death and a century after he commanded the Army of the James in Virginia, in September 1964 Colby College's *Library Quarterly* devoted a special issue entirely to the institution's most important and influential Civil War alumnus. The issue contained three articles, one each by Richard Cary, then the college's curator of rare books; Ernest C. Marriner, the college's official historian; and Harold B. Raymond, a distinguished Harvard-trained professor and my immediate predecessor as Colby's Civil War historian. Cary's and Marriner's articles focused on the Butler material housed in the college library's Archives and Special Collections Department and on the general's four years as a student at then–Waterville College, from which he graduated in 1838 and also received an honorary degree in 1853 and again in 1862. In contrast, Raymond's article—by far the longest of the three—offered a meticulous "reappraisal" of Butler as a soldier, politician, and citizen. Raymond argued that, "when stripped of their more dramatic overtones," Butler's "weaknesses" were, in fact, unremarkable, no more noteworthy than "those of the typical Northern politician, businessman, and amateur soldier." Moreover, he concluded, although Butler surely had "his full share" of human flaws, nevertheless his many accomplishments and successes "made a substantial contribution to the preservation of the Union and the advancement of social justice" in the United States.[6]

I agree.

In the introduction to his article, Raymond observed that each of Butler's three most recent biographers (at the time he was writing) had unfairly reinforced long-standing negative, Lost Cause–inflected depictions of the general as, among other things, an "incompetent" and corrupt military leader who not only "mistreated the citizens of New Orleans" but also "came home from the war with pockets stuffed full of graft and stolen spoons." "It is neither possible nor desirable," Raymond declared, "to retouch Butler's historical portrait so that the horns of dubious popular tradition" become "an equally improbable halo." He reminded readers, however, that while Butler was alive, "his friends and defenders included some of the most eminent men of the day," and went on to explain why.[7] As I suggested above, and will demonstrate below, one has only to consider the number, stature, and commentary of the many individuals affiliated with Butler's funeral to know that Raymond was right.

Nevertheless, even at his alma mater Butler's posthumous experience has hardly been smooth. These days, a life-sized, elaborately framed oil portrait of the general in uniform, seated in his tent in Virginia in 1864 and holding a military map marked "Dutch Gap," greets visitors as they enter Colby College's Schair-Swenson-Watson Alumni Center. In July 1889, three and a half years before his death, Butler returned to campus to speak at the commencement exercises, sailing up the Kennebec River on his nearly twenty-three-foot-long "yacht," as he called it—the *America*—and bringing the portrait with him as a gift.[8] "Nothing has happened for some time so pleasing to the majority of the students than the announcement that Hon. Benj. F. Butler will deliver the oration next Commencement," wrote one eager student in advance of the general's arrival, adding that anticipation of Butler's visit had aroused "a livelier enthusiasm on the part of students" than could be expected from "any other public man" of the day. An eyewitness later recalled that when he presented the portrait, Butler commented that "he was getting along in years, and as he had no fitting place where the portrait could be preserved, he wanted to feel that it was where it would be well taken care of."[9]

Given his high hopes for the portrait's future, Butler would surely be interested to know that the massive painting has been treated, like the man himself, with both esteem and disdain at different times since he delivered it to the campus. Painted in 1864 by John Antrobus, better known for his depiction of Ulysses S. Grant at Chattanooga, the Butler portrait hung for many years in the library of Colby's Memorial Hall on the original downtown Waterville campus. (Memorial Hall—completed in August 1869—was the first building on a US college campus dedicated to honoring the Civil War's Union dead.) Then, at some point during the 1930s or 1940s, the portrait moved with the campus up to Waterville's Mayflower Hill, subsequently spending several decades hanging conspicuously at the top of the north staircase in Miller Library before being taken down, supposedly just for restoration, in the early 2000s. Over the next several years the college received numerous inquiries about the absent painting, notably from descendants of the proud, extensive Butler family, many of whom attended Colby, too. During these years some at the college expressed concern about the high cost of restoration. Others suggested—as had been done periodically since the late 1970s—that it might be prudent to leave the portrait permanently in "storage," or place it somewhere less well-traveled (like the Chapel) to shield the institution from any negative public relations fallout, given the general's contentious reputation. To many on this side of the discussion, free speech martyr Elijah P. Lovejoy—a native of nearby Albion, Maine, who had graduated from the college a dozen years before Butler—was a more appealing Civil War–era alumnus to promote. After leaving Waterville, Lovejoy went on to become a journalist and was subsequently murdered in Illinois in 1837 for his refusal to cease publishing newspaper articles attacking slavery. Despite his virulent anti-Catholicism, Lovejoy was both a local and a campus hero with apparently none of Butler's famous reputational "baggage."

Perhaps it was best to let Lovejoy represent Civil War–era Colby and allow Butler's memory to fade?[10]

Eventually, however, in conjunction with the college's 2013 bicentennial celebrations, the decision was made to return the now professionally restored Butler portrait to public view in the lobby of the grand new alumni center. A new legend posted nearby explained why, down to the present, Butler's memory had remained inseparable from epithets like "Beast" and "Spoons." At the same time, however, the legend now offered important reasons why members of the campus community could and should be proud of this bold and influential alumnus. As Hal Raymond once wrote, "If Colby students would champion the underprivileged as fiercely and uphold the American Republic as faithfully as Benjamin Butler," they too "would deserve to be honored by the college."[11]

WHY THIS BOOK MATTERS

The chapters that follow draw on years of intense research into the abundant available sources—primary, secondary, archival, published and unpublished—in Colby's Archives and Special Collections, at the Library of Congress, and at numerous other fine repositories from Maine to Louisiana. Predictably, the sources' perspectives run the gamut, from those of Butler and his closest allies to those of his most virulent opponents; collectively they constitute a fascinating and complex historical record. Over the last several years, in my encounters with and analysis of these rich and diverse sources, I have worked diligently to bring the best critical skills from my professional training to bear, but I would be lying if I claimed that the results of my efforts were somehow pristinely "objective." I have been a careful, mindful historian throughout, but history is not objective; it cannot be, because historians are human. When I began this work, I mostly hoped to expand—judiciously and credibly—upon Hal Raymond's impressive reappraisal of the general, which I found both evenhanded and revelatory. Over the years, even as that original goal remained in place, I admit that I also came to feel considerable affection and admiration for Mr. Butler, which is perhaps the almost inevitable hazard—and blessing?—of being a biographer (though I can certainly think of historical figures I could never learn to love). So there is that. Moreover, in the time that I have been engaged in this work, many of the issues that concerned Butler most have resurfaced with a troubling (but not terribly surprising) vengeance. Most recently, I have been struck by how much we might benefit today from Butler's wisdom and leadership on issues like racial and economic justice, even as I am hardly blind to the ways he was limited by his circumstances, personality, and the horizon of his times.

In any case, what I offer here is a depiction of Butler as I read him: a brilliant, complicated, funny, annoying, loving, beloved, frequently brash individual who was unquestionably ambitious and could be opportunistic, but who also exhibited a rather stunning capacity for ideological growth and development and an impressive and genuine dedication to bringing about the kind of social and cultural transformation so many Americans still seek today. Butler's life span—1818–1893—coincided with the rise and much contested consolidation of American industrial capitalism and the beginning of the Gilded Age, the birth and advancement of the movement for women's rights as well as the expansion of the electorate to include landless White men, massive waves of both immigration and anti-immigrant nativism, the fierce political struggle over slavery that gave way to America's brutal Civil War, Emancipation, and the expansion, at least fleetingly, of African Americans' civil and political rights during Reconstruction, as well as the violent reemergence of white nationalism with all of its anti-egalitarian, antidemocratic consequences. As I often say these days, What a time to be alive! And what a time to have been in the position to actually make a meaningful difference, as Butler was, and as he tried to do, for so many years.

Indeed, in the numerous positions of power that Butler held over the course of his momentous lifetime—as a lawyer, wartime general, US congressman, governor—his own personal development, deepening political commitments, and keen intelligence, along with his special blend of arrogance, stubbornness, wit, and scorn for shallow praise and blind party loyalty, enabled him to support, and at times simply enact, policies that had very real consequences for individuals, communities, and the nation itself, not least in terms of its potential for progress toward racial and economic justice. In his recent book, *How to Be An Antiracist*, Ibram X. Kendi observes that "the history of racist ideas is the history of powerful policy-makers erecting racist policies out of self-interest, then producing racist ideas to defend and rationalize the inequitable effects of their policies, while everyday people consume those racist ideas, which in turn sparks ignorance and hate." Racism, writes Kendi, can only be eradicated if we first carefully identify the *policies* that underlie racial (and economic, and gender) inequality, and then eliminate them.[12] I believe Benjamin Butler would have enjoyed a good long conversation with Professor Kendi. I also believe that in his own way, in his own time, Butler had a visceral understanding of what Kendi seeks to teach us in ours. As I understand Butler, his personal experiences, sharp mind, and capacity for both change and tenacity, led him increasingly and in diverse settings to throw his weight behind policies he hoped would yield practical positive change in the direction of racial, economic, and even gender justice, including Black and women's suffrage and the rights of labor. In so doing, as nineteenth-century Black Americans, women's rights activists, and workers clearly recognized, he helped destabilize—alas, only temporarily—some of the ideological structures that opponents deployed to defend centuries-old discriminatory, elitist, and patriarchal arrangements. Depending on their own social positions, Butler's contemporaries found him confusing, inspiring, delightful, charming, infuriating, and/or downright dangerous. As for me, I would paraphrase Hal Raymond and argue that if all Americans "would champion the underprivileged as fiercely and uphold the American Republic as faithfully as Benjamin Butler," we too "would deserve to be honored" by history.

Acknowledgments

Many, many people helped make this book possible. The first to come to mind are my colleagues and friends in Colby College's Special Collections and Archives Department: Pat Burdick, Erin Rhodes, Maggie Libby, and Jim Merrick. Over the last several years we have spent hundreds of hours together as I steadily made my way through the college's wonderful (and little used) Butler collection and we puzzled through different questions about his life and work together. During these years, Pat, Erin, and I also designed and team-taught several individual classes on Butler—always both fun and illuminating!—during which we enjoyed introducing students to the man *and* to the whole process of critically engaging archival sources. As the manuscript reached its final stages, Maggie and Jim graciously provided invaluable help choosing and then preparing images for the book. Two fine student workers in Special Collections also deserve mention: Meghan Kelly and Makhieba Simon. I am grateful to all of them for their kindness, generosity, friendship, and abiding good humor.

There would be no book at all without the Library of Congress's excellent Manuscript Division staff, especially (but by no means only) Michelle Krowl, Bruce Kirby, Patrick Kerwin, and Edith Sandler. I have been making research visits to the Manuscripts Reading Room several times a year since I began working on my dissertation three decades ago, and I have never failed to come away refreshed by the work and uplifted by the blend of professionalism, respectful camaraderie, and sense of shared stewardship of our nation's history that prevails there. I hope I have been an easy researcher to deal with. I know I have been a predictable one. Locker number 1 is mine when I'm in town!

I extend deep thanks, too, to all the talented and helpful archivists at the other repositories I visited for this project, especially the University of Massachusetts Lowell's Center for Lowell History; Emory University's Stuart A. Rose Manuscript, Archives, and Rare Book Library and Robert W. Woodruff Library; Tulane University's Howard-Tilton Library and Amistad Research Center; the Boston Public Library; and the Ames Mansion in North Easton, Massachusetts. Special thanks go to the staff of the Special Collections Department at Smith College who assisted me during my research time there, and to Kate Long, who later produced high-quality digital images for me from Smith's Ames Family Collection, despite the challenges presented by COVID-related library restrictions.

In almost thirty years of teaching at Colby College, I had the good fortune to work alongside a number of brilliant historians; some also became great friends. Two I must mention here are Raffael Scheck and Rob Weisbrot, whose collegiality, kindness, respect, encouragement, and standards of excellence (also, occasional silliness) sustained me in good times and bad. Thank you. I am grateful, too, to Earl Smith, Colby's most recent institutional historian, who may well have been the first to suggest that I write this biography and who encouraged me every step of the way. The dedication page offers my very specific appreciation of Hal Raymond.

Consciously or not, numerous colleagues elsewhere have also been profoundly important to this process, offering insights, advice, information, and references, cheering me on, helping me stay on track, keeping me honest. At the risk of forgetting someone, I will not name names here, but I hope you all know who you are! As for the two superb readers of the original and then revised manuscript: their deep reading and detailed guidance made this book much, much better and they should certainly not be held responsible in any way for its flaws.

I would also like to thank Richard Strand, author of the play *Butler*, which focuses on Butler's decision in May 1861 to accept the runaways from slavery at Fort Monroe and declare them "contraband of war." My very dear stepsister and stepbrother-in-law, Lenore and Paul Sundberg, first alerted me to the existence of this play, and Mr. Strand was kind enough to send me a copy of the unpublished script while I was working on the manuscript for this book. A couple of years ago my Colby Special Collections and Archives buddies and I also had the opportunity to actually see the play in Portland, Maine, and I got to participate in a lively discussion with the audience afterward. If you haven't seen the play yet, you should!

My deep gratitude goes to the excellent staff at University of North Carolina Press, and especially to Wyndham Robertson Editorial Director Mark

Simpson-Vos, for welcoming this book into their house and shepherding it along with such kindness, wisdom, and patience.

Finally, I want to thank all the beloveds in my large, extended, blended family, though I will only name three. My father, the Rev. Richard Leonard—a retired Unitarian Universalist minister and author himself—taught me many things, including how important it is to be prompt ("better an hour early than five minutes late"). And his lifetime of dedication to civil rights, social justice, and humanitarianism created the foundation for my understanding of and engagement in the world. And I am immeasurably grateful to my two precious sons, Anthony Bellavia and Joseph Bellavia—my greatest treasures!—who have grown into such fine young adults and without whom I would be quite lost.

Elizabeth D. Leonard
WATERVILLE, MAINE

BENJAMIN FRANKLIN BUTLER

I have the satisfaction of knowing that I am feared and loved by all honest
good men, but the bad hate and fear me for I am a terror to evil doers.
—JOHN BUTLER TO CHARLOTTE ELLISON BUTLER, JUNE 1813

The stock from which one comes is very material.
—BENJAMIN FRANKLIN BUTLER, 1892

A Life Begins
1818–1840

Charlotte Ellison Butler was twenty-six years old and only slightly younger
than the United States itself when she gave birth to Benjamin Franklin Butler on November 5, 1818, the same year the brilliant future abolitionist and
orator, Frederick Douglass, was born into slavery on Maryland's Eastern
Shore. On that cold afternoon in Deerfield, New Hampshire, exhausted from
the delivery of her second son and third child, Charlotte surely pondered the
many challenges that lay ahead for her as the mother of three children and
stepmother of three more, with a beloved husband who was nevertheless
frequently absent and whose record as a provider was spotty. As she considered her family's precarious future, others in the state were bidding farewell
to flocks of southward-migrating birds. With winter on the way, observed an
article in the weekly New Hampshire *Farmer's Cabinet*, "numbers of the birds
which, during summer, had lived and found food in our fields, woods, and
gardens, quit our climate for other countries." This annual avian migration
to warmer regions, the author opined, was an indication of the "admirable
guidance of Providence" in caring for his creatures. "Will he not with equal
goodness guide us whom he has vouchsafed to endow with reason?" Steeped
in Calvinism, Charlotte Butler must have wondered if Providence would
care for and guide her family in the days ahead. Providence certainly did *not*
seem to be taking very good care of the folks in bustling downtown Boston,

about sixty-five miles south, where a dramatic fire had just demolished the grand Exchange Coffee House hotel along with many nearby structures. The flames from that fire, the *Farmer's Cabinet* reported, "exhibited at once the elevation and brilliance of a volcano" that could be seen from many southerly places in New Hampshire, perhaps including Deerfield.[1]

Just how and when Charlotte Ellison first met her husband and newborn Benjamin's father, John Butler, is unclear. John hailed from Nottingham, a good day's horseback ride southeast of Charlotte's family home in Northfield. Ten years Charlotte's senior, John had been married before; his first wife, Sarah Batchelder, had died in February 1809 after giving birth to Polly (1804), Sally (1806), and Betsey (1808). What *is* clear is that by November 1810, as steamboats were first beginning to operate along major American rivers like the Hudson and the Ohio, Charlotte and John had fallen in love and begun a correspondence that sustained their relationship even as his various business and other endeavors increasingly took him far from home, and her. Not long before he and Charlotte began courting, John, who loved the sea, received authorization from the state of New Hampshire to operate a merchant vessel out of Portsmouth. The document recognized him as a legitimate "man of business" who deserved all the respect and protection available in the ports where his travels took him. When John sailed, Charlotte prayed and wrote him loving letters, addressing him fondly as "My Dear Friend" and emphasizing how much she hated their separation and worried about his safety. Charlotte urged John to do as she did: to seek God and pray regularly, including for their swift reunion. John and Charlotte married in August 1811.[2]

Even after they married, however, John and Charlotte's time together was limited. Averse to leaving his new, nineteen-year-old wife alone to care for Polly, Sally, and Betsey while he pursued his business ventures, John brought them all to Nottingham where she could have the support and companionship of his mother (his father had died in 1800). Then, a year after they wed, political developments and family tradition combined to take John in a different direction. His late father, Zephaniah Butler, originally from Woodbury, Connecticut, had served in both the French and Indian Wars and the colonies' war for independence; his mother, Abigail Cilley, was the daughter of revolutionary war officer Joseph Cilley, an early member of the Society of the Cincinnati in New Hampshire. According to Betsey, when the War of 1812 broke out, her father, John (a descendant of military men), was already serving as adjutant in the Nottingham militia and "was among the first to spring to arms."[3]

In March 1812 John accepted a captain's commission in the Second Regiment of United States Light Dragoons, a cavalry unit. "I shall hold myself in readiness to obey any commands the Government may give me," he promised a superior officer as he set about recruiting, training, drilling, and providing uniforms and other supplies for a group of "brave, patriotic young men who may wish to engage in the service of their country." Meanwhile, that May, Charlotte gave birth to their first child together, whom she and John also named Charlotte. Following little Charlotte's birth, and in anticipation of his departure to the northern front, John moved his wife, infant daughter, and two older daughters, Polly and Sally, about ten miles northwest to Deerfield to be near the family of his brother Benjamin, whom he had appointed the children's guardian, while Betsey remained with Grandmother Abigail in Nottingham. Soon John's orders took him to northern Vermont and then New York, where he spent a good deal of his time handling prisoners, smugglers, counterfeiters, and British and American Tory spies who were trying to make their way to Canada.[4]

During the long months away John wrote Charlotte frequently, expressing his deep affection as well as his frustration that she wrote so much less often than he did. Lonely and struggling to resist the "temptations of the flesh" that apparently presented themselves daily, John proved unsympathetic regarding Charlotte's relentless domestic responsibilities; he tended instead to scold. "You say you would write longer letters only the care of the family takes up so much of your time," he grumbled on May 16, 1813. "I am sorry you should suffer such a trifling excuse to prevent your pleasing your husband. You would think hard of me if I was to let my family [the soldiers under his command] hinder me from writing to you." John believed strongly that he must fulfill his patriotic duty at the risk of returning home dishonored, but he missed Charlotte and the children keenly. "I long much to see you and those dear little girls," he wrote on July 4. As the war continued, his growing distaste for certain aspects of his military service made the situation even more painful. In particular, John complained about the many southerners he encountered among the officer corps, including Gen. Wade Hampton, whose grandson later served in the Confederate army. In contrast with "freeborn Yankees" such as himself, John considered most of the southerners he met "negro drivers" unworthy of his respect. It bears noting that John himself was hardly unacquainted with slavery: the 1790 census, taken when John was about nine years old, indicates that his father, Zephaniah, owned at least one of the 158 slaves remaining in New Hampshire at that time.[5]

Early in January 1814 John fell and broke his ankle, permanently disabling him for field duty. Unable to travel, he asked Charlotte to leave the children behind with a hired caretaker and come visit him for a few weeks at his winter quarters, in Burlington, Vermont, which she did. Then, in February, he was reassigned to recruiting duty and returned to Deerfield, but his career as a soldier was effectively over: his injury and the poor medical care he had received made both walking and horseback riding extremely difficult. At the same time, his relative youth, his family obligations, and his adventurous spirit precluded a quiet retirement, and at the beginning of the following year, even as the war was coming to an end, an advertisement in a Portsmouth newspaper announced, under his name, that a new stagecoach line was now "running between Portsmouth and Concord, by way of Deerfield," and he was working for the new line's "proprietors." Soon John Butler was back at sea, having "fitted out a privateer" with the help of some friends. A number of sources indicate that John sailed to New Orleans at least once to carry messages to Gen. Andrew Jackson, whom he admired enough to use the general's name for his first son, Andrew Jackson Butler, born in February 1815. John may also have sailed at one point under a letter of marque signed by South American independence hero Simón Bolívar.[6]

Sadly, by March 1819 Charlotte's deepest fear was realized: her thirty-seven-year-old husband was dead on or near the Caribbean island of St. Kitts, a victim of yellow fever. Although she and her now six children, including infant Benjamin, still had John's birth family to lean on, Charlotte's financial situation had abruptly become even more tenuous, further exacerbated by the first waves of the national economic collapse known as the Panic of 1819, which actually lasted into the mid-1820s. Unable to care for all of the children herself—her skills as a seamstress could only bring in so much money—Charlotte left four-year-old Jackson with his guardian in Deerfield and moved with Benjamin, little Charlotte (now seven), and her stepdaughters Polly (now fifteen) and Sally (now thirteen) back to the Butler family homestead in Nottingham with Grandmother Abigail and Betsey. They stayed there for two years, by which time the toddler Benjamin had begun to exhibit a fondness for books that his mother hoped might eventually purchase him a brighter future. When the local school proved too distant for him to attend regularly, she returned with him and little Charlotte to Deerfield so Benjamin could attend a small local school run by Winthrop Hilton. Subsequently, however, her financial struggles drove them back to Grandmother Abigail's in Nottingham, where Benjamin continued his schooling and also frequented the local library. There is no doubt that the sustained and considerable instability of his earliest years—along with his mother's heavy burdens and persistent financial insecurity—left a lasting impression on Benjamin Butler and profoundly shaped his worldview, even as the harshness of these years was eased in some measure by the support and affection of various family members (his mother first and foremost) and by the structure and promise of words, books, school, and learning.[7]

In 1825, Charlotte sent seven-year-old Benjamin back to Deerfield to board at the home of an elderly, unmarried woman known as "Aunt" Polly Dame while he attended—likely at his guardian uncle's expense—the Deerfield Academy, then run by James Hersey. Hersey, Butler wrote many years later, was "the most intelligent teacher of the English language I ever knew," and, given her strong Calvinist faith, Charlotte undoubtedly appreciated Hersey's unwavering dedication to the "correct formation of the youthful mind and character." Years later Butler recalled his youthful self as a great lover of books—especially after a local shoemaker gave him his first, a copy of *Robinson Crusoe*—and as physically "puny" but also "quiet, gentle, and eager to learn." Reflecting on these early years, Butler spoke with deep and abiding affection of his mother's devotion, and with amazement and abundant gratitude for her unfailing courage in the face of myriad financial and other challenges. Moreover, Butler wrote, Charlotte taught him not just about the value of books—especially the Bible—but also about the beauty of nature, taking him outside at night to examine the stars and identify the constellations. She was, he declared, the one "whom I love, honor, and revere beyond any other person ever on earth." As will be seen, many of the choices he made and the actions he took in the course of his personal and professional life reflected his understanding and appreciation of his poor widowed mother's heavy burdens as well as her determined and tireless exertions on his and his siblings' behalf.[8]

As Benjamin Butler approached the age of ten, the financial situation for Charlotte and her children became even more precarious, although her stepdaughters, at least, were moving into their own new families. In 1823, at the age of nineteen, Polly had married Theodore Hilton—possibly a younger brother of Deerfield schoolmaster Winthrop Hilton—and together they relocated to Cornville, Maine. Betsey and Sally wed in 1827 and 1828, respectively: Betsey, nineteen like Polly, married Daniel Barber Stevens and Sally, at twenty-one, married Jonathan Meloon. They both remained in New Hampshire. Meanwhile, "Aunt" Polly Dame, with whom young Benjamin had boarded while attending Deerfield Academy, died in 1827. So did Grandmother Abigail, whom Butler later described as "the most imperious person

I have ever seen" at nearly six feet tall in her stocking feet. Grandmother Abigail, Butler recalled, was also the family member who most energetically shared his emerging love of history, particularly American history. He further attributed to her a sharp disdain for the principle of inherited social status. It was she, he insisted, who taught him that the law and public policy often enshrined fundamental social inequities, including between women and men, providing—with his mother—a crucial source of inspiration for his own egalitarianism and commitment to democracy. But now Grandmother Abigail was gone, soon to be followed by Uncle Benjamin Butler, who died the next year. To all intents and purposes, by the late 1820s Charlotte Butler and her three younger children were on their own.[9]

Charlotte's deepening financial struggles come through vividly in her ensuing and largely unsuccessful efforts—and those of her surviving brother-in-law, William Butler—to find a new guardian to secure the children's future and sort out the confusing and protracted inheritance implications of the deaths of Grandmother Abigail and Uncle Benjamin, who in any case did not leave much wealth behind. At the same time, Charlotte's ongoing commitment to Benjamin's education is evident in her decision, no matter what, to send him next to New Hampshire's esteemed Exeter Academy. Having marked him as the more intellectually promising (and perhaps also curious) of her two sons, Charlotte hoped that Benjamin would eventually attend college and then become a Baptist clergyman. Toward this end she asked Deerfield Academy's James Hersey to apply to Exeter on Benjamin's behalf, citing the family's poverty as a reason to accept the gifted boy on a scholarship. Happy to oblige, Hersey advised the Exeter trustees that young Benjamin had clearly demonstrated "proficiency in his studies" and should they offer him a scholarship, Benjamin personally, and the world more generally, would enjoy a "lasting benefit." The trustees agreed, and Uncle William Butler escorted Benjamin to the school in early 1828. Meanwhile, unable to resolve the financial crisis that faced her in New Hampshire, Charlotte left Deerfield with thirteen-year-old Jackson and his sixteen-year-old sister, Charlotte, and moved about fifty miles south to the booming mill town of Lowell, Massachusetts. There, with the help of a local Baptist clergyman, Enoch W. Freeman, Charlotte Ellison Butler became one of the dozens of boardinghouse keepers whose lodgings belonged to the proliferating textile mills then fueling the town's financial growth. Over the next two decades she oversaw several different boardinghouses—on Gorham, Lawrence, Charles, and Center Streets—all affiliated with the Merrimack Manufacturing Company.[10]

First explored by British colonists in the 1630s, Lowell occupied a four-square-mile area carved out of the town of Chelmsford, Massachusetts, with Dracut to the north and Tewksbury to the southeast. Originally known as East Chelmsford, in 1826 the area was renamed "Lowell" to honor Francis Cabot Lowell, who was instrumental in developing the region's textile factory system after the War of 1812, which had revealed the need to strengthen American domestic industry. With its two fine rivers, the Merrimack and the Concord, and the impressive thirty-foot drop of the Merrimack's mighty Pawtucket Falls, Lowell emerged in the postwar period as an ideal site for "an active industrial city." Indeed, Lowell quickly became the new nation's preeminent center for textile manufacturing, earning it the nickname "Spindle City."[11]

But Lowell was more than just a site for factory-based textile production. Francis Lowell died in 1817, the same year construction on New York's Erie Canal began, and a number of those who followed in his wake envisioned American industry operating differently from the British model. An industrial city, they believed, could also be a kind of utopian community, revolving around a contented workforce—including many young women—under the benevolent control of (and committed to) the corporation, which in turn provided jobs, housing, schools, commons for recreation, even a company-centered church, paid for by taxes on the workers. In line with this thinking, in 1824 the Merrimack Manufacturing Company constructed not only factories (five) and boardinghouses (about a hundred) but also St. Anne's Episcopal Church under the leadership of Rev. Theodore Edson, who played a major role in developing the city's public school system as well. One early historian described Lowell in these years as "an exemplar of the principles of 'welfare work.'" Lowell's founders, he wrote, "took into their consideration the proper upkeep of men [and women] as well as machines." As former mill worker Lucy Larcom put it in her rosy memoir, "From the beginning, Lowell had a high reputation for good order, morality, piety, and all that was dear to the old-fashioned New Englander's heart." Lowell's population of about 2,500 in 1826 grew to about 18,000 over the next ten years, almost two-thirds of whom were girls and women who typically lived in company boardinghouses managed by older widows like Charlotte Butler.[12]

As Charlotte, Jackson, and "little" Charlotte settled in to life in Lowell, Benjamin continued his formal education at Exeter, apparently without much enthusiasm for the school itself. Despite his mother's high hopes for the academic training he would receive at such a highly regarded institution, Butler recalled that he learned very little and was eager to leave the school

Charlotte Ellison Butler. Artist unknown. Courtesy of the Ames Family Papers, Sophia Smith Collection, SSC-MS-00003, Smith College Special Collections, Northampton, Massachusetts.

and rejoin his family in Lowell as soon as possible. Indeed, his description of his own eventual arrival in the Spindle City positively glows, in part, surely, because he prepared it for the city's semicentennial celebration in 1876, but also because his memory was infused with the delight he experienced as a child in being reunited with his family. Butler fondly recalled his entry into Lowell on a "cloudless spring afternoon" as a small, thin boy wearing a "fox skin cap closely drawn over his ears" and a "linsey-woolsey jacket, tightly buttoned to his throat" against the cold. He spoke of being dazzled by the view from the top of Christian Hill as he approached Lowell from the north: "the panorama of the valley at the confluence of the Concord and Merrimack rivers," including "three small, and what would now be deemed insignificant brick mills of the Merrimack corporation flanked by two rows of detached two-story buildings," which were boardinghouses. At the time, he noted, Lowell was "by far the largest town he had ever seen," a place that offered myriad new adventures, such as the possibility of eating his first oysters, which he found "strange" and unappetizing.[13] One imagines that his anxious mother's first impressions of Lowell were far less optimistic.

In his extensive 1892 autobiography, Butler indicated that he studied at Exeter for one term only—the winter term of 1828–29—before leaving for Lowell that spring, and, further, that he spent the time until the newly established Lowell High School opened in December 1830 reading classics in a local judge's office and working in a nearby bookstore to help support his family. The elderly Butler's memory of these details, however, turns out to have been somewhat flawed. Although it may well have been printed before he departed, the Phillips Exeter Academy catalog for 1829–30 still listed him as a student. Also, Lowell High School did not actually open until late 1831. Most likely, then, young Benjamin actually left Exeter at the end of 1830, at age twelve, spent much of 1831 working at the bookstore and perhaps also reading at the judge's office, and then, at age thirteen, began attending Lowell High School. In any case, at the public school Butler quickly demonstrated his advanced intellectual skills to his strong teachers, including recent Yale College graduate Thomas March Clark, who went on to become an Episcopal minister and bishop in Rhode Island, and J. Milton Clapp—"the most bitter pro-slavery and states-right gentleman I ever knew," Butler later wrote. (Clapp later became the editor of the vehemently secessionist *Charleston Mercury.*) In addition, he had both boys and girls of diverse class backgrounds for schoolmates, including Gustavus V. Fox, the son of a physician, who subsequently became President Abraham Lincoln's assistant secretary of the navy. Sadly, the historical record is elusive when it comes to Butler's brother's education (or experiences more generally) during this period. As for his sister, at nineteen when Lowell High School opened, "little" Charlotte would have been too old to attend. In 1830, however, a Charlotte Butler from Lowell, Massachusetts, was enrolled in the "female department" of the Academical and Theological Institution of New Hampton, New Hampshire— about eighty-five miles north of Lowell—where "the studies [were] similar to those pursued in the two English Departments of the Male Branch, with the addition of Painting, Drawing and Ornamental Needlework, and the

Latin and French Languages." Keenly aware (like her late mother-in-law) that women could not always count on men to "provide" and should therefore take steps to enhance their capacity for self-support and financial independence as well as intellectual growth, it seems that Charlotte Ellison Butler strove to provide her daughter, too, with some formal education.[14]

Benjamin Butler graduated from Lowell High School in 1834, having forged friendships there that followed him into the next phase of his life and beyond. "Shall I talk of the goodly town of Lowell," reminisced George L. Balcom from his lodgings at Harvard College two years later, "and of our good old school, of our former classmates, of the pretty damsels who there enlivened us with their presence, of the pleasant evenings which we have spent together, with a few friends of both sexes and there talked of *love and politics*?" Many years later, as the nation was descending into civil war, James M. Flagg wrote from Providence, Rhode Island, to share fond memories of the "desperate snow ball battles" that he, Butler, and other friends had engaged in behind the "little old schoolhouse" during the long Massachusetts winters. In 1834, however, as he looked ahead from high school graduation, Butler's attention was on matters other than snowball fights and flirting with girls. Not least among the questions he pondered was why he should be heading north—"very unwillingly," he recalled—to study at a small institution in central Maine called Waterville (now Colby) College, when what he really wanted to do was attend the United States Military Academy at West Point, perched above the Hudson River in New York.[15]

Indeed, Butler had long dreamed of going to West Point, which offered not only a solid education in engineering and military science but also possibilities for both adventure and social advancement. But the archival trail indicates that his hopes only took a practical turn after he had already completed his first year in Waterville. Writing to Charlotte Butler in September 1835, Senator Isaac Hill of New Hampshire expressed his willingness to "render any assistance" he could on Benjamin's behalf and requested that she send her district's congressional representative—now Caleb Cushing, who had become a member of Congress from Massachusetts the previous March— "the certificate of [Benjamin's] instructors and the scientific gentlemen who personally know him and his qualifications, scholarship, age and moral character." These documents in hand, Hill advised Charlotte, Cushing could then recommend Benjamin to the secretary of war for an appointment.[16]

A few months later, Rev. Edson, the influential Lowell clergyman, joined the effort to secure a West Point cadetship for Butler, portraying him in a letter as "a young gentleman of good moral character" and a person "esteemed" in Lowell for his "interesting and pronounced talents." One of Butler's writing instructors at Lowell High School, S. R. Hanscom, added his influence, describing his former student as possessed of "good native talents" and a "moral character" that merited "the confidence of an enlightened community." William Graves, a Lowell physician "well acquainted" with Butler, called him "an excellent scholar" and "a young man of industrious habits" who was "highly respected in this town." "If any man deserves the assistance of friends to obtain him a place" at West Point, Graves concluded, "it is Benjamin Butler." In February 1836, however, soon after these testimonials were dispatched, Congressman Cushing crushed Benjamin's hopes for an appointment: all of the vacancies at the academy allocated to Massachusetts and New Hampshire had already been filled for that year. Although he noted that Charlotte was free to renew Benjamin's application in the future, Cushing did not encourage her to do so.[17]

Charlotte did not try again. For one thing, she would have had to wait until Benjamin was more than halfway through his career at Waterville College, by which time he would be thoroughly out of step developmentally with the young men then beginning their training at West Point. Even more important, Charlotte herself remained committed to educating him at the Maine school, which had been founded by the Baptist Church less than two decades earlier, in 1818, as the Maine Literary and Theological Institution. (The college's trustees changed the name to Waterville College in 1822.) Charlotte's deep Calvinist faith, her desire that Benjamin become a clergyman, and the guidance of her Baptist pastor in Lowell, Enoch Freeman—himself an early Waterville College graduate—all pushed in this direction. Interestingly, at this time Brown University in Providence, much closer to Lowell than Waterville, was also affiliated with the Baptist denomination. Presuming Benjamin could have been accepted at Brown, Charlotte nevertheless seems to have preferred that her son travel the 175 miles through their native New Hampshire to central Maine—no easy trip in the years before the railroad—perhaps because he could stop with family along the way. In addition, Benjamin's half-sister Polly and her family now lived in Cornville, Maine, just over twenty miles, or a good day's walk, from the college. In the end, Butler spent all four years at Waterville College, where, like other less-privileged students, he helped offset his tuition and expenses by making chairs in the college's carpentry shop for thirty cents a day and teaching in a small Cornville school during the eight-week-long winter break.[18]

An early history describes Waterville in the 1820s and 1830s as "the trading center of a growing agricultural community" that had taken root along the powerful Kennebec River but would have to wait until the early 1850s for industry and the railroad to arrive. At the time Butler first saw it, Waterville College's physical plant consisted of only two brick buildings: South College, built in 1821, and North College, built in 1822; a third building, Recitation Hall, was constructed between 1836 and 1837, its progress slowed by the financial woes that had dogged the school since its founding. The college grounds, too, were "rough and untended" when Butler arrived on campus to join the thirty-five-man class of 1838, and there were only four regular faculty and two "tutors" on staff for between seventy and a hundred students across four classes. Although its ties to the Baptist Church remained strong for decades, within two years of its establishment the then-all-male institution began welcoming students from all religious denominations and, by the early 1830s, effectively set aside a portion of its original purpose—"to provide the church with an educated, competent, and significant" clergy—to focus on the rest, namely, providing Maine with "leaders of reliable character." Still, in this era of religious revival and the Second Great Awakening, conservative Protestant ideas, practices, and requirements persisted, such as the stipulation that students attend chapel twice a day from Monday through Saturday as well as public worship once on Sunday. Many and perhaps even most students during Butler's time at the college attended Waterville's First Baptist Church, still standing today at the corner of Elm and Park Streets, whose pastor was Rev. Samuel Francis Smith, an instructor of modern languages better known for having composed the anthem "America." In addition to routinely attending religious services on campus and off, students were encouraged to engage in missionary work and required to avoid tobacco, alcohol, and card playing, among other sins.[19]

Many years later Butler recalled how irksome he found the religious features, underpinnings, and expectations of the college, although they were precisely the aspects of the school that appealed most to his devout mother. Butler did not share his mother's Baptist faith, however; indeed, he viewed many of Christianity's earthly representatives—at the college and elsewhere—as deeply flawed and even hypocritical, and considered Calvinism itself absurd, especially its concept of predestination. As Butler saw it, if God had already determined every individual's fate in eternity, then salvation could not possibly be achieved, nor damnation avoided, through worship or other expressions of purposeful piety. So why bother? Why pretend such things mattered? "My whole mind," Butler wrote, "rebelled against this teaching," which he considered the illogical and unjust relic of a "superstitious, witch-burning age." For this reason, Butler repeatedly asked to be excused from chapel services and sometimes skipped them without permission at the risk of being fined, suspended, or even expelled, not to mention having to face his mother's grave disappointment. Butler also relentlessly prodded his instructors, no doubt to the considerable frustration of some if not all of them, with complex theological questions that, he claimed rather boldly, "it was impossible for them or any one else to answer." Now coming into adulthood, Butler discovered rich sources of strength, intellectual development, personal identity, and purpose not only in the financial and other hurdles he and his family had faced and the superior formal education he continued to enjoy, but also in his ongoing resistance to the Waterville institution's religious constraints, obligations, and principles.[20]

Butler was hardly alone in his disdain for certain types of secular as well as sacred authority and control. Toward the end of his sophomore year he received a letter from classmate Joseph W. Russell in which Russell spoke bitterly about the college faculty, especially President Rufus Babcock, or "Baboon," as some of the students called him. "I wish the Devil had him," Russell wrote, urging Butler—whom he must have known lent a sympathetic ear—to "tell the whole Damn [bunch] of them that hell is too good a place for them." Looking back, Butler and others recognized these Waterville College years as formative with respect to another enduring character trait besides his tendency to resist authority he found questionable: "where I thought myself in the right," Butler later wrote, "I never counted the number of my opponents in shaping my action." Not only was he willing to do battle with principles and persons he found problematic; he was willing to do so regardless of the odds seemingly stacked against him or the number of allies who stood with him.[21]

As a boy Butler had loved learning about the stars and the natural world from his mother, and as a college student this inclination matured into a strong and lasting interest in science. Indeed, at Waterville Butler came to believe that "chemistry and its adjuncts were to be the means of opening a very great field of highly promising labor and research to benefit all mankind." He drew particular inspiration from the teaching of George Washington Keely, the British-born professor of mathematics, natural philosophy, and astronomy from 1829 to 1852, whom histories of the college describe as "a man of genius and taste" and "a profound scholar" possessed of "splendid powers of mind and heart" and "yet more splendid common sense." Students like Butler cherished Keely, too, for his unflagging commitment to them as individuals and thinkers, and his willingness to side with them in their occasional conflicts with the college administration.[22]

Butler's college years coincided with the rise of antislavery sentiment in New England and elsewhere across the northern states, an effect of the Second Great Awakening's demand for social reform and the repudiation of sinful institutions and practices. Indeed, Lowell—whose textile industry was inextricably interwoven with slavery—had hosted its first antislavery meeting the same year Butler began his time in Waterville, and antislavery ideas were circulating in Maine, too. The year before Butler matriculated, Boston's fiery abolitionist William Lloyd Garrison, founder of the *Liberator* and the American Anti-Slavery Society, gave a speech in Waterville that many of the college's students attended, leading some to establish an antislavery society on campus. Additionally, Butler was a nineteen-year-old senior at the college when, on November 7, 1837, newspaper editor and Waterville College alumnus Elijah Parish Lovejoy (class of 1826) of Albion, Maine, was shot to death by proslavery thugs in Alton, Illinois, after repeatedly refusing to stop printing antislavery articles in his *Alton Observer*. News of Lovejoy's murder appeared across the nation's press, including in Maine and, of course, in Waterville.[23]

All that said, evidence suggests that the growing national conflict over slavery generally—and Lovejoy's murder specifically—did not play a vivid role in Butler's consciousness or his mental and political development at this point in his life. College men in the decades before the Civil War typically understood themselves to be training for leadership in professions that valued skills in public speech and argumentation, and most joined social groups that dedicated time to debate. For his part, Butler notably did *not* seek membership in either the college's antislavery or its colonization society. Rather, he belonged to—and may also have cofounded—a more general college debate group, the Erosophian Adelphi Society (EAS). He also served as the EAS's first historian, a role he took seriously, urging the group "to obtain a locked box for preservation of their records" (almost two centuries later, the records of the EAS remain intact), oversaw the purchase of library books, and organized and participated in a number of the group's debates. In only one, however, in April 1838, did he touch on slavery. To the question, "Was the course pursued by the Rev. Mr. Lovejoy at Alton right and expedient?" Butler argued in the affirmative, and he won a close victory. But that, of course, does not necessarily mean Butler believed his own argument, only that he presented it more compellingly than his opponent presented his. The other debates in which Butler participated dealt with temperance, the significance of "the manner of an orator's delivery," the impact of President Andrew Jackson's attack on the national bank, the best way for the nation to absorb and naturalize immigrants, and the proper scope of international law. In these years, it is difficult to see Butler as anything other than indifferent to the enslavement of Black people in the American South. Over time and under different conditions, that would change.[24]

On April 28, 1838, after a somewhat bumpy campaign and in the final months of his time at Waterville College, Butler became the EAS's president. It was a significant honor, hard to square with both his self-proclaimed rebelliousness and the many enduring stories about his student days that depict him as, at best, a jolly prankster and, at worst, a dislikeable, self-serving troublemaker. Among the stories of mischief, "daring," "cunning," and generally bad behavior that have clung to the popular representation of Butler's college years—some of which he cheerfully perpetuated himself—are that he at one point stole (or just silenced) the chapel bell, and that he occasionally pilfered "signs and gates, pigs and chickens," got into numerous brawls, proposed to a local girl and then shamelessly jilted her, stiffed a local merchant for a suit of clothing he purchased for graduation (finally paying the merchant several years later), and only received his diploma "because the faculty were glad to get rid of him." One 1883 newspaper story reinforces the impression of Butler as a scamp whose many failings included a complete absence of antislavery sentiment. This same article goes on to describe Butler as once having boasted of paying a local farmer to allow him to catch the swallows in the farmer's barn. He and some friends then released the birds during a meeting of abolitionists at a local church, temporarily creating mass confusion and offering fleeting opportunities—as the wind from the swallows' wings extinguished the candles that lit the room—for the boys to quickly kiss any girls they found sitting nearby in the pews.[25]

Colby College historian Ernest C. Marriner, who recounts numerous tales of Butler's questionable conduct, nevertheless observes that the college's official records actually depict young Butler as "one of the best behaved and most respected" students during his years in Waterville. And perhaps by now it comes as no surprise that the historical record reveals Butler to have been both admired *and* reviled, adored *and* despised, well behaved *and* mischievous, honorable *and* dishonorable. One thing is clear: Butler, whose financial situation was likely more precarious than many of his classmates', was not entirely reliable about paying his bills in Waterville: a full year after he left town, merchants he had patronized while a student were still pursuing him for his unpaid debts. In September 1839, F. G. Cook asked Butler to settle his account for matches, oil, and other miscellaneous items (Butler owed Mr. Cook $2.29); a month later, a debt collector from nearby

Augusta, Maine, demanded payment on a bill for $11.25, owed to Waterville merchants Gould & Newman; that December, Eben Freeman requested that Butler reimburse him for a loan.[26]

The Butler family's ongoing financial instability hardly offers a satisfying excuse for his failure to deal responsibly with his debts. At the same time, if he was unreliable in the eyes of some of his creditors, frustratingly confrontational toward some of his faculty, and determined on many occasions to challenge college norms and protocols he found stale and unreasonable regardless of the consequences, Butler also won the admiration of many with whom he interacted regularly at Waterville College. In 1887 a fellow alumnus recalled Butler as "a generous, manly boy, shrewd and witty, always ready with an answer whenever assailed, but always displaying good temper. Whoever attacked him was always sure to 'get as good as he sent,' but he never harbored anger, or resentment, or revenge." Butler, this former classmate insisted, "stood well in his class." Similarly, although an 1893 *Boston Globe* article criticized him for having "a hot temper" and tending to be "somewhat antagonistic," the college newspaper, the *Echo*, years later and drawing on recollections from Butler's classmates, depicted him much more affectionately as a "picturesque character" whose congenital strabismus—a condition where the eyes do not line up together to focus, which in Butler's case was compounded by droopy eyelids—"gave him an uncertain, quizzical expression in his facial landscape." He was, the *Echo* piece continued fondly, someone who "kept the college from being dull." In 1924, another aged former classmate emphasized Butler's capacity for "acute observation" and praised his remarkably "retentive memory" and his "daring, fearless, inquisitive disposition," while also waxing nostalgic about his "pugnacity," his "fondness for controversy," and his penchant for "creating a sensation and focusing all eyes on himself," often by "espousing . . . the wrong or unpopular side of a question." Evidently, those who knew Butler best as a college student recognized in him a complex, inspiring, and infuriating nature, a young man with tremendous intellectual ability, capable of boorishness, discourtesy, and disdain for others' needs, as well as great kindness, generosity, and leadership.[27]

As with Lowell High School, friendships Butler forged at Waterville College endured. Among his correspondents in future years was Arthur Fuller Drinkwater of Mt. Vernon, Maine (class of 1840), who became a lawyer, judge, and editor of an Ellsworth, Maine, newspaper, the *American*. In July 1839, Drinkwater, a fellow member of the Erosophian Adelphi Society, tugged hard on this connection, urging Butler to return to Waterville for that summer's commencement ceremonies. In another letter Drinkwater vaguely invoked a memory of their somewhat fraught interactions as students with the local community, writing, "Village folks are the same as ever, and you ought to know what that is." In a manner that seems timeless, Drinkwater cheerfully recalled the many "scrapes" in which he, Butler, and other college chums used to find themselves, some of which were the result of too much "drinking of wine."[28]

In later years Butler had other correspondents from his Waterville days, too. Among them was classmate Moses J. Kelly of New Sharon, Maine, also a member of the class of 1838 and an Erosophian who became a clergyman and instructor of theology and during the Civil War served as chaplain of Sixth Maine Infantry Regiment. Just as the war was getting started, Kelly invited his old friend to visit Maine soon, and perhaps give a lecture. Around this same time Butler also heard from former classmate Edgar Harkness Gray, originally of Bridgeport, Vermont, who, like Kelly, became a clergyman and who served from 1864 to 1868 as chaplain of the US Senate. In the late 1860s Butler also heard from Lucius L. Scammell, who overlapped with Butler at Waterville College from 1834 to 1836 before transferring to Dartmouth. Now living some forty miles southwest of Lowell in Hopkinton, Massachusetts, Scammell joked about having been suspended from Waterville as a result of his undefined "incorrigibleness in the matter of the *Erosophian Adelphi*." He also marveled at the directions their lives had taken since their college days and reminisced about other old friends, including George Whitefield Bosworth who, in 1869, was the featured speaker at the dedication of the college's Memorial Hall, built to honor alumni who had given their lives in the Civil War.[29]

Butler graduated from Waterville College in August 1838 with a bachelor of arts degree. That same year his sister Charlotte married Horace Holton of New Hampshire, a hotel operator. The Holtons moved to Springfield, Illinois, the same booming western town to which Abraham Lincoln had relocated the previous year, but their married life was brief: "little" Charlotte died in 1839, probably in childbirth. Meanwhile, Butler's brother Andrew Jackson Butler moved to Missouri and married Joanna Clifford. They had two children: George, born in 1840, and Charlie, who was born a decade later and died when he was only three. At the time he left Waterville, Butler's own health was frail: now nearly twenty, he weighed under a hundred pounds, well below the optimal weight even for a man of his diminutive height (five feet four inches). Butler attributed his poor physical condition that summer to a "severe cold" he had contracted as his senior year drew to a close, but it seems more likely that two decades of financial instability with the associated lack of access to good nutrition and reliable health care had taken their toll.[30]

Distressed to find her son so debilitated when he returned from Waterville, Charlotte Butler sent him cod fishing along the Labrador coast for a few months with one of his late father's friends. Butler's recollections of that adventure evoke the image of Theodore Roosevelt overcoming his asthmatic youth by engaging in strenuous exercise. According to Butler, when he arrived to join the ship's crew, the "old fisherman" in charge scornfully dismissed his efforts to bring a box of books on board, urging Butler instead to use the time to "become a sailor," in other words, a *man*, in the mid-nineteenth-century meaning of the word. Caught off guard at first, Butler confessed that in the end he "took all the old man's advice." And while that advice "was not delicate," it was beneficial. "I took my place and was taught to 'knot, reef, and steer,' and very soon the crew became very kind and very fond of me." With its hard labor and fresh air, along with his abundant consumption of cod liver oil (Butler somewhat dubiously claimed he drank the oil "with as much relish as I ever drank anything in my life"), the trip served the young scholar well. He gained both weight and strength, greatly enhancing his personal and physical confidence and setting him up for a lifetime of rarely interrupted good health. "Since that time," Butler boasted late in life with some exaggeration, "I have never been sick in my life to a degree requiring me to spend half a day in bed."[31]

But a life at sea did not appeal to Butler in the way it had to his father, and once he returned to thriving Lowell—now officially a city rather than a town—young Butler began studying law in earnest. For in addition to having been drawn to the sciences in college, Butler had developed an interest in the legal profession, particularly after he witnessed a gifted and prominent attorney in action at a jury trial he attended during his junior year. The lawyer was Jeremiah Mason, a former US senator, state legislator, and state attorney general from New Hampshire, whom one eulogist in 1848 described as an "extraordinary" individual whose "intellect, wisdom, and uprightness gave him a control over the opinions of all the circles in which he lived and acted." Watching Mason in court inspired the already ambitious Butler to contemplate "the possibilities which were open to me in the profession of law," not least, one suspects, the longed-for opportunities for fortune and fame he had frequently discussed with his college friends.[32]

Toward this end, Butler apprenticed himself to a respected local attorney, William Smith, who specialized in real estate law and was also a Massachusetts state legislator. Smith had offices in Lowell and Boston and an exten-

Young Butler, with dog, daguerreotype by Lorenzo G. Chase. Courtesy of the Ames Family Papers, Sophia Smith Collection, SSC-MS-00003, Smith College Special Collections, Northampton, Massachusetts.

sive professional library, to which he gave Butler full access. Butler committed himself to his legal studies with a degree of dedication his Waterville College professors would have loved to see. "I used to begin reading at half past seven o'clock in the morning," he later wrote, "stopping at twelve for dinner, beginning again before one and stopping at six. I then returned to the office at seven, and closed usually at ten." At the same time, Butler got some practical training: Smith paid him to perform a variety of less advanced legal tasks that resulted in Butler appearing on a regular basis in police court, a venue that his early years in poverty may have made less intimidating for him than it would have been for others. As Smith's protégé, Butler studied hard. But having learned the health benefits of regular physical exertion, he also made sure that he closed his books periodically in order to take some exercise, including going horseback riding around town a few times a week on his "small gray saddle horse."[33]

Eager now to do whatever he could to help lift himself and his family out of their perpetual financial straits, and perhaps also in the hope of being able to pay off his own lingering debts, in the fall of 1839 Butler somewhat ironically assumed the role of family debt collector. That November he wrote to J. M. Damon of Lancaster, Massachusetts, requesting that Damon reimburse brother Andrew Jackson Butler for the fifty dollars he had borrowed under what Butler described only as "peculiar circumstances." In addition, Butler briefly took employment as head of a small, coeducational private school in nearby Dracut. As it happens, Butler had not enjoyed teaching during the semester breaks at Waterville College, once grumbling bitterly about having to exchange home "and all its joys in winter season"—warm fires, lively parties, nuts and cider with friends, skating and sledding—for "a district school and ten dollars per month," where "the privilege of being a pedagogue" was to "instill erudition into one end of a thick s[k]ulled boy by beating on the other." His experience in Dracut was no better. The school enrolled only students who had been expelled from other institutions and were therefore already accustomed to ignoring discipline. Butler, however, considered himself "by habit of mind" a "disciplinarian" of the sort the students simply could not disregard. He was right. Instead of disregarding his efforts at discipline, soon more than half of the students had simply quit the school. Then Butler quit, too, having completed only a single term but apparently satisfied that he had delivered to many of the students "a thrashing, the remembrance of which would last . . . a lifetime."[34] For better or worse, such comments reflect what became Butler's enduring impatience with those who could not meet his own high standards for labor and dedication to a task.

In September 1840, mentor William Smith encouraged Butler, then just shy of twenty-two years old, to apply for admission to the Massachusetts bar. Because he had been studying with Smith for less than three years, Butler was required to pass an examination before a judge. Unfazed, he approached this particular hurdle in the same supremely self-confident manner that many of his friends, schoolmates, and, ultimately, professional associates would surely have recognized, some with deep affection, some with eye-rolling, some with disgust. In Butler's account, although the judge urged him to take a little more time to prepare for the examination, he not only pressed on but also brazenly questioned the judge's ruling in a particular case, in the end arguing his own point to such good effect (as he recalled it) that the judge actually changed his ruling. It is impossible to know whether this story is true in all of its details; it is certainly vintage Butler. In any case, the historical record clearly indicates that he was admitted to the Massachusetts bar just two years out of college and thereafter began to build his own practice.[35]

Not unlike today, lawyers in the years before the Civil War commonly engaged in both private practice and politics. "The middle decades of the nineteenth century were marked throughout the United States by political exuberance," wrote one historian of Lowell, where the complicated political environment involved not only diverse party affiliations but also pro- and anti-textile-corporation factions. Butler was no exception. Indeed, right around the time he took his examination for the bar, Butler gave his first political speech, in favor of the New York Democrat Martin Van Buren's reelection as president of the United States (Van Buren lost to William Henry Harrison).[36] Just how Butler found his way into the Democratic Party is unclear, though his Scots-Irish heritage, his family's working-class status and years of relentless financial struggle, and the egalitarian views he had absorbed from his grandmother inclined him in that direction. There is evidence, too, that although the two never met, Butler's father had been an unrepentant Democrat at a time when adherents to the party essentially "lived under a social ban" in New Hampshire. John Butler, one source observes, "was a personal friend and political backer of Isaac Hill of the New Hampshire *Patriot*, the paper which taught Democracy till even New Hampshire listened." It was this Isaac Hill, too, who had offered to help Charlotte Butler place Benjamin at West Point. Although the effort was unsuccessful, Hill's promise of assistance surely earned Butler's gratitude and may also have influenced his political views and party affiliation.

In the period between his graduation from Waterville College and his admission to the Massachusetts bar, two more important building blocks of Butler's future professional and personal life fell into place. First, he met and became good friends with Fisher Ames Hildreth, the only son of Dr. Israel Hildreth and his wife, Dolly, whose family had lived in the area for generations and "numbered among the most excellent citizens of Lowell." Born the same year as Butler, Fisher too was "an ardent and sincere democrat" who "loved politics," and who "by the natural bent of his mind was eminently calculated to shine therein," at least according to his direct descendants. Like

Butler, Fisher studied for the law, but in the end he chose to become a farmer instead of an attorney, a course that brought him considerable success. The friendship that took firm root between Butler and Fisher Hildreth in 1839 lasted until Fisher's premature death in July 1873. By far its greatest consequence, however, arose from the fact that Fisher had a beautiful and beguiling sister named Sarah, an aspiring actress who captured Butler's interest immediately.[37]

During this period Butler also enlisted, like many young men in town, in the local militia company, the Lowell City Guard. Butler spent three years as a private with the Guard, during which, he remembered fondly, "I carried my musket" cheerfully and "encamped with the company, either in conjunction with the regiment to which it belonged"—the Massachusetts Volunteer Militia (MVM)—"or in our private encampments, from five to nine days every year" in order to "learn the duties of a soldier." Butler found his military training time-consuming but thoroughly enjoyable. Perhaps it made up in some measure for having been denied access to West Point. At the same time, service with the MVM helped to shape Butler's attitude regarding the distinctions between "regular," academy-based military training and the status it conferred, and the training and status of volunteer citizen-soldiers. "We were armed with arms issued by the United States," he recalled with pride, "and in all things we observed, as far as we could, the tactics and regulations of the army of the United States." Among other things, Butler came to see the *motivations* of the militiamen as far nobler than those of the regulars. "We went through our drill," he explained in his autobiography, "because we loved to do it; they went through theirs because they were made to do it." Moreover, Butler maintained that he already knew he would someday be summoned "to perform those duties as a soldier in actual war." As it turns out, he must have demonstrated at least some capacity for mastering military training on an intellectual level, as well as an aptitude for generating loyalty and enthusiasm among those with whom he served. For he soon began receiving promotions, rising "step by step through all the gradations of military rank" and eventually becoming—by election—colonel of his regiment.[38]

From my earliest vote I became deeply interested in politics. . . .
From my earliest youth I had been taught to believe in democracy.
—*BUTLER'S BOOK*, 1892

If this nation of ours ever comes to naught, it will be because the few,
under one pretext or another, holding the power, have oppressed the many.
The history of the world may be examined with a vision aided by the highest
microscopic power, and it will appear that the few have ever oppressed
the many when they could get the power to do it; but the many have never
oppressed the few, although they have always had it in their power to do so.
—*BUTLER'S BOOK*, 1892

Butler's Antebellum Journey
1840–1860

In the early 1840s, as White settlers laid new claims across the North American continent and, in the South, sought to take their "colored" human property west with them, and as debates over the future of slavery that William Lloyd Garrison and others had fostered throughout the previous decade grew steadily more heated, Benjamin Butler's attention remained focused primarily on his own personal and professional concerns. Not least important, he sought to develop a successful legal practice in and beyond Lowell, an enterprise for which, he later claimed with uncharacteristic modesty, he was "illy prepared." Still, he loved his profession, with its logic, precision, and opportunity for argument. "I tried my cases critically," he later recalled, "catching at every point in the faults of my opponents, and of course was immediately called 'sharp'" by the opposing attorneys, "who frequently begged of me to overlook their blunders." Butler ignored such pleas. "I was," he confessed, "inexorable." By the mid-1840s Butler had made significant progress: he enjoyed an abundance of casework, a solid income, an appointment to the position of local justice of the peace, and admission to practice in all courts in Massachusetts as well as the United States Supreme Court.[1]

During these years Butler's law office was situated in an elegant building on the corner of Central and Merrimack Streets that he and Fisher Hildreth had purchased together when Hildreth was still considering becoming a lawyer and perhaps even joining Butler's practice. In the end, however, though their friendship remained strong, Hildreth chose a different path. Between 1843 and 1845 he served as Dracut's representative to the Massachusetts state legislature. Then, disenchanted by his experience with lawmaking and legal wrangling, Hildreth turned to farming and newspaper work, becoming the publisher of Lowell's weekly Democratic newspaper, the (seemingly paradoxically named) *Republican*. Subsequently, he and others merged the *Republican* with two other papers, the *Advertiser* and the *Patriot*, to establish the *Lowell Patriot and Republican*. In addition to his administrative work, Hildreth wrote politically robust articles and editorials; supporters and opponents agreed that he "wielded a ready and trenchant pen" that greatly benefited the Democratic Party, its causes, and its local and state candidates.[2]

Butler and Hildreth transformed the building they had purchased—originally the town's First Freewill Baptist Church, built largely by donations from the Lowell factory "girls"—into a theater, museum, and office space known as the "Museum Building," which provided them with some rental income. (More real estate investments would follow.) There Butler took on a variety of cases. "Police court cases [adulterers, murderers, thieves, debtors] fell to him by the hundred," wrote biographer Richard S. West. Butler's name consequently "became a household word" in and around Lowell, and "the zeal and vigor with which he fought his courtroom battles, together with his high percentage of favorable verdicts, brought many new cases to his docket, and with them financial independence."[3] Professional success had arrived.

In addition to his police court cases, a sizeable portion of Butler's legal business involved the state's female factory operatives, thousands of whom were employed in Lowell alone. As already noted, Lowell in the 1820s had reflected an attempt to the build an idealized, factory-centered world in which the "mill girls" played the role of contented laborers who served the nation and, simultaneously, their own economic and intellectual uplift. By the early 1830s, however, work speedups and other efforts by the mill owners to increase their own profits had upended this ideal, leading to a series of strikes and other acts of labor resistance. By the 1840s, these same capitalist pressures drove most of the original operatives—so many of them proud, native-born daughters of New England farm country—to seek other options for labor, like schoolteaching in the expanding western settlements. Into the vacancies they left behind flooded Irish immigrants, whose choices were much more limited and whom the employers squeezed even tighter. His own family and life experience led Butler to sympathize deeply with the struggles these women faced, and he became known locally for taking on the cases of operatives who were brave enough to sue the manufacturing companies "for wages withheld on one pretense or another." Individually, such cases were by no means lucrative, bringing in perhaps no more than two dollars apiece. Butler was unerringly committed to them, however, having long watched his mother strain to keep the family from descending irrevocably into financial ruin. At Charlotte's boardinghouse table, too, Butler frequently heard first-hand the operatives' complaints and concerns. "With such people I spent my boyhood," he later wrote. "I knew all their wants; knew their sicknesses and the causes thereof; saw the deterioration in their bodily health from year to year." The premature and heartbreaking death of his younger sister further sharpened Butler's awareness of the physical and other challenges women faced, especially working-class women, and surely strengthened his decision to help them. Charles Dickens, who visited Lowell briefly in 1842 and spoke relatively favorably of the factories there, would nevertheless have been pleased to learn of Butler's work on behalf of the factory "girls."[4]

As he built his law practice and professional reputation, Butler also began involving himself more in Democratic Party politics at every level, in the fall of 1844 campaigning in Massachusetts and New Hampshire for presidential candidate James Polk. Looking back from the vantage point of old age, Butler described himself ideologically as a life-long "Jeffersonian Democrat," in the sense of being perennially opposed to aristocrats and the institutions and customs that uncritically sustained their power. Simultaneously, he noted that his politics were always "practical," aimed at improving "the condition and welfare of the citizen"—regular folks—rather than ensuring the success of a particular political *party*. "The full and only end of government," Butler wrote in his autobiography, "is to care for the people in their rights and liberties . . . to protect them in equality of powers, equality of rights, equality of privileges, and equality of burdens under the law, by carefully and energetically enforc[ing] provisions of equal laws justly applicable to every citizen."[5] Certainly Butler crafted his self-definition, in 1892, at least in some measure to explain his willingness over the years to move from one political party to another, depending on the values that party espoused. That does not mean he was dissembling. Butler's earliest work as a lawyer on behalf of the Lowell operatives exhibited precisely the political philosophy he later claimed to have had—and also unquestionably displayed—throughout his life.

As he laid the foundation of a long and highly successful career as a lawyer, politician, and businessman, Butler's ongoing service with the state militia reinforced his sense of himself (and his reputation) as a dedicated citizen-soldier available for active duty. Meanwhile, Butler took crucial steps to ensure a future of great *personal* happiness. On May 16, 1844, amid "falling apple blooms" that "carpeted the farm roads" around Lowell, Rev. Theodore Edson—the prominent local clergyman who almost a decade earlier had recommended Butler for a West Point cadetship—presided over the wedding ceremony at St. Anne's Episcopal Church that united Butler, now age twenty-five, with his friend Fisher's sister, Sarah Jones Hildreth, almost twenty-eight. Butler later recalled first meeting Sarah in the fall of 1839, when he attended Thanksgiving dinner at the Hildreths' elegant home as Fisher's guest. On that occasion, Sarah's "personal endowments, literary attainments, and brilliancy of mind" instantly drew him to her. Whatever Butler noticed or felt when he *first* met Sarah, one newspaper article at the time of his death claimed that he actually only fell irreversibly in love with her—"a lady of surpassing beauty"—upon seeing her perform in a play a few years later in Cincinnati. According to this account, Butler spent two straight weeks watching Sarah onstage before he finally worked up the courage to reintroduce himself, confess his love, and propose. Hardly eager to quit acting and perhaps still uncertain about Butler's professional prospects, Sarah demurred. In the end, however, his earnest and persistent "wooing," his steady professional advances, and, surely, Fisher's encouragement, brought forth "a favorable conclusion."[6]

Sadly, not one of Butler's birth family members could attend the wedding. By May 1844 his sister Charlotte was dead and his stepsisters in Maine and New Hampshire were too far away and busy with their own households. National conquest had lured his older brother and his family west to Liberty, Missouri (they later moved to Sonoma, California), and mother Charlotte had relocated temporarily to Missouri, too, in order to assist Jackson's wife and surviving son, George, during Jackson's frequent travels for business and other ventures. Even so, the wedding of Sarah Hildreth and Benjamin Butler was a joyful occasion, after which the newlyweds settled into a comfortable new routine together, initially residing in the Central Street boardinghouse Charlotte Butler had managed and where Butler had lived since his return from college, just a short walk from his office in the Museum Building. A few months after the wedding, Butler proudly informed Charlotte that Sarah was "in excellent health and quite happy I believe in her new mode of life," and he praised his new wife in what were likely the highest

Butler family home in Lowell, Massachusetts. Photographer unknown. Courtesy of the Prints and Photographs Division, Library of Congress, Washington, D.C.

terms he could conjure, as "fully worthy of our loved and best Charlotte," his late sister. Just over a year into their marriage, on June 8, 1845, Sarah and Benjamin welcomed their first child, whom they named Paul. Two years later, on March 2, 1847, Sarah gave birth to their daughter, Blanche, whom Butler nicknamed "Buntie."[7]

As his family, financial investments, political commitments, and legal practice grew and thrived—one source notes that within the next decade or so Butler's "law practice netted more than eighteen thousand dollars a year, the most lucrative in New England"—the Butlers purchased a much larger home on Andover Street in the elegant Belvidere neighborhood overlooking the Merrimack River; eventually Butler also bought a home for his aging mother on nearby Willow Street. In addition, he established a second law office on State Street in Boston, to which he began to commute regularly, and took on at least one law partner to help manage his expanding caseload: Dartmouth graduate (class of 1838) William Prentiss Webster, who not only worked with Butler for many years but also married Sarah Hildreth Butler's younger sister Susan. In 1846 Butler also joined the Freemason's Pentucket

Lodge in Lowell. Membership in the centuries-old Freemasons commonly coincided with an anti-elitist, prolabor (including pro-foreign-born labor) political stance and, in this period, a commitment to *Jacksonian* Democracy, much like Jeffersonian Democracy but even more egalitarian (for White men, anyway); President Andrew Jackson himself was a Freemason. At the same time, these very aspects of the fraternal organization, along with its secretive rituals, provoked opponents to declare freemasonry antithetical to "native" or "true Americanism," by which they often meant ideals associated with the Federalist Party and, later, the Whigs. Predictably, the perennially scrappy and unabashedly antielite Butler was unfazed and perhaps even somewhat emboldened by such opposition. Moreover, his highly respected father-in-law, Dr. Israel Hildreth, was also a longtime member of the same lodge, which likely contributed to Butler's decision to join in the first place. In the end, his practical involvement with the organization seems to have been rather half-hearted. Although he eventually advanced to the degree of "Royal Arch Mason," an old friend later recalled that he rarely attended meetings and, in a familiar echo of past financial delinquency, was even briefly suspended for nonpayment of dues.[8]

Butler was unfazed, too, by the fact that Lowell itself, like Massachusetts generally in this period, was dominated politically not by Democrats but by Whigs, who were overwhelmingly allied with the powerful owners of the town's numerous manufacturing corporations and who frequently lived in Boston and elsewhere. Butler's relationship with local and state members of the Whig Party was, simply put, rocky. He was by no means uniformly critical of those he opposed politically, or their political views; he was, after all, a businessman, too, who over time came to hold a good deal of mill stock in addition to his law practice. Indeed, Butler was comfortable crediting Whig mill owners with having done wonderful things for Lowell and its residents, especially in the earliest years of the town's development as an industrial center. "It is but just to say," he wrote, that many of them had supported "humane, philanthropic, and far-sighted economic business regulations"; educational opportunities for the town's children, like himself; and moral development through religious organizations. For the factory operatives, such moral training took place in affordable and secure boardinghouses, like the several his mother managed. But there was no getting around the fact that since Lowell's earliest days, even the most benevolent provisions and regulations were fundamentally designed to benefit the mill owners above all. "The great men who founded Lowell knew that good morals were the prime qualification for good working people," Butler noted. And good working people would produce greater profits. Still, as time passed, the "great men's" desire for profits inevitably outstripped their desire to provide for the welfare of the "good working people" who made those profits possible.[9]

If some of Lowell's leading Whig capitalists and other elites turned their noses up at Butler for joining the Freemasons, more surely did so when they read his "occasional editorials" for the *Vox Populi*, a local newspaper dedicated to "oppos[ing] corporation control of the city." One imagines them shaking their heads and rolling their eyes even more vigorously when, in the late summer of 1847, the spirited Butler was arrested for contempt of court. According to the *Boston Daily Atlas* (a Whig newspaper), in the course of prosecuting a particular case Butler insulted, cursed, and used menacing gestures toward the Lowell police court judge, for which the judge had Butler taken into custody. Butler subsequently protested his arrest and denied all the charges against him, insisting that he always aimed to behave respectfully in court, though he did admit to becoming a bit overzealous in support of his client on that particular day. (It would not be the last time.) The judge released him.[10] Word of Butler's behavior, both initially and in responding to the contempt charge, disgusted opponents and delighted allies, echoing the range of responses his words and actions had elicited in college and that would follow him throughout his life and beyond.

At the end of the 1840s, Butler's political views combined with his dedication to the Lowell operatives led to what he considered his first meaningful "political action," namely, an effort to pressure the Massachusetts state legislature to make the ten-hour workday standard for laborers. Back in 1840 Democratic President Martin Van Buren had instituted a ten-hour workday for federal employees and contractors, but in 1848, fourteen hours with a short break for a midday meal was still typical in Lowell and across Massachusetts. Meanwhile, the steady ratcheting up of demands on labor in the mills had produced "almost continuous agitation" by the operatives and their allies, mostly in the form of petitions to the legislature signed by hundreds, even thousands of supporters, calling for the establishment of the ten-hour workday. In 1844 Sarah Bagley, "the most prominent female labor leader of the 1840s," and others formed the Lowell Female Labor Reform Association (LFLRA), for a time the leading organization in New England's labor movement. "For the last half century," Bagley declared in Boston in June 1845, "it has been deemed a violation of woman's sphere to appear before the public as a speaker; but when our rights are trampled upon and we appeal to legislators, what shall we do but appeal to the people? Shall not our voice be heard and our rights acknowledged here; shall it be said again to the daughters of New England, that they have no political rights and are not subject to legislative action?"[11]

In the 1840s the female operatives notably did not engage in work stoppages, as they had on more than one occasion the previous decade, and one source claims that among those who dissuaded "the girls" from striking was Butler, who "believed it was easier to change the law" first than to alter "the habits of profit-motivated businessmen" through walkouts. In any case, male and female workers eventually joined forces to pressure the state legislature in what came to be known as the Ten Hour Movement. But women predominated, often vividly expressing their frustrations and reporting their activities in the *Voice of Industry*, a bold Massachusetts labor newspaper that ran from 1845 to 1848, became the official media organ of the New England Workingmen's Association (with which the LFLRA merged), and was for a time published in Lowell. On one occasion in 1847, the paper referred to the Lowell operatives sardonically as the "living machinery" of the "Cotton Lords of Lowell," a clear reference to the interconnection between the institution of slavery and the textile industry that depended on it, as well as the abusive dominance and greed exhibited by both slave owners and mill owners. Two months later, the paper announced a visit to Lowell of the antislavery orator and activist Frederick Douglass, who had escaped from bondage in Maryland less than a decade earlier, the year Butler graduated from Waterville College.[12]

By publicly and energetically aligning himself with the labor movement and against the interests of the mills' managers and owners, Butler ensured that every "bad name that could be used" against him by his powerful opponents would be "liberally bestowed" upon him. "In the opinions of the mill managers and their principal workmen," Butler later wrote, apparently with considerable pride and no hint of regret, a "more unpopular movement" than the Ten Hour Movement "could not have been made," though it bears noting that his native New Hampshire had passed a ten-hour law in 1847, as did Maine in 1849. Indeed, apart from the laborers themselves, Butler quickly became one of the cause's most provocative and vocal proponents in Lowell and beyond. "The manufacturing newspapers," he wrote, "exhausted their billingsgate upon me." Meanwhile, as the *Voice of Industry* published steadily on the topic, Butler and other like-minded activists strove to persuade the state Democratic Party to adopt a series of ten-hour resolutions.[13]

In the midst of all this, an up-and-coming lawyer and congressman from Illinois made his one and only visit to Lowell, on a campaign stop for Zachary

Taylor, who was running for president as a Whig.[14] On the September 1848 day he visited, reported the favorably inclined *Lowell Journal and Courier*, Abraham Lincoln gave a speech "replete with good sense, sound reasoning, and irresistible argument" to a gathering of local Whigs. Understandably, as Frederick W. Coburn observed in his massive 1920 history of Lowell, at the time Lincoln's "greatness" had yet to be "fully recognized." Indeed, recalling Lincoln's visit many years later, one Lowell resident described the future president on this occasion as basically unimpressive, "slightly stooping, as tall men sometimes are, with long arms which he frequently extended in earnest gesticulation" and "strong and homely features." This same observer, however, remembered being struck by Lincoln's eyes, "which now kindled into brightness in earnest argument or quiet humor, and then assumed a calm sadness."[15] The historical record suggests that Butler took no particular notice of Lincoln's visit, or Frederick Douglass's, or, for that matter, the country's recent and highly consequential—if geographically distant—war with Mexico, despite his party's fervent support for it.

As the 1840s gave way to a new decade, Butler's legal practice continued to prosper, and a number of his more colorful cases elicited the attention of the press, contributing both positively and negatively to his growing celebrity. "I was quite successful in my defences of criminals," Butler recalled. In early 1850, however, he and Sarah suffered a terrible loss on the deepest personal level: the death of their first child, Paul, just two months shy of turning five, from what appears to have been a form of inflammatory bowel disease. This personal tragedy cut sharply into the satisfaction that came from Butler's many advances, which now included his progress up the ranks in the Massachusetts state volunteer militia, first to lieutenant colonel and then colonel of the Fifth Regiment of light infantry. How very happy Benjamin and Sarah must have been, therefore, to welcome their second son in 1852, whom they also named Paul. According to one biographer, this new child grew into a "cheerful youngster with a fondness for swimming and boating," though at some point in his childhood he apparently "fell down a feed chute in the barn, and his legs, crippled in this accident, failed to develop to normal size." Two years later, in a Christmas letter to Sarah, Butler rejoiced in the years of happy family life they had forged, and spoke affectionately of her many fine attributes. Having spent time "looking at the portraits of the *belles* and wives" of the heroes of the American past, Butler wanted Sarah to know that "no more noble and intelligently beautiful face is limmed by the burn of the engraver" than hers, which had cast light on his life's path "for so many years." No individual, indeed, could "more fully, sweetly" blend the roles of woman, wife, and mother than she.[16] At this stage in his journey, Butler was both professionally and personally a happy man.

He was a mindful one, too, whose legal acumen, love for his family, and personal experience of life's fragility now prompted him to draft his first will. In it, Butler directed, first, that in the event he predeceased her, his estate should provide an annual allowance for his beloved mother. He then allocated the required third of his remaining estate to Sarah, noting that if she should remarry, her portion of the estate must remain *outside* her new husband's control. Butler divided the remains of his estate between his (then) two children, Blanche and Paul. As he had done with Sarah, Butler stipulated that should Blanche (or any future daughter) marry, her portion of the estate must also remain outside the control of her husband, suggesting a belief that even married women must retain at least some control over their economic affairs. He named his dear friend and brother-in-law, Fisher, as "protector" for Sarah and the children in the event of his death; he named Sarah executrix.[17]

Revealingly, and perhaps presciently, Butler did not arrange to leave any of his growing wealth or assign any future responsibility to his only brother, Andrew Jackson Butler. It seems that Butler worried that his brother was unreliable, even capricious, not unlike their father. Charlotte Butler shared Benjamin's concern, complaining in September 1847, in the context of the US war with Mexico, that Jackson had left "his wife and child to the mercy of the world" in order to "throw his life away in that miserable Mexican war and bring upon me sorrow upon sorrow." Andrew Jackson Butler survived the war, but his future was unclear. So was the nation's, for although US victory meant the acquisition of vast new lands (the "Mexican Cession"), these new lands in turn dramatically exacerbated sectional tensions over slavery that had already been building for decades. In this turbulent context Benjamin Butler undertook a new and seemingly unlikely political initiative: to help forge a coalition between Democrats—who officially endorsed the principle that "the Constitution recognized slavery" and therefore "nothing could be done towards its abolition except through an amendment to the Constitution"—and emerging antislavery Free Soilers, for the common purpose of diminishing the Whig Party's power. Fisher Hildreth, too, became "one of the spirits that gave life and soul to the Coalition," and Middlesex County, in which Lowell was situated, "was the head and front of this movement" in Massachusetts.[18]

Democrats' and Free Soilers' temporary alignment in Massachusetts, as elsewhere, had its roots in their shared commitment to overcoming the Whigs, which Butler and others characterized as the party of "oppressive anti-labor legislation . . . under the lead of the manufacturers." Significantly, the coalition also endorsed the ten-hour labor law. At this point in his life and development, Butler had not yet become an avowed opponent of chattel slavery, as he himself freely admitted. But he also insisted—perhaps somewhat evasively—that his ongoing affiliation with the Democratic Party, which was fraying along sectional lines—did not reflect an unqualified endorsement of the "peculiar institution," either. Still, even as the sectional divide deepened, Butler's primary focus remained on the sort of "slavery" he witnessed in Lowell on a daily basis: the oppression of waged labor, much of it female, by greedy mill owners. "Although a Democrat," he later wrote, "I was ready to join with anybody who would ameliorate" the "quasi slavery" the New England factory operatives experienced. That said, Butler also apparently felt no obligation to obey the Fugitive Slave Law of 1850 and "go bounding over the graves of my fathers to catch a fugitive slave who was seeking Canada."[19]

In 1850, with Butler's active assistance, Massachusetts Democrats and Free Soilers struck a series of deals that enabled them to gain control of the governorship and the state legislature. Leading Whigs were stunned. According to Butler, Benjamin R. Curtis, then serving as a representative in the Massachusetts House of Representatives (who went on to become a US Supreme Court justice and issue a stinging dissent in the 1857 *Dred Scott* case), "was so far thrown off his balance by the horrors of the coalition that he wrote and published an elaborate pamphlet solemnly arguing his opinion that our political understandings and arrangements" were "an indictable conspiracy at common law, and ought to be prosecuted as such." Alas for the Whigs, such reactions had no practical impact, at least not immediately. Rather, the coalition's electoral successes meant that Democrat George S. Boutwell became the state's twentieth governor (serving from January 1851 to January 1853); Democrat Nathaniel Prentiss Banks became speaker of the newly Democratic-led Massachusetts legislature (1851–52); and Henry Wilson became president of the Massachusetts senate (1851–52). The coalition also led to the Free Soil candidate and abolitionist Charles Sumner's becoming a US senator, an office he held from April 1851 until his death in March 1874. All four of these men went on to have long and illustrious careers that frequently crossed paths with Butler's. Meanwhile, Fisher Hildreth, described by a favorable source as "cool, clear-headed, and far-reaching, with a wonderful insight into the motives which govern and actuate men" and a great "facility" for "moulding the opinions of others to his own," became Middlesex Country's "high sheriff" and later, Lowell's postmaster.[20]

In his autobiography Butler recalled one particularly unsavory consequence of the coalition's efforts, namely, the brazen attempt by *anticoalitionists* in Lowell to frighten voters on the other side—especially workers or allies of labor who endorsed the "Ben Butler ten-hour ticket"—into not casting their ballots in the state elections of 1851. A notice posted on the Hamilton Manufacturing Corporation's gates, Butler remembered, bluntly warned employees they would be fired if they voted for coalition candidates. True to form, in response to such threats, Butler doubled down on his commitment to the cause, at one point giving a rousing speech at City Hall to a gathering of factory workers whose "ten-hour feeling was pronounced." On that occasion, Butler emphatically endorsed the principle of self-government and insisted on the right (at least, men's right) to vote freely. If "working men," he wrote, "can be deprived of their freedom and rights by threats of starvation of themselves and their wives and children, when they act according to the laws and their own judgments, then they had better be slaves indeed, having kind masters, instead of being freemen who are only at liberty to do what their task masters impose upon them, or starve." Butler declared his strong advocacy of mandatory secret ballots, against his opponents' predictable claim that secrecy was unnecessary. To Butler, the secret ballot was the only means by which voters could express their political will undaunted by the threat of coercion from employers and others who had influence over them. The secret ballot, the right to cast a free and independent vote, he believed, was essential for sustaining democracy.[21]

Whatever faith Butler actually had in the principle he articulated, that "undeserved newspaper abuse, however vile, will never ultimately harm a man who lives an honest, proper, and independent life," he never did forgive or forget the unrelenting criticism he faced during the coalition period, especially from the Whig *Journal and Courier* and its senior editor, John H. Warland. At the time, Butler sued both the newspaper's publisher and Warland for libel after they published an article that referred to him as a "notorious demagogue," "political scoundrel," and "dangerous character," and even accused him of having been drunk at the time he gave his City Hall speech. The *Journal and Courier* article also took the tiresome tack of mocking Butler's physical appearance—a recurring theme throughout his life—comparing him to a "Bornese ape" to whom "Nature" had given "a face, which, like a wrecker's light, warns all whom it may concern to be on the lookout while in the vicinity." It bears noting, however, that what the article's author clearly intended as a damning *accusation*—that is, that Butler did not care if the mill owners' and stockholders' profits were reduced, so long as the rights and "hard earnings" of the operatives were protected—one might also consider a badge of honor, as Butler surely did. In any case, the jury quickly decided that Warland and the *Journal and Courier* were not guilty, and the pro-Whig *Boston Daily Atlas* insinuated that even some of Butler's own "best friends" believed he had gone too far by challenging "the fair fame and name of our old friend John H. Warland," not to mention "the corporations." Even the judge who heard the case in the Boston Court of Common Pleas, Ebenezer R. Hoar, himself a Free Soiler, declared that Butler was inordinately brash and primarily self-serving in his challenge to Warland and the paper—perhaps the first skirmish of what became a decades-long personal war between Hoar and Butler. Meanwhile, although the coalition effort clearly had some success, it failed to produce the ten-hour legislation Butler had hoped for, which only got on the books in Massachusetts in 1874.[22]

Still in his early thirties in the early 1850s, Butler already enjoyed a growing family, satisfying finances, a steadily expanding professional portfolio, a gratifying reputation as a determined fighter against entrenched power on behalf of those with less, and increasing political influence within the Democratic Party, both within Massachusetts and beyond. In late 1852—the year Harriet Beecher Stowe published *Uncle Tom's Cabin*—Butler accepted the nomination to represent the Bay State's Eighth District in the US Congress, his first outing as a candidate for elected office. Butler lost the election but won a seat in the Massachusetts state legislature, where he served for a year (1853). During that year Butler advanced a bill to provide relief for an Ursuline convent and school in Charlestown that had been the victim of arson almost twenty years earlier and had struggled financially ever since. Like his efforts on behalf of factory operatives, Butler's support for the Catholic nuns during this era of rising anti-Catholic nativism engendered lavish praise from some and stinging opposition from others; he swatted away the latter as "virulent religious clamor." When Butler's bill failed, some who had opposed it celebrated the failure as a victory for their general anti-Catholicism. For Butler, the dispute simply underscored what he called his "unhappy condition of mind which has ever led me to be with the under dog in the fight when I thought he had been wronged."[23]

In 1853 Butler also served as one of over 400 delegates to the state's third constitutional convention, which met in Boston from May into early August,

Antebellum Butler, seated. Artist unknown. Courtesy of Special
Collections & Archives, Colby College Libraries, Waterville, Maine.

in the course of which he received the news that his Waterville alma mater
had awarded him an honorary "magistratem"—likely master's—degree,
presumably in recognition of the positive ways his professional advance-
ments and increasing political prominence reflected on the college. In contrast with the view from Waterville, anti-Democratic newspapers expressed
wariness about Butler's potentially strong influence at the convention,
calling him a "radical" and a "revolutionary" and cautioning readers about
his views on broadening political representation by nonelites. As he had
grown accustomed to doing, Butler brushed the attacks aside as the sort of
"libels" that "by propriety of life and conduct one can always easily" endure.
Then, when the delegates gathered, Butler validated his opponents' fears by
pressing for significant adjustments to the state constitutional guidelines
for political representation that would reduce the power of cities vis-à-vis

BUTLER'S ANTEBELLUM JOURNEY

towns and limit the possibility of political power becoming centralized in the hands of the few. On June 24, 1853, the *Boston Daily Atlas* grumbled that Butler opposed allocating more representation to Boston even though the city's wealthy residents paid higher taxes than residents elsewhere. The *Atlas* was right: in Butler's view, state government should not "give the rich man a right to cast more votes than a poor man" simply because he was rich. In the end, the convention ended up agreeing on only eight propositions, none of which offered meaningful changes to the system of representation but some of which surely had Butler's support, such as a ban on imprisoning debtors except in cases of fraud. That fall, all eight of the convention's successful propositions were defeated by the state's voters, a result, Butler declared, that sharply undermined his and others' efforts to "benefit the common people."[24]

The failure of the proposed constitutional revisions may seem, especially from this distance, like a nonevent. But it contributed to the collapse of the fragile coalition of Democrats and Free Soilers that had temporarily altered the state's political map. Then, in 1854, the US Congress passed Illinois senator Stephen Douglas's fateful Kansas-Nebraska Act, calling for "popular sovereignty" on the issue of slavery in the first portion of the Mexican Cession to seek statehood, further inflaming sectional passions and laying the foundation for the terrible violence known as "Bleeding Kansas." The collapse of the Whig Party followed, creating a space for the sudden rise of the anti-immigrant, anti-Catholic Know Nothings in Massachusetts, where they captured the governorship and a significant number of seats in the state legislature in the 1854 elections. Despite the fleeting power of this "bigoted and unscrupulous party"—which had emerged suddenly "like a mushroom in the night," as Butler later wrote, both in Massachusetts and elsewhere across the northern United States—they managed to produce an amendment to the Massachusetts state constitution depriving illiterate individuals and non-English speakers of the right to vote or hold political office. Butler was incensed. "I do not hold, and never shall believe, that the matter of reading and writing should determine the capacity of a man to govern himself," he wrote. "An examination of the pay-rolls of that revolution which established the liberty of this country will show that much the larger number of soldiers were such as could not have voted under the strict application of this rule." Given Butler's inescapable penchant for self-congratulation, some might wonder if this declaration was an example of self-serving hindsight, Butler falsely praising himself for having stood up for those whom others ground down. It seems not, however: in the mid-1850s, the pro–Know Nothing

Lowell Daily Citizen and News attacked Butler for his support for immigrants (including the Catholic Irish) and for advocating their speedy naturalization and enfranchisement. The paper even declared Butler the state's preeminent enemy of Know Nothingism, declaring that Butler had heaped more invective on the American Party than anyone. "Butler," the paper insisted, "is the Irishmen's Napoleon."[25]

In January 1855—the same year he and Sarah joyfully welcomed a new son, whom they named Ben-Israel but usually called "Bennie"—Butler also clashed directly and openly with the Know Nothings' successful candidate for Massachusetts governor, Henry J. Gardner. Gardner had "scarcely got warm in his chair," Butler recalled, when he ordered Butler to disband Company A of his Massachusetts Volunteer Militia command, the Fifth Light Infantry Regiment. Company A included many Irishmen (perhaps as many as two-thirds of the total) who were naturalized citizens of the United States. Convinced that the men's Irish heritage and their Catholic faith would never override their loyalty to Massachusetts and the nation, Butler took what he considered the only possible action that his disdain for the governor, and the Know Nothings' xenophobia, allowed: he refused to execute the order and, further, explained to Gardner why the order was illegal. Should this act of defiance lead to a court-martial, the frequently critical *Boston Daily Atlas* jokingly predicted, Butler's "legal talents will outshine his military abilities and we shall probably have the opinion of the Supreme Court upon the powers of the Commander-in-Chief on the premises."[26]

Governor Gardner himself may well have feared contending with Butler's undeniable "legal talents"; in a court-martial, one newspaper observed, "Ben would have proved a troublesome fellow." Instead of taking that chance, therefore, Gardner simply exploited Butler's refusal to obey orders as a reason to remove him from command. Even the *Salem Register*, frequently critical of Butler like the *Atlas*, declared Gardner's decision to fire him "most extraordinary." "We have no political, personal, or other particular partiality for Col. Butler," the paper averred. But "we had supposed" that "we were living under a Republican form of government," and that "citizen soldiers as well as all others were protected by the Constitution and its laws." Now it seemed "we have got beyond this old fashioned doctrine, and that there are powers 'incident to the office,' which give the Governor full leave and liberty to exercise a sway more arbitrary and unlimited than was ever exercised by any Governor or President" in the past. The *Register* called Butler's removal from command "entirely unauthorized by law" and cautioned that the governor's next act might well be to disband the militia entirely.[27]

Instead, Gardner tried a different approach: he reorganized the state militia units so that the Fifth Regiment was no longer associated with Lowell and the surrounding area, causing Lowell instead to be associated with the Sixth Regiment, which already had its own commander. In May 1857, however, Butler's fellow MVM officers took matters into their own hands, electing him not *colonel* of the *Sixth* Regiment, but *general* of the entire organization's Third Brigade, Second Division. Butler recalled with considerable pleasure the irony of receiving his new commission from none other than the much-discomfited Governor Gardner. This happy development was soon followed by a particularly flattering appointment by then-Secretary of War Jefferson Davis to serve on the board of visitors for the annual examination of the cadets at West Point. That June, Butler finally made it to West Point, where he met the now seventy-one-year-old commanding general of the US Army and veteran of the War of 1812, Gen. Winfield Scott. And thus, declared the *Salem Register*, "the whirligig of time brings about its revenges."[28]

The sudden rise of the Know Nothings had far reaching implications for the political party system, not the least of which was enabling the formation of yet another new party, the Republican Party, which explicitly prioritized an antislavery agenda over anti-immigrant xenophobia and in which even some former Know Nothings found a new home when the American Party itself collapsed. In 1857, the year of the US Supreme Court's momentous *Dred Scott* decision, Nathaniel Banks—a former mill worker in Lowell and nearby Waltham who had worked with Butler in the coalition movement, served as speaker of the Massachusetts House of Representatives, and also presided over the 1853 state constitutional convention—was elected governor, a position he held for three terms until January 1861. Having previously been a Democrat and, briefly, a Know Nothing, Banks was now a Republican, and during his years as governor the state as a whole became more and more heavily Republican, too. In addition to returning Banks to the governorship, the 1858 state elections produced a state senate with thirty-seven Republicans and only three Democrats, and a house of representatives with 177 Republicans and 32 Democrats. For his part, Butler still felt ideologically most at home in the nevertheless disintegrating Democratic Party and was concerned that the Republicans' antislavery focus would result in national rupture. In June 1856 he chaired the Massachusetts delegation at the Democratic National Convention in Cincinnati. While in the Queen City of the West, although his focus was politics, Butler still found time to entertain "a cloud of sweet memories" of having seen his beloved wife, Sarah, perform on the stage there more than a dozen years earlier.[29]

The Cincinnati convention nominated the lackluster James Buchanan for president. Butler was disappointed. As one of his correspondents noted, Buchanan "excited no enthusiasm" at the convention, in part because of the vagueness of his political positions, and in part because his speechmaking skills were so poor that they "would have ruined any man less eminent." Unenthusiastic about Buchanan, Butler nevertheless exerted considerable impact on the party platform, which ultimately reflected his and others' fading hope for compromise between the sections. To that end, the Cincinnati platform endorsed state's rights, "popular sovereignty" ("let everyone mind his own business," Butler phrased it in one speech), and noninterference by the federal government on the institution of slavery. Bleeding Kansas and the brutal assault by a slavery apologist on Massachusetts senator Charles Sumner had not yet persuaded Butler to reject slavery; the dangers of an increasingly likely national conflict over the issue seemed far more pressing. Butler also may have been considering the implications of such a conflict for Lowell itself, where the raw materials of slavery and the engine of the town's economy (and, by association, his own) were inseparable. To a number of Butler's most avid supporters at the convention, the procompromise Butler represented a refreshing, "moderate" alternative to those they derided as "Black Republicans" with their uncompromising antipathy to slavery. Butler was even briefly on the vice presidential ballot at Cincinnati, but the prize, such as it was, went to Kentucky's John C. Breckinridge instead.[30]

Butler returned home to Massachusetts and, despite his lack of enthusiasm for Buchanan, immediately began campaigning for the Democratic presidential ticket, provoking the *Lowell Daily Citizen and News* to describe him as, like Buchanan himself, a "doughface": a northern Democrat whose views were more closely aligned with those of the southern wing of the party. In truth, Butler was closer to Stephen Douglas in his politics: that December, speaking to a grand meeting of Massachusetts Democrats in Boston's Faneuil Hall he still openly endorsed Douglas's deeply problematic principle of "popular sovereignty," despite the violence it had produced in Kansas. On the issue of slavery, Butler declared, "let the people govern themselves as they think best." On that occasion Butler also expressed opposition to the interference of Congress or the president in any matter that "comes within the limit of state legislation," including slavery. Years later in his autobiography Butler mounted a vigorous self-defense against the decades of criticism that his late-antebellum views had elicited. He reminded readers that back in 1787 the US Constitution could never have gone into effect had it not endorsed slavery, and that as a lawyer, soldier, and citizen he had felt bound to uphold the Constitution *as it was written*, despite the fact that slavery itself "was repugnant to the moral feelings of a great many citizens." On the question of how repugnant the institution was to him personally in the pre-war period, he did not elaborate. It seems clear, however, that in the years before the war, Butler's concern about the suffering and abuse of industrial wage laborers in his immediate community and beyond outstripped whatever concern he felt about the unique horrors of chattel slavery and the terrible suffering of those held in its grasp.[31]

By the fall of 1857, Butler was well positioned to make a run for the Massachusetts state senate. Predictably, his political opponents came out in force to stop him, the *Lowell Daily Citizen and News* breathlessly branding him the leading light of the state's "Irish ragamuffinism" and representative of a party "hated, despised, and deserted of all honest men!" The paper urged voters to choose Lowell's Arthur P. Bonney instead, and Bonney won. (Butler lost this election but went on to win the same seat the following year, despite the continued dire warnings of the *Daily Citizen and News*.) Meanwhile, Butler expanded his business investments, now purchasing a controlling interest in the Middlesex Woolen Mill, where he appointed Richard Fay Jr. the mill's treasurer and immediately enacted a ten-hour rule for the operatives as well as overtime pay regulations. In November 1858 Butler stood for election to the US House of Representatives from Massachusetts's Eighth District (he lost to Republican Charles R. Train of Framingham) and simultaneously submitted his name for nomination as the state Democratic Party's gubernatorial candidate, an honor that went to Erasmus Beach of Springfield, whom Butler quickly endorsed. Despite these electoral ups and downs and the loud and virulent opposition that dogged him, Butler's political star was indisputably on the rise, though perplexity regarding his precise views on chattel slavery—the nation's preeminent problem—persisted. As the *Hartford Courant* observed in October 1858, "He is in favor of Douglas's doctrine of popular sovereignty in the territories, and believes that the Dred Scott decision is not a correct one, and that slavery is not carried into the territories by the Constitution. All this he fully believes." Meanwhile, perhaps in an ironic case of "he doth protest too much," while visiting Washington, D.C., after the 1858 election, presumably on legal business, Butler wrote to Sarah expressing distaste for the capital city. "I think a fortnight longer here would quite cure me of any desire to go to Congress."[32]

As a state senator in 1859 Butler sat on the Militia and Judiciary Committees, voted for his old friend and mentor Caleb Cushing to become one of Massachusetts's US senators (Republican Henry Wilson was reelected by a wide margin), introduced a series of resolutions pertaining to the various issues that interested him and his constituents, served on a committee to review and possibly revise the state's statute laws, and recommended an increase in the salaries of judges on the state Supreme Court so as to enable broader socioeconomic representation on the bench. He also continued to hone his already advanced skills in argumentation, participating in heated arguments with senate colleagues on subjects large and small. On one occasion, Butler spoke adamantly and at great length in opposition to any efforts to impose anti-immigrant, Know Nothing–inspired restrictions on state voting rights. "He denounced this scheme in bold terms," reported one newspaper, "and criticized its provisions with much shrewdness. His speech was not answered, for the good reason that it could not be." The *Pittsfield Sun* observed that Butler's arguments on all fronts were "clear and pointed," and that "nearly everybody" knew Butler possessed "a pretty good share of the ability in the Senate." The *Boston Semi-Weekly Courier* agreed, declaring that Butler stood "at the head of the Senators for legal erudition and general ability," and commending renegade Republicans from his district who had joined with Democrats and others to vote him into office. The paper went on to describe Butler as a "forcible" if sometimes inelegant and occasionally sarcastic orator with a "ready wit and great readiness at repartee." Although Butler's previous lack of legislative experience occasionally led him to treat the state senate more like a courtroom than a legislative chamber, it had not hindered him in any other way. "Mr. Butler's legal knowledge and clearness of insight," the paper concluded, "is of great service in matters of ordinary legislation," and "personally" Butler was very "popular" with his colleagues.[33]

As the decade drew to a close, in contrast with his views on slavery, Butler's stance on the question of immigrant rights remained firm and unambiguous. In September 1859, a month before John Brown's momentous antislavery attack on the federal arsenal at Harpers Ferry, Virginia, Butler continued to argue that the parameters of citizenship for naturalized immigrants should be equal to those for native-born citizens. "Between citizens," he insisted in a letter to the *Boston Post*, "the Constitution and the laws know no distinction, and the government of the United States ought not and cannot know the adopted from the native." That same month at the Democratic Party's state convention in Worcester, he opposed lengthening the naturalization period for immigrants seeking citizenship. When it came to selecting the state party's candidate for president, the convention endorsed Illinois senator Stephen Douglas and his principle of "popular sovereignty" and then nominated Butler for governor. In the weeks ahead, Butler's energetic campaigning—which included speeches in favor of protective tariffs and of immigrants, but also *against* allowing Black men to enroll in the state militia—elicited stern criticism from the abolitionist (Worcester) *Massachusetts Spy*. In contrast with Republican candidate Nathaniel Banks's explicitly antislavery position, observed the *Spy*, Butler came across as, at best, only slightly uncomfortable with the idea "that under our federal constitution pigs and slaves are on the same footing, both being property."[34]

That fall, the *Spy* and the increasingly antislavery and increasingly numerous Republican voters of Massachusetts found Butler's equivocal public stance on slavery thoroughly unsatisfying, and Banks won reelection by a substantial margin (58,780 votes to 35,334). It bears noting, however, that shortly *after* John Brown's October raid, Virginia's *Richmond Whig* expressed alarm about an assertion Butler had made in a recent letter, to the effect that the nation's laws on slavery were not fixed in perpetuity, could in fact be changed, and then, potentially, the institution could be destroyed. "Slavery exists no where by natural right," the *Whig* quoted Butler as writing, "but only because of some positive enactment, embodied either in the Constitution or statute law of the community in which it is found." The *Whig* worried that Butler's equivocation might eventually give way to legal activism against the "peculiar institution." For its part, the *Patriot and State Gazette* of Butler's birth state, New Hampshire, seemed more in line with the *Whig* than the *Spy*, observing with disgust "how much higher the negro is esteemed than the naturalized white man, by the black republicans of Massachusetts."[35]

Butler lost his latest race for Massachusetts governor, but he enjoyed other successes. For one thing, his legal practice continued to thrive in both Lowell and Boston. Additionally, he soon learned that he would be the Eighth District's delegate to the following spring's Democratic National Convention in Charleston, South Carolina, where his old friend Caleb Cushing would preside. As the new decade began, Butler also received special public recognition for his most recent, visible work on behalf of the state's mill workers. In this case, Butler was instrumental in the effort to raise funds for the victims of the terrible Pemberton Mill collapse in nearby Lawrence in January, which produced "scores of both dead and mangled and wounded" workers, including one man who was so "deeply buried in the ruins" that he concluded that "there was no possibility of being extricated" and chose to "cut his own throat to end his sufferings."[36]

In mid-April 1860 Butler headed to Charleston, nearly a thousand miles from Lowell, for his party's national convention. From onboard the steamer

Spaulding Butler wrote cheerfully to Sarah that the trip from Boston had been "very pleasant, " and that while others, like his brother-in-law Fisher, had become "very sea sick" on the way south, he himself comfortably "ate five times a day, slept soundly, worked incessantly, and drank sparingly." Butler further informed Sarah that his detour to visit a private Catholic girls school just outside of Washington, D.C.—now Georgetown Visitation Preparatory School—where he and Sarah were considering sending "Buntie," had convinced him that they were doing the right thing. In Washington, Butler also met briefly with Senator Douglas regarding the upcoming convention. When he reached Charleston, Butler reported, he and others were required to spend the night "on the quarantine ground" before entering the city, which they found alive with excitement, with "flags flying guns firing and drums beating all in the finest style." He was, he hastened to add, both homesick and lovesick. "I long to be with you at home again," he assured Sarah, "with an inexpressible longing."[37]

The 1860 Democratic National Convention began on April 23, delegates gathering at Charleston's Masonic Hall to devise a party platform and select a candidate for president in the context of unprecedented national tension and political upheaval over the issue of slavery. For his part, Butler served as a key member of the Committee on Resolutions, where, with John Brown's provocative raid and martyrdom weighing heavily on his mind, he proposed that the convention adopt, unchanged, the compromise platform he had been key to devising in Cincinnati four years earlier. The committee, reported one paper, "had a stormy time of it." Butler, it appears, hoped above all—perhaps with some willful blindness and even hubris—to keep the party and the Union intact. "Having become satisfied that there was danger of an attempt to sever the Union of the States upon the slavery question," he later wrote, "I sedulously devoted myself to an endeavor to keep the peace, and keep the Democratic Party together, because I looked to that as the only source of safety in the Union." Sectional divisions within the party, however, soon scuttled Butler's proposal: more than half of the thirty-two state delegations present demanded, at the very least, amendments to the Cincinnati platform that would provide additional guarantees for slavery. According to these delegates, "Congress had no power to abolish Slavery in the Territories," and, moreover, "Territorial Legislatures had no power to abolish Slavery in any Territory, nor to prohibit the introduction of Slavery therein, nor to exclude Slavery therefrom, or to impair or destroy the right of property in slaves by any legislation whatever." Clearly, wrote one observer, the slave states "were united, evidently by pre-concert, in a determination to demand from the people of the Free-labor States further and most offensive concessions to their greed for political domination." Butler and others pressed again for adoption of the more conciliatory and by no means antislavery Cincinnati platform, but angry proslavery delegates, including those hailing from Alabama, Mississippi, Louisiana, South Carolina, Florida, Texas, and even Delaware, began to withdraw, "in an evident condition of weariness and fretfulness," before agreement on a platform could be achieved.[38]

By the time balloting to select the party's presidential candidate was set to begin, the possibility of cross-sectional party unity at the convention had slipped away entirely. "The Northern Democrats have yielded as much as they could," reported the *Boston Recorder*. In contrast, the unreasonable demands of the slave states' delegates had provoked even the previously equivocal Butler to make what the *Recorder* lauded as "a very good anti-slavery speech." The balloting proceeded, and in the end a majority of the remaining delegates in Charleston chose Stephen Douglas, but not enough votes were cast for him to clinch the nomination. Having lost some of his earlier support among northern Democrats who considered him responsible for the Kansas violence and the attack on Charles Sumner, Douglas had wisely backtracked somewhat from his pure "popular sovereignty" position. In his 1858 debates with Abraham Lincoln, Douglas offered what came to be known as his "Freeport Doctrine," which allowed that territories could explicitly *exclude* slavery if they chose to do so. This move brought a number of former supporters back into the Douglas fold, but Butler was not among them. "Mr. Douglas was my personal friend," Butler wrote later, and "the district which had sent me to the convention was undoubtedly in his favor." Butler himself, however, had lost confidence that "the Little Giant" could lead the Democratic Party to victory in the upcoming presidential election.[39]

Still, when he met with Douglas in Washington on his way to Charleston, Butler had promised he would cast up to five ballots for him at the convention, and when the balloting began, he did just that. Increasingly, however, Butler became convinced that the number of southern delegates willing to accept Douglas's nomination would never reach the necessary threshold (nomination required two-thirds of the gathered delegates' support), and he quietly began to shift his loyalty to Kentuckian James Guthrie, whom he deemed "a clear-headed man, of quick perceptions, of careful and conservative reflections upon all subjects, and of a well-balanced mind," who "looked upon the preservation of the Union as infinitely beyond any question in regard to slavery." Then, when it became clear that Guthrie's support at the convention was even weaker than Douglas's, Butler switched his support to Jefferson Davis, the candidate he considered most likely to defeat a Republican nominee. If his decision to endorse Davis was an obvious one to Butler, it was definitely not so for many of the devoted Douglas supporters who had sent him to Charleston in the first place. Davis, the *Lowell Daily Citizen and News* growled, was "the sworn enemy alike of Douglas and his policy" and "the chieftain of the southern fire-eaters." Indeed, pro-Douglas and anti-Davis ire rained down on Butler not only during and immediately after the convention but also for the rest of his life and beyond. For his critics, the nearly sixty votes Butler ultimately cast for Davis in Charleston provided all the evidence they needed that he was uniquely politically fickle. Not everyone agreed, however. Indeed, the often disparaging *Massachusetts Spy* praised Butler's voting strategy as an example of "pluck under somewhat trying circumstances," and a "rebuke of those delegates who gave their sympathies, and whatever aid they could, to the advocate of the slave code and the disunionists."[40]

For his part, Butler explained switching his support to Davis in purely pragmatic terms. At first, he explained, he had hoped that a few votes for Davis would persuade proslavery southern delegates of his and other northerners' genuine willingness to accept a southern candidate. Then, when he eventually began to vote for his actual favorite candidate, Guthrie, as he planned to do, the mollified southerners would follow suit. Butler's original plan went awry, of course, and once Guthrie's nomination, too, became impossible, he determined that the best move *for the party* was to stick with Davis who, he pointed out, was not strictly a "southern candidate" in any case but had genuine national credentials. For although Davis was certainly a Mississippi slaveholder, and although within a few short months he would reveal his determination to protect the institution of human bondage in perpetuity at the expense of the Union, at the time Butler voted for him in Charleston Davis was best known as a veteran soldier and officer of the US Army who had fought in the Mexican-American War, served as secretary of war under Franklin Pierce, and was now a US senator. In the course of his career Davis had taken multiple oaths to defend the US Constitution and as of the spring of 1860 he had expressed not a hint of "ultra" secessionist sentiment. Rather, Davis had distinguished himself with his "great reach of thought and great belief in the future of the country." In Butler's view, therefore—and it is not an entirely unreasonable one given what he knew in April 1860—the decision to support (and stick with) Davis made perfect sense. Moreover, he was certain, some of the attacks he subsequently endured for it grew out of his attackers' loyalty to Stephen Douglas the *man*, who could not win the nomination, rather than to the Democratic *Party*, which, with the "right" candidate, still might win the election and save the Union.[41] In other words, the attacks on Butler's voting record at Charleston that continued up to and beyond his death reflect knowledge Butler did not have in the spring of 1860, namely, that in January 1861 Davis would defy his oath of office, walk out of the Senate, and go on to become president of Confederate States of America.

With its business unfinished and sectional acrimony raging, the convention adjourned on May 3, agreeing to meet again in Baltimore in mid-June, by which time, presumably, flaring tempers would have cooled. By then, too, the Republicans gathering for their convention in Chicago would have chosen their nominee, whom Butler and so many others expected to be the ardent antislavery New Yorker, William H. Seward. The *Spaulding* left Charleston for Boston on May 4. The following day, William Locke of Bedford, Massachusetts, wrote to Butler, identifying himself immediately as a staunch Republican who had never supported Butler in the past. Locke echoed the praise of the *Massachusetts Spy*, noting that he had "watched the doings of the Charleston convention" and believed Butler's actions there were merited. Moreover, Locke insisted, "if my vote would make you President of the U.S. you should have it."[42]

On May 15, back in Lowell's Huntington Hall, Butler reported at length to a rowdy crowd of about 300 mostly Douglas supporters who, although they had fully expected Butler to throw his weight behind Douglas in Charleston, dispersed after reluctantly endorsing the course of action he had pursued. Still, the question of what would happen when he attended the Baltimore (re)convention in June left many unsettled. Butler promised doubters that if Douglas seemed to have a shot at the nomination when the delegates met again in Maryland, he would vote for him. But he reiterated that his aim was to vote for whichever Democrat he believed could win the presidential election in the fall, a stance the *Boston Courier* praised as "the party first and men afterwards." "Mr. Butler," observed the *Boston Daily Advertiser* on May 18, "plainly supposed himself to be sent to Charleston to nominate a candidate who should win." That is what he had done and what he would do again. From this perspective, the *Advertiser* insisted, he had "acted like a democratic tactician" in choosing Davis.[43]

On June 18, Butler took his seat at the Front Street Theater in Baltimore for his party's second attempt to nominate a presidential candidate capable of satisfying both northern and southern Democrats and winning the November election. Southern delegations that had bolted the gathering in

Charleston had now in many cases been reconfigured to include more at least putative Douglas supporters, who simultaneously proved even more fervently supportive of protecting slavery than the delegates they had replaced. Meanwhile, as if to ensure that Douglas got the nod, some threatened to demand revocation of the long-standing two-thirds rule for winning the nomination, ripening the conditions for sharp conflict. Indeed, a tumultuous week of "despicable strife, vulgar brawls, and bitter vituperation" followed, in the course of which Butler contributed at least one "defiant speech" protesting the southern delegates' increasingly uncompromising demands. Among other things, reported the *Lowell Daily Citizen and News*, Butler castigated proslavery conventioneers who apparently meant not only to defend the institution in its current form but also to expand it into the territories and even reopen the slave trade. Butler then led a walkout of members of the Massachusetts delegation, provoking vigorous cheering from the supposedly pro-Douglas and certainly proslavery attendees. "There was loud applause, with cries of 'good,' 'good,' 'go along,' when they retired," reported the *Salem Register*. Butler and the rest of the Massachusetts delegation then joined representatives from other states who had also walked out for yet a third convention—also in Baltimore—where they nominated the sitting vice president of the United States, John C. Breckinridge of Kentucky, but only after Breckinridge had given—reassuringly and in person—what Butler described as "the strongest possible declaration of his devotion to the Union and the Constitution" as well as "a particular disavowal and repudiation of the cry then ringing through the South, that if the Republican Party came into power, the South would secede."[44] Meanwhile, as expected, the delegates still gathered at the Front Street Theater nominated Stephen Douglas.

Reaction to the turbulent events in Baltimore was, put mildly, mixed. Back in Massachusetts, the *Boston Herald* declared that by abandoning Douglas, Butler and the Massachusetts delegation had "proved themselves traitors of the blackest kind" who were prepared to do the "dirty work" up north for fire-eating southern nationalists who showed "about as much regard for them" as they did for their slaves. Butler and the delegation had "disgraced the people who have lifted them into stations which they have proved unworthy to fill," the *Herald* scolded. Once again, Butler gave a speech "of several hours in length" to a gathering at Huntington Hall, defending his action. Opponents remained unappeased. "Can Mr. Butler tell the Massachusetts democracy the way whereby they may possibly turn her electoral vote against Lincoln?" asked the *New York Herald*, now that the Republicans had selected their candidate. "If he can, let him speak." Meanwhile, repre-

sentatives of the national "Breckinridge for President" campaign urged Butler to get out on the stump as quickly as possible in light of Butler's "well
known ability as a speaker" and his "devotion to the great cause in which we
are engaged."[45]

How much campaigning Butler actually undertook for the Breckinridge
ticket is unclear. As summer gave way to fall, the fracturing of the national
Democratic Party was fully reflected in his state, which held three distinct
state conventions in mid-September, in Boston (the Breckinridge faction),
Springfield (the Douglas faction), and Worcester (supporters of the newly
formed Constitutional Union Party ticket, John Bell of Tennessee and Massachusetts's own Edward Everett). The Breckinridge faction unanimously
and quite hopelessly nominated Benjamin Butler for governor, after which
Butler quickly made it clear that he had no interest in forming a coalition
with the supporters of Douglas or Bell simply in order to advance his candidacy, which was likely to go nowhere anyway. Meanwhile, Massachusetts Republicans nominated John A. Andrew for governor after Banks
announced that he would not run again. The *Boston Courier* described
Andrew, an otherwise "kind-hearted and courteous gentleman," as an
"extreme abolitionist" who "would set all the slaves free, without regarding
the fact that it would be letting loose millions of helpless creatures, whose
only resort must be beggary and crime—starvation for multitudes of them,
and, only too probably, the ultimate forcible extermination of the rest." For
its part, Butler's hometown paper, the *Lowell Daily Citizen and News*, insisted
that the Maine-born Andrew, a graduate of Waterville College's rival, Bowdoin College, was "at once honest, able, and thoroughly devoted to the great
interests of free labor." His reputation, the paper noted, "is unsullied." When
Lincoln was elected president in November, his Massachusetts ally, Andrew,
won a resounding victory as governor, earning more than 100,000 votes to
Butler's 6,000.[46]

Observers noted that in his previous run for governor, Butler had done
significantly better, and on November 16, even William Lloyd Garrison's *The
Liberator* reported that Butler had a made poor showing, payback from the
state's Douglas Democrats, no doubt, for Butler's "betrayal" in Charleston.
Notably, the same issue of the paper pondered the meaning of a recent case
in Lowell in which Butler defended a Black plaintiff who had been manhan-
dled and ejected from a concert at Huntington Hall. In commenting on the
case, the paper praised Butler's spirited and successful argument on behalf
of the plaintiff, to whom the jury awarded $200. Noting that the case indi-
cated good things about Butler's stance and "sentiments" with regard to "fair

play for black men" in Massachusetts, *The Liberator* observed that Butler did not hesitate "to rightfully apply the law" for the Black man in the same way he would have done for a White one. Apparently, *The Liberator* speculated, Butler's "practice" when it came to issues of racial justice was more advanced than his "theory," as far as that "theory" was detectable. Some weeks later, the *Lowell Daily Citizen and News* reported that Butler did not oppose the state's personal liberty laws, by means of which Bay Staters could justify resisting the federal Fugitive Slave Law, which required them to participate in the capture of runaway slaves.[47] It seems that Butler's journey toward active antislavery was underway.

All hail to Butler.
—*NEW YORK HERALD*, MAY 16, 1861

Gen. Butler has been fighting theoretical abolitionism for thirty years, and now the slaves are running to him in flocks for freedom and protection. Thus circumstances have made him the first practical abolitionist we have had.
—*REGISTER* (SANDUSKY, OHIO), JUNE 4, 1861

Into the Civil War
1861–April 1862

In January 1860, Benjamin Butler's "Memoranda of Estate & Liabilities" listed an impressive catalog of assets: a twelve-acre family homestead valued at $31,000; the Museum Building along with a contiguous city block that housed the post office, valued at $37,500; an additional plot of land (with buildings) in downtown Lowell, valued at $5,000; his mother Charlotte's property, valued at $1,500; ten other pieces of real estate, not all in Lowell; and about $10,000 worth of personal property: "furniture, books, pictures, plate, household stuff and plants . . . horses, carriages, harness, stable furniture, tools, implements, and stock . . . library safe and office furniture . . . and books." Butler's assets further included his stock holdings in the Middlesex woolen mill and other area mills, valued collectively at about $22,000, plus a number of claims against debtors—his perennially floundering and unsettled brother among them—totaling around $4,000. Butler's liabilities—bank loans, life insurance payments, and various "floating debts"—amounted to far less than his nearly $100,000 in assets.[1]

Even as the nation itself was heading for collapse, Butler and his family were thriving financially and otherwise. Meanwhile, life at home had changed in one significant way: thirteen-year-old Blanche was now a homesick boarding student at Georgetown's Catholic Academy of the Visitation, to which her father had escorted her at the end of the summer.

Late in September, Sarah sent words of comfort to her lonely daughter. "You must consider my dear," Sarah wrote, that "the next few years must be devoted to study. And you would find the consequent confinement as irksome in one place as another." In October, Sarah offered some tips for overall health—"When you are out," she advised Blanche, "walk about briskly and get as much exercise as you can"—and she promised that "Buntie's" feelings of isolation would fade. As it happens, Blanche was one of only a few New Englanders at the school and the only student from Massachusetts. The other girls, Sarah wrote reassuringly, "will like you better when they know you longer." Still, she added with evident regional vanity, "Do not mind what they say of your pronunciation" and "by no means adopt theirs."[2]

Blanche's devoted father provided advice, too. "That you should be ambitious to excel, and obtain the rewards of merit," Butler wrote, "gives me much pleasure." But he reminded her that "progress at school" was valuable only to the extent that "it gives assurance that you are endeavoring to prepare yourself for the future," though precisely what sort of future Butler envisioned for Blanche he did not say. He went on to offer words of praise, caution that the family's "happiness" was "bound up in your welfare," and to remind his daughter that she must work hard and represent Yankeedom well now that she was, essentially, in the South. Butler closed his missive with news about her brothers, who were both attending local schools, noting that little Bennie, now five, "gets his usual share of unlucky tumbles, but picks himself up again with the same good humor as ever." As for eight-year-old Paul, he had recently "cut a fine little gash in his forehead but that is healing up cleverly after having let out, as I tell him, some of his bad blood." In another letter Butler scolded Blanche for her persistent melancholy. "Pray do not pain me by hearing that you are homesick," he wrote with perhaps exaggerated sternness. "Never say it. Never feel it, never think it." Butler had sent Blanche to Georgetown, he explained, not just for academic reasons but also that she might "see other manners, other customs and ways, than those around you at home," believing as he did that "one used to a single range of thoughts and modes of life soon comes to think all others inferior, while in fact they may be better, and are only different." This, he added, "is a provincialism, and one of which I am sorry to say that Massachusetts people are most frequently guilty." At the same time, like Sarah, Butler encouraged Blanche to "hold fast" to her own way of pronouncing words and "not adopt the flat drawl of the South."[3] Diversity of experience was important, but regional pride was too.

As Blanche slowly settled in at school in Georgetown, the bonds holding the nation together in late 1860 continued to unravel with the breakdown of President James Buchanan's cabinet, South Carolina's December 20 declaration of secession, and rumblings of war growing louder. On December 28, South Carolina sent a group of "commissioners" to Washington—allegedly as "ambassadors from a sovereign power"—to directly advise the flustered and indecisive lame-duck president of their determination to ensure South Carolina's independence. To this end, the commissioners demanded the removal of all remaining Federal military forces from South Carolina, specifically those under the command of Maj. Robert Anderson, who had recently moved his men from Fort Moultrie to Fort Sumter in Charleston Harbor. Butler—whom Buchanan briefly considered as a replacement for Secretary of War John B. Floyd of Virginia after the southern nationalist resigned—was in Washington when the commissioners arrived and advised Buchanan to arrest them immediately and have them tried for treason. For Butler, who had so recently and energetically endorsed sectional compromise, South Carolina's assertion of independence was, simply, a game changer. The Union was now being actively dismantled, and its defenders must exact swift and unequivocal retribution on those who were engaged in tearing it apart. "Of course it was impossible for a man of Mr. Buchanan's temperament and training, however honest and conscientious, to adopt so decisive a course," Butler later recalled. "He thought it would lead to great agitation." Looking back, Butler remained certain that if Buchanan had arrested the commissioners as he suggested, "the question of secession could have been settled then in a manner that would have saved life and treasure incalculable." While Buchanan dithered, Butler met with a number of political leaders from around the country, including Senator Jefferson Davis, to discuss the developing crisis. His conversation with Davis, he wrote later, convinced him "that war was inevitable."[4]

South Carolina's declaration of independence soon provoked similar pronouncements from other Deep South states as well as the departure from Washington of their many senators and congressmen. At least as troubling was the defection of hundreds of US Army officers from their posts and the rapid surrender to southern nationalist rebels of a multitude of federal properties, both civil and military, across the region. Perhaps the most shocking of these acts of disloyalty was the surrender by Gen. David E. Twiggs, a veteran of the War of 1812, of the entire Department of Texas. Alarmed by all these developments, in early January Kentuckian Joseph Holt—the former postmaster general Buchanan had ultimately selected as Floyd's replacement in the War Department—ordered the first naval expedition to resupply Major Anderson and his men at Fort Sumter. Led by the steamship *Star of the West*, the expedition returned north immediately upon taking enemy fire. The drums of war grew louder. From school in Georgetown, Blanche Butler anxiously urged her mother "to ask Father what he thinks about Civil War."[5]

Butler saw the war coming, and from the start he aimed to play a substantial and meaningful role in the rebellion's defeat. For a man with his combination of ability, drive, and genuine devotion to the Union, the looming conflict offered an ideal opportunity to deploy many of his most impressive qualities: his intellectual and organizational acumen, his strong will, his robust ego, his fearlessness, his seemingly unflappable self-confidence. On a personal level, the war provided an opportunity to make up in some measure for the loss of his dream of attending West Point, which his service in the Massachusetts Volunteer Militia had only partially assuaged. Possessed of considerable self-awareness, Butler would have readily admitted, too, that a successful showing in the war could advance both his personal and professional prospects. All that said, it would be wrong to see Butler's determination to carve out an important place for himself in the defense of the nation as merely a manifestation of naked ambition and overweening self-regard. In the end, like virtually every other Civil War military leader, *including* those trained at West Point, Butler stumbled on the battlefield more often than he liked to admit, which his opponents during his life and after took great pleasure in highlighting. Equally true, however, is that Butler sacrificed boldly and generously for the nation's cause throughout the war and accomplished much while he was in uniform that was to the country's, and not least African Americans', benefit.[6]

Even before Abraham Lincoln assumed the presidency in early March 1861, and even as he remained busy with his professional responsibilities, Butler began taking steps to prepare the citizen-soldiers of the Massachusetts Volunteer Militia for service. In late January the *Lowell Daily Citizen and News* reported that the MVM's Sixth Regiment—which Brigadier General Butler now commanded, along with the Eighth—had authorized Col. Edward F. Jones to place it under Governor Andrew's control for the national defense, if necessary. The Sixth, Colonel Jones reported to Governor Andrew, comprised four companies from Lowell, two more from Lawrence, and one each from Acton and Groton, all men "who earn their bread by the sweat of their brow" and "are willing to leave their homes, families, and all that man holds dear, and sacrifice their present and future as a matter of duty." MVM regiments from elsewhere in the state drew their enlistments from men with similar backgrounds and motivations. And as Butler and others immediately noted, they all needed uniforms, guns, and ammunition, which would be expensive. But "what is the cost in money to the State of Massachusetts," Jones asked, "when compared to the sacrifices we are called upon to make?"[7]

With Colonel Jones, Butler pressed Governor Andrew for the supplies the men would need if deployed to an active battlefront, especially if deployment took place before the weather grew warmer. In a letter some years later, Butler praised the governor for his "sagacity," "patriotism," and "fidelity to the Union" in response to these urgent requests; together, he recalled, they worked expeditiously to put the state's militiamen "into a state of readiness." In his 1870 history of Massachusetts, Edward Everett Hale observed that the Democrat Butler and the Republican Andrew may have been political opponents, but at this moment "they were both Massachusetts men." On Butler's recommendation, Hale wrote, Andrew called on the state legislature to make an emergency appropriation to purchase supplies, including winter coats, which came to be known as "Andrew's overcoats." The fact that the cloth came from the Middlesex woolen mill later provoked Butler's opponents to accuse him of self-dealing: Butler, it has been noted, owned considerable stock in the mill. In Hale's view, however, what mattered was not the source of the cloth or which mill got the contract but that the cross-party collaboration of Butler and Andrew made the required coats available quickly.[8]

By mid-February 1861, even as the nation's capital buzzed with preparations for Lincoln's inauguration, invasion from the newly created Confederate States of America threatened. There was, Blanche observed from Georgetown, "a great deal of excitement in Washington." Then, in mid-April, South Carolina forces attacked Fort Sumter, resulting in the surrender of Major Anderson and his garrison and their departure north to safety. In response, President Lincoln summoned 75,000 state militiamen for three months service to suppress the rebellion and "repossess the forts, places, and property which have been seized from the Union." Lincoln simultaneously called upon "all loyal citizens" to "favor, facilitate, and aid this effort to maintain the honor, the integrity, and the existence of our National Union, and the perpetuity of popular government; and to redress wrongs already long enough endured." As an experienced commander of state militia, an individual with an impressive record of professional accomplishments, and a loyal citizen of the United States, Butler was influenced by the overwhelming "rage militaire" that gripped men of all political persuasions across the North. "But one sentiment finds expression," reported the *Massachusetts Spy*. "Party feeling and party prejudice are lost sight of in the greater and more solemn purpose to stand by the constitution and the government." Butler now dove deeper into the work of defending the nation, and specifically its capital.[9]

On April 15, the same day Lincoln called for troops to put down the rebellion, Governor Andrew directed the Massachusetts Volunteer Militia's Third, Fourth, Sixth, and Eighth Regiments to proceed to Washington. Although technically not the MVM's senior brigadier general, Butler did command the Sixth and Eighth Regiments and therefore requested that Andrew detail him as the state forces' overall commander. Butler sweetened his appeal by offering to put his long-standing friendship with a Lowell bank president, James G. Carney, to good use, soliciting a $50,000 line of credit from Carney that dramatically increased Governor Andrew's ability to continue supplying the state forces, as the legislature, with its responsibility for appropriating funds, was now out of session. On April 17, Andrew's Special Order No. 21 confirmed Butler as commander of the four MVM regiments that had been summoned, "and also of such other regiments and companies as may be attached thereto." That same day, an old friend from Lowell High School now living in Providence, Rhode Island, wrote to lament the "terrible times" that had "arisen in this our hitherto glorious & happy land," and offering his services as a member of Butler's staff. Similar offers abounded.[10]

On April 17 and 18, as a "Secession Convention" of over 150 delegates voted in favor of Virginia's joining the Confederacy, the Third and Fourth Massachusetts Regiments departed by ship to Fort Monroe, located off the tip of the peninsula that juts out between the James and York Rivers in that state. The militiamen of "the Old Bay State" were "in the field," the *Massachusetts Spy* reported proudly. The Third traveled on the *Spaulding*, the same ship that had carried Butler to Charleston for the Democratic National Convention in 1860, enjoying an enthusiastic salute from a nearby telegraph station "by discharges of cannon and dipping of the American flag" as they passed the lighthouse in Boston Harbor. Soon the Sixth, too, headed south, traveling by train from Boston through New York, Philadelphia, and Baltimore under the command of Colonel Jones. Meanwhile, Butler remained behind in Boston waiting for the men of the Eighth to reach the city, issuing orders, and arranging his business and professional affairs in anticipation of a perhaps protracted absence. Butler, the *Boston Daily Advertiser* reported, "was busily occupied at his head-quarters" in the Massachusetts State House, "making arrangements" while "couriers were constantly coming and going." No one, the paper noted, "seemed more enthusiastic or energetic in their labors than General Butler himself, whose eyes and ears were open to every detail."

Meanwhile, thousands of excited civilians welcomed the gathering troops. "The crowd about Faneuil Hall and Quincy Markets," the *Daily Advertiser* informed its readers, "was immense," with representatives "from all ages and both sexes" offering "touching examples of loyalty and patriotism." Finally, following a march and addresses by Governor Andrew and Butler ("You are the advance guard of freedom and constitutional liberty," Butler proclaimed), the men of the Eighth and their commander embarked by train toward Springfield, New York, New Jersey, and Philadelphia, with plans to reunite with the Sixth in Washington. Traveling with them as a civilian aide to the general was his brother, Andrew Jackson Butler, who had recently returned from California. Butler's business associate from Lowell, Richard S. Fay, went too, as Butler's military secretary and aide-de-camp.[11]

The planned route to Washington for both the Sixth and Eighth Massachusetts Regiments passed through Baltimore, where pro-Confederate sentiment predominated. That spring, writes one historian, "bellicose Marylanders swept both city and State government before them like straw upon a flood," and as the Sixth passed through town in advance of Butler and the Eighth, they were met by a raging, violent crowd. "The Massachusetts troops were attacked in Pratt Street," Butler telegraphed Governor Andrew from Philadelphia near midnight on April 19, and were "assaulted" not just with angry words but "with stones and pieces of iron." Butler assured the governor that the men initially endured the attack "with utmost patience," but when "a prominent citizen of Baltimore told them to fire upon the mob," they did so. Chaos ensued, some of the rebellious citizens fired back, and by the time the Massachusetts men were finally able to escape the city, at least two of their comrades were dead. Over thirty more were injured, some severely enough to be left in Baltimore for care, others having been transferred to Washington. Baltimore civilians also suffered casualties, and some of the injured locals later died.[12]

As the Massachusetts troops departed, irate Baltimoreans took action to prevent any more northern soldiers from coming through town on their way to Washington, not just lobbying civic leaders to forbid the soldiers' passage but also wrecking the relevant tracks and bridges used by the Baltimore and Ohio Railroad. Decades after the war Butler rightly recalled that "while the attack upon the Sixth Regiment in its march through Baltimore was in fact of small moment, in view of the subsequent events of the war," it had a dramatic effect "upon the country and upon public sentiment." Among other things, hopes for a bold uprising of pro-Union sentiment across Maryland and the other border states receded, as did dreams of a swift and perhaps even bloodless solution to the national crisis. Communities across the North, South, and West began organizing to provide for a dramatic influx of men into volunteer military service. Among those who could not serve in a military capacity, and particularly among women, preparations got underway to care for the many sick and wounded soldiers the conflict would surely yield. The events in Baltimore further evoked profound questions about the extent to which the federal government was required, in a time of severe political conflict, to protect the civil rights of individuals who sought, or even just countenanced, its destruction.[13]

The immediate and most pressing problem for Butler and the Eighth, however, was how to get to Washington now, given that passage through Baltimore was no longer possible. With speed and ingenuity, Butler and the president of the Philadelphia, Wilmington, and Baltimore Railroad, Samuel M. Felton, forged a solution: send the troops by train to Perryville, Maryland, then by ferry to the state capital at Annapolis, home of the US Naval Academy, and on to Washington from there. Hoping to navigate safely the conflicting sentiments rattling his state, Maryland governor Thomas H. Hicks quickly declared his opposition to this plan, advising Butler instead to find another route. In response, Butler unleashed a torrent of outrage over the Baltimoreans' mistreatment of his troops and then reminded the governor that Maryland was still a part of the United States of America and therefore subject to its laws and power. "I am sorry that your Excellency should advise against my landing" in Annapolis, Butler wrote coldly. Having found "the ordinary means of communication cut off by the burning of Railroad bridges by a mob," however, he and his troops had no choice but "to make this detour."[14]

On April 20, Butler explained his plan to Governor Andrew: he and the Eighth would join with the Seventh New York Regiment and their commander, Col. Marshall Lefferts, and together they would head, 1,500 strong, to Annapolis, which they would occupy "and thus call the state to account for the death of Massachusetts men, my friends and neighbors." As it happens, however, Lefferts was reluctant to advance without additional reinforcements and, even more important, without official authorization from Secretary of War Simon Cameron. Less concerned about such details, Butler decided not to wait. He and the Eighth made their journey as planned, arriving early on April 21 at the Naval Academy's Annapolis wharf, where their unexpected appearance thoroughly disrupted the normal routines of the school. The New Yorkers arrived the following day. For his part, Governor Hicks anxiously continued to object to the entire operation, but to no avail. Upon reaching Annapolis, Butler wrote an upbeat letter to Sarah, noting that he had "worked like a horse" and "slept not two hours a night" but had landed safely and was now "about to march on Washington." "I think," he boasted, "no man has won more in ten days than I have. We will see."[15]

Understandably, Governor Hicks and others feared that the presence of Butler's forces in sharply divided Maryland would not only incite further violence by the state's proslavery southern nationalists but also inspire Maryland's human property to rise up in violent rebellion against their White owners. Eager to encourage Unionist sentiment in the Old Line State, in the days ahead Butler worked to tamp down such fears, reflecting the "soft war" approach Lincoln advocated early on, and which has commonly been associated with commanders like Gen. George B. McClellan. In doing so, however, Butler arguably also revealed—in ways that the rush to arms had temporarily effaced—that his views on the issues of slavery and race, including the supposedly inherent "savagery" of the country's 4 million bondspeople, remained several steps behind those of many of his Republican political opponents and his state's abolitionist governor. In an April 23 letter from Annapolis, Butler promised Hicks, and through him other White, proslavery Marylanders, "that the forces under my command"—which, by order of President Lincoln, would soon include any US troops "assembled at Annapolis"—"are not here in any way to interfere or countenance any interference with the laws of the State," including laws pertaining to slavery. Rather, his troops were prepared "to cooperate with your Excellency in suppressing most promptly and efficiently any insurrection vs. the laws of the State of Maryland" and "to act immediately for the preservation and quietness of the peace of this community." Butler's promise pleased Governor Hicks who, Butler later recalled, "was not at heart a secessionist" but "only a very timid and cautious man" desperate to keep the state's population—both White and Black—under control.[16]

In contrast, Governor Andrew quickly and bluntly condemned Butler for "tendering Governor Hicks the assistance of our Massachusetts troops to suppress a threatened servile insurrection." A revolt by Maryland's bondspeople, Andrew argued, was a problem for secessionist Marylanders to deal with, and soldiers from overwhelmingly antislavery Massachusetts who had been deployed to protect the government and integrity of the United States should not be reassigned to duty protecting antigovernment, proslavery rebels or their property, human or otherwise.[17] It is easy in retrospect to see the justice of Andrew's position. It bears reiterating, however, that whatever he himself thought about slavery at this point, Butler's approach to the possibility of an uprising by the enslaved was, for the time being, entirely in keeping with Lincoln's overall "soft war" strategy, especially relative to border states whose loyalty might still be preserved. Moreover, in these earliest days of the war, the complex question of how US forces should respond if enslaved Blacks took advantage of the conflict to claim their freedom remained unresolved. At the same time, the disagreement between Butler and Andrew was almost certainly not just about slavery but was also inextricably intertwined with their longer-standing political rivalry, and that of their respective allies in Massachusetts and elsewhere.

In any case, by early May the two men's correspondence spilled indelibly into public view, and there is simply no denying Butler's lingering racism, displayed in his use of ghastly, all-too-common tropes in his letters to Andrew about, among other things, the horrors that a rebellion of "worse than savages" would inflict "upon the defenceless women and children of the country, carrying rapine, arson, and murder . . . among those whom we hope to reunite with us as brethren." Frederick Douglass, for one, protested fiercely, asking why Butler did not welcome enslaved men as fellow warriors for the Union instead of denying their right to rebel against their bondage. In sharp contrast, one female correspondent from Wilmington, Delaware, spoke for many Whites living on the border between slavery and freedom when she praised Butler "in behalf of the wives, mothers, & sisters of these Border States" for his "humane and patriotic sentiments" and his merciful approach to dealing with rebeldom. Also supportive was "An Elector of Washington County, New York," who opined that "however much the institution of slavery with all its demoralizing tendencies may be deprecated and abhord [sic] by an enlightened Christian world," nevertheless, "humanity shudders & shrinks, and all Christian graces blush, at the thought of exciting that uncontrollable mass of ignorance embodied in the slave population to a servile insurrection, thereby to bring upon the heads of thousands of innocent women & children torture and death, and the destruction of millions of property by the faggot, lost forever to the world." In the period that Maryland's loyalty was most uncertain, and to his opponents' lasting glee, Butler's determination to maintain order overshadowed all other considerations.[18]

For the Eighth Massachusetts, the remainder of the trip to Washington was reasonably uneventful, facilitated by many of the men's skills at repairing tracks and rolling stock. It could easily have gone differently. For one thing, as one historian writes, "a more timid citizen soldier" than Butler "might have waited at Annapolis, fearful of what lay down the rail line, leaving Washington cut off even longer, with unpredictable results." Similarly, someone other than Butler "might have considered every sullen Marylander in the state capital an enemy, shot some of them as exemplary punishment, and thereby provoked a violent reaction," which might in turn have pushed Maryland into the Confederacy. Instead, "Butler's dogged course, which avoided either extreme, served Lincoln well." And indeed, by April 25, the Massachusetts men were in Washington, to the great relief of those who had been living for weeks in fear of an imminent, hostile invasion. "God bless you for what you have done," wrote a friend from Boston on April 30. "Everybody here [is] overflowing in their praises of you & your troops." "All the accounts, both public and private, which are received from the Massachusetts regiments," wrote Governor Andrew, setting their recent friction aside, "convey to us a most favorable impression of the intelligent efficiency of yourself and your command." Butler's early efforts to serve the nation—and save the Union—were proving successful. He welcomed the praise, and he did not hog it. "To you, under God," Butler reminded his veterans a few years after the war, "it was given to save the National Capital from traitors," and they did.[19]

With his regiments now in their proper stations, Butler remained in Annapolis to reinforce the area and oversee the movement of additional troops through the Maryland capital to Washington. Delighted with the work he had done so far, Butler colorfully promised Sarah that he would "either bring back my shield as a proud trophy to you, dearest," or "come back upon it with a name which you will not be ashamed to bear and teach our children to love and reverence." Together they pondered how much the advent of war might endanger Blanche, who was still in school in Georgetown but seemed anxious to return to Lowell as soon as possible. "Nearly all of the girls are going home," Blanche wrote, urging her father to find someone to escort her north. One "Sister Bernard," perhaps the head of school, downplayed Blanche's fears, reassuring Butler that the students were all "perfectly safe" and there was no need for alarm. Perhaps Sister Bernard worried that a mass exodus of the students would result in the Georgetown school's closure, a problem that other schools—including Butler's Maine alma mater—also faced. Indeed, the wartime departure of students from Waterville College caused such severe financial problems that the institution likely would have closed had not a philanthropist by the name of Gardner Colby come to the rescue. Colby's $50,000 donation kept the doors open and led to the school's change of name to Colby University. In any case, despite Sister Bernard's assurances, by the end of April Sarah's sister Harriet Hildreth Heard was en route to Georgetown with a Mr. Read to collect Blanche and bring her either home or to Annapolis. "And now how do you like this life?" Sarah asked her husband. "Will the glorious excitement more than balance the labour and anxiety? I hope so." For her part, Sarah felt quite melancholy without him or Blanche in Lowell, but she was glad that Butler had his brother for company. "Jackson," she wrote, "must be of infinite service to you in every way. I am so glad he is with you now. To think of you there alone would be intolerable." Increasingly, Sarah wondered if she, too, should make the trip south.[20]

Newly appointed commander of the Military Department of Annapolis, Butler soon received orders from the overall commander of US forces, Lt. Gen. Winfield Scott, authorizing him not only to reinforce the area against Confederate invasion but also, if necessary, to suppress pro-Confederate sentiment by suspending the writ of habeas corpus "at any point on or in the vicinity of the military line" between Philadelphia and Annapolis. As such, he assumed he would be remaining in place for several more months. Butler therefore urged Sarah to "shut up the house" in Lowell, send sons Bennie and Paul to stay with her parents or her sister Laura, put the horses out to pasture, pack her summer clothes, and "come on" to Maryland, bringing the family coachman, Gilman Jones, with her. His Annapolis headquarters, Butler informed Sarah, occupied "a very excellent house" that was staffed with "a good corps of servants." Arriving in Annapolis at the beginning of May, Blanche concurred. "You ought to come on Father's account," she coaxed her mother. "He would be so much happier if you would." Blanche described the "great big house" with its a "beautiful little garden" and "the nicest servants [all of them Black] that you ever saw." She even encouraged Sarah to bring nine-year-old Paul along. "There is not the least danger here," Blanche wrote confidently, "and you know what pleasure it would give him to be with four thousand troops."[21] Defending the Union, Blanche seemed to suggest, could be a family affair.

Meanwhile, rarely content to sit still and "let things take their course," and emboldened by his previous successes, Butler actively surveyed the conditions in and around Annapolis to see what more he could accomplish on the nation's behalf. Like Lincoln, he remained concerned that Maryland might yet slip into the welcoming arms of the Confederacy, encouraged by prosecession activists in Baltimore and insufficient action on the part of the United States, either offensively or defensively. Butler worried, further, what the secession of Maryland would mean for any military stores the state currently possessed, especially in Baltimore, and especially now that Confederates under the command of Col. Thomas J. Jackson had occupied

Harpers Ferry in Virginia, only about seventy miles away, with its arsenal. A demonstration of Federal military strength in Baltimore, Butler believed, could effectively squelch secessionism there, ensure Federal control over the city's armaments, and give Massachusetts troops yet another opportunity to avenge the April 19 attack they had endured.[22]

And so, having analyzed the situation to his own satisfaction, and with orders in hand from General Scott that permitted him, if necessary, "to seize property, arms, ammunition, and provisions in Baltimore"—but notably *without* explicit orders to occupy the city itself—in mid-May Butler undertook another bold expedition. It involved, first, capturing and occupying the Relay House of the Baltimore and Ohio Railroad that served the lines between Washington and Baltimore, on the one hand, and between Washington and Manassas and Harpers Ferry, on the other. Then, on the night of May 12–13, Butler and roughly a thousand soldiers seized and occupied Baltimore itself, aided by a thunderstorm that helped mask the sound of their steps as they marched into town. "I believed and knew," Butler later boasted, "and it so turned out, that it was comparatively as easy to capture Baltimore as it was to capture my supper. I knew it, but Scott did not. Was I not justified in acting upon my knowledge?"[23]

Butler and his soldiers quickly asserted their control of the rebellious city—and by extension, Maryland as a whole—by taking possession of Baltimore's Federal Hill. To ensure that residents understood his purposes, Butler promptly issued a proclamation proposing "to give every good citizen protection"—a promise that implicitly excluded enslaved people, who were not technically citizens—and "to deal properly with every enemy of the United States." Butler then met with the city's political leadership to demand the surrender of all Federal military stores. Soon some "fifteen dray loads" of stores were in his command's possession, and a subsequent raid on a warehouse in town produced still more. For good measure, and as a warning to others that antigovernment behavior would not be tolerated, Butler also ordered the arrest of a wealthy, elderly local rebel named Ross Winans, accused of supplying the mob with weapons on April 19 to thwart the Massachusetts soldiers' passage through town. In contrast with the uproar of the previous month, Butler's actions in Baltimore met virtually no local resistance. "The city is very quiet," one newspaper reported, "and there seems to be a general disposition to co-operate in sustaining the laws." Not everyone was content, of course. "The obvious purpose of the government is not to prevent Maryland from seceding," growled the *Baltimore Exchange*, "but to subjugate and hold her for the benefit of the North."[24]

Despite having achieved what many northerners deemed a masterful stroke that might even end the entire rebellion within a few days, on the morning of May 15 Butler received an angry message from General Scott conveying the general's stern disapproval. In Scott's view, Butler's capture of Baltimore was precipitous, dangerous, and—perhaps most damningly— insubordinate. And even if Scott himself had to admit that the overall result was positive, he demanded an explanation. Fiercely proud of what he had accomplished, confident that Maryland was now safely held for the Union, and convinced that Scott was mostly just jealous that Butler had captured Baltimore according to his own devices rather than by following some per- haps more elaborate plan Scott might have devised for him, Butler brashly chose not to answer right away. Years later he claimed that Scott had once been "a good soldier," but by the time the Civil War began he had become "a pompous old man, magnified [by] his office," not to mention "a little irri- table." Butler's stonewalling and unapologetic self-confidence only further exasperated the lieutenant general, who issued an order removing him from command.[25]

If he was disappointed by Scott's harsh response to his capture of Balti- more, Butler was nevertheless pleased the following day when President Lincoln promoted him to the rank of major general of US volunteers, mak- ing him the Union army's senior civilian general. In the days ahead, Lincoln promoted former governor of Massachusetts Nathaniel Banks (June 5) and New York's John A. Dix (June 14) to the same rank, their commissions dat- ing back, like Butler's, to May 16, 1861. Butler's appointment letter came first, however, which provided him with strong and gratifying evidence of his seniority over the other two. In tandem with his military achievements thus far, word of Butler's promotion generated scores of enthusiastic letters of support and admiration. "You can have no idea of the universal praise bestowed on you by your fellow citizens in Mass. regardless of former par- tisan associations," wrote John Ryan from Boston, adding that some Bay State Republicans now seemed prepared to endorse Butler for president. "I can only say that tears often start when I see [that] in the crisis of my coun- try's destiny, one whom I have ever reckoned as a special personal friend, is among the very foremost of her champions & defenders," wrote M. J. Kelly of Jefferson, Maine, a classmate from Waterville College. "May the God of armies prosper you & your future military career be more glorious if pos- sible than the past." Another college classmate, E. H. Gray, recalled how often, "when planning for the future in my room at Wat. College, you used to remark, 'Well Gray if you & I live you will hear from me by & by'? Your prophecy seems to be rapidly fulfilling." Gray was sure his old friend would soon go on to capture the Confederate capital. "I intend to hold a jubilee when you *crush out the vipers* at Richmond!" he wrote.[26]

Despite Butler's impertinence, General Scott knew the Union cause could not spare him, and on May 18, he issued new orders placing Butler in command of Virginia's Fort Monroe. In these orders Scott provided broad directions for the handling and welfare of the 10,000 troops who would now be under Butler's authority, several thousand of whom, he noted, should be considered "disposable for aggressive purposes." Still deeply vexed by Butler's handling of the capture of Baltimore, however, Scott strove to clarify the military chain of command and Butler's place in it, cautioning Butler to exercise "great circumspection" and "be sure to submit your plans and ask instructions from higher authority" whenever possible. Initially, Butler resisted being reassigned. Why should he be transferred away from Annapolis, where Sarah and their son Paul were now comfortably ensconced? (Blanche had returned to Lowell for the summer to help her Aunt Harriet care for Bennie.) "What does this mean?" Butler queried Secretary of War Cameron. "Is it a censure upon my action" in Baltimore? "Is it because I have caused Winans to be arrested?" Butler even briefly considered leaving the army and returning to Lowell. Instead, having let off sufficient steam, he departed for his new post near the very spot where the first African captives had been delivered to the Virginia colony in 1619. "I am to go to Virginia to prosecute the war vigorously into the heart of the enemy," Butler wrote to his law partner and brother-in-law, William Webster. "God only knows what may be the result." For her part, Sarah was convinced that Butler's burdens at the fort would be "frightful." But neither she nor her husband could possibly have anticipated the momentous consequences of his deployment there, for the war and for the future of slavery in the United States.[27]

Butler reached Fort Monroe on May 22, two days after North Carolina joined the Confederacy and the day before Virginia voters affirmed their April 17 Secession Convention's decision to join as well. As Butler later wrote, Fort Monroe was "one of the strongest and best" military installations in the United States, "and certainly the largest" at that time, "a bastion fort about sixty-five acres in extent, with a water battery casemated on its sea front and some guns mounted *en barbette*"—elevated so that they could fire over the parapets. The fort was also surrounded by a six-foot-deep moat, which made it "assailable only by bombardment." On the whole, Butler was impressed. Sarah joined him there before long, as did his twenty-year-old nephew, George H. Butler, who joined Butler's staff. This was by no means the last time that Butler tried to help his nephew, just as he routinely tried to help his brother. Both George and his father, "Jackson," were sources of perennial trouble and worry; as will be seen, Butler struggled for many years to help by giving them work and frequently bailing them out of financial and other messes.[28]

Soon, however, Butler had a more immediate and ultimately consequential problem to solve at his new headquarters: what to do about the arrival at the fort of three bondsmen—Frank Baker, Sheppard Mallory, and James Townsend—whose rebel owner, Col. Charles K. Mallory, had impressed them into service constructing a battery across Hampton Roads at a place known as Sewall's Point. The three men had bravely escaped by boat and, having surrendered to the pickets at Fort Monroe, now requested federal protection. Initially, Butler ordered Baker, Mallory, and Townsend "fed and set to work" while he considered his options. Then, when Colonel Mallory's emissary, Maj. John B. Cary, appeared at the fort on May 24 to retrieve the men, Butler resolutely declined to hand them over. "We met at the time and place appointed," Cary later recalled, and over the course of several hours of conversation, "I maintained the right of the master to reclaim them." Butler in turn "positively refused to surrender them," on the principle that they were "contraband of war."[29]

As it happens, in the hours between the bondsmen's arrival at the fort and Cary's, Butler had met with each of the runaways separately to hear their stories, his sharp legal mind slowly reasoning its way to the position that Virginia's recent claim of independence from the United States meant that escapees from bondage there—unlike, for example, in still-loyal Maryland—were no longer subject to the US Fugitive Slave Law. Moreover, in Virginia and throughout the self-declared Confederacy—again in contrast with the case for the loyal slave states—US authorities no longer had an obligation to lift a hand to suppress a rebellion by the enslaved. "I am under no constitutional obligations to a foreign country, which Virginia now claims to be," Butler recalled informing Cary, though he offered to return Colonel Mallory's human property if the colonel would simply come to the fort and swear an oath of allegiance to the United States. Looking back, Butler later explained, "I do not claim for the phrase 'contraband of war,' used in this connection, the highest legal sanction," and "the truth is, as a lawyer I was never very proud of it." However, "as an executive officer" in the volunteer army of the United States, committed to saving the Union, "I was very much comforted with it as a means of doing my duty." Following Cary's visit, Butler wrote to General Scott, with a copy to Secretary of War Cameron, explaining

ORIGIN OF THE WORDS "CONTRABAND OF WAR," APPLIED TO SLAVES—FIRST USED BY GENERAL BUTLER

Butler at Fort Monroe with the original "contraband"
fugitives, by James E. Taylor. Courtesy of Special Collections &
Archives, Colby College Libraries, Waterville, Maine.

his decision and emphasizing that Baker, Mallory, and Townsend could provide much needed labor at the fort—labor which, if they were returned to Colonel Mallory, would surely be deployed on behalf of the rebellion. He also asked for further direction.[30]

While he waited for instructions from Scott and Cameron, Butler shared with Governor Andrew back in Massachusetts a portion of his communication with Scott, perhaps hoping it would help settle their ongoing dispute over his promise to Maryland's Governor Hicks a month earlier. How much his actions actually succeeded in mollifying Andrew is not clear, but they certainly had that effect on some of Andrew's allies. "General Butler's refusal to deliver fugitive slaves to their pretended owners," declared the *Lowell Daily Citizen and News*, "has given so general satisfaction that his parley with Gov. Hicks is almost forgotten. 'Actions speak louder than words,' and right action is really of more practical account that abstract theories, right or wrong." Meanwhile, Butler ordered that within the bounds of his command, "the rights and private property" of *peaceable* citizens—including their *human* property—"must be respected." But he also authorized his quartermaster to issue rations not for three but for fifty runaways, to be shared among the rapidly expanding number of bondspeople arriving at the fort, many of them hungry. Clearly the news was spreading that Baker, Mallory, and Townsend had not been turned away.[31]

Indeed, as Butler recalled, once he offered the US Army's protection to the first three escapees who requested it, "the negroes came pouring in day by day," and soon "more than $60,000 worth of them," some dozens of individuals—"men, women, children, sick and well"—were taking shelter at Fort Monroe. They came in "by twenty's, thirty's, and forty's," recalled Edward L. Pierce of the Third Massachusetts, to whom Butler assigned primary responsibility for managing the influx. According to Pierce, by July 30 Fort Monroe housed some 900 "contraband," and soon "the number ran up into the thousands." To those seeking freedom from slavery, he added, "the renowned Fortress took the name of the 'freedom fort,'" local Blacks guiding one another to safety there by means of some "mysterious spiritual telegraph." "The decision of Gen. Butler pronouncing slave property contraband of war," observed the *Massachusetts Spy*, "proves to be popular among the slaves," whose "readiness to run to the Union flag," observed the *Hartford Daily Courant*, belied their "much boasted fidelity" to their White owners. "Our Government is taking a wiser and more humane course towards those of the slaves who succeed in getting within the lines of our army," wrote Frederick Douglass, who had previously criticized Butler for his willingness to suppress slave rebellion in Maryland. Now, as he observed Butler's actions at Fort Monroe, Douglass had reason to hope "that better ideas are beginning to control the action of our army officers," Butler perhaps first and foremost. News of developments at Fort Monroe continued to spread. "*All* our patriotic papers" were supportive of Butler's actions, wrote Cornelius Baker from New York on May 28. "We cannot conciliate slaveholders." "Your decisions at Fortress Monroe upon the Fugitive Slave Law have given us infinite delight," wrote George Morey of Boston. The June 1, 1861, issue of the popular illustrated *Harper's Weekly's* featured Butler on its front page, along with a detailed, lengthy, and admiring article.[32]

On May 29, Postmaster General Montgomery Blair wrote Butler that when Lincoln's cabinet met to discuss the situation at the fort, he personally planned to propose that Butler be allowed to continue using his "discretion" with regard to the contraband, while emphasizing that the goal was "not emancipation"—at least, not yet—but military victory. Soon both the president and the War Department gave tacit approval to Butler's contraband policy and practices, in the form of an absence of instructions other than to continue doing what he was doing while keeping an "accurate account of the value" of the work the runaways were providing. "Your action in respect to the negroes who came within your lines from the service of the rebels is approved," wrote Secretary Cameron. "It is understood that Gen. Butler's course in the matter is endorsed by the administration," concluded the *Massachusetts Spy* on June 5. "I had found work for them to do," Butler explained in his autobiography, and "had classified them and made a list of them so that their identity might be fully assured" in case their owners should capitulate to federal authority. In addition, Butler named a "commissioner of negro affairs" whose job was "to take this business off my hands, for it was becoming onerous." It bears noting that Butler's decision to put the escapees to work on behalf of the Union has provoked some criticism in recent years, with some historians arguing that the enactment of a work requirement undermines any claim that Butler's actions constituted, in any conscious way, "a prelude to the Emancipation Proclamation" or even a sign of his growing sympathy for the bondspeople. From this perspective, Butler's contraband policy was nothing more than "an act of military necessity that developed in response to the question of political refugees," and Butler was simply and perhaps even cynically "capitaliz[ing] on the labor power that fugitive slaves could provide."[33]

Other historians, however, agree that while Butler's contraband policy "did not recognize the personal liberty and free status of escaped slaves," to do so would have pushed the military well beyond where the federal government's policy making had yet gone (one thinks of George McClellan's 1862 Harrison's Landing letter). Moreover, his plan "contained useful ambiguities" that could and *did* help prepare resistant northern Whites for eventual emancipation. Butler's policy was, in short, "agreeable to conservatives," even if it failed to completely satisfy abolitionists, "who believed that slaves should be recognized as persons under the Constitution with equal rights" and simply set free. Further, Butler's contraband policy "clearly" helped lay a tangible foundation for future developments in the long, complex process of destroying slavery. How could it not? For it encouraged hundreds, even thousands of enslaved people to abscond with their labor. At the same time, "in view of the prejudice against blacks in the North, the constitutional limitations on federal power over slavery in the states, and the long-standing disavowal of abolition purposes by Republicans," it "made the drift toward emancipation easier and more acceptable than it would have been if justified on the high ground of antislavery moral principles."[34]

As one historian writes, if Butler was "feeling his way," he was definitely "not flailing around blindly," and it is worth emphasizing that "a different Union general, one less willing to attack the social basis of the southern rebellion" than Butler proved to be, "would have returned Colonel Mallory's slaves without hesitation." Notably, many of Butler's contemporaries also firmly believed that his actions on behalf of the runaways had irrevocably "shaped the policy for the administration" on one of "the most difficult questions in this contest," namely, "the policy to be pursued in relation to the negroes." Doing so came with a cost, too, for "in providing a haven for slave refugees and extending even modest rights to them," Butler "made his first steps toward becoming, among whites, the single most despised leader in the country, both South and North," even as, among Black Americans, enslaved and free, he was also taking steps toward becoming "the most revered general in the Union army." "It is evident," observed the *Springfield (Mass.) Republican*, on June 15, 1861, "that the slaves themselves are impressed with the belief that 'their time is come,' or that it is very soon coming," and that Butler had positioned himself as an agent of their liberation. Meanwhile, it is telling that southern newspapers began ratcheting up the nasty rumors they were already circulating about him, calling him "Picayune Butler," or "Strychnine Butler," claiming that he had been "so drunk" during his time in Baltimore "that he required the assistance of two men to put him on his horse," declaring that he was secretly more *proslavery* than southern slaveholders because he considered the fugitives "things" rather than people, and suggesting that he himself was "the son of a negro barber in New Orleans." By end of the summer the US Congress offered its own answer to Butler's contraband policy by passing the First Confiscation Act, which permitted the confiscation of human and other property that was being used to support the rebellion, though it did not (yet) clearly permit emancipation. Late that summer, with Butler's encouragement and support, efforts to educate the contraband also began in and around Fort Monroe, starting with the establishment of a school in nearby Hampton run by a free Black woman named Mary Peake. Peake's school "was not only the first one at Hampton but the first of the kind in the South."[35]

From a historical perspective, Butler's contraband policy and actions were undoubtedly the most momentous aspect of his period of command at Fort Monroe. To Butler himself, however, a raft of other concerns demanded his attention over the course of his time in Virginia, not the least of which was the question of what *else* he and the soldiers under his command could be doing to disrupt and perhaps even defeat the Confederate rebellion. As he debated his options, Sarah and Paul arrived from Annapolis with her sister Laura in tow. In letters to Harriet, still in Lowell with Blanche and Bennie, both women described the curious pleasures a commanding officer's family members could enjoy in the context of war, including a "splendid sail" from Annapolis and, now, residence in the general's "very pleasant" house, with its "pretty garden" of roses that were just getting ready to bloom. "The beach here," wrote Sarah, "is one of the finest I ever saw," with stunning "green and foamy waves" that "roll in and break to pieces," though she found the social burdens of the commanding general's wife quite onerous. "Fourteen at table every meal," she wrote, and sometimes more, including, on occasion, such elevated figures as Secretary Cameron. In addition, Sarah missed her family back home and observed that Paul "would rather go home and play" with Bennie. Like Butler himself, Sarah, Laura, and even Paul were compelled for the first time ever to confront directly both the horrors of slavery and the suffering of its victims. It was, Laura wrote to Harriet, "a sad sight to see the poor creatures, homeless, not knowing when or where they were to get their next meal," but finding hope under Butler's protection.[36]

Even as the runaways continued to pour in to Fort Monroe, the press raised the same questions Butler was raising for himself regarding what lay ahead for him and his command. Would they perhaps advance soon and maybe even capture Richmond, which was, after all, less than a hundred miles away? Butler certainly hoped General Scott would soon order him to advance, but Scott was reluctant, and on June 6, the *New York Commercial Advertiser* informed its readers, "there is no positive intelligence that General Butler will move forward at this time." For his part, Postmaster General Blair believed Scott would never assign Butler a sufficient number of offensive troops "to make any great blow" because Scott was a jealous man, eager to "monopolize all the reputation to be made" and determined to treat Butler "as he has always treated those whom he knew would be effective if he gave them the means." Blair insisted that he, too, was eager to see the US forces act decisively against the rebels soon, but he advised Butler to "work on patiently," avoid overestimating his own and his limited command's capabilities, and not attempt "more than in your cool judgment the force you have can effect."[37] Whatever the merits of Blair's analysis of Scott's hesitation, the lieutenant general surely also remained wary of Butler's capacity for acting on his own authority.

Perhaps it was the rumor some newspapers were circulating, to the effect that Butler was about to be superseded in overall command at Fort Monroe by Nathaniel Banks, that provoked Butler to act, although the *New Haven*

(Conn.) Columbian Register declared the idea of subordinating Butler to Banks "simply ridiculous." Butler, after all, was Banks's superior "in everything that goes to make up the brave and successful leader on the field of battle." Perhaps it was news of the June 3 clash of arms 300 miles away at Philippi, Virginia, where Union forces under George McClellan enjoyed a bloodless rout of their unprepared Confederate opposition. Perhaps it was simply the predictable result of Butler's own willfulness, especially in the context of the "loose, clumsy, and inharmonious" state of the US forces at this time. "The aged Scott reigned without really ruling," writes one historian. "He had three armies . . . which he failed to coordinate, and whose commanders all distrusted him." In any case, in early June, Butler authorized an advance from Fort Monroe toward Richmond, bringing on what many consider the first real battle of the war on land.[38]

"There was a point nine miles from the fort on the road leading from Hampton to Yorktown [Big Bethel] which I learned the rebels intended to entrench and hold," Butler later recalled, "because they expected a move toward Richmond to be made very soon." And so, after "carefully reconnoitering the position," Butler decided to attack, ordering a "rapid, but not hurried" nighttime advance on June 10 by about 3,500 soldiers starting from two different locations, all under the command of Gen. Ebenezer W. Peirce of Massachusetts. Almost immediately, the plan went awry. General Peirce, it appears, was "incompetent," using "faulty old maps" and handling his two columns of men so poorly that they ended up shooting at each other, which alerted Confederates in the area to the impending attack and gave them time to reinforce Big Bethel. In the clash that followed, Peirce's forces suffered roughly eighty casualties—including nearly twenty dead—in contrast with a tenth that number on the Confederate side. The Union forces withdrew. The Union dead included Lt. John T. Grebel of Pennsylvania, the first West Point graduate to die in the war, as well as Maj. Theodore Winthrop, a volunteer soldier and author from Massachusetts. It was, the Boston Daily Advertiser reported the next day, "a sad reverse of our arms," although given the nature and scope of the battles that were to come, it amounted to little more—in Butler's words—than a "skirmish."[39]

Both at the time and subsequently, Butler faced a great deal of criticism, much of it justified, for the failed attack on Big Bethel, not least because he had delegated command of the attack rather than leading it himself. To his discredit as the commanding general who ordered the advance, Butler acknowledged that the attack was "utterly mismanaged" but did not accept responsibility. Still, although he was subjected to stinging criticism—including from Peirce, who demanded a court of inquiry so that any blame for the outcome could be "placed where it belongs"—Butler also had defenders. On June 12, for example, the *New York Commercial Advertiser* noted that confusion in the dark, casualties from friendly fire, and being misled by bad information were hardly unprecedented in the history of war. "We cannot join some of our contemporaries," the paper declared, "in their unqualified condemnation of General Butler . . . nor even of General Peirce." Military commanders, the paper continued, "are no more infallible than are other men," and given Butler's successes to date, "it does seem to us unjust and even cruel to assail him in harsh terms for a seeming blunder, even before he has had opportunity to say a word in explanation." Indeed, the paper warned, northerners should resist the temptation to assume that "every movement made by our troops in this war will be a great and triumphant success." Good advice indeed, given the much more dramatic reverses that were coming not far down the road. As the *Hartford Daily Courant* put it optimistically, "Does anyone dream that the spirit of Yankee soldiers will be broken" by the events at Big Bethel? "Nay; it will rise higher and higher with every such temporary obstruction and annoyance."[40]

As the debate continued over what exactly had happened and who was responsible, other events in the developing war, and especially the debacle of First Bull Run, soon began to overshadow the clash of arms at Big Bethel. "We have heard the sad news from Manassas," Butler wrote to Postmaster General Blair on July 23. But, he added, "we are neither dismayed nor disheartened. It will have the same good effect upon the Army in general that Big Bethel has had in my Division, to teach us wherein we are weak and they are strong, and how to apply the remedy to our deficiencies." Meanwhile, Butler stayed busy with the day-to-day work of commanding at Fort Monroe, including regularly soliciting the War Department for more troops. Instead, he received disappointing orders to send several regiments to Baltimore to fend off any attack from there on Washington. Doing so required consolidating the forces that remained in the department and bringing them closer to the fort, thereby denying protection to hundreds of runaways from slavery who had settled in the area around the fort and who had believed themselves under the army's protection even though they did not reside within its walls. Many now fled in fear that the Confederates would return. "It was a most distressing sight," Butler complained to Secretary Cameron on July 30, "to see these poor creatures, who had trusted to the protection of the arms of the United States, and who aided the troops of the United States in their enterprise, to be thus obliged to flee from their homes." What should he do

"Major Gen. Benj. F. Butler," lithograph by Currier & Ives. Courtesy of Special Collections & Archives, Colby College Libraries, Waterville, Maine.

for these suffering people? he asked, revealing a degree of empathy that his constant exposure to their plight could not help but elicit. Equally important, but as yet unanswered by the government, Butler wondered, "What is their state and condition?" And "are these men, women, and children slaves? Are they free?" Some weeks earlier, Butler had urged Governor Andrew to allow him to use "but partially worn out" Massachusetts soldiers' uniforms and fatigue clothing for the "poor, distressed" contraband.[41]

There were other problems to solve, too, such as getting permission from Secretary Cameron to rid himself of a number of company officers he deemed incompetent. During this period Butler also explored the benefits of an emerging technology that might be useful for reconnaissance, communicating regularly with John La Mountain, a balloonist, regarding hot air balloons' feasibility for that purpose. At the same time, through his friend, business associate, and former aide-de-camp Richard Fay, who had returned to Massachusetts in mid-July, Butler monitored his professional commitments in Lowell, some of which had direct connections to the army. The Middlesex mill, Fay wrote on July 27, "is full of work," including an "immense Govt. contract to be given out on Monday." Fay also checked on conditions at the Butler family homestead, reporting that "the place looked beautifully," and expressing amazement that Butler had been willing to exchange such a splendid home "for the annoyances of your present life." For her part, Sarah continued somewhat begrudgingly to fulfill her social obligations as the commanding officer's wife. "Yesterday I had a most fatiguing day," she complained to Harriet. "The Secretary of War, his wife, Mrs. [Ambrose] Burnside and son, two Misses Chase, daughter of the Secretary of the Treasury, Gen. [George H.] Thomas, wife and daughter, and a half dozen gentleman without ladies, all came down to pass the day at Fortress Monroe," and "of course, it was my duty to play the courtier to the people who have it in their power to send troops here and everything else that is wanted!" In early August, Sarah and Paul rejoined Blanche and Bennie in Lowell, but soon Sarah was missing her husband badly and hoping they could be reunited before long, especially if his military plans remained on hold due to insufficient numbers of "effectives." (With so much faith in her husband's abilities, no other explanation was possible.) "Many who like you best," Sarah observed, "have thought you would resign and come home unless you are to be better supplied with means of action."[42]

Restlessly, Butler considered his next military move. Should he attempt another advance on Richmond? And if so, how much support might he expect from Washington? Rumors that Banks would take over the department seemed unfounded: instead Banks assumed command in Maryland. But the troops Butler had requested still did not come, despite the Confederates' invasion and destruction of nearby Hampton in early August that the contraband had predicted and feared, and which Butler observed with dismay. Then Butler learned that he was to be superseded at Fort Monroe after all, not by Banks, but by seventy-seven-year-old Maj. Gen. John E. Wool of New York who, like Winfield Scott, was a veteran of the War of 1812. President Lincoln, it turns out, had decided to send Butler on a recruiting expedition to New England with a goal of enlisting 5,000 soldiers for the Union cause. Butler was furious. "This move has come from my enemies," he wrote angrily to Sarah, "and I shall have to fight it out." When he discovered that Sarah's loneliness in Lowell had temporarily overshadowed her interest in his problems, he displayed a rare flash of temper toward her, scolding Sarah harshly for both her indifference and her melancholy. "You claim to be a woman of mind," he admonished her. "Why not exert that mind in making yourself and me happy—not miserable?" Meanwhile, he suspected that the decision to remove him from command at Fort Monroe might be related to statements he had begun making publicly, to the effect that slavery as an institution was dying and, frankly, should be hurried on its way into history. "The negro will be free," he wrote bluntly in mid-August. "It is inevitable. We may patch it as we please but the fact will work itself out." Butler's experience with the flood of contraband in and around Fort Monroe—not to mention the runaways' courage and determination to be free—made that clear.[43]

As he prepared for his departure, Butler expressed his hope that the soldiers whose leadership he was handing off to General Wool would soon have an opportunity to "signalize their bravery" and demonstrate their "gallant conduct" on the field of battle, just as they had already proved "their patriotism by fortitude under the fatigues of camp duty." Although his future with the army was uncertain, friends urged Butler not to resign, arguing that doing so would only encourage the notion that he was not up to the job of command. Truth be told, Butler was not averse to undertaking the recruiting expedition Lincoln had assigned him, especially if he could expect to be given command of the men he enlisted. But he still yearned to do something *in the field* that would serve the Union cause more immediately, while simultaneously enhancing his reputation for decisive and meaningful action on the battlefield and his opportunity for military glory. On August 21, he got his chance: General Wool put him "in command of the Volunteer forces in this department [the Department of Virginia and North Carolina] exclusive of those at Fort Monroe." The following week, on Wool's orders and with the support of the navy, Butler and over 800 men undertook an expedition to capture a series of Confederate batteries at Hatteras Inlet on the North Carolina coast, in conjunction with the Federal effort to establish a blockade of southern ports.[44]

"If anything befalls me," Butler promised Sarah from onboard the *Minnesota* on August 27, having resumed his usual loving tone, "you will know that my last thoughts were of you [and] the children." Three days later he wrote again, now reporting "a glorious victory": the capture of "more than 700 men, 25 pieces of Artillery, a thousand stand of arms, a large quantity of ordnance, stores, provisions," and more. Indeed, Butler's Hatteras Inlet expedition seized the forts in a manner "so sudden and easy" that "it seemed an adventurous lark," and reminded those who had been disappointed by the events at Big Bethel of his many earlier accomplishments for the Union cause. "Permit me to congratulate you," wrote James S. Whitney from Boston on September 3, "upon the brilliant success of the movement" by which "you have again placed your countrymen under renewed obligation which, I trust, they will not fail to appreciate." In his autobiography Butler—who was never reluctant to claim credit for deeds well done, even as he hesitated to accept blame for his failures—reflected with enormous pride upon the expedition, cheerfully boasting that his "hazardous bravado" in disobeying a portion of his orders (by *not* destroying the inlet by filling it with sand) revealed his shrewd military savvy in contrast with the "wonderful stupidity at Washington." The successful expedition, he was certain, laid a firm foundation for Gen. Ambrose Burnside's subsequent victory in the region.[45]

Soon after the Hatteras Inlet foray Butler traveled to Washington, where he met briefly with his old Lowell high school friend, Gustavus Fox, now assistant secretary of the navy, and also gave his report to the president and his cabinet. In addition, Butler and Lincoln discussed techniques for effective recruiting, especially of so-called War Democrats, which both he and Lincoln considered essential to proving that the current struggle was for the *nation's* survival, not simply the Republican Party's. In July Congress had authorized the enlistment of hundreds of thousands of additional volunteers for three-years' service, but, as Butler observed, "recruiting was very dull in New England," and "Massachusetts had not furnished her quota of troops." Friends and supporters believed that enlistments would abound if potential recruits knew they would come under Butler's command, and by mid-September he was back in Massachusetts to "raise, organize, arm, uniform, and equip a volunteer force for the War in the New England States, of such arms, and in such proportions, and in such manner" as he deemed appropriate. Toward that end, Butler announced the establishment of the Department of New England with headquarters in Boston not far from the Massachusetts State House, and began making arrangements for recruiting and supplying men from across the region. As he dug in to this new assignment, Butler gladly received accolades from many of his fellow New Englanders—some of whom now pressed him to run for the Massachusetts governorship. Butler's handling of slavery's runaways at Fort Monroe, along with the larger potential implications of his contraband policy, continued to garner him favorable attention and high praise. "I believe under God," wrote one Connecticut correspondent that fall, "you are the right man in the right place, to whom our bleeding country must look for its redemption from *Slavery*."[46]

In late October, Butler—a firm believer in science ever since his college days who ordered that "every regiment, battalion, or detached company of United States Volunteers" in his department must be "carefully vaccinated" against the scourge of smallpox—informed Secretary of War Cameron that his recruiting efforts were going reasonably well. Indeed, he relished the support of all of the New England governors *except* his own. Their old political rivalry resurfacing, Governor Andrew claimed that Butler was now encroaching upon his authority as the state forces' commander in chief by personally selecting officers to command the Massachusetts recruits and unilaterally making arrangements to provide for the recruits' families, including offering to pay for the necessary resources himself. As Andrew saw it, and not without reason, Butler aimed to set himself up as the governor's equal in terms of "official dignity" and "rank" in Massachusetts, which in turn raised important questions about the proper relationship between civilian and military—and federal and state—power. This new source of friction between the two men also revived their earlier dispute over Butler's offer to suppress a slave uprising in Maryland. As one observer noted, the latest argument between Butler and Andrew over recruitment in Massachusetts was really just an offshoot of "an old feud between the old parties. Butler is a democrat and the opposite side are against him."[47]

As before, this dispute, too, spilled out into public view through the local newspapers, and by mid-November Butler was exceedingly frustrated. "I have failed utterly in my attempts to arrange [matters] with Gov. Andrew," he complained to Blair, though he claimed to have "abased myself trying." "I have made every proper proposition to Governor Andrew," Butler insisted to Secretary Cameron a couple of days later, "consistent with the dignity of the United States. He refuses them all, and has now gone to Washington to see you and the President and get you to interfere with me." Butler traveled to Washington, too, in an effort to sort out the conflict, to no avail. Meanwhile, some soldiers in the new Eastern Bay State Regiment received troubling notices, apparently from Governor Andrew, indicating that they were "irregular forces raised by General Butler against the lawful authority of the State, and the United States." These notices, Col. George F. Shepley protested, had engendered a certain amount of "restlessness" among the men, as they seemed to suggest that despite the privations the men had already suffered, they were not, in fact, "in the service of the United States" and "owed no obedience to their officers." Shepley marveled that the soldiers' "murmurings" had not yet "broken out into the actual insubordination the letters seem intended to have incited," which he attributed to the fact that no one really believed that Governor Andrew could have written or authorized such inflammatory documents. "Surely," Shepley suggested, Andrew "could never have so far forgotten what was due to his country, to his state, and to himself, as to have written such letters."[48]

As the dispute over recruitment in New England churned, Butler asked Lincoln to appoint him major general in the *regular* army. Butler's failed quest to attend West Point left him perennially touchy on the distinction between "regular" soldiers and officers, on the one hand, and volunteers and politically appointed officers like himself, on the other; presumably, Butler also hoped the appointment would enhance his stature vis-à-vis Governor Andrew. Lincoln denied the request but in late November authorized Butler to begin deploying troops to Ship Island, a "desolate and barren" strip of sand off the coast of Mississippi, along with a support staff that once again included Butler's brother, now as "civilian commissary of subsistence." For now, the troops would serve under Brig. Gen. John W. Phelps of Vermont, an ardent abolitionist who quickly and controversially proclaimed that he and his command would be actively working to end slavery in the region. And if that was not enough to stir popular interest both North and South, new rumors surfaced that General Butler himself would soon lead a major expedition in the Gulf of Mexico. Planning for such a mission was in fact underway in connection with the federal government's desire to capture and control the all-important Mississippi River. But the details of the expedition remained unclear, as a February letter from Butler's brother indicated: "General Phelps is doing nothing but waiting for you," Jackson reported somewhat anxiously from Ship Island. "The fleet has all gone to different places, and if the rebels don't take us it is for want of enterprise."[49]

Meanwhile, Butler traveled to Washington to meet with the new secretary of war, Democrat Edwin M. Stanton, whom he described as "an old political and personal friend of mine" with whom he was "on the most intimate terms," and from whom he hoped to get more clarity about what lay ahead. "Has Father started for 'Dixie' yet?" wrote Blanche to Sarah on January 2 from Georgetown. The answer was no. Moreover, troubling rumors suggested that George McClellan, who had replaced the retiring Winfield Scott as general-in-chief of the US Army, opposed the mission. On February 20, however, McClellan proved the rumormongers wrong, shutting down the Department of New England and assigning Butler to command of the newly created Military Department of the Gulf, comprising "all the coast of the Gulf of Mexico west of Pensacola Harbor, and so much of the Gulf States as may be occupied." "The Head Quarters for the present," McClellan ordered, will be "wherever the Commanding General may be." To Butler, McClellan wrote directly, "You are assigned to the command of the land forces [more than 15,000 soldiers] destined to co-operate with the Navy in the attack upon New Orleans," whose capture by means of an expedition up the Mississippi River was "of vital importance." The overarching goals of the Gulf mission were massive: in McClellan's words, "first the reduction of New Orleans and all its approaches, then Mobile and all its defenses, then Pensacola, Galveston, etc." Here was yet another big opportunity for Butler to serve the nation and perhaps achieve military glory.[50]

"We came on board at eleven o'clock," wrote Sarah on February 25, 1862, to her sister Harriet, who resumed caring for the Butlers' sons in Lowell along with her own five-year-old daughter, Hattie. Sarah penned her letter from the *Mississippi*, anchored offshore near Fort Monroe as it prepared for the trip to the Gulf. "It is expected we shall be off tonight." Five hundred miles further south and a few days later she wrote again from Port Royal, South Carolina, describing the "agonizing suspense" and "despairing misery" of the journey, during which the *Mississippi* had gone aground on the "Frying Pan Shoals" near Cape Fear, North Carolina, following a treacherous storm. Having suffered considerable damage, the ship was now undergoing repairs and was soon back in working order. "I have the great pleasure in informing you," Butler wrote proudly to Gen. William T. Sherman, then serving in the Department of the Mississippi, on March 10, "that I have succeeded at last in putting my vessel in a proper condition to proceed on her voyage in safety, and that I shall sail immediately." Butler blamed the accident on the ship's captain, whom he suspected of disloyalty, and had him arrested.[51]

After yet another fierce storm at sea, Butler, Sarah, and the roughly 1,400 soldiers who had traveled with them arrived about ten days later at Ship Island, where they were greeted by over 10,000 more Union troops. "The Island," Sarah observed, "is attractive seen from the ship; a long curving line of smooth beach, where the surf rolls in and breaks gaily in foam on the white sands." From the deck she could see the commanding officer's lodgings, "the house or room we are to have in addition to the tent." Situated close to water on three sides, Sarah joked that a stiff wind might blow their quarters right into the Gulf. More seriously and with some anxiety, she noted that her husband would begin his expedition up the river in just a few days, leaving her alone. "When you say your prayers," she advised her young sons back home, "pray that we may get back to you again in safety. You are master of the home now," she reminded Paul, who was about ten.[52]

In the latter part of March, Butler set about inspecting the troops on Ship Island and establishing a thorough sanitation infrastructure, a focus of concern he would soon bring to the city of New Orleans as well. Toward this end, Butler ordered all regiments on the island to construct "proper sinks"—troughs dug into the ground for use as temporary toilets. These sinks, Butler explained, should be dug in such a way that seawater could flow in and carry out the waste. At the same time, he strove to ensure that the soldiers and everyone else on the island had sufficient fresh water. "The sand on this Island is our great reservoir for pure water," he wrote, and it must be kept clean in order to avoid disease. "Cleanliness is next to godliness," Butler added with somewhat exaggerated piety. "The men must and shall be confined to their sinks." Butler held regimental commanders responsible for carrying out his orders, including promoting good moral behavior among the men by maintaining his ban on the sale and consumption of alcohol except for official medicinal purposes.[53]

On March 30, Butler informed Flag Officer David G. Farragut, in command of the US Navy's Gulf Expeditionary Force—"twenty-four wooden warships carrying 245 guns, nineteen mortar boats, and 15,000 soldiers"—that the mission up the Mississippi River to New Orleans was about to begin. He awaited only the completion of the naval squadron's preparations, as their gunboats would be spearheading the assault on the forts guarding the river. "It is 'bustle, bustle' now," Sarah wrote, "the vessels loading and unloading" in preparation for the expedition. "If they are successful," she added, "we shall be in New Orleans in two or three weeks"; if not, "woe betide us, we must seek a lodgment somewhere else." Sarah expected her brother Fisher's arrival on the island any day, and perhaps also that of Richard Fay, whose son sent word that Butler's business in Lowell was still doing well, thanks in part to continuing and substantial government contracts with the Middlesex mill. Meanwhile, she brooded over Governor Andrew's continuing antipathy, including its possible implications for the tenuous channels of communication and supply that stretched between Massachusetts and the Gulf. "Seven thousand men are shipped and ready to start," she informed Harriet on April 18. "Mr. Butler leaves with them tonight," she added. "On this action hang the hopes of thousands." Sarah briefly considered going along, simply for the thrill of being able to witness the capture of New Orleans personally and, if necessary, to help caring for any wounded. In the end, she remained safely behind, where she could nevertheless hear the "distant sound of heavy artillery" from the forts on the river. As she waited for news,

Sarah strove for patience. "I must neither hope, nor fear, exult or weep," she wrote Blanche, "until I have seen the messenger."[54]

The story of David Farragut and the navy's impressive running of the Mississippi River forts has been well told many times elsewhere. Suffice it to say that Butler was pleased to congratulate Farragut on April 24, "upon the bold, daring, brilliant and successful passage of the Forts of your fleet this morning. A more gallant exploit," he added, "has never fallen to the lot of man to witness." Two days later, Butler informed Sarah that he was about to land his infantry and proceed with the capture of New Orleans, though he was somewhat frustrated that Farragut and the fleet seemed to have now abandoned him and his thousands of infantrymen and headed up river "in the race for the glory of capturing" the city without completely disabling the forts they had passed so bravely. By April 29, however, Butler assured Secretary Stanton that the Confederate garrisons at Forts Jackson and Philip were now fully in his possession and that he was on his way "up the river to occupy the City with my troops." "Now we are in the Father of rivers," wrote one of Butler's infantrymen, B. B. Smith, in his diary. "The water looks muddy but tastes cool and good." Three days later, Smith felt less cheerful. "We are all getting tired of the old ship, as we are all crowded together like a lot of hogs." Still, Smith was struck—as Butler himself must have been—by the very different world he now encountered in the Deep South. "There is some very large & fine plantations along up the river," Smith wrote on April 30. "There is some very large sugar fields, with any amount of slaves of both sex[es] at work," he noted. "The scenery here is the finest I ever see."[55]

Upon arrival, Butler found the Crescent City in chaos and "under the domination of the mob," one of whose ruffians—a man named William Mumford—quickly and unapologetically "insulted our flag" and tore it down "with indignity" from where it hung in front of the US Mint. Outraged, Butler promised to punish the offender "in such a manner as in my judgment will caution both the perpetrators and abettors of the act, so that they shall fear the *stripes* if they do not reverence the stars of our banner." Indeed, writes one historian, "New Orleans was a city on the verge of anarchy. Fires burned unchecked; looters roamed at will; all commerce, including the delivery of foodstuffs, abruptly stopped." Even the mayor, John T. Monroe, initially "encouraged citizens to resist Union authority," though in the end Monroe, the city council, and the angry crowd were all forced to capitulate to Butler and his occupation forces. And so, provoking "intense chagrin and resentment" among its "high-spirited population," the all-important commercial center of New Orleans came under Union army control, the Confederacy having "lost its greatest city with scarcely a real battle." For his part, David Dixon Porter, commander of the expedition's mortar fleet, confidently (and erroneously) predicted that "the backbone of the Rebellion is broken." "We consider this the greatest event of the war and the hardest blow to the rebels yet administered," wrote Addison Gage and others to Butler on May 3. "Allow us to congratulate you on the success."[56]

No event during the war has exercised an influence upon the public mind so powerful as the capture and occupation of New Orleans, and to you, and to the gallant officers and soldiers under your command, the Department tenders cordial thanks. Your vigorous and able administration of the government of that city also receives warm commendation.
—EDWIN M. STANTON TO BUTLER, JUNE 1862

I thought of calling on you, and while bidding you a loving farewell, informing you of the true light with which your departure is viewed by us. Self-respect, however, prevented me from doing so, as I feared contamination by even breathing the polluted air with which you are surrounded. Ever since you came among us, we have felt for you *hatred* so violent that no words can express it. We have always regarded you as a monster in whose composition the lowest of traits were concentrated; and "Butler the brute" will be handed down to posterity as a by-word, by which all true Southerners will "remember *thee* monster, thou vilest of scum."
—"ONE OF YOUR SHE ADDERS" TO BUTLER, DECEMBER 1862

New Orleans
April–December 1862

Of all the chapters in the story of Benjamin F. Butler's long and complicated life journey, the one that comprises the seven and a half months he commanded the Federal occupation of New Orleans has drawn the most historiographical and cultural attention. This is, arguably, appropriate: Butler's approach to governing in New Orleans and the surrounding area brought him nothing less than "international notoriety and the undying hatred of Southerners." In New Orleans, observes one historian, "every move Butler made created controversy." At the same time, Butler's months in New Orleans undeniably also produced important and highly lauded successes for the Union cause, while further advancing his own personal development on the issues of slavery, race, and the burdens and responsibilities of federal power, among others. Whole books, ranging in tone from hagiographic to scathing, have been devoted to this phase of Butler's military career.[1]

And still today, conversational references to Butler commonly evoke responses that allude, usually pejoratively, to some aspect of his command style or some action he took (or supposedly took) to exert authority over the rebel city. Even at his alma mater in Maine, mentioning Butler typically elicits some epithet derived from the Lost Cause reinterpretation of the war, one that positions Butler as a heartless, self-dealing purveyor of violence and grift against the noble, victimized Confederate population of the Crescent City. Such labels fail to acknowledge the fullness of the historical record, including the unprecedented burdens and expectations under which Butler was operating in rebel Louisiana, over a thousand miles from Washington, D.C., and just one year into the rapidly expanding and changing war. They fail to reckon, too, with the fact that in the spring and summer of 1862 New Orleans was, among many other things, a major cosmopolitan and racially complex southern city where slavery, commerce, and international relations intertwined, underpinning the city's wealth and prominence. It was, therefore, a unique testing ground for the shape—or shapes—that Union conquest, occupation, and reconstruction should take. Moreover, legends—as well as jokes—about Butler's supposed tyranny and corruption have roots not only in the resentment shared by many (but by no means all) proud New Orleanians during and after the war but also in the tiresome and demeaning criticism deployed by his political opponents in Massachusetts and elsewhere, many of whom gleefully echoed Confederate talking points in order to undercut Butler's postwar political ambitions and his formidable and enduring appeal to the poor, to laboring men, to Blacks, and to women.

This is not to suggest that Butler's every move in New Orleans was brilliant or perfectly thought through in advance, or that his administration of the occupation was flawless. It is not to deny, either, Butler's substantial ego and his personal weaknesses. It is, however, to suggest a more balanced reconsideration of his months of command in Louisiana, including his many impressive accomplishments, especially given the limited and often undefined parameters of his authority, his relative isolation from Washington, and the profound social and political difficulties of the job he had been sent to New Orleans to perform. Two months into the occupation, former secretary of war Simon Cameron commended Butler for a hard job well done. "I hasten to offer you my thanks," Cameron wrote, "for the great service you have rendered our country, and my congratulations on the able, firm, and statesmanlike conduct you have exhibited since you came into possession of the city of New Orleans." Around the same time, Secretary of the Treasury

Salmon P. Chase wrote similarly, "Your success at New Orleans and your general course of administration there has given the greatest satisfaction to all your friends." Both during the war and after, of course, whatever gave satisfaction to Butler's friends typically enraged his opponents; his time in New Orleans offered both groups a deep well of resources upon which to draw for argument's sake.[2]

"New Orleans is in our possession," Sarah wrote exultantly to her sister Harriet on May 2, 1862, describing the expedition up the Mississippi, the "sullen and dangerous" nature of the local population when the US forces arrived, and the poverty and hunger they found running rampant among a sizable proportion of New Orleans's residents. "I was excited," Sarah wrote of her own entrance into the city, but "felt no fear." Having landed his troops, Butler worked quickly to establish his own and the federal government's authority, taking up residence with his staff (and Sarah) at the elegant St. Charles Hotel, setting up his headquarters at the massive Custom House, summoning the mayor and other civic leaders to meet with him, declaring martial law, ordering a regimental band to play lively and loud patriotic songs, and proclaiming to recalcitrant city residents his intent "to restore order, maintain public tranquility, and enforce peace and quiet under the laws and constitution of the United States." "There is here," Butler confided to Secretary of War Stanton on May 8, "a violent, strong, and unruly mob that can only be kept under by fear." As one historian writes, the city was "a powder keg ready to explode." Butler demanded that residents hand over their firearms, forbade "any displays of flags or emblems other than those of the United States," called for loyalty oaths, banned the use of Confederate money, and shut down newspapers that printed material he deemed "derogatory of U.S. authority." Envisioning himself as an agent of unyielding federal government authority against the rebellion, Butler meant "to rule with a stern hand" in New Orleans. At the same time, and surely recalling his family's own financial woes as well as his years of effort on behalf of the mill operatives and other struggling workers in Lowell, Butler meant to act as a "benevolent tyrant," reaching out vigorously to the provide the city's poor with desperately needed relief.[3]

Among the many concerns weighing heavily on Butler's mind as the occupation began was the problem of supplying his own soldiers at this remote post. "I have already expended $5000 of my private funds to enable the Quartermaster's men to get on at all," he informed Quartermaster General Montgomery Meigs on May 8, just a week after the Federals had arrived. As summer loomed, Butler worried, too, about the very real possibility of a

GEN. BUTLER HOLDING THE MOB IN CHECK AT NEW ORLEANS.

"Gen. Butler Holding the Mob in Check at New Orleans," by
Charles Stanley Reinhart. Courtesy of the Prints and Photographs
Division, Library of Congress, Washington, D.C.

yellow fever epidemic, with its particularly dangerous implications for his
northern troops, who had no experience with the disease and no immunity from it. A recurring problem in the Gulf region, a yellow fever outbreak
seemed even more likely once enslaved people, who had learned of the Union
occupation, began abandoning farms and plantations in and around the city
and seeking freedom under the authority of the man who had created the

contraband policy eleven months earlier. New Orleans, wrote surgeon Robert K. Smith to Butler on May 5, had been spared an eruption of the fever for over a year, but that was no guarantee of continued protection. Indeed, at the time the Federals arrived the disease had already begun spreading downriver and was poised to attack the city as well, evoking fears of streets flooded with "black vomit." Butler heard rumors that "the rebels were actually relying largely upon the yellow fever to clear out the Northern troops."[4]

In Butler's view, there were two keys to preventing an outbreak. First, he must develop effective quarantine processes for outsiders entering the region, particularly from the Gulf. "My experience for twenty-five years in this climate," advised William Marvin from Key West in late May, "induces me to . . . suggest to you the importance of establishing a rigorous quarantine of all vessels, cargoes, and persons coming to the port of New Orleans." Marvin recommended a fifteen-day isolation period and urged that "quarantine regulations should be made and enforced as military regulations." Second, as he had done on Ship Island, he must act quickly to improve the city's sanitation infrastructure. "I desire to call your attention to the Sanitary condition of your streets," Butler wrote the mayor and the city council on May 9. "Resolutions and inaction will not do. Active, energetic measures, fully and promptly executed, are imperatively demanded by the exigencies of the occasion." From an old Waterville College friend Butler gratefully received a copy of a "learned report" on a yellow fever epidemic in 1853. "It is the best work on the subject," wrote Erastus Everett from Brooklyn, "and I send it as a token of esteem with the hope that you may gather from it some useful hints for the improvement of the sanitary condition of your command."[5]

Butler's efforts to upgrade the city's sanitation infrastructure in order to stave off a highly contagious disease had the corollary result of amplifying his awareness of the particular vulnerability of many of the city's residents, especially those suffering from high levels of poverty and hunger. As early as May 9, Butler commented publicly on the "deplorable state of destitution and hunger of the mechanics and working classes of this city," a crisis whose origins he unequivocally laid at the feet of the city's "wealthy and influential" citizens, whom he equated with the Crescent City's Confederate leadership. Although he had not originally expected to have to use army provisions and any other resources he could requisition to feed the city's downtrodden, Butler nevertheless promised, "to the extent possible, within the power of the commanding general, it shall be done." Butler's commitment to provisioning the city's neediest residents caught the attention of his soldiers, many of whom were themselves all too familiar with financial hardship. Butler, noted B. B. Smith in his diary, "is agoing to begin to relieve the poor in this city tomorrow. There is a great deal of want and suffering."[6]

Like so many of the problems he faced in New Orleans, widespread hunger and poverty had no easy solution, and deep into the summer Butler acknowledged that "the need of relief to the destitute poor of the city requires more extended measures and greater outlay than have yet been made." One possible strategy was to tax the city's rich who, Butler was confident, were in fact some of the very same people who had brought the war on in the first place, and with it, the increased suffering of those further down the social ladder. Perhaps reminded of his earlier battle to protect the secret ballot in Lowell, Butler noted that "middling and working-men" in New Orleans had never been able to exert an independent influence at the ballot box—"unawed by threats and unmenaced by 'Thugs' and paid assassins"—and thus could hardly be blamed for Louisiana's secession, or the economic problems it had produced (or exacerbated) in New Orleans. Even worse, many of the destitute were the wives and children of men who had been duped into serving in the Confederate army. As such, justice required that the fortunes of the leaders of the rebellion be tapped to provide for its local victims. It bears noting that Butler's concern for the neediest in New Orleans extended to the Black poor as well. "We have with us a great many Negro women and children, barefoot and half naked," he wrote to General-in-Chief of the US Army Henry Halleck. "May I ask in what way, in view of the coming winter, these are to be clothed?" Although Butler reported that he was shipping food into the city as best he could and "distributing in various ways about $50,000" worth of it to the city's White residents and double the amount of rations required by his own troops to Black residents, still, he noted, "more is needed."[7]

In early June, Butler had also begun taking steps to combine his commitment to feeding the poor, his determination to prevent a yellow fever outbreak, and his desire to punish the wealthy local Confederate leaders: he put thousands of needy residents, Black and White, to work on sanitation duty cleaning the city's streets and sewers and performing other tasks, like repairing levees, and paying them with the taxes he collected from the rich. Further, he demanded that property owners "clean up their grounds" (or pay workers to have it done), promising to arrest those who refused. In the end, Butler's efforts to stave off both yellow fever and mass starvation at the expense of the city's financial and political elite were successful, although they predictably infuriated local elites who could not even bring themselves, in most cases, to admit the salubrious effects of his innovative policies.

"Perhaps in no other occupied city of the Confederacy," writes one historian, "did the residents need the Federal government so much, yet acknowledge its help so little." Local Unionists, in contrast, made a point of expressing their deep gratitude; in late June one anonymous "Union Man" sent Butler a brace of pistols to thank him for everything he and his troops had done, starting with "the re-establishment of Federal rule in place of the tyranny practiced by Jeff Davis & his followers."[8]

Some of the actions Butler took in New Orleans provoked outright fury, not just among local opponents but also far beyond Louisiana's borders. Among the most famous of these was his General Orders No. 28, frequently called "the Woman Order," which he issued on May 15. In it, Butler advised local Confederate women that if they continued to actively protest the occupation as they had been doing since the Federals' arrival, they should expect to be treated, in essence, as prostitutes, and thrown in jail. "See where we were," Butler explained in a letter to an old college classmate. "We had come into a city where the dirt and pistol had ruled for ten years at least" and the women, even "more bitter in their secession than the men, were everywhere insulting my soldiers; deliberately spitting in their faces and upon their uniforms, making insulting gestures and remarks, tending to provoke retort, recrimination, and return of insult, which would have ended in disgraceful and murderous riot." Butler asked, "What was there to be done?" and, "Is a she-adder to be preferred to a he-adder when they void their venom in your face?" Butler, one historian observes, "especially resented the way in which ladies in New Orleans would withdraw from pews in church should a Union man choose to sit nearby," and "would depart from streetcars should a Yankee board," and "gather up their skirts and desert the sidewalk rather than to pass close by a federal soldier." When one woman spat in two Federal officers' faces, Butler decided he had had enough. Sarah agreed. "Their insolence," she wrote, "is beyond endurance, and must be checked." Many correspondents expressed their vigorous approval of the Woman Order, including B. W. Richmond of Albion, New York, who commended Butler's "gallantry and quick insight into the remedy to be applied to the wicked aiders to this rebellion—who wear petticoats." Any woman who behaved "like a whore," he wrote, "should be judged by Christ's maxim: the tree is known by its fruit."[9]

City leaders and their elite allies, however, were appalled. Mayor Monroe described General Orders No. 28 as "extraordinary," "astounding," and dangerous, nothing less than a "reproach to the civilization not to say the Christianity of the age," and a license to Union soldiers to "commit outrages" against supposedly "helpless" (White) women and girls. "Few things," notes one historian, "could more effectively make nineteenth-century white men, North or South, feel that their society was under attack than questioning the behavior or morality of white women," as Butler's order had done. And "by holding women accountable for what they did and said in public," General Orders No. 28 "discarded the idea of female innocence and made white southern male protectors superfluous," even as it "challenged the moral righteousness of all of southern society and also announced that white southern men had not been exercising their authority over their subordinates properly." In the end, "an insult of that magnitude could not be taken calmly," for "it threatened white men's very identities as men." Rumblings of opposition to the order could be heard not just among White men across the South, but in the North as well, and even across the Atlantic.[10]

In practical terms, the order did suppress the bulk of local Confederate women's misbehavior. As Butler explained to his old friend from Waterville, the Woman Order "executed itself," and once he issued it, public insults against his soldiers ceased. "Why, these she-adders of New Orleans themselves," he informed another friend, were quickly "shamed into propriety of conduct by the order." This was not entirely true, however. In early July, almost two months after he issued the Woman Order, Butler learned that Eugenia Levy Phillips—who had been imprisoned in Washington, D.C., the previous year—had been seen celebrating the death of a Union officer as his funeral procession passed below her balcony. "Mrs. Phillips," Butler growled, had for some time been "training her children to spit upon the Officers of the United States at New Orleans." Now she was discovered "laughing and mocking" at the remains of one Lieutenant DeKay. Adding insult to injury, when Butler asked her whether she had indeed engaged in such disrespectful behavior, she "contemptuously" answered, "I was in good spirits that day." Rather than charge her under the earlier Woman Order, Butler issued a special order declaring Phillips an "uncommon, bad, and dangerous woman, stirring up strife and inciting to riot," and had her arrested and confined on Ship Island. Phillips spent nearly three months in detention before Butler released her on parole in mid-September. "I did not carry on war with rose-water," he wrote later.[11]

Needless to say, local "she-adders" and wealthy Confederate leaders were hardly Butler's only opposition during the occupation of New Orleans, or his only targets for punishment. As noted above, even as Federal forces were arriving to take control of the city, a professional gambler and rebel named William Mumford tore down the flag that Federal soldiers had hoisted at the US Mint, dragged it through the streets, and made a public display of destroying it. In late May, Butler organized a military commission to consider the charges against Mumford, namely, that he had committed the offense "for the purpose of opposing the force of the United States and of showing his contempt for its laws," as well as "to excite animosity and resistance to the lawful authority of the Government of the United States among the citizens of said city of New Orleans." The commission found Mumford guilty and sentenced him to death, and Butler promptly approved the sentence. On June 7, William Mumford was hanged on a scaffold that federal officials had constructed directly in front of the Mint, "under the flagstaff from which he had taken the flag." At his wife's request, Mumford's body was later buried at what was known as the Fireman's Cemetery.[12]

From across the Confederacy and beyond came howls of protest over what many called murder. Mumford's execution only intensified the rage the Woman Order had provoked and confirmed Confederates' and their allies' assessment of the hardline Union general as "nothing less than a 'Beast,'" by far the most enduring of all the nicknames that followed Butler after the war. On June 10, a Missouri newspaper attacked the general as a "miserable hireling" guilty of "playing the tyrant with a high hand," and, in a telling use of racist language, pointed to Butler's "savage instincts," which the paper claimed "are far ahead of the most ferocious native of Dahomey or Patagonia." In contrast, the paper described William Mumford as a good and decent man who had "died as a patriot should die—with great coolness and self-possession." The paper rejected any claim that Mumford had simply "received the reward of his treason and madness," as well as any attempt to justify the execution as a reasonable, if terrible, act of war in the context of a violent rebellion against the national government.[13]

In the months that followed, Butler continued to arrest and imprison other troublesome locals, including a bookseller, whom he put in jail "for allegedly displaying the bones of a Union soldier in his front window," and a judge, accused of wearing a cross made of the same macabre material. By the fall, dozens of political prisoners were in confinement on Ship Island, a clear indication of Butler's "determination to make secessionists pay for their continued defiance of U.S. authority." Among them was Pierre Soulé, a powerful local figure whom Butler described to Secretary Stanton as an "ex-member of Congress and former Minister to Spain" who had been (and still was) "engaged in plotting treason against the United States Government" by means of his role as the city's sheriff and his membership in a secret society, the "Southern Independence Association," and related treasonable activities.[14] And yet, whether Butler felt chastened, which is unlikely, or simply decided that he had made his point with sufficient force in the Mumford case, there were no more executions.

As already noted, some historians have accused Butler of behaving like a "czar" in New Orleans, and certainly there were many in and around the city who saw him and his administration in the same brutal light, even before the execution of Mumford. Indeed, not long after the occupation began, one self-proclaimed "wife of a Southern Planter" lambasted Butler (whom she mockingly called "your majesty"), claiming that "one and all" people like herself in New Orleans "detest your government, and feel your orders as insults to our common sense." This elite correspondent warned that "when our gallant [Gen. P. G. T.] Beauregard," a native of the area, "comes to deliver us from the inflated myrmidon of the tyrannical Buffoon at Washington, we shall see with intense joy the noble Picayune Butler flying from the *Vatican*, in finished *Bull Run* or *Bethel* style, with all his Yankee rabble infesting our City at his heels." "Our hearts," she warned, "you can never, never subdue."[15]

Words of condemnation also flowed freely from the state's Confederate political leaders, including Governor Thomas O. Moore, who accused Butler, among other things, of trying to incite class warfare to his own benefit. "General Butler's attempt to excite the poor against the more wealthy is characteristic of the man," wrote Moore in a public statement addressed "to the Loyal People of New Orleans." Butler, he declared, deploying a familiar proslavery argument, "comes from a section of country that has done more than any other to degrade and cheapen labor and reduce the laboring man to the condition of slave," and he cautioned that "the real object of the war," epitomized by the bully Butler, "is to turn loose an ignorant and servile race that would desolate the land when once freed from the restraint which they have learned to respect as well as fear." The Yankees "are sowing to the wind, but fear the harvest," Moore proclaimed, and "we would advise General Butler to make the most of his ill-gotten power, for his reign will be short." Moore promised that the "bitter humiliation" of surrendering the city to the Federals had neither "created despondency, nor shaken our abiding faith in our success," and he swore, "our recognition as a Nation is one of those certainties of the future which nothing but our own unfaithfulness can prevent."[16]

Not surprisingly, some of the virulent opposition Butler faced while attempting to manage the turmoil in New Orleans seemed likely to result in violence against him personally. "Mr. Butler gets letters almost daily," Sarah wrote to Harriet, "that he will be poisoned or assassinated, and that leagues are formed, sworn to accomplish it." But, she added bravely, "we shall not be driven out." "Heaven preserve you from the hell-hounds of secession," wrote Joseph B. Quinby of Cincinnati in July. "When so many inducements are held out, and rewards offered, by the secession villains for your assassination, it behooves you to be ever on your guard." Quinby reported reading a newspaper article about a "secession devil" from Mississippi who had offered $10,000 to anyone who would kill Butler in cold blood. "The secession she-devils," he added, were "getting up a subscription for the same purpose," and he counseled Butler to observe "eternal vigilance, prudence, and caution." Undaunted but not reckless, Butler took to keeping lists of people in the area who were presumed to be disloyal, paid some in the community to keep their eyes and ears open for signs of trouble, and gratefully received any and all relevant information, including from local Black residents.[17]

In addition, Butler strove to identify opponents—his own and the federal government's—by imposing loyalty oaths, an effort that in the end proved only minimally successful simply because so few residents—perhaps around 10 percent—agreed to them. By October, Butler accelerated the program, requiring residents who had not yet taken the loyalty oath to "register with a Federal provost marshal, reporting the names of all members of their household and listing all the family's property." But defiance continued. In November, Butler further attempted to separate the loyal from the disloyal by demanding that the latter hand in their weapons, which resulted in the collection of "about six thousand guns" but still failed to solve the basic problem of lingering resistance to Federal authority. At one point, notes one historian, Butler even "fired the civilian police force for refusing to take the oath of allegiance," which actually increased the burden of keeping order for the US troops until he hired a new force.[18]

Meanwhile, guerrillas active in the region were busy doing whatever they could to destabilize the Federal occupation. Determined to stop them, and in keeping with the Union's overall shift from a soft war to a hard war policy in this period, Butler adopted an approach that was "just as punitive as any policy he initiated against the citizens of New Orleans." In early July he ordered that guerrilla fighters who attacked Union troops be punished "with the last severity" and their property summarily destroyed, including their homes. In a letter to Secretary Stanton, Butler further suggested that a $1,000 reward be offered for every captured guerrilla, as well as freedom to any enslaved Blacks who participated in the capture. It was time, he declared, to enact a policy of "fire set to fire" that "would bring that uncivilized system of warfare to sudden termination by an equally uncivilized remedy." As it happens, Butler's suggested approach did not come fully to fruition, proving itself "more fiery rhetoric than actionable policy." Still, Butler seemed ready if not eager "to push the limits of 'civilized warfare' when dealing with the guerrilla problem" if doing so would enable him to keep New Orleans under control and in the Union's grip.[19]

In addition to irregular military operatives in the region, Butler's occupation forces faced steady threats of attack from the north by regular Confederate soldiers. And indeed, in early August, a fierce battle erupted in Baton Rouge when Confederate general John C. Breckinridge—the same man Butler had unenthusiastically ended up supporting for president in 1860—attacked the Federal soldiers newly stationed there. The Confederates temporarily threw the garrison into chaos, killed Union general Thomas Williams, and stunned Butler "with the ferocity of their onslaught" before the Federals, with naval support from the river, managed to stop them. To Sarah, recently returned to Massachusetts for the unhealthful summer months, Butler reported, "our casualties in that battle are very large," including "some 90 killed and two hundred and fifty wounded." The battle, he admitted, had brought to his own and his forces' attention "the strong realities of war." Nevertheless, the Confederate attempt to advance had been stopped, and as a result Butler claimed a "glorious victory." In the wake of the battle, Butler pondered revenge, ordering Baton Rouge "destroyed" and the Federal troops stationed there brought back to New Orleans. Butler later rescinded the first part of his order, but not before Federal soldiers had exacted a measure of retribution on the city: according to one source, soldiers "cut down its massive shade trees, plundered its homes, and crated up its public art for shipment to New Orleans," leaving residents fearful that worse lay ahead. "All good citizens are called upon to lend their influence to the United States," Butler reminded Louisianans some weeks later, and "all that do not do so are enemies of the United States. The line is to be distinctly and broadly drawn. Every citizen must find himself on the one side or the other."[20]

Meanwhile, the cosmopolitan nature of New Orleans as a major commercial trading center brought Butler into regular contact with representatives of other nations: consuls and other diplomats who were stationed there, only some of whom cooperated readily with his administration. Like the Civil War generally, Butler's occupation of New Orleans had international dimensions. "I find that the British Consul here has complicated himself and his countrymen with the rebels in every form," Butler advised Secretary of State William H. Seward in the early days of the occupation. "The precise contrary course I believe has been taken by the French consul." A few days later he addressed the British consul directly, promising to protect "all Neutrals and foreigners who have kept aloof from these troubles which have been brought upon the City," including their property. "They shall have," Butler vowed, "the same hospitable and just treatment they have always received at the hands of the United States Government." At the same time, he warned against representatives of foreign nations even seeming to take the side of the Confederacy, and threatened that "unworthy" agents would be summarily "routed out."[21]

Among the foreign agents who quickly came into direct conflict with Butler's administration was the Dutch consul, A. Conturié, who claimed that Federal soldiers had "forcibly entered" the consulate, held him prisoner, and "subjected" him to "indignity" and "severe ill-usage" while they searched the premises. Having learned that Conturié was harboring "a large amount of specie," Butler had indeed ordered soldiers to raid the Dutch consulate, where they found thousands of dollars' worth of "Mexican coin" rather suspiciously "bearing the mark of the Citizen's Bank of Louisiana." Butler refused to return the money, insisting that Conturié had acted in bad faith against the United States and now wanted to claim neutrality and "perfect immunity from the ordinary laws of war" for himself and for his native country's supposed property. Such "pretensions," Butler insisted to Secretary Stanton, "are too absurd to be for a moment entertained."[22]

In early June, Secretary Seward tried to smooth things over with the Dutch envoy in Washington, Theodorus Marinus Roest Van Limburg, without either attacking or fully endorsing Butler's actions. Rather, Seward advised Van Limburg that President Lincoln had recently appointed a military governor for Louisiana—George F. Shepley, a former member of Butler's staff who had also worked with him recruiting in New England—who had been instructed, somewhat vaguely it would seem, to "pay due respect to all Consular rights and privileges." Seward further explained that a "Commissioner"—Reverdy Johnson—was on his way to New Orleans to investigate and, hopefully, resolve the dispute "according to international law and justice." (Butler and Johnson had clashed the previous year over Butler's arrest of the Baltimore rebel Ross Winans, whose release Johnson, a native Marylander, had eventually engineered.) Seward directed Colonel Shepley to "afford all reasonable facilities to Mr. Johnson to perform the trust confided to him," as "the utmost delicacy is required in transactions with consuls and with foreigners, so as to avoid not only just cause of complaint, but groundless irritation in a critical juncture." Seward simultaneously cautioned against any assumption that by sending Johnson to New Orleans he was casting aspersions on Butler's actions or leadership. "I am by no means to be understood as prejudging, much less censuring, Major-General Butler, whose general course of administration seems to me to have been eminently judicious and energetic." For his part, Butler's friend Postmaster General Blair objected to the whole arrangement. "I don't know what Johnson will do," he wrote. "I confess I don't expect much good of him, but I hope you will study your part in dealing with him very closely."[23]

Meanwhile, Butler further aggravated existing tensions with the city's international residents by issuing his General Orders No. 41, which required "all foreigners claiming any of the privileges of an American citizen, or protection or favor from the Government of the United States" to take the oath of allegiance. Some foreigners considered this a violation of "the ordinary obligations of probity, honour, & neutrality," or at least so they claimed. Many who fell under the order openly protested it, as did some native-born observers who felt Butler was being unnecessarily pugnacious and simply insulting the Crescent City's foreign residents without cause. On June 24, Seward informed Stanton that Lincoln wanted Butler to stand down from demanding the oaths, even though he technically had the right to insist upon them. "The expediency of requiring oaths from those who do not owe a permanent allegiance to the Government," wrote Seward, "is so doubtful that I am directed by the President to request you order him to discontinue that practice for the future, and to cancel any such obligations which may thus have been compulsorily contracted."[24]

Later that month Seward reemphasized the importance of balancing the demands of federal authorities, the protocols of foreign diplomacy, and the benefit of advancing international commerce through New Orleans. "The President regards the renewal of commerce at New Orleans, and on the Mississippi and its tributaries," he explained to Reverdy Johnson, "as a most effective means of bringing this unhappy civil strife to an end, and restoring the authority of the Federal Government" by depriving other nations "of all excuse for sympathy with the insurgents." In mid-July, Charles Francis Adams, US minister to the Court of St. James's, took a more directly critical approach, scolding Butler all the way from London for his behavior vis-à-vis the consuls and decrying the embarrassment he now felt as a US emissary abroad. "Altho' you have been invested with high honors and power," Adams wrote, "it must not be supposed that you can act as the veriest despot without being judged by the tribunal of the *Civilized World*." Moreover, Adams continued, "the Consuls whom you have treated with so much contumely *have rights*," and Butler's disdain for those rights had now thoroughly embarrassed America's diplomatic envoys.[25] How much store Butler put by Adams's criticisms and protests is impossible to measure, but one suspects it was minimal.

It is important to note that as troubling and dangerous as the possibility of foreign recognition of the Confederacy must have felt to Lincoln, Seward, and others in Washington and across the Atlantic, to Butler on the ground in distant New Orleans, concern over individual foreigners' practical engagement with and support for the local rebels—hard as they were to keep in check—must have felt significantly more tangible and immediately problematic. As a result, throughout his occupation of the city Butler determinedly and unapologetically resisted all pressure to treat foreign residents and their diplomatic representatives with kid gloves. In mid-August, for example, he reminded the French consul, Count Eugène Méjan, that even foreign-born residents who failed to take the oath of allegiance were expected to hand over their arms to the federal government. When Méjan replied that he needed weapons for self-defense in case of a slave rebellion, Butler noted that he, too, had been observing the "disquiet" that had become increasingly evident among the region's enslaved Black population as they demonstrated their desire for freedom. Butler understood, too, why the enslaved might choose to rise up, if for no other reason that "their masters had set them the example of rebellion against constituted authorities." Butler then shrewdly backed Méjan into a logical corner: "Surely," he wrote, "the representative of the Emperor, who does not tolerate slavery in France, does not desire his countrymen to be armed for the purpose of preventing the negroes from breaking their bonds."[26]

For all the opposition Butler and his occupation forces faced in New Orleans, from a variety of quarters, it is also true that many locals were grateful—sometimes immensely so—for the federal authority and basic order and control that Butler and soldiers had imposed. "This day being the anniversary of our Glorious Independence, so dearly bought," wrote M. M. White on July 4, "I raised upon my balcony the noble emblem of our loved Country, and also to testify the joy I felt for our recent deliverance from the despotic power, which has ruled us for the past nineteen months." Among those who were most thankful for the arrival of the Federal forces were, predictably, the region's bondspeople, many of whom may have already known of the contraband policy Butler had initiated at Fort Monroe the previous year. Surely there were others who knew of Gen. David Hunter's recent order declaring "forever free" persons "heretofore held as slaves" in the states of Georgia, Florida, and South Carolina that comprised the Military Department of the South. Lincoln quickly rescinded Hunter's order, but that did not stop the flow of runaways to Union lines. Indeed, virtually from the moment he reached New Orleans, Butler began receiving complaints from local slave owners about their human property absconding, along with demands for their immediate return. On May 10, for example, Theodore Laussade, a rice planter in the Parish of Plaquemines south of the city, reported that two days earlier, "six of my slaves, viz: Edmond, Victor, Charles, Pierre, Ulysse, and Helain, stealthily and during the night left my premises and went to Fort St. Phillip where they can be found and restored to me." On May 22, Polycarpe Fortier whined that "my slaves who have never left me before and who were satisfied with my treatment are now running away."[27] Similar letters accumulated daily.

Before long, large numbers of runaways were gathering at Camp Parapet west of the city limits, which was under the command of Gen. John W. Phelps of Vermont. Having previously announced at Ship Island that he and his soldiers fully intended to undermine slavery to the best of their ability, Phelps welcomed them all. As early as May 22 he had compiled a "List of Persons White & Black in Camp Parapet" that was five sheets long, which he forwarded to Butler with the comment, "Colored persons unemployed are continually varying in number coming and going. The old system of labor seems [to be] breaking up, so much so as hardly to be worth the while to try to save it." As Butler had done at Fort Monroe, Phelps at Camp Parapet aimed to put as many of the new arrivals as possible to work, including the women, whom he employed as cooks, laundresses, and hospital workers. "With regard to the Negro women connected with our Hospital Department," wrote one surgeon, they "fill a place well that men from the ranks would be but poor substitutes for." The "female 'contrabands,'" wrote another officer, "are invaluable to us as servants, & on the ground of morals no well founded objection can be raised to their presence, as they are quartered separately & allowed to have no improper connection with the men."[28] Phelps employed every runaway from slavery he could find a job for, and he hoped to protect those who were unable to provide labor, too.

Unlike at Fort Monroe, however, Butler remained uncertain how to handle this admittedly predictable development. At least one historian has argued that Butler purposely chose to go in the "opposite direction" of Hunter (and John C. Frémont in August 1861) after he observed the commander in chief's negative (and perhaps humiliating) response to their emancipation orders. According to this theory, Butler's primary goal was to protect himself from a similar fate by ordering that, at the very least, the escapees who could not be put to work should be turned away. This interpretation seems unduly harsh, however, attributing to Butler a degree of callous, raw ambition that does not take into its calculation the complexity of the situation Butler faced in Louisiana. It must be remembered, first of all, that at Fort Monroe, the runaways had clearly been escaping from the control of avowed rebels against the federal government who meant to put them to work on behalf of the Confederacy. In New Orleans, the lines were blurrier. Some enslaved Blacks were fleeing determined Confederates, but some were running from owners who were either already Unionists or might well be persuaded, with a little coaxing, to take the oath of allegiance. Moreover, in the early days of the occupation Congress had only passed the First Confiscation Act; it would not pass the Second Confiscation Act until July, allowing for the emancipation of the enslaved who came under Union control. And Lincoln himself was still months away from taking a firm, public stand on emancipation, though he had already begun to set aside his faith in the soft war strategy. In addition, the capture of New Orleans had for the first time truly put the question of wartime Reconstruction powerfully and unavoidably on the table. How might the federal government most easily and smoothly undertake the process of bringing rebels, and rebel states, back into the Union, and how did the preservation or destruction of slavery factor into those considerations? Given the parameters—and limits—of his authority as a military officer (again, one thinks of George McClellan's much-criticized Harrison's Landing Letter later that summer), Butler opted for what must have seemed to him a reasonable compromise commensurate with advancing the likelihood of White Louisianans' return to the Union. On May 23 he ordered Phelps to accept only those runaways who were able to perform labor, and reject the rest.[29]

The abolitionist Phelps pushed back quickly, and on May 27 Butler heard from one of Phelps's frustrated subordinate officers that the soldiers under Phelps's command were now being "allowed to range the country, insult the planters," and not just welcome runaways into camp when they came on their own but also "entice negroes away from their plantations," especially if there were indications that the bondspeople at a given location were being treated poorly. "While, Sir, such acts are permitted," this disgruntled officer wrote, "it is utterly impossible to call upon the negroes for any labor, as they say they have only to go to the Fort to be free, and are therefore very insolent to their masters." More than one local slave owner agreed: Phelps's policies were having "a demoralizing effect on the serving population, not alone of this Parish, but of the whole state." Another urged Butler to put a halt to Phelps's antislavery activities, if only to convince Whites in the region that "the war is to restore the Union and not for abolition." "You can be in peaceful possession of Louisiana in less than a month," this correspondent advised Butler, unless Butler decided to endorse Phelps's program of military emancipation, in which case the Union could never be saved.[30]

As early as May 25, just a year since he had established his contraband policy at Fort Monroe, Butler sought guidance from Secretary Stanton. What, he asked, is the "state of negro property here and the condition of the negroes as men?" Whether they liked it or not, he observed, New Orleans's Whites, including slave owners, had largely capitulated to federal power, as Marylanders had done the previous year. Were they not therefore due the protection of the federal government's laws, including the Fugitive Slave Law? "To this city and vicinage," Butler continued, "has been pledged the Government protection and inviolability of the rights of property under the laws of the United States so long as the conditions of peace and quiet shall be preserved," and in many cases, he noted, "that pledge has been accepted by the good, loyal, and peaceful." Moreover, even "the wicked" were becoming more compliant, whether or not they were loyal in their hearts. As for the enslaved, who represented "a large portion of property here," their labor was essential to the local economy. "They till the soil, raise the sugar, corn, and cotton; load and unload the ships; they perform every domestic office, and are permeated through every branch of industry and peaceful calling." While it seemed clear—as it had in Virginia, and as Congress had declared—that the Black men, women, and children who belonged to Whites "actively in arms" against the Union could and should be "confiscated," the question remained, what of those seeking Union army protection whose owners freely took the oath of allegiance? And if the federal government's answer was to take some but not others—"*It is a physical impossibility to take all,*" Butler emphasized—how was he to decide, in a judicious manner, whom to protect and whom to return to bondage? "If coming within our lines is equivalent to freedom," Butler asked, "and liberty is a boon, is it to be obtained only by the first that apply?"[31]

Once again, Washington's reply to Butler's questions—both practical and profound—came slowly and was, initially, vague. "It has not yet . . . been deemed necessary or wise," Stanton wrote rather unhelpfully in late June, "to fetter your judgment by any specific instructions in this regard." Instead, "it is confidently hoped that, exercising your accustomed skill and discretion, you will so deal with this question as to avoid any serious embarrassment to the Government, or any difficulty with General Phelps." A few days later, Stanton provided a bit more clarity, conveying the president's opinion that "under the law of Congress," the runaways of diehard rebels simply "cannot be sent back to their masters," and moreover, "in common humanity they must not be permitted to suffer for want of food, shelter, or other necessaries of life." These escapees should, rather, "be provided for by the Quartermaster's and Commissary's Departments," and if they proved fit for labor on behalf of the United States, they should be "set to work and paid reasonable wages." Nevertheless, Stanton reiterated, "in directing this to be done, the President does not mean, at present, to settle any general rule in respect to slaves or slavery, but simply to provide for the particular case under the circumstances in which it is now presented." Butler must have appreciated the words of support he received from Treasury Secretary Chase. "It is quite plain," wrote Chase, "that you do not find it so easy to deal with the contraband question as at Fortress Monroe. Of course, until the Government shall adopt a settled policy, the commanding General will be greatly embarrassed by it." Chase was of the opinion that the government should go ahead and abolish slavery. "That the United States Government under the war power might destroy slavery I never doubted," he wrote. "I only doubted the expediency of the exercise." However, he explained, all doubt vanished "when I saw that to abstain from military interference with slavery was simply to contribute the whole moral and physical power of the Government to the subjugation of some four millions of loyal people, to save three hundred thousand disloyal rebels."[32]

On July 17, Congress passed the Second Confiscation Act and soon thereafter Lincoln shared with his Cabinet the preliminary Emancipation Proclamation he would finally issue two months later. "The Government," Butler informed Sarah with some concern, "have sustained Phelps about the Negroes, and we shall have a negro insurrection here I fancy. . . . God help us all." And yet, he admitted, if "the negroes are getting saucy and troublesome," who could blame them? Still, the situation in New Orleans specifically remained unresolved, and Phelps and Butler had not yet come to terms. For his part, writes one historian, "Phelps understood that the act of running away from their masters was a decisive intellectual and emotional break for slaves," which in Phelps's view "made them 'ripe for manumission.'" Moreover, Phelps was surely encouraged by Lincoln's view "that Southerners had only themselves to blame" for Phelps's "presence among them," and that "they could easily get rid of Phelps by bringing themselves back to a firm allegiance to the U.S. government." Meanwhile, Butler continued to puzzle his way through the situation's legal and moral complexities, as he had done in Virginia. Receiving and protecting the runaways was one thing, employing them for wages was another. And how, exactly, to employ them? As laborers only? As soldiers? And what about the free Blacks in the area who had already been formed into *Confederate* regiments for the defense of the state? For as it happens, within a month of his arrival in New Orleans, Butler had been visited by some of the officers of those free Black regiments, Black men themselves, who sought to discuss, as he explained to Stanton, "the continuance of their organization," and "to learn what disposition they would be required to make of their arms." Noting that, "in color, nay, also in conduct they had much more the appearance of white gentlemen than some of those who have favored me with their presence claiming to be the 'Chivalry of the South,'" Butler inquired, what should happen to them?[33]

Not surprisingly, Phelps advocated turning all Black men who were available for military service—enslaved or free—into US soldiers. Not only could the army use their help, but for the formerly enslaved, military service would serve as "a useful tool to facilitate the transition" from slavery to freedom "when the inevitable collapse of Southern society occurred." Indeed, aware that Congress had also recently passed the Militia Act, which opened the door to Black men's military service, Phelps was already planning to organize male runaways at Camp Parapet into units and arm them, with or without Butler's approval. Toward that end, on July 30 Phelps requested "arms, accouterments, clothing, camp and garrison equipage, etc.," from Acting Assistant Adj. Gen. R. S. Davis "for three Regiments of Africans which I propose to raise for the defence of this point." Phelps was sure he could raise the regiments quickly, as with little effort and "without holding out any inducements, or offering any reward," he already had the names of "upward of three hundred Africans" who were "willing and ready to be put to the test." These men, Phelps added pointedly, had proven themselves "willing to submit to anything rather than slavery," and he cautioned that if the federal government rejected them, the men would surely begin seeking freedom elsewhere. Should they be turned away by the United States, Phelps wrote, "any petty military Chieftain, by offering [them] freedom, can have them for the purpose of robbery and plunder." As such, "it is for the interest of the South as well as for the North that the African should be permitted to offer his block for the Temple of Freedom."[34]

The following day, on Butler's instructions, the acting assistant adjutant general denied Phelps's request. "The Commanding General," Davis wrote, "wishes you to employ the Contraband in and around your camps in cutting all the trees, etc., between your lines and the Lake, and in forming abatis according to the plan agreed upon," but not as soldiers. Again, Phelps pushed back, insisting that "while I am willing to prepare African Regiments for the defence of the Government against its assailants, I am not willing to become the mere slave driver which you propose, having no qualifications that way." He tendered his resignation. Now Butler stepped in directly, reminding Phelps that he lacked the authority to organize Black regiments and must desist, and refusing to accept his resignation or even grant him a leave of absence. Phelps held firm, arguing that by ordering the employment of the runaways as laborers only, Butler was requiring him to do something that was "wholly opposed to my convictions of right as well as of the higher scale of public necessities in the case." He again refused to comply and declared that he would request the president directly to "liberate me from that sense of suffocation, from that darkling sense of bondage and enthrallment," which "is entangling and deadening the energies of the Government and the Country, when a decisive act might cut the evils and liberate us from their baneful and fascinating influence forever."[35]

"Phelps has gone crazy," Butler announced to Sarah on August 2, his exasperation surely clouding the pleasure that came with learning that his Waterville alma mater had recently awarded him a second honorary degree, this time a doctorate of laws. A couple of days later he coarsely informed Sarah that Phelps was, in fact, "mad as a March Hare on the 'nigger question.'" To Phelps himself he wrote more judiciously, but he still refused to let his subordinate resign. "I pray you to understand," Butler wrote, "that there was nothing intended to be offensive to you in either the matter or manner of my communication in directing you to cease military organization of the negroes. I do only carry out the law of Congress as I understand it." Observed one federal government official in New Orleans, "The controversy between Generals Butler and Phelps is much regretted by the best Union men. Gen. Phelps is beloved by his soldiers, and no man has suspected his integrity and disinterestedness." The same, this official added, was "not strictly true of Gen. Butler, for while all admire his great ability, many of his soldiers think him selfish and cold-hearted." Others, however, joined Butler in questioning Phelps's sanity, or at least his impatience. "I know Genl. Phelps well," wrote Brig. Gen. John Gibbon in mid-August, "and the only excuse that can be offered for him is that his mind is undoubtedly affected."[36]

Treasury Secretary Chase continued to push Butler in the direction of Phelps's perspective. "We must either abandon the attempt to retain the Gulf States in the Union," Chase wrote, "or we must give freedom to every slave within their limits." Moreover, he continued, were he in Butler's place, he would immediately inform local slaveholders that *they* must start paying their Black laborers. Doing so, Chase argued, "would settle it in the minds of the working population of the State that the Union General is their friend" and would therefore incline them to offer the Federals important assistance, including as scouts and spies. Chase also observed that popular views on the question of slavery and emancipation were changing across the North generally: far more northerners now understood and accepted that saving the nation might depend on slavery's destruction. Chase believed, further, that, "Negro slavery should first fall where it has done most mischief, and where its extinction will do most good in weakening rebellion." And, he added flatteringly, who better "to begin the work than my friend Gen. Butler?"[37] It was a question Butler had apparently been asking himself.

As the dispute continued, Phelps conceded to Butler that he understood "the difficulties of your position," and he praised the "varied abilities, patriotism, and untiring diligence which you have shown in meeting them." But he continued to press his case, insisting that "at a crisis in our national affairs so important as this," he would be remiss to remain silent and not do what he knew was right and what the times and conditions required. Phelps urged Butler again to approve the arming of Black troops for the Union's cause. "Society here is on the verge of dissolution," he wrote urgently on August 6. Now was the time for the government to harness all available energy to combat impending "disorder and anarchy." The Black man might have been made "ignorant and benighted" by his bondage, Phelps admitted, and "yet newly-awakened to liberty," that same man could become either "a fearful element of ruin and disaster" or a source of strength, if armed and organized "on the side of the Government."[38]

Even as Butler struggled to control his subordinate—reminiscent of how Winfield Scott and others had tried to control Butler himself—Phelps's arguments, and Chase's, were having an influence. Indeed, by mid-August Butler was ready to federalize the free Black regiments previously known as the Louisiana Native Guard, whose officers had approached him earlier. First he gave Sarah a preview of his plans. "I shall arm the 'free Blacks,' I think," he wrote her, "for I must have more troops, and I see no way of getting them save by arming the black brigade that the rebels had." Then he wrote to Stanton. "We are now threatened by the whole western division of the southern army," Butler informed the secretary of war on August 14, recalling the recent Battle of Baton Rouge. Moreover, "disease and discharges" had sharply diminished the forces assigned to his command, and they were in great need of reinforcement. Therefore, Butler advised Stanton, in the case of a targeted attack on New Orleans itself, he planned to "call on Africa to intervene," and he anticipated an enthusiastic response. Butler further assured Stanton that the loyalty of "the free colored men who were organized by the rebels into the 'Colored Brigade,' of which we have heard so much" could be trusted.[39]

In fact, some weeks earlier Stanton had authorized Butler to recruit 5,000 *White* men from the region into the US service, both to create new regiments and fortify older ones whose numbers had declined. Butler's efforts on this front had quickly proved successful. Late in August, George S. Denison, collector of internal revenue in New Orleans, informed Secretary Chase that the White First Louisiana Regiment was "ready for service," and that Butler had enlisted almost enough locals to create a second such regiment. According to Denison, the recruits were "generally foreigners—many Germans" who could be counted on to "do good service." Now, a full month before Lincoln's preliminary Emancipation Proclamation, Butler issued General Orders No. 63, officially beginning the process of enlisting *Black* men into the US Army. These orders began by explaining the April 1861 formation of the original Louisiana Native Guard units and then officially called those same units into US service by repurposing much of the original language the Confederates had used to summon them in the first place. "Now, therefore," Butler wrote,

> the Commanding General, believing that a large portion of this militia force of the State of Louisiana are willing to take service in the Volunteer forces of the United States, and be enrolled and organized to "defend their home from ruthless invaders"; to protect their wives and children and kindred from wrong and outrage; to shield their property from being seized by bad men; and to defend the Flag of their native country. . . . Appreciating their motives, relying upon their "well-known loyalty and patriotism," and with "praise and respect" for these brave men, it is ordered that all the members of the "Native Guards" aforesaid, and all other free colored citizens recognized by the first and late Governor and Authorities of the State of Louisiana as a portion of the Militia of the State, who enlist in the Volunteer Service of the United States, shall be duly organized by the appointment of proper officers, and accepted, paid, equipped, armed, and rationed as are other Volunteer Troops of the United States, subject to the approval of the President of the United States. All such persons are required at once to report themselves at the Touro Charity Building, Front Levee Street, New Orleans, where proper officers will muster them into the service of the United States.[40]

The Native Guard regiments Butler reclaimed for US Army service originally comprised approximately 1,400 free Blacks, many of whose ancestors "had fought alongside Andrew Jackson in the Battle of New Orleans in 1815," who had responded—"albeit halfheartedly," writes one historian—to the Confederate government's summons to defend Louisiana against Federal invasion. Once the Federals occupied the city, however, these same men readily answered Butler's call to serve the Union, a call he sweetened by declaring his willingness to accept their Black officers as well. By the end of November 1862, and while "specific approval" was still pending from the War Department, Butler had taken command of three such regiments, the First, Second, and Third Native Guards, now comprising about 3,000 men and including hundreds of runaway bondsmen. "The free negroes of Louisiana," George Denison assured Secretary Chase, "are certainly superior, as a class, to the Creoles (descendants of French and Spanish settlers). They are intelligent, energetic, and industrious, as is evident from the fact . . . that they own one-seventh of the real estate in this city. This is their own work, for they commenced with nothing, of course." And he added, "These men will be good soldiers." On September 9 Denison further advised Chase that one whole regiment of the "Free Colored Brigade" was now full, "and about 500 more are already enlisted." The men had excellent "physical qualities," not the least of which, in his view, was (not surprisingly, alas) the fact that "most of them are very light color." Denison expressed admiration for the "characteristic shrewdness" Butler had displayed throughout the process that brought them into the US Army. "By accepting a regiment which had already been in Confederate service," he wrote, Butler had "left no room for complaint (by the Rebels) that the Government were arming the negroes." At the same time, he pointed out, when new recruits arrived to enlist, questions about their previous status relative to the institution of slavery were left unasked. "Better soldiers never shouldered a musket," Butler claimed with enthusiasm and pride. "They were intelligent, obedient, highly appreciative of their position, and fully maintained its dignity. They easily learned the school of the soldier," and "they learned to handle arms and to march more readily than most intelligent white men."[41] By the fall of 1862, many of the racist biases and assumptions Butler had internalized and taken for granted for decades in predominantly White New England were irrevocably fading away. Change was possible.

Throughout the fall, Denison kept Chase apprised of the Black regiments' progress. "To-morrow the first Regt. receives arms and joins the army," he wrote in late September, adding that a second regiment was now full and in training, and a third was being organized. Within a few weeks, two regiments were deployed to guard a railroad line extending west about a hundred miles from the city. "They have done well," Denison reported in November, "and accomplished all that has been given them to do." Denison reiterated his praise for the regiments' Black company officers, all of whom he declared "educated men" who were bilingual at the very least and sometimes could speak additional languages, too. Soon, he informed Chase, Butler planned to give the Black soldiers an opportunity to prove themselves in combat. "He designs attacking Port Hudson," Denison wrote, "a strong position on the river."[42]

Not surprisingly, some White officers resisted calls to take command positions with the new Black regiments. Even Godfrey Weitzel, whom Butler considered "one of the ablest men and best loved members of my staff" and a "life-long friend," said no. Having himself committed to organizing, developing, and deploying the regiments, Butler was now keenly disappointed with those who turned down the opportunity to help. "That you should have declined the Command," he wrote to Weitzel in early November, "is the occasion of regret," adding that he found Weitzel's reasoning particularly troubling. Weitzel claimed that he had no confidence in the Black soldiers' willingness to fight, to which Butler bluntly responded, "You have failed to show, by the conduct of these free men so far, anything to sustain that opinion." Conversely, well before they even had a chance to prove Weitzel wrong, the Black regiments were becoming a source of enormous pride among Black Louisianans. "Allow me to present to you," wrote C. C. Antoine to Col. Spencer H. Stafford, commanding the First Louisiana Regiment of Volunteers (Colored) Native Guards, on October 22, "this emblem on behalf of the First African Baptist Church of New Orleans, as a token of their esteem for you & your Regiment." Antoine urged the soldiers to remain cognizant, not least "when you are upon the battlefield and meet your enemies, those that have robbed you of your liberty," of the "duties which have devolved upon you." He called on them to "look upon this flag and thank Providence that he has afforded an opportunity of showing your Bravery in defense of your Liberty that you may bring it back untarnished."[43]

On September 22, following the terrible Battle of Antietam, Lincoln issued his preliminary Emancipation Proclamation. Two days later, George Denison happily informed Chase that the development of Butler's ideas and plans vis-à-vis slavery, Black freedom, and the Union cause had reached a new phase: having resolved to protect and employ rebel Louisianans' runaway human property and having undertaken to transform the Black Louisiana Native Guardsmen into US Army troops, Butler had finally come to believe that the institution of slavery itself "must be abolished." Moreover, he was prepared to "do his part" however circumstances enabled him to do it.[44] Denison was right. And in the weeks ahead, among the ways Butler determined to "do his part" to end slavery once and for all was by creating the basic framework of a "free labor" system for Black workers to replace the institution he had finally rejected.

Butler's Special Orders No. 441 began by observing that Confederate owners of some local sugar plantations had abandoned their land, and that the crops were now in danger of "running to waste." Should that happen, the profits the sugar could produce "will be lost as well to the late owner as to the United States." Noting the increasing number of runaways from slavery whose labor could and should be harnessed, he therefore appointed a man named Charles Weed to "take charge of said plantations, and such others as may be abandoned along the River between the city and Fort Jackson, and gather and make these crops for the benefit of the United States, keeping an exact and accurate account of the expenses of each." Butler charged Weed with hiring Black laborers first, in consultation with "the several Commanders of Camps for laborers." In such case as the number of available Black laborers proved insufficient for the task, he authorized Weed to employ White laborers "at $1.00 per day for each ten hours of labor."[45]

By mid-November, Denison observed that Butler's "free labor" plan—like his efforts with the Black regiments—was working beautifully. "I lately visited this plantation," Denison wrote, "which is a few miles below the city, and never saw negroes work with more energy and industry. This single experiment refutes theories which Southern leaders have labored, for years, to establish." Two weeks later, responding to an inquiry from President Lincoln, Butler echoed Denison's evaluation. "Our experiment in attempting the cultivation of sugar by free labor," he wrote, "is succeeding admirably." Indeed, he noted, in contrast with the common proslavery argument that Blacks would only work if Whites forced them to do so, it was becoming obvious that free Black laborers were even *more* productive than chained ones. Butler then offered to send Lincoln "a Bbl. of the first sugar ever made by *free black labor* in Louisiana," and expressed confidence that the experiment would continue "without loss to the Government, and I hope with profit enough to enable us to support for six months longer the starving Whites & Blacks here, a somewhat herculean task." Butler took this opportunity, too, to remind Lincoln that he was still feeding 32,000 Whites and 10,000 Blacks daily, "without drawing on the treasury."[46]

When examining the extent of Butler's official duties, actions, responsibilities, and conflicts in New Orleans, it can be all too easy to forget that he was not only a commanding officer in the US Army in wartime but also a husband, father, and brother. For the most part, of course, during the time he spent in New Orleans, Butler's three children were virtually beyond the realm of his authority and companionship: Paul and Bennie—now ten and seven, respectively—remained safely in Massachusetts, where they occasionally received letters from their busy father at the front; Blanche, now fifteen, spent the summer in Massachusetts with her mother and brothers and the spring and fall at school in Georgetown. "I send you a model of a piece of field artillery," Butler wrote to Paul in mid-July, "complete with its caisson and equipment, also a model of a mortar for throwing bombs, of which you have heard so much," as well as "a gun on a Barbette carriage such as is used in fortification." From so far away, Butler nevertheless sought to exert some paternal influence, emphasizing to all three children the importance of their schoolwork and encouraging them always to "love justice and tell the truth," and to "not do a mean thing." As the months of separation piled up, Butler asked Sarah to send along some photographs of the children, "the best you can get."[47]

"Has Paul blown himself up with the cannon yet?" Butler asked Sarah in late July. Despite his abundant responsibilities, Butler felt lonely and yearned for letters from his family members, sometimes threatening punishment if he did not receive them. "Why does not Blanche write," he demanded. "She has nothing else to do." And he warned, "I won't love her a bit if she don't write." For her part, Sarah split her time between Lowell and New Orleans, in accordance with Blanche's school schedule, and when they were not together, Butler missed her sorely. He relied on Sarah's deep and abiding faith in his capabilities, which bolstered his morale and provided him with a wellspring of support and confidence. "New Orleans would not be ours today but for the untiring energy of Mr. Butler," she wrote Harriet characteristically on one occasion. "And could he have left this town with the fleet directly after our arrival, Vicksburg would now be ours, and the river open."[48]

Butler enjoyed Sarah's company and support, but he worried about her health, particularly in the summer months, though his efforts to protect the city from a yellow fever outbreak seemed to be working, and though she had removed back to Lowell for safety. Still, he wrote, "you are not strong." At the same time, Butler clearly felt a little sorry for himself in her absence. "You are quite home now," he complained after she had returned to Massachusetts, "and I am sweltering here under the Summer Sun." Butler asked Sarah to send him copies of the local Lowell newspapers so that he might feel closer to home. Sarah was lonely, too, of course, but when she allowed her loneliness to spill into her letters (along with her fear that perhaps he did not miss her quite as much as she missed him), Butler sometimes grew annoyed. "If you knew how my heart is full of kindness and love, yearning to see you," he replied to one sad missive, "you would not write me so." At the same time, he repeatedly urged Sarah not to worry about *his* health, and often made light of his tribulations, including the notoriety the "Woman Order" had brought him. "It is right, it was right. It will be right, and be the most popular act of my life. You said it was right at the time, and therefore I knew it was right." Some of their exchanges were more romantic than others, even mildly erotic, such as when he declared "that you are the best of good, dear, kind, and thoughtful and affectionate wives," and that "if I were in the vestibule now of our house, and you had come to let me in, and everybody didn't see me, I could tell you what I mean and not say a word."[49]

Ambitious in her own right and always eager to advance her husband's career, Sarah served as more than Butler's beloved companion and champion: when they were apart she occasionally sent him information from their contacts back home about happenings in Washington, the latest political and military machinations that had come to her attention, and how Butler's fortunes seemed to be faring in the eyes of the administration and other military leaders. In one particularly long, detailed, wide-ranging, and rather confusing letter that included commentary on McClellan's tenuous status, the preliminary Emancipation Proclamation and its consequences, party politics, Black regiments, and the current dynamics among Lincoln's cabinet officers, she summed up her thoughts by saying that from all she could tell, "I think your position satisfactory." On the one hand, she warned her husband not to "venture dangerous experiments." On the other, she suggested that his military and political future might benefit from the clearest possible demonstration, to Lincoln and the Republican Party, that he endorsed the Emancipation Proclamation and meant to carry it out in the area under his command. Certainly, some of his recent public statements and actions had alienated many Democrats, and indeed, she remarked, "at present you are outside of all parties." But bold steps—perhaps even going so far as to "*organize insurrection*" of the enslaved, as she put it (albeit, under the control of White commanders)—might yield a position of power among the Republicans. Still, she cautioned in closing, "there is but a step sometimes between a crown and a gibbet, and in days like these one cannot tell to which his labors will lead."[50] Butler aimed to navigate that narrow terrain as best he could with a combination of boldness and prudence.

One family member gave Butler quite a bit more trouble than any of the others during his time in New Orleans: his brother Andrew Jackson Butler. Jackson's various activities while serving in a largely undefined role on Butler's staff led many contemporaries and others long afterward to conclude that both he and the general were "engaged in deep, widespread, profiteering," and both "quietly amassed personal fortunes" as a result of their corrupt collaboration. And although more than one historian has observed that "nothing illegal" was "ever proved against the general himself," nevertheless, accusations of shameless grift, even outright theft, have followed him and are reflected in another of his long-surviving nicknames, "Spoons," a reference to a mass of Confederate silver he supposedly confiscated in New Orleans and never returned. It is certainly true that Butler "had a great talent for personal financial advancement and harbored a sincere love of profit," but that hardly proves that Butler and Jackson "initiated a scheme for a quasi-legal plundering of their conquered domain," including "speculating heavily in rum, sugar, salt, cotton, and even Texas beef cattle" and "employing soldiers and sailors to carry contraband of war to New Orleans for auction." Indeed, one historian accuses the Butlers of conspiring with local planters to devise a system of "bribes and kickbacks" that further enhanced their profits, all the while exploiting the government's policies on confiscation to "target the homes and estates of Confederate soldiers" with a combination of "intimidation and reward," as "forfeitures to the Republic," and selling the goods—especially "war-rare staples"—to "eager Yankee merchants and factory owners" at a massive profit, thereby enlarging "the Butler empire."[51]

The Butlers did get involved in trying to restore economic activity in New Orleans, which had been "the South's premier commercial emporium" until the Union blockade sharply interrupted commerce there. By the time of the occupation, Lincoln's administration was looking for ways to use the power of the federal government to revive commerce and thereby forge in the public mind a clear connection between the city's fortunes as a trading center and its loyalty to the United States. As early as May 16, just two weeks after he arrived, Butler addressed this same idea in a letter to Secretary Stanton. "We need their products and they need ours. If we wish to bind them to us more strongly than can be done by the bayonet let them again feel the beneficence of the United States Government as they have seen and are now feeling its power." By the middle of June, Butler had made effective use of his personal and professional connections and his military authority to reopen a north-south trade in goods like cotton, sugar, and other local products. Butler intended the profits from this trade, however, to be deposited not in his *own* accounts but in the US Treasury, a practice that Quartermaster General Meigs deemed "wise and patriotic," though Meigs worried that it could appear otherwise to opponents who believed Butler was using his "official power and position" unfairly. Later that month, Butler's business associate Richard Fay echoed Meigs's concern about the possible appearance of impropriety, noting the difficulty of persuading wealthy New Orleanians, whose personal financial gains were now being circumscribed by the government's plans, "that they have not been plundered somewhere."[52]

Butler's late June transfer of his residence from the St. Charles Hotel into the elegant New Orleans home of Gen. David E. Twiggs, infamous for surrendering his entire Texas command to the Confederacy while still in his US Army uniform, also raised his enemies' hackles, and their suspicions. On June 26 he issued General Orders No. 46, declaring that "all the property in New Orleans belonging to Gen. D. E. Twiggs, and of his minor son . . . consisting of real estate, bonds, notes of hand, Treasury notes of the United States, slaves, household furniture, etc., is hereby sequestered, to be held to await the action of the United States Government." Butler had already inventoried the property, including Twiggs's swords, his and his son-in-law's silver, and other items of value. "So you see," he joked to Sarah, "plundering still goes on." That Butler unabashedly used the language of "plunder" for his confiscation of Twiggs's goods no doubt fed opponents' distrust as well as their bitter resentment of his policies. Perhaps it did not even matter that instead of stashing them away for his own enjoyment Butler instead sent three of Twiggs's swords directly to Lincoln with the observation that he had, ironically, found the swords in the custody of one of Twiggs's bondsmen. "A more lamentable instance of the degradation to which this rebellion has reduced its votaries can hardly be imagined," he wrote. "Swords given to a General for courage and good conduct in the armies of the Union as tokens of admiration by his fellow-citizens and the gratitude of a State and Nation . . . at last find a depository with a negro, for the sake of enslaving whom even the double crime of treachery and rebellion had been consummated."[53]

On July 19, even Richard Fay expressed regret that the profits gained by selling some of the confiscated goods would not accrue to Butler's own financial benefit but would be used to help cover the enormous costs of the occupation instead. "I am very sorry that you will not have the profit upon the merchandise shipped," he wrote, "as it has paid best of all." But, he noted, "my first thought and effort has been to guard your personal reputation in official transactions intact and unspotted. In this I believe I have been entirely successful." Some days later, Butler declared, "I will assure safe conduct, open market, and prompt shipment" of whatever property came under his control. Questions about Butler's commercial trading arrangements persisted even among his friends, with increasingly negative attention going to the problematic role his brother Jackson was playing in the arrangements, which only lengthened the shadow opponents were eager to cast over the general's integrity. "Col. Butler," George Denison informed Secretary Chase in late August, using the unofficial military title Jackson enjoyed,

came out with the army, and immediately commenced doing business. He is not in government employ. He is here for the sole purpose of making money, and it is stated by secessionists—and by some Union men— that he has made half a million dollars, or more. I regret his being here at all, for it is not proper that the brother of the Commanding General should devote himself to such an object. It leads to the belief that the General himself is interested with him, and such is the belief of our enemies and some of our friends. The effect is bad.

At the same time, Denison remarked, "General Butler seems entirely devoted to the interests of the Government" and did not seem to be connected to his brother's "speculations." "I believe Gen. Butler is disinterested," he reiterated, "and that he is a most able officer, though in a difficult position."[54]

On September 9 Denison contacted Chase again, repeating his observation that some people in the area, both soldiers and civilians, were losing faith in Butler's "disinterestedness" in his brother's apparent self-dealing. "Sometimes circumstances look very suspicious," Denison admitted, but, he added when questioned, Butler always seemed able to explain things in a way that made sense, and "suspicion almost entirely disappears." Butler was so smart, of course, that it would be "difficult to discover what he wished to conceal," Denison acknowledged. Perhaps even more important, Butler was a devoted and widely respected defender of the Union cause whose place could not easily be filled by anyone else. In a later missive Denison observed that Butler worked harder "than any other man in Louisiana," and his "every thought" seemed to be "given to the interest of the Government." Butler, Denison added admiringly, "learns everything and forgets nothing. He comes in contact with the best minds in the State, and is equal, or superior, to them all."[55]

For her part, Sarah—who over time had lost any of the fondness she once felt for her troublesome (and troubled) brother-in-law—worried that whatever else was happening, Jackson was doing serious harm to her husband's reputation and future. Jackson, she advised Butler, had "done, and is doing you vast injury," as "all his deeds are reflected on you." Indeed, she wrote, "a more obnoxious person to invest with power could not be found." Sarah did not expect her husband to agree with her, knowing as she did his affection for his brother as well as his principles of fraternal loyalty and responsibility. "I know," she wrote, "you will say this is prejudice and ill-feeling on my part." But she could not stop herself. "You think you control him and know his acts," she advised. "On the contrary, though subservient to your face, he controls where he wishes, insults and overbears everywhere," and, she insisted, "it is only a question how far you are willing to suffer in estimation and position for his advancement."[56]

By early October, even George Denison had begun to feel less sanguine about Butler's handling of the claims of corruption that were circulating in connection with Jackson's activities. "Ever since the capture of this city," Denison observed to Chase, "a brisk trade has been carried on with the rebels by a few persons under military permits, frequently with military assistance, and, as I believe, much to the pecuniary benefit of some of the principal military officers of this Department." In an effort to halt this trade, Denison had begun an investigation, and Jackson Butler's involvement was undeniable. Moreover, although Jackson held no official military position, yet many people understood him "to be the partner or agent of Gen'l. Butler." And in any case, he seemed to be making a lot of money with his commercial activities, perhaps as much as $2 million. Even more concerning to Denison was his belief that the brilliant and all-seeing general *must* be aware of his brother's illegal profiteering, as well as Jackson's use of some seized riverboats for transport and of Federal soldiers to guard the freight. And yet he was not taking the situation and its possible repercussions seriously. "The amount of goods smuggled from this point to the enemy has been trifling," Denison admitted, but the general's reputation was in peril, both with locals and even some of his own soldiers, who would "want to go home, not wishing to risk their lives to make fortunes for others." Subsequently, though,

Denison returned to his basic faith in Butler: "Gen. B. has always carried out (so far as I know) the wishes of the Gov't.," he wrote. The real problem was his brother, though Butler had clearly stumbled by allowing Jackson to act with impunity to line his own pockets.[57]

Chase agreed with Denison and urged Butler to distance himself or, even better, use his influence and authority to bring Jackson's problematic activities to a halt. "So many and seemingly such well-founded charges against your brother, Col. Butler, have reached me and other members of the administration, as well as the President," Chase wrote on October 29, "that I feel bound to say to you that in my judgment you owe it to yourself not to be responsible, even by toleration, for what he does." In reply Butler admitted that Jackson had indeed been "engaged in commercial adventure in New Orleans," and had been "successful," but by no means "more successful than many others." Moreover, he believed "every transaction" Jackson had undertaken was "legitimate." As for the rumors about his own involvement, Butler insisted he had done nothing in his official capacity to assist his brother, and had heard nothing to suggest that Jackson's activities "in any way interfere[d] with the Army of the Gulf or with the department." Still, he was "determined" that "no appearance of evil shall exist to rob me of the fair earnings of a devotion of life and fortune to the service of my country," so he asked his brother to leave New Orleans, which he did.[58]

Sarah was elated. "Your Uncle" who "has caused me so much grief," she wrote with great satisfaction to Blanche in mid-November, would soon be leaving New Orleans for good. "Are you not pleased for my sake?" In a letter to Harriet two weeks later, Sarah described a newspaper article from London that claimed her husband and his brother were in collusion in New Orleans to increase their personal fortunes. Perhaps now, she wrote angrily, her husband would understand the dangers he courted by letting his brother act unchecked. At least Jackson was being sent packing. "But is this any consolation to me," she asked, "who knew what the result must be from the first, and have nearly died because I could not prevent it?" According to Sarah, Jackson had actually begun causing trouble the previous year at Fort Monroe, though she did not specify how. "Is it not enough to make one mad," she asked, "that two years of agony which I have borne, and after I had proved to him that Jackson was the cause of his failure at Fortress Monroe, yet again that he should bestow all power and give all confidence once more, to have his reputation assailed, and the power he has and might yet gain, slip from his grasp and crumble to nothing?" From her perspective, Jackson's misdeeds in New Orleans were just the tip of a profoundly troubling ice-

Rare image of Butler with beard. Engraved by H. Wright Smith. Courtesy Special Collections & Archives, Colby College Libraries, Waterville, Maine.

berg. Fortunately, the situation was finally getting under control. Denison agreed, emphasizing again to Chase that Butler was "a man not to be spared from the country's service," not least because he had proved himself "bold and enterprising enough to undertake the raising of a large crop of sugar by free labor—which, a little while ago, was slave labor—in opposition to the Southern idea, long established, that Sugar and Cotton can be successfully raised only by compulsory labor."[59]

About a month before Jackson left New Orleans, Sarah began packing for her return, looking forward to being reunited with her husband but unenthusiastic about the long journey from Lowell and weary of the war's ongoing impact on her family and the peripatetic life it demanded. "Oh, how I long to have done with the roving," she sighed to Blanche, "to be home again in quiet with the family all at home. When will that time ever come?" Butler was eager to have Sarah back at his side. "You will come, won't you?" he wrote plaintively. "Then, dearest, dearest, we won't plague each other any more!" By October 21 they were reunited, following Sarah's eight-day voyage, during which she was apparently sick most of the time. "We are here safe and comfortable," she informed Harriet. "Mr. Butler was rejoiced to see me, and says it is the first time we have been so long apart since we were married, and it shall be the last." Predictably, Sarah now missed the children. Still in Georgetown, Blanche, too, longed to have the family reunited. She especially yearned for a visit with her father, whom she had not seen for months. "Tell Father," Blanche wrote, "I shall forget how he looks if I do not see him soon," and she added, "be sure to tell him that he must not wear a beard, for it he does, I shall not want to kiss him."[60]

By the time Sarah returned to New Orleans, Butler was about two months shy of being removed from command there. Indeed, as early as September 1, he began complaining to General-in-Chief Halleck about rumors of his impending replacement. "I learn by the Secession newspapers," Butler wrote with some asperity, "that I am to be relieved of this Command. If that be so, might I ask that my successor be sent as early as possible, as my own health is not the strongest, and it would seem but fair that he should take some part of the yellow fever season." To Sarah he pretended not to care. "The 'Secesh' newspapers say that I am to be relieved from my command," he had informed her while she was still in Lowell. "Be it so. I shall be very glad to get home to you and the children." Rather than feeling "aggrieved" about the possibility of removal, he insisted defensively that "it is all for the best for me personally." Moreover, should the rumors of his impending dismissal prove true, Butler promised to bring home an excellent new hired female servant, a former bondswoman whom he described as "the nicest washer, mender, ironer, and chamber girl you ever saw," who "takes the best possible care of my clothes," "has no possible fault but a devil of a temper," and "is much *attached* to your humble servant."[61]

For all her desire to have the family quietly reunited in Lowell, Sarah was nevertheless distressed by the possibility of Butler's possibly abrupt and ignominious removal from command, and the idea that he might be forced to sit out the rest of the war on the sidelines. The federal government, she insisted proudly, "cannot allow a man like you to rest quietly at home. You have shown such efficiency there would be clamor if you were not employed in these disastrous times." Sarah strove to analyze the situation from a practical standpoint. As long as there was a threat of Confederates attacking

New Orleans, she predicted, "you will be retained." That threat eliminated, however, "I think you will be superseded." Butler's allies strove to squelch the rumors of his impending removal as they continued to spread, and to encourage him. "If any fool shall remove you it will be your gain every way," wrote Maj. Joseph M. Bell bracingly from New York, "but there is no danger of that."[62]

On November 9, President Lincoln quietly made the rumors official, issuing the order that would remove Butler from command in the Department of the Gulf and replace him with Nathaniel Banks, his long-standing political and military rival. Because Lincoln's order would not actually go into effect until mid-December when Banks finally reached New Orleans and presented it to Butler, however, uncertainty persisted. Indeed, some, even the highly placed Secretary Chase, remained under the impression that Lincoln was sending Banks to the Gulf to take up an independent command further west. "Gen. Banks goes to New Orleans," Chase assured Butler on November 14, "to conduct an expedition to Texas while you are engaged nearer to your present Headquarters."[63] For his part, Butler was skeptical, unable to imagine how such a plan would work. Even if Banks *was* headed ultimately to Texas, would not federally occupied New Orleans be his base of operations? And in that case, would not having two commanding generals of nearly equal rank and seniority there cause problems and confusion?

Writing directly to the president at the end of November, Butler reminded Lincoln—unnecessarily, for sure—that he was the senior general in the nation's volunteer army. He then painstakingly listed his eighteen months' worth of accomplishments. "I beg leave to call your attention," Butler began,

> that since I came into the field . . . I have ever been in the frontier line of the rebellion—Annapolis when Washington was threatened, Relay House when Harper's Ferry was being evacuated, Baltimore, Fort Monroe, Newport News, Hatteras, Ship Island, New Orleans. . . . I have lived at this station exposed at once to the pestilence and the assassin for eight months, awaiting reinforcements which the needs of the Government could not give me. . . . And now they are to be given to another. I have never complained. I do not now complain. I have done as well as I could everything which the Government asked me to do. I have eaten that which was set before me asking no questions.

If the rumors were true, therefore, and he was not being sent into the field or even allowed to retain his New Orleans command, Butler urged Lincoln to openly declare why he considered Butler unqualified for either assignment.[64]

As late as December 12, Massachusetts senator Charles Sumner continued to offer reassurances: "The President says that you shall not be forgotten," Sumner wrote. "Those were his words to me." Two days later, Secretary Chase reported that Lincoln had acknowledged to him personally all of Butler's contributions and achievements to date but had said nothing about Butler's future. From other sources, however, Chase had now learned for certain that Banks would in fact be replacing Butler in command of the occupation of New Orleans. By way of consolation, presumably, Chase offered his friend generous praise. "In my judgment," Chase wrote, "you have done more work and more important work and have done it better than any General whom the President has commissioned; and I believe this to be the judgment of the country." Preemptively, Chase urged Butler not to resign from the army altogether.[65]

On December 15, shortly after Banks's arrival in the Crescent City, Butler issued his final orders to the soldiers under his command, showering them with accolades. In the days ahead, he received many letters, some of them— like the one signed by "One of Your She Adders"—positively gleeful about the prospect of his imminent departure. In contrast, many of his fellow officers in the region conveyed their appreciation and their dismay. "For your kindness to the soldiers," wrote Capt. John F. Appleton, "you will ever be held in loving remembrance and your past services will be remembered by the country and be rewarded." Particularly gratifying, one imagines, was the letter he received from Colonel Stafford, commanding the Black First Regiment of Louisiana Native Guards, whose soldiers, Stafford noted, had asked him to address Butler on their behalf. "As men and soldiers," he wrote, "they look upon you [Butler] as their Creator and their Father," "they regret the parting," and "they will, when opportunity offers, seek to prove themselves worthy of you, who made them what they are." Stafford promised, "Wherever you go there will their hearts be also, and their pride will grow on whatever honors you may win." At noon on December 16, Butler turned over command of the Department of the Gulf to General Banks.[66]

"All is over for the present," Sarah informed Harriet the following day. "The Department of the Gulf has passed into other hands." Soon after, Butler offered his farewell to the citizens of New Orleans, in which he provided a brief but powerful interpretation of the war as he had come, over the months in Louisiana, to understand and approach it, and the ways in which his own ideas had been transformed by the experience. As time passed, "I saw that this Rebellion," Butler explained, "was a war of the aristocrats against the middling men, of the rich against the poor; a war of the land-owner against the laborer; that it was a struggle for the retention of power in the hands of the few against the many. . . . I therefore felt no hesitation in taking the substance of the wealthy, who had caused the war, to feed the innocent poor, who had suffered by the war." Now, Butler explained, he left New Orleans "with the proud consciousness that I carry with me the blessings of the humble and loyal, under the roof of the cottage and in the cabin of the slave," and "content to incur the sneers of the salon, or the curses of the rich." One more time he urged Louisianans to reassert their loyalty to the federal government.[67]

Meanwhile, that same day, Confederate president Jefferson Davis essentially declared war on Butler with his General Orders No. 111, in which he pronounced the departing commander a "felon deserving of capital punishment." Referencing what he called Butler's "deliberate murder" of William Mumford as well as "numerous other outrages and atrocities"—which he listed in detail—Davis ordered that Butler "be no longer considered or treated simply as a public enemy of the Confederate States of America but as an outlaw and common enemy of mankind." Should Butler be captured, he should be "immediately executed by hanging." Of particular relevance were the direct connections Davis drew between Lincoln's Emancipation Proclamation (which he declared a sign of Lincoln's "effort to excite servile war") and Butler's protection of slavery's runaways and decision to arm Black soldiers against the Confederacy. Henceforth, Davis proclaimed, "no commissioned officer of the United States taken captive shall be released on parole before exchange until the said Butler shall have met with due punishment for his crimes." "I am sure," declared one Butler ally in response, "that you will treat the fulmination of the bogus rebel President as Martin Luther did the Pope's bull of excommunication." Davis's only possible reason for attacking Butler specifically, this friend added, was Butler's "superior vigilance, boldness, and efficiency in curbing the insolence and suppressing the machinations of the rebels."[68]

A comparison of Jefferson Davis's official condemnation of Butler with the letters of adulation he received from others as he was leaving New Orleans recalls to mind historian Harold B. Raymond's observation, a hundred years after the war, that when it came to their overall evaluation of his administration in New Orleans, "most of the standard histories" had "pictured Butler in an unfavorable light." Over a half century since Raymond wrote these words, the same is still true. But, as Raymond himself pointed out, "in his own lifetime" Butler's "friends and defenders" were abundant, steadfast, and "included some of the most eminent men of the day." Moreover, to a great extent their praise was merited. For over the course of American history, as Raymond noted, few commanders tasked with occupying conquered territory had a more "formidable" assignment than Butler in New Orleans, namely, "to restore the full authority of the federal government" in a deeply, violently rebellious major commercial southern city that was rife with internal racial and social divisions and remote from other centers of federal power and supply. In fact, according to Raymond, Butler did exactly what he was charged with doing. Moreover, although "every account of Butler's career" in New Orleans "describes the execution of Mumford, the 'woman order,'" and other harsh actions he took to force the rebel population into compliance with his authority and that of the United States, "few have noted his acts of generosity and kindness," or, for that matter, his significant accomplishments. As another historian observes, Butler "gave New Orleans the most efficient and healthful administration it had ever known. He cleaned up the foul sewers, established new drainage systems and health regulations, and embarked on an ambitious public works program that provided jobs for the poor and the unemployed," even if it meant confiscating public and private Confederate property to fund it. And he revived the local economy in the process.[69]

There is no question that Butler took considerable satisfaction from explicitly positioning himself as something of a Robin Hood figure in New Orleans. He cheerfully and without remorse commandeered resources (including confiscated property, taxes, and the like) from the wealthy, many of whom he associated with the rebel leadership, to support the town's poor, White and Black alike, whom he understood to be, collectively, the war's most grievously suffering victims. It would be a mistake, certainly, to exonerate him for his personal weaknesses and his blunders, including his indulgence of his brother's self-dealing. Still, one recalls how frequently Butler's brash and largely unapologetic personality, strong ego, stunning cleverness, willingness to cut through red tape to achieve certain ends, and frequent imperviousness to criticism and control had contributed early in the war to northern public faith in him as one of the great heroes upon whom the Union's survival depended. Why, then, did these very same qualities, put into action in New Orleans against wealthy White Confederates, come to underpin his enduring image as a "beast"? And how much of this shift can also be attributed to his growing support for Black freedom?

In this work of freeing and elevating the African race
in our country, you are writing your name in letters of living light.
—MASSACHUSETTS SENATOR HENRY WILSON TO BUTLER, DECEMBER 1863

I am daily accused of every crime in the Decalogue, and if I should begin by contradicting
or explaining these accusations, and should fail to meet a single one, perhaps not seeing
it, I should be taken to have confessed it by my silence. Therefore I have preferred
to allow all to go on. If I am the man my enemies (and they are also the enemies of
my country) would fain have me believed to be . . . sure if not swift punishment will
overtake me. If I am not guilty, a life spent in the public eye will vindicate me.
—BUTLER, MARCH 1864

5

To Virginia and Beyond
1863–1865

Following his mid-December 1862 replacement by Gen. Nathaniel Banks—
which coincided with the Union army's Fredericksburg, Virginia, debacle—supporters and foes freely expressed their thoughts about Benjamin
Butler's handling of affairs in the Department of the Gulf, and the reasons
for his removal from command there. "There are two families in England
whose name is Butler," wrote one bitter critic all the way from Liverpool,
who went on to say that Butler's administration in New Orleans had so thoroughly "outraged decency, religion, and all morality," that both families had
now "petitioned Parliament to change their name, execrable in every sense
of the word." More generous by far were the comments of George Denison,
still serving as the US tax collector in the Crescent City, who insisted that
Butler deserved his country's and his government's acclaim and reiterated
that Butler's only misstep in New Orleans had been to allow his brother to
operate freely and thereby accrue "large sums of money" to his own and perhaps also some of his friends' accounts. "I wish I could see and thank you
for your services at New Orleans," wrote Edward L. Pierce, "where you have
done so nobly and well." Pierce, who had served with Butler at Fort Monroe

in 1861, urged the general to ignore "the calumniators," for "God never deserts, the American people never desert, a man determined to do his duty." "In my opinion," advised New Orleanian P. H. Morgan, Butler would still be serving there had not "several things conspired" to bring about his removal, including rumors that Banks was actually being considered as a replacement for Secretary of War Edwin Stanton, which had made Stanton eager to have Banks "out of the way."[1]

Somewhat curiously, and perhaps also disingenuously, Massachusetts senator Charles Sumner suggested that Butler's replacement by Banks was the direct result of Banks's more vigorous public endorsement of Lincoln's Emancipation Proclamation. According to Sumner, once Lincoln issued the proclamation, Stanton was determined to have a commander in the Gulf "to whom the Proclamation would be a living letter," and Butler simply had not proved that he fit that profile. Still, Sumner added, had Stanton known Butler's "real position with regard to the Proclamation," he "would have cut off his right hand before he would have allowed anybody to take your place." In the hope of settling the ongoing debate, the popular biographer and staunch Butler supporter James Parton offered to write a history of Butler's time in New Orleans, "for the vindication of the country as well as to do honor to one who, in this most difficult of all wars, has shown a capacity equal to the occasion." Butler accepted the offer, though he urged Parton not to distort the record to please him.[2]

Leaving New Orleans, Butler may have planned to return with Sarah straightaway to Lowell. Before he could do so, however, President Lincoln summoned him to Washington. "I am contemplating a peculiar and important service for you," Lincoln wrote mysteriously, "which I think, and hope you will think, is as honorable as it is important." According to one historian, despite his growing list of accomplishments in the Western Theater of the war—Forts Henry and Donelson, Shiloh, Iuka, Corinth—rumors of Gen. Ulysses S. Grant's occasionally excessive consumption of alcohol were already circulating by late 1862, and a "worried" Lincoln was pondering sending Butler west to take his place. Some allies wondered if Butler was about to be given a cabinet post; still others urged him to begin positioning himself for a run for the presidency. According to Sumner, Lincoln might even send him back to New Orleans and, in any case, was clearly "anxious" to "keep you in the public service." Treasury Secretary Chase was under the same impression, and indeed, on January 23, Lincoln proposed to Stanton that Butler be returned to the Gulf by the beginning of February, but only if the appointment could be made without simultaneously offending Banks, whose "original wish," after all, had been an independent command in Texas. If an arrangement between the two generals proved impossible, Lincoln still believed that Butler must be retained in some capacity, not least because of his political influence, including with War Democrats, and his undeniable administrative talents. "I think we cannot longer dispense with General Butler's services," Lincoln observed to Stanton. Having met with Butler once already, on January 28 Lincoln summoned him for further conversation.[3]

Meanwhile, many in New Orleans yearned for Butler's return. "Come back," begged George Denison on February 10. "The new troops and your old regiments, equally, will hail your return with joy." Denison promised that Butler would find himself with "even more friends than when you left," and insisted that the work ahead in the region "can be accomplished only by you." Among Denison's gravest concerns was Banks's poor handling of the Black Louisiana regiments. "Gen. Banks," he wrote, "seems to be much guided by his West Point officers, most of whom for some reason or other, have prejudices against negro troops." On their advice, Banks had replaced the regiments' Black commissioned officers with White ones, a move the enlisted men understandably resented. Meanwhile, although Secretary of State Seward continued to oppose Butler's return to the Gulf on the basis of his thorny interactions with the foreign consuls during his previous tenure, at the end of February orders were in fact drafted to send him back. Would he actually accept the command? "As your friend," urged Treasury Secretary Chase, "allow me to say that you cannot rightfully or wisely withhold yourself from the true post of duty at this time. . . . Go to New Orleans, General, and the sooner the better."[4]

Butler was certainly gratified by the offer, which he considered "a most complete personal vindication" of his administration and which, therefore, "entirely satisfied any personal wish I could entertain on the subject of my relief from the Department." Still, to return to command there now seemed like a hopeless, thankless assignment. For one thing, Banks had made a mess of things with the Black troops and "it will take months," Butler was certain, "to restore in the negro in Louisiana that reliance upon the Justice, that confidence in the power, that appreciation of the good will, and that trust in the good faith of the Government of the United States which he had on the 15th day of December last," when Banks took over. Additionally, as far as he could tell the plan for his return did not include providing him with the soldiers he would need to "finish the work on the Mississippi and in the Gulf," by which he meant depriving the Confederacy of any and all control of the river and the region. Butler also suspected the command arrangements between himself and Banks would simply be too difficult to sort out. So he turned the offer down, and by early March 1863 he and Sarah were back in Lowell. "Your letter came almost immediately on our arrival home," Sarah wrote to Blanche in Georgetown on March 5. "We staid one night in Baltimore, on our return, then I think in N. York. I spent another day in shopping." Once again, Sarah confessed her deep weariness of the war: "I do not know when I shall ever get rested," she admitted. A week later Sarah observed that life in Lowell had resumed some of its prewar regularity: "The two boys," she told Blanche, "have gone to bed, and your Father is down at the office." But in other ways, the war remained supremely and inescapably present. A local Sanitary Commission fair had brought in $5,000, Sarah noted proudly, "a remarkable thing for Lowell" which "shows how enthusiastic and ready the people are to aid the soldiers on in sickness, indeed, to aid the war in any form."[5]

As he awaited his next orders, Butler gave a number of speeches, notably at the Academy of Music in New York City on April 2, where he basked in the grateful praise of the city's Republican mayor, George Opdyke, for his "judicious management" of Baltimore in the earliest days of the war, his shrewd contraband policy, and his excellent command in New Orleans. "Your friends," declared Opdyke, "knew that in a position so environed with difficulties as this, no ordinary commander could hope to acquit himself with credit." Butler's "capacious and fertile mind," along with his "resolute will," "dauntless courage," and "earnest patriotism" had suited him above all others for the job. In his own speech, which he later published and much of which he included in his autobiography, Butler proudly reviewed the details of his military service to date and then discussed how his views on the rebellion had changed over time. At the start of the war, Butler explained, he had perceived the Confederates as nothing more than "our erring brethren." Now, however, he realized they were much more dangerous. They were, in fact, "our alien enemies, foreigners, carrying on war against us, attempting to make alliances against us, attempting surreptitiously to get into the family of nations." And as for the rebellion itself, he no longer saw it as a family squabble but rather as a fearsome attempt by the rebels at "revolution, the rightfulness or success of which we," he insisted, "never will acknowledge." Nor, henceforth, could he support a peaceful return to the status quo antebellum. "I am not for the reconstruction of the Union as it was," Butler now declared. "I think we can have a better Union next time." In order to accomplish that goal, the seceded states must be conquered and then reduced to territorial status until they met whatever requirements the United States imposed for their return to statehood. By early 1863, Butler's wartime journey had brought him a long way from where he stood in Charleston in 1860, and far closer—not least on the complex questions of slavery, national reunion, and reconstruction—to the views of Radical Republicans like Thaddeus Stevens. Increasingly observers attributed to him "the conviction that there is no middle or neutral ground between loyalty and treason; that traitors against the Government forfeit all rights of protection and of property; that those who persist in rebellion . . . must be put down, and kept down by the strong hand of power and by the use of all rightful means, and that, so far as may be, the sufferings of the poor and the misguided, caused by the rebellion, should be visited upon the authors of their calamities."[6]

Predictably, not everyone gushed with praise for Butler in the aftermath of his speech in New York. The following day an anonymous writer, addressing him as "The Beast, of Big Bethel Notoriety," mocked the Academy of Music event as a "demonstration of a party of thieves and abolition fanatics" who "listened to [your] egotistical jargon about what you have done, and you would do, and what you wouldn't do with the South." This writer further advised Butler that "many of the crowd" at the Academy had attended purely out of "curiosity to see the Bully and Braggart, the most adroit thief in America, and the defamer of the fair sex." For good measure, he also threatened Butler with assassination, warning him to "wear your steel armor and put it on when you go to bed."[7]

For his part, Butler remained as dismissive of such attacks as he was of the more abundant adulation he received. What really concerned him, what he really wanted, was a military assignment where he could do some concrete good for the nation. And while he waited he felt useless and frustrated, not least because he found himself being "asked a hundred times a day, 'when are you going into service?'" Moreover, despite the sensation of "vindication" he had experienced when it appeared that he might be returned to the Gulf, the collapse of that plan left him feeling "disgraced in the eyes of the country and especially in the eyes of foreign nations," not by his own actions but by the way the government had treated him. Indeed, not for the last time he wrote to Secretary Chase that he was considering leaving the army altogether unless he was given a significant and practical way to express his loyalty to the Union cause and exercise his military and administrative acumen. Among other things, he had a good deal to offer by way of analysis of the Union's military situation. As he observed to Chase, the uncoordinated use of several different smaller armies that had been the Union's approach thus far would never result in victory. "Have we not got over that absurd idea yet?" he asked, foreshadowing the plan Grant would advance in 1864 when he assumed command of all Union forces. Additionally, to the US Congress's Joint Committee on the Conduct of the War—upon whose members, especially the Radical Republicans, he apparently "made an excellent impression"—Butler "urged the employment of Negro troops" to assist in crushing the rebellion. Meanwhile, supremely and perennially conscious of issues relating to prestige and authority, he fretted over what he considered the government's failure to properly acknowledge (and reward) his status as the senior ranking major general "on the active list in the service of the United States."[8]

As the weeks passed and the US forces experienced yet another stunning defeat at Chancellorsville in early May, Butler's mystified supporters continued to offer theories about and suggestions for his future. Some remained certain that Lincoln would yet tap him to replace Stanton, Grant, Halleck, or someone else. Some remained convinced that he would eventually be returned to New Orleans. Others recommended that he run for governor of Massachusetts, or, as had been proposed earlier, president of the United States. "It seems too bad to have you idle at Lowell," wrote Edward L. Pierce, now stationed at Port Royal, South Carolina. Writing on July 2, the second day of the great and terrible clash of the armies at Gettysburg, Pierce wondered how it was possible for Butler to be left idle, "when so much is going on in which you ought to bear a part." Meanwhile, life went on in Lowell, where Sarah, for one, eagerly awaited the return of "Buntie" from Georgetown. "I need not say how I long to have you with me," she wrote as her daughter's spring term came to an end. "Leave your books" behind, Sarah advised, but "take your music. I must hear you play and sing."[9]

Then came the New York City draft riots, a week-long eruption of violence caused by a dangerous combination of "antidraft and antiblack discontent" in the city, during which "mobs of Irish workers roamed the streets, burned the draft office, sacked and burned the homes of prominent Republicans, and tried unsuccessfully to demolish the New York Tribune building," all while targeting the city's Black population with lynchings and other acts of brutality. When the riots began on July 13, a number of prominent New Yorkers called for the deployment of Federal forces under Butler's command to bring the city under control. Butler's stern administration in New Orleans, they believed, made him "the preferred replacement for the irresolute General Wool," the War of 1812 veteran who had taken over for Butler at Fort Monroe in 1861 and who had recently been sent with troops to New York to contain the mob. In the end, the official order did not come, and Butler remained on the sidelines. "I am still unemployed," he wrote Chase despondently in October. Butler bided his time by tending to his private and professional affairs, giving speeches, campaigning across party lines for the reelection of Republican Andrew Gregg Curtin as governor of Pennsylvania, and consulting with interested parties regarding his views on the Union's war effort.[10]

In early November 1863, Butler finally received his new assignment, as commander of the Department of Virginia and North Carolina, with headquarters once again at Fort Monroe, and on November 9 he and Sarah headed back to their old stomping ground. This new command, the army's "counterpart of the North Atlantic Blockading Squadron," encompassed Fort Monroe and its surroundings, as well as "Norfolk, the Cape Hatteras islands, and some scattered outposts around Pamlico and Albemarle sounds." According to one historian, Lincoln chose Butler for the assignment precisely because, despite its closeness to Richmond, the department was considered, at least for the time being, "relatively insignificant" and was manned by only somewhere between 23,000 and 40,000 soldiers. Here, therefore, Butler's limited and uneven *combat* experience would be unimportant, while his well-established *administrative* skills would prove essential, a reminder in and of itself that the capacity of the army to function, let alone succeed in its battlefield objectives, depended not only on good fighters and field commanders but also on astute and effective bureaucrats. This post, Lincoln and Stanton expected, would play to Butler's strengths. "Know you," wrote an old friend from Waterville College, "that in addition to our approval of *every word* and *deed* of yours, we suspect that whatever may be the want of brains elsewhere, the vacancy is not under your hat." "The great body of the people," wrote John D. Kellogg from New York, "are fully impressed with your great administrative and executive ability, which was so brilliantly displayed while you were in command of the Department of the Gulf." Expressing more confidence than some that Butler could also be successful on the field of battle, Kellogg added that he hoped it would also "fall to your lot to take Richmond, and to thus restore the 'old Dominion' to her true position in the Union."[11]

On their way back to Virginia the Butlers stopped briefly in Washington to bring Blanche back to school. While he was in the capital, Butler and Stanton discussed the details of his new assignment, such as where to house any prisoners of war who should come under his authority and, more generally, how to handle the whole vexing prisoner exchange issue, especially in light of Jefferson Davis's December 1862 threat—in the same proclamation where he declared Butler a "felon" and an "outlaw"—that he would execute

Butler with other key army and cavalry officers, by Augustus Tholey. Courtesy of the Prints and Photographs Division, Library of Congress, Washington, D.C.

captured Black soldiers and their White commissioned officers. "No one will go farther in exerting every power of the Government in protecting the colored troops and their Officers than myself," Butler insisted. While Butler and Stanton pondered such weighty matters, Sarah took Blanche to call on First Lady Mary Todd Lincoln, and was pleasantly surprised to be invited in for a visit by the president instead. A few days later, having arrived with her husband at Fort Monroe (Paul and Bennie followed once their parents were settled), Sarah once again confronted one of the tiresome shortcomings of army life as a commanding officer's wife, which her enjoyable visit with President Lincoln may have temporarily effaced. "Dirt, dirt, dirt" everywhere, she grumbled in a letter to her sister Harriet. "My skirts were full of it." And she added, "I do not like this place, never did."[12]

On May 22, 1863, the War Department's General Orders No. 143 had finally established the Bureau of Colored Troops, and even as he continued to reflect on how to manage the prisoner exchange problem—especially as it now related to the United States Colored Troops (USCT) and their White commissioned officers—Butler earnestly took up the work of recruiting more Black soldiers from among the free and unfree Black population in the

TO VIRGINIA AND BEYOND

area now under his command. On November 29 he informed Stanton that it had taken him only three days to raise the Union army's first company of "colored cavalry," which he hoped to expand promptly into an entire regiment. A few days later Butler issued his own General Orders No. 46, in which he reiterated that "the recruitment of colored troops has become the settled purpose of the Government," and that he planned to pursue that goal vigorously. Not everyone in the department was pleased with this development: Butler received numerous anxious, sometimes angry, letters from local Whites who feared that armed Blacks would soon "make war" on "helpless" White women and children. Instead of enlisting Black men in the army, one White correspondent pleaded with Butler to relocate all enslaved and free Black people as far away and "as fast as possible, to avoid farther trouble," claiming, "we [meaning "we Whites"] have become a loyal people, and will look to our Government for protection." Fully committed to the project of expanding the USCT, and recalling the trustworthiness and courage of the Black troops in Louisiana, Butler was unmoved by such pleas. "If you do not die until the negroes hurt you," he responded, "you will live forever."[13]

In fact, Butler's extensive and detailed General Orders No. 46, dated December 5, mapped out his plans not just for Black recruitment but also for management, organization, and protection of the sizable Black civilian population that now came under his jurisdiction. Among other things, the orders declared it the duty of all US soldiers and military officers under his command to support and advance the general welfare of the local Black population, "irrespective of personal predilection" and not only to ensure the recruitment project's success. "The former condition of the blacks," he declared, with some lingering paternalism, "their change of relation, the new rights acquired by them, the new obligations imposed upon them, the duty of the Government to them, the great stake they have in the war, and the claims their ignorance and the helplessness of their women and children make upon each of us who hold a higher grade in social and political life, must all be carefully considered." He authorized a ten-dollar bounty for each Black enlistee as well as subsistence provisions for his family, to be managed by Lt. Col. J. Burnham Kinsman, the department's newly appointed "general superintendent of negro affairs," and his assistants. So long as the soldier remained in good standing, those provisions would continue, including for six months after his death should he die in the service. Butler further expressed his desire that the Black soldiers' uniforms, arms, equipment, and other materials should be the same as those supplied to White soldiers, which he considered "an act of justice." Unfortunately, he was bound by the federal policy of paying Black soldiers ten dollars per month instead of the thirteen dollars received by Whites, and of charging Black soldiers a three-dollar clothing fee that Whites did not have to pay. Butler considered the discrepancy indefensible, for a "colored soldier," he insisted, "fills an equal space in the ranks while he lives, and an equal grave when he falls."[14]

Although Butler believed that the "best use during the war for an able-bodied colored man, as well for himself as the country, is to be a soldier," his orders also stipulated that Black civilians in his department who were laboring on behalf of the government must be paid promptly. "Political freedom rightly defined," he observed, "is liberty to work, and to be protected in the full enjoyment of the fruits of labor." This principle cut both ways: Blacks able to work must be offered the opportunity—but must not compelled, unless by "imperative military necessity"—to do so. At the same time, however, those who freely chose *not* to work would *not* be supported. Additionally, families would be kept together, and racial insults, abuse, and ridicule of Blacks by Whites were proscribed and would be punished. Butler further called for "an accurate census" of all Black residents in his department, in order that they might be properly cared for. And he proclaimed that those "religious, benevolent, and humane persons" who had come to the area to educate the local population must be treated with absolute respect and assisted in whatever way possible. Butler's development on the profound issue of Black rights—their rights as human beings and as Americans—was clear. A few days later, abolitionist Robert Dale Owen, a leader of the benevolence organization known as the American Freedmen's Inquiry Commission, thanked Butler for devising such a "comprehensive" and "effective" system of "protection and improvement" for the Black men, women, and children in his department. General Orders No. 46, wrote Owen, "will contribute more than any other similar document issued since the commencement of the war to the solution of one of the hardest problems that has arisen in the course of it," namely, the future of the former bondspeople. From the Office of the Special Commissioner of the War Department, H. S. Olcott praised Butler as the "deep-thinking, practical statesman" the country needed to resolve "the great question of the day." "God bless you for what you have done and are doing for the cause of a wronged and despised race," wrote Massachusetts senator Henry Wilson.[15] Through his actions and policies in his department, Butler's move toward racial egalitarianism offered hope for broader social and cultural transformation.

White residents in the Department of Virginia and North Carolina, of course, generally condemned and resisted the ways that the war, the Emancipation Proclamation, the enlisting and arming of Black soldiers, and But-ler's orders especially were reshaping local and regional racial dynamics. Some expressed their discontent in complaining letters; others engaged in violent guerrilla activity, especially against Blacks both in and out of mil-itary uniform. In one of the many cases that came to Butler's attention, a group of supposedly "respectable" Whites "organized a riot, broke into a negro's house, beat his wife with a table leg and carried him off, an old man, into slavery, lying about it by saying that they were going to carry him to the Yankees." On another occasion, guerrillas simply captured and brutally executed a Black soldier. Such "lawlessness," Butler insisted angrily, "must cease."[16]

With that goal in mind, not long after he issued General Orders No. 46, Butler authorized Edward A. Wild and two regiments of Black troops to launch an antiguerrilla raid into Pasquotank County, North Carolina, which stretched from the southern boundary of the Great Dismal Swamp to Albe-marle Sound. During the raid, General Wild and his troops tore through the area, liberating perhaps as many as 2,000 enslaved people. They also cap-tured Daniel Bright, a local guerrilla and deserter from the Sixty-Second Georgia Infantry who was known, Butler later wrote, for "carrying on rob-bery and pillage in the peaceable counties of Camden and Pasquotank." They burned Bright's house to the ground. Subsequently, a court-martial presided over by Wild found Bright guilty of guerrilla activity and sentenced him to death, and on December 13, Bright was hanged. Predictably, the hanging of a White man who had been captured by *Black* soldiers—most if not all of them formerly enslaved—provoked a storm of protest among those who objected to the very principle of arming Black men, let alone deploying them to sub-due White rebels. Some local Whites produced extravagant claims about "child murder, arson, and mistreatment of white women" by Wild's soldiers; Confederate major general George E. Pickett angrily asserted that Butler had clearly planned to "let loose his swarm of blacks upon our ladies and defenseless families," to "plunder and devastate the country," and to "hang everyone they could capture." Some evidence suggests that Wild and his men did get somewhat "carried away" with their "notions of righteous vengeance" against the guerrillas and their supporters: one witness claimed the raiders had "crudely embarrassed and humiliated" a number of White women whom they held for a time as hostages, by insisting they "relieve themselves in the street while under the eye of a black soldier-guard." For his part, Butler staunchly defended Wild and his men, insisting to Secretary Stanton that Wild had "done his work with great thoroughness" even if he may have acted with "perhaps too much stringency" in his burning of guerrilla property and taking of hostages in return for the guerrillas' own depredations. Butler further praised the Black soldiers for "conduct[ing] themselves with propriety" despite the persistent prejudice and hostility they faced even, he noted, not infrequently from their own White officers.[17]

Wild, too, emphatically defended his soldiers, and in the aftermath of the raid he and his men only "grew fiercer" in their clashes with local guerrillas and even Confederate regulars who, in keeping with Jefferson Davis's December 1862 proclamation, "rarely took black prisoners." Local Whites' persistent bitterness over Bright's execution came into sharp relief when some Pasquotank County residents discovered the lynched and lifeless body of a Black enlisted man, Samuel Jones, in mid-January 1864 and sent the body to Butler. A note pinned to the corpse explained that Jones had been murdered specifically in retribution for Bright's hanging. The ratcheting up of hostilities, which increasingly afflicted loyal civilians as well as disloyal ones, no doubt contributed to Butler's decision to issue his General Orders No. 10 on January 16, 1864, in which he reminded both soldiers and officers of their responsibility to "afford just protection to peaceable and quiet citizens from unauthorized and lawless acts, and to enable them to obtain speedy redress and remuneration therefor." The private property of "peaceable inhabitants," he added, "shall be seized only when needed for the use of the troops," and enemy property could be "taken or destroyed" only to prevent its use against the US troops or the government, or as punishment for the same. Butler appeared to be trying to rein his men in. At the same time, he vented his rage in a letter to James W. Hinton, Confederate commander of North Carolina's state troops, advising Hinton and other Confederate leaders and provocateurs to consider "whether the kind of warfare carried on for the past year" in the region could possibly have the desired effect, namely, "to set up the Confederate Government among the nations of the earth." President Lincoln, too, strove to bring calm to the Department of Virginia and North Carolina by staying all executions in the area.[18]

Meanwhile, on December 17, Maj. Gen. Ethan A. Hitchcock, serving as the Union's commissioner of prisoner of war exchange, had handed over the reins to Butler, placing all prisoners then housed at Point Lookout and Fort McHenry in Maryland, and Fort Norfolk in Virginia, under Butler's charge along with "such others as will be sent to you from time to time." According to Hitchcock, "Colored troops and their officers will be put upon an equality in making exchanges," and, further, "Colored men in civil employment, captured by the enemy, may also be exchanged for other men in civil employment taken by our forces." Pointedly, Hitchcock emphasized to Butler that, "in conducting this delicate, and perhaps difficult matter" of prisoner exchange, "you will see to it that in no degree the protection of the Government is withdrawn from colored soldiers of the United States, and the officers commanding them." Butler agreed: in prisoner exchange as in other matters, Black soldiers and civilians must receive the same treatment and protection as Whites.[19]

Soon, Butler and his Confederate counterpart, Robert Ould, were in communication, prompted in part by Butler's concern about an outbreak of smallpox among Union prisoners being held at Belle Isle prison in Richmond. As he had done in New Orleans, Butler sought to prevent the spread of a highly communicable disease by encouraging proper scientific protocols; he therefore dispatched to the prison "a quantity of vaccine matter" sufficient to inoculate as many as 6,000 individuals. On the basis of Butler's swift action on the Belle Isle prisoners' behalf, the *Army and Navy Journal* expressed optimism that his new authority in connection with prisoner exchange meant that "our brave fellows" would not only survive the disease outbreak but would also "before long be returned from their trying captivity." Ould, however, objected fiercely to Butler's appointment and threatened not to cooperate with him. "When one who has been proclaimed to be so obnoxious as General Butler is selected," he explained to Hitchcock, recalling Davis's proclamation, "self-respect requires that the Confederate authorities should refuse to treat with him." The *Army and Navy Journal*'s early optimism faded. "The negotiations for the exchange of prisoners are again at a stand-still," the paper observed on January 2. "The rebel Commissioner refuses to have anything to do with General Butler, whom Jeff. Davis has declared an outlaw."[20]

As it happens, however, Butler had already quietly begun devising a creative plan for dealing with at least some of the Confederate prisoners who now fell under his purview, at least so long as Federal prisoners of war remained in limbo. "Is there any objection," he asked Secretary Stanton on December 27, 1863, "to my enlisting as many prisoners as may desire to do so, after they know they can be exchanged, either in [the] regular or volunteer force of the United States, or that of any state?" After some consideration, Stanton approved the plan, and in early January Butler ordered Brig. Gen. Gilman Marston—commander of Point Lookout, one of the largest prison camps in the United States—to prepare for enrolling Confederate prisoners who desired "to enlist in the service of the United States, either in the Army or the Navy." The following day Butler sent Marston a list of questions, drafted and delivered to him by Lincoln's secretary, John Hay, which were designed to determine a prisoner's viability for US service. Those who met all the requirements came to be known most commonly as the "galvanized Yankees"—they were also called "repentant rebels" or "transfugees"—and over the next two years their numbers reached several thousand. By late March 1864, Butler reported that he had a regiment's worth of men ready to be organized and armed in this way. These particular men, the First US Volunteer Infantry Regiment, were "assigned to routine police duties" in Virginia; subsequently, "under the hard driving of young Colonel Charles Dimon and his eager New England officers," they "became a first-class body of soldiers" who served mostly in the Western Theater. Several more regiments followed.[21]

In the midst of his pressing administrative responsibilities, in February 1864 Butler suffered a serious personal blow: the death of his brother, Andrew Jackson Butler. Late in January, Butler's old friend and business associate Richard Fay had informed him that Jackson, then in New York City, was severely ill with what one doctor later identified as "consumption." According to Fay, Jackson was then "in pretty good spirits and confident" about his chances for recovery," but another friend was less certain. Thomas Richardson warned Butler that his brother's strength had recently and quite suddenly deteriorated, and he urged the general to come to New York as soon as possible. "He is a very sick man," agreed Butler's chief of staff, J. W. Shaffer, who had gone to New York to assess the situation. "I don't think he will live through the Spring." For her part, Sarah—who had so vividly expressed her dislike and distrust of her brother-in-law in the past—seemed indifferent: her known letters from this period do not mention Jackson, focusing instead on her own state of mind and, often, her loneliness. "I have been round the ramparts twice alone," she wrote mournfully to Blanche from Fort Monroe on February 21; "the day is *very* lonely." In this letter, Sarah noted that her sister Harriet, niece Hattie, and nine-year-old son Bennie were all sick, that twelve-year-old Paul was off with his father visiting Point Lookout, and that she missed Blanche terribly. But she did not say a word about Jackson, who had died on February 11, just two days shy of his forty-ninth birthday.[22]

Butler had surely hoped to see his ailing brother alive again. But in addition to the daily burdens of managing his department; grappling with the prisoner exchange question; recruiting, training, and protecting the rights of Black soldiers; providing for and employing Black civilians; and keeping the rebellious portion of the local White population under control, he was—

in keeping with his perennial yearning for action—in the midst of plotting an attack on Richmond. As he explained to Brig. Gen. Isaac J. Wistar in early February, the goals of the proposed attack were ambitious: to liberate the Federal prisoners in the Confederate capital, destroy public buildings, devastate Confederate resources, and "capture some of the leaders of the rebellion, so that at least we can have means to meet their constant threats of retaliation and hanging of our men white and black." To Butler's great disappointment, however, in the end the movement was a flop. "We chronicle this week," reported the *Army and Navy Journal* on February 13, "another serious attempt to capture Richmond," and "are sorry to add, another failure," although the plan had been a bold one.[23]

Led by General Wistar, the Federals had advanced to within ten miles of Richmond. But the city's defenders, having learned of Butler's plans from a deserter, had prepared for the Federals' arrival by destroying a crucial bridge and blocking the main road into the city with felled trees. "We were obliged to retire," Butler reported to Stanton. Days later, the frustrated general finally traveled to New York City to attend his brother's funeral and prepare the remains for return to Lowell. Subsequently, although his sister-in-law was still living, Butler began to assume more responsibility for Jackson and Joanna's troubled son, George, then twenty-three. Given his brother's untimely demise and his latest military reverse, Butler surely found some solace during this period in the many letters of support and encouragement that continued to flow in, some of which recommended—again—that he consider a run for the presidency that fall. "Gen. B. is more dreaded" by Lincoln's supporters "as a Presidential candidate than anyone spoken of," claimed one correspondent exuberantly. Others showered praise on Butler for his service in New Orleans and urged him, again, to return there.[24]

At the beginning of March, having rebounded from the poor results of the previous operation, Butler authorized another attempt on the Confederate capital, this time prompted by information he had received from Elizabeth Van Lew, a staunch Unionist in the city with whom he had struck up a secret correspondence. Butler first became aware in December 1863 of Van Lew's willingness to serve as the army's eyes and ears in Richmond. His direct communication with her began in mid-January 1864, mostly in the form of letters whose true messages were written in invisible ink that had to be revealed with heat and acid. It was Van Lew who notified Butler of a Confederate plan to send Union prisoners of war south to the newly constructed (and soon to become infamous) prisoner of war camp at Andersonville, Georgia, and she who urged him "to send a force of forty thousand to rescue the prisoners before they could be carried off." On Van Lew's recommendation, Butler ambitiously decided to try, convinced that "if he could get forty thousand troops into Richmond, he might as well capture the city," too. Lincoln and Stanton responded with understandable caution, in the end authorizing a much smaller force than Butler had requested: 3,500 cavalry troopers under the leadership of Gen. H. Judson Kilpatrick and Col. Ulric Dahlgren. Once again, the attempt failed. Moreover, twenty-one-year-old Dahlgren was killed. On March 11 Butler sadly requested that Ould return Dahlgren's body so that it might be "delivered to his afflicted father," Rear Adm. John A. Dahlgren, commander of the South Atlantic Blockading Squadron, "who is waiting here to receive it." The military consequences of this second unsuccessful escapade were not significant; potentially more problematic were the long-term political implications of the Confederates' claim to have discovered papers on the young Dahlgren's body indicating that he had been ordered, if possible, to assassinate Jefferson Davis.[25]

Less than a week after what came to be known as the Dahlgren Raid, on March 8, 1864, President Lincoln formally commissioned Ulysses S. Grant commander of all Union forces, with the rank of lieutenant general. Four days later, Butler's chief of staff, Colonel Shaffer, suggested this might be a good time to request additional troops for the department, given his belief that Grant "has a high and correct opinion of you" and was eager to begin an aggressive spring campaign in which the Department of Virginia and North Carolina would surely play a crucial role. As Shaffer predicted, Grant soon began devising and implementing his "grand strategy" for Union victory, whose principal features were simultaneous, coordinated movements against all Confederate armies in the field and the annihilation of Confederate civilians' will to continue the struggle. Grant did indeed have a plan for Butler, which included appointing him commander of the newly designated Army of the James, a combination of the Tenth and Eighteenth Corps in which the USCT regiments, including the now-famed Fifty-Fourth Massachusetts, had a substantial presence. "The regiments composing this field force of 34,000 men," writes one historian, "had little combat experience." Still, "the men were of good quality, and they could learn how to handle themselves under fire just as they had learned how to do all the other tasks normally assigned to soldiers." According to this historian, "The most serious weakness in the Army of the James lay in its high command," namely, Butler, who was "among the least deserving of available candidates." Other historians evaluate Butler's leadership of the Army of the James more favorably. "Butler's abilities," writes one, "were unquestionable, and he was a forcible administrator" as well as "a master of quick, clever marches, feints, ruses, and shrewd surprises." True, he could be "endlessly troublesome," but he was also "endlessly useful," so much so that "only a Dickens could do justice to his remarkable combination of gifts, faults, and picturesque anfractuosities." Butler's weaknesses were certainly compounded by those of his two most important subordinates, corps commanders Maj. Gen. William "Baldy" Smith and Maj. Gen. Quincy A. Gillmore, both West Point graduates who could be as prickly, argumentative, and glory-seeking as he was.[26] The combustible combination of Butler, Smith, and Gillmore hardly boded well for their ability to succeed as a team in the portion of the grand strategy General Grant assigned to them.

At the beginning of April 1864, Grant met with Butler at Fort Monroe to discuss the spring campaign. As he later explained to Gen. George Gordon Meade, commanding the Army of the Potomac, Grant envisioned a coordinated action, "so far as practicable," of all the armies "towards one common centre." Grant's expectation was that "simultaneous with the movement of the Federal forces elsewhere," Gillmore, Smith, and Butler would spearhead an advance designed to "seize City Point" and, with naval support, to "operate against Richmond from the south side of the river" and force the Confederates there to abandon their defenses. On April 2, Grant laid this plan out to Butler in person, emphasizing the desirability of beginning the operation "at as early a day as practicable." Butler's task, Grant further explained, was to gather his available forces and, as soon after April 18 as he could—once the order to move was issued—"take City Point with as much force as possible" and then entrench there. After that, Grant would send him further directions. "Richmond is to be your objective point," Grant reiterated, but he left "all the minor details" of the advance to Butler's discretion. It is perhaps a sign of Butler's delight at being chosen for such a momentous assignment that he wrote to Lincoln that same day inviting him to make a social visit to Fort Monroe, which he promised would provide "a pleasant and necessary relaxation from official cares." "Long hampered and limited," writes one historian, Butler "at last rejoiced in an independent and important theater of action."[27] Undoubtedly the invitation to Lincoln also reflects Butler's ambitious, even occasionally hubristic nature.

As plans for the campaign took shape in the days ahead, Butler's headquarters swarmed with visitors. "The reason I have not written earlier," Sarah explained to Blanche on April 13, "is we have a great deal of company. The mornings slip by before we are aware in entertaining them, and the evenings are devoted to the same thing." From Sarah's perspective, there was one good thing about having all these high-level visitors: their coming and going seemed to underscore her husband's stature and augured well for his future. "Your Father is not likely to be removed from here," Sarah observed with satisfaction. On April 25 she wrote again, "I fear you will think I have delayed too long in writing you, but the days slip by and I accomplish nothing." Still, she admitted, she had no desire at this point to return to Massachusetts, "as there are movements" of the army "to be made that will interest me to be near as possible." Sarah wondered if the bustle around the fort might even mean the war would soon come to an end. "I do not think you should be away from me much longer," she wrote. Even so, she wondered how, if her husband chose to continue his military life after the war, "we are to be together."[28]

As Sarah entertained both a flood of guests and her visions of the future, Butler corresponded with Grant and others regarding the campaign's details and how he planned to complete his particular assignment. He also sought Grant's guidance on the increasingly vexing issue of prisoner exchanges, particularly those that involved Black soldiers, who, he rightly emphasized, faced even greater personal risks in Confederate hands than White prisoners did. On this score, Grant, who had basically halted all exchanges soon after being promoted to overall command, remained unyielding. Some of Grant's replies also suggest that his patience with Butler's many questions and suggestions was wearing thin. "I do not pretend to say how your work is to be done," he wrote on April 16, "but simply lay down what, and trust to you, and those under you, for doing it well." Careful planning for the coordinated movement of the armies consumed time; persistent rain further delayed any movement throughout the month, and, by the end of April, signs of trouble brewing between Butler and his subordinates were unmistakable. Finally, on the evening of May 5—as Meade's Army of the Potomac was becoming brutally entangled in the Battle of the Wilderness—Butler informed Grant and Stanton that he had landed part of the Army of the James at City Point and more at nearby "Bermuda Hundreds," just north of the juncture between the James and Appomattox Rivers. The following day Butler reported that all of his troops had now "taken the positions which were indicated to the Comd'g General at our last conference, and are carrying out that plan."[29]

Nearly 200 miles away in Georgetown, Blanche heard rumors that her father and his army were on the move. "I know that you must be very lonely," she consoled her mother on May 8, "if it is true that Father has gone into the field," though she admitted that there were "so many conflicting reports that one hardly knows what to believe." What would happen next to the army, Blanche wondered, and, perhaps even more important, how would the outcome of the spring campaign affect her family? "Are you going to remain at the Fortress until the campaign is over?" she asked, or "or do you think of joining Father as soon as he stops marching?" Like Sarah and surely most northerners, Blanche hoped "the decisive battle" of the war would come soon, and with it, war's end. Back at Fort Monroe, Sarah expressed "absorbing interest" in all the activity. "Our troops," she wrote, "have taken possession of and now occupy City Point and Bermuda on the opposite side of the river," and, she added proudly, "your Father is there of course." In light of these developments, Sarah pondered whether to take her sister and the children—Paul, Bennie, and Harriet's daughter, Hattie—back to Massachusetts or remain in Virginia, where she could "hear the exciting news from day to day." In the end, aside from a brief excursion to Philadelphia, Sarah stayed at Fort Monroe so she could be close to her husband. "We shall be very glad," she confessed to Blanche on May 21, "when this campaign is over."[30]

Sarah worried about her husband's safety. Ever ambitious on his account, she also hoped the current campaign would crown him with the sort of glory that had seemed more attainable in the earliest days of the war, when many in the North had believed Butler would bring about the Union's swift salvation. "There must be fearful fighting," she wrote to him on May 8, and "if it comes your way, I pray you to act with *caution. . . .* No display of *personal courage* merely will have any weight compared to the glory you will win if your part of the grand movement is carried through without a mistake." Having landed so many of his forces successfully at Bermuda Hundred, Butler, too, had high hopes for further triumphs, as did the War Department. "I congratulate you and your gallant command upon the skill, energy, and success of your operations," wrote Stanton encouragingly on May 10. "Reports say that Lee is retreating and Grant pursuing with his whole army." "Everyone expects you to enter Richmond," wrote Sarah optimistically from Fort Monroe the same day. "I will send you a cake tomorrow if possible." Butler, too, was confident that his portion of the campaign had gone well thus far. "I have now done all I agreed to do with Grant," he wrote.[31]

However, as Grant, Meade, and the Army of the Potomac slogged their way south toward Richmond following the terrible fighting at the Wilderness, Butler found that he and his men were virtually immobilized. Sarah wondered anxiously what was happening. "Would it not be possible for you to give me an item of news a little more frequently?" she implored on May 15. Two days later, her confidence returned, at least temporarily. "I will send you coffee, cakes, and bread tomorrow morning," she promised; "we shall soon be in Richmond." Throughout the month of May, the *Army and Navy Journal*, too, watched hopefully for further developments. Even if Butler could only manage to "interrupt permanently the direct communication between Richmond and the South," the paper declared on May 14, "it will cause much distress in the [Confederate] capital." A week later, the paper observed that Butler had "abandoned his apparent intention to advance," and seemed to have "undertaken the siege of Fort Darling," or Drewry's Bluff, fifteen miles to the northwest and high above the James River, "the preliminary operations of which," the paper added hopefully, "were progressing with gratifying success at the date of our latest advices."[32]

Hope, however, was unsustainable. "Our right flank," reported the *Army and Navy Journal* on May 28, "seems to have been so nearly turned as to necessitate a withdrawal from our advanced position, back to Bermuda Hundred." The promising attack on Fort Darling had in fact "failed when at the point of fruition." Observing from Fort Monroe, Sarah counseled, "I hope you are strongly intrenched, for if Beauregard is at Fort Darling," his rebel forces "will come down upon you." Like so many observers as the ruthless Overland Campaign proceeded, Sarah could not help commenting on its tremendous human cost. "If one could win these battles by stratagem rather than rivers of blood," she wrote, "it would surely be better." Butler strove to reassure her of his own safety at least: "All well," he wrote, "and do not be uneasy." Moreover, he maintained confidence in the ultimate success of his portion of the campaign, so much so that he once again boldly proposed to Lincoln that he be considered to fill a vacant commission in the regular army. Lincoln thanked Butler for his recent accomplishments but demurred on the proposal. "As to the major-generalships in the regular army," the president advised, "I think I shall not dispose of another, at least until the combined operations now in progress . . . shall be terminated."[33]

By late May it became clear that no further advance on Richmond, or offensive action period, could be expected from Butler's command, at least for the time being. "I fear there is some difficulty with the forces at City Point," wrote Grant to General-in-Chief Halleck. Three weeks later, the *Army and Navy Journal*, too, observed that Butler and his soldiers were idle, perhaps permanently immobilized. "There has been little fighting during the past week in the neighborhood of Bermuda Hundred," the paper reported on June 14. "It has been suggested that the remainder of General Butler's Army is penned into an uneasy position, with a river on either side, and a watchful and petulant enemy stretching his hostile cordon across from the James to the Appomattox." Still, the paper added, Butler's army was "in a very safe and very excellent position. Its communications and supplies are beyond all doubt safe and perfect. Its flanks are thoroughly covered by gunboats. And, with its entrenchments, it could hold a greater force than itself at bay." The paper further argued that Butler's landing of the Army of the James at Bermuda Hundred had been essential to Grant's effort to force Gen. Robert E. Lee and his Army of Northern Virginia into a defensive stance around Richmond, which was all to the good. For her part, Sarah offered to join her husband at the front once the military situation seemed relatively stable; he urged her instead to wait at Fort Monroe. While she waited, Sarah used the time not occupied by caring for the children and her now-ailing sister Harriet to visit the soldiers hospitalized nearby. "The Hospitals are full of wounded men in every stage of suffering," she wrote sadly to Blanche. "I have been in a number of times but what I can do is trifling among so many and surely it is a melancholy sight."[34]

Meanwhile, tensions between Butler and his subordinates Smith and Gillmore had erupted into bitter, open conflict and a complicated blame game. Each man publicly and privately enlisted his supporters to participate, and the press joined in enthusiastically. In early June, Sarah raged about the difficulties of her husband's position to their friend James Parton, who that year published an uncritically admiring study of Butler's command of the occupation in New Orleans. "I have read with surprise and a feeling of indignation," she wrote, "a series of articles . . . calling on Gen'l. Butler for defence, while well aware that an officer is not allowed to make one, no matter how bitter the condemnation or to what humiliation he may be subjected." Sarah offered her own interpretation of the basis for the three men's dispute, representing her husband as both brilliant and blameless. "Gen'l. Butler," she explained, "surprised and captured City Point and Bermuda Hundreds to the amazement and consternation of the rebels and the astonishment of our own people, by a strategic move not surpassed during the war. It was done by finesse and celerity." Moreover, Butler's operation had been "bloodless," unlike other recent battles "where blood flows like water," and which were "appalling to nature and fill the country with gloom." Several pages of detail and anger later Sarah concluded loyally that her husband had "done all that he was ordered or expected to accomplish." She further theorized that his troops were now being withdrawn out from under him by the tens of thousands and being redeployed "for political" rather than militarily strategic reasons, largely out of concern that he would be *too* successful and thereby cast others, maybe even Lincoln, into the shadows. From the start of the war, Sarah complained, her husband had "shown ability and power to produce great results with less means than any other man engaged in it." The Confederates hated him because he had done so much to harm their cause, and his various enemies in the North were attacking and undermining him now because he posed such a threat to their own power and, potentially, to the president. "He is the foremost man of the times," she wrote with proud, if flawed, confidence.[35]

When he penned his personal memoirs two decades later, Ulysses Grant looked back on Butler's overall performance in the spring of 1864 with considerable disappointment. In seizing City Point and Bermuda Hundred—a position of "great natural strength"—Butler had indeed accomplished "the first step contemplated in my instructions," Grant observed. After that, however, Butler had achieved little else offensively in the campaign: despite limited opposition, he had failed to destroy the relevant railroad lines that facilitated Confederate movements around Petersburg and Richmond, and he had initiated no meaningful attacks in the area in the period before General Beauregard was able to gather his reinforcements. Beauregard then managed to block the route to Richmond and "limit very materially the further usefulness of the Army of the James as a distinct factor" for the duration of the campaign. Grant conceded that even though Butler and his troops ended up unable to move in force toward the Confederate capital from the south, they were situated in such a way as to be "perfectly safe against an attack," which in turn made it possible for Grant to have troops from Butler's position "brought round by water" as needed to reinforce the Army of the Potomac.[36] But he had hoped for more.

"Although Butler did not achieve his objective," writes one recent historian, "his army nevertheless joined supporting naval units of the North Atlantic Blockading Squadron to prevent Confederate reoccupation of the Peninsula." And then, in June, when General Grant shifted his army from north of Richmond to south of the James, these units successfully blocked Confederate naval efforts in the area. Elaborating on a phrase he used at the time to describe Butler's situation at Bermuda Hundred, Grant recalled in his memoirs that it was "as if Butler was in a bottle," and "the enemy had corked the bottle and with a small force could hold the cork in its place," although the units from Butler's command that proved extractable were certainly useful. In the mid-1880s, the dying Grant kindly expressed regret for having launched his famous description in the first place, knowing how quickly and for how long it became a catchphrase for heaping blame and ridicule on Butler for developments that were not entirely his fault and, in many cases, not entirely negative. "I desire to rectify all injustice that I may have done to individuals, particularly to officers who were gallantly serving their country during the trying period of the war," not the least of whom was Butler, who "certainly gave his very earnest support to the war; and he gave his own best efforts personally to the suppression of the rebellion."[37]

At the end of May, Sarah prepared to send her sister, niece, and the boys back to Massachusetts for the summer. Meanwhile, Blanche fretted in Georgetown, eager to be with her family and for the war to end. For his part, Butler struggled against "a tide of deep, bitter disappointment" to summon hope that he would soon have renewed opportunities for military glory. "My time will come," he wrote mournfully, "and that not long delayed, when either a quiet grave or full power to right myself will be mine." Unfortunately for his military ambitions, a number of other plans Butler devised either to capture Petersburg and open the way to Richmond, "or at least to rip up railroads and destroy bridges" over the Appomattox River to the north, "proved abortive." On June 9, writes one historian, "when Butler took another stab" at Petersburg, "it came as no surprise"—not even, apparently, to Butler himself—"that it failed." Butler had assigned responsibility for that particular effort to General Gillmore, in whom he had little confidence, and as it got underway he predicted privately to Sarah, "it will fail from that cause."[38]

A subsequent attempt led by General Smith in mid-June also proved futile. Indeed, Butler and his subordinates' infighting, the soldiers' weariness, and the hot, exceedingly dusty, and debilitating weather all gradually combined to dispel even the thought of further offensive action by the Army of the James and provoke a discussion at the highest levels about perhaps removing Butler from command once and for all. "Whilst I have no difficulty with General Butler," wrote Grant to Halleck on July 1, "finding him always clear in his conception of orders and prompt to obey, yet there is a want of knowledge how to execute, and particularly a prejudice against him as a commander that operates against his usefulness." At the same time, Grant admitted that Butler had "no superior" as an administrator, and he wondered if a western command might be the answer. As Union casualties in the Overland Campaign mounted, northern morale plummeted, and the presidential election drew closer, the question of what to do with Butler seemed even more complicated. "Changing Butler's assignment," one historian notes, "presented political problems," not just military ones. "Mr. Lincoln was renominated this morning," Stanton wrote to Butler on June 8, with Andrew Johnson replacing Hannibal Hamlin as the candidate for vice president. With everything else that was going on, Stanton and others feared that removing—and likely alienating—Butler might well lead many of his supporters to express their resentment at the ballot box and vote for Lincoln's opponent, Democrat George McClellan.[39]

In addition, Lincoln had recently accepted the resignation of Treasury Secretary Chase, "a favorite among many Radical Republicans," and had pocket-vetoed the stern and uncompromising Wade-Davis Bill, "which embodied the notions of many" on the left flank of the Republican Party with regard to the issue of reconstruction. If Radical Republicans decided to run a candidate against Lincoln, and removing Butler meant stirring up opposition among his supporters, the president might end up facing both angry Democrats *and* a split in the Republican vote. With all this in mind, Grant, Stanton, and Lincoln decided to hold Butler in place and remove his subordinates instead, sending Gillmore to Fort Monroe and then on to Washington on recruitment duty, and accepting Smith's request to be relieved of command altogether. "General Butler has my confidence in his ability and fidelity to the country and to me," declared Lincoln bracingly on July 26, "and I wish him sustained in all his efforts in our great common cause." "The political cauldron is boiling," Butler observed to Sarah, "until one hardly cares who comes uppermost." He focused instead on defending the Black soldiers under his command against the accusation that they were responsible for the Federal army's problems in Virginia. The men of the USCT, he insisted, "ought to bear all their share of the odium which attaches to the failure[s], but no more."[40]

Even as command difficulties in the Department of Virginia and North Carolina stumbled toward a temporary if not entirely satisfying resolution, Butler also embarked on an engineering project that involved cutting a canal across an island in the James River to facilitate the passage upriver of Union ironclads. "We should have for a fifty feet cut but about 55,000 cubic feet of excavation," amounting to roughly "10 days' labor for a thousand men," he informed Grant on July 28, describing the "Dutch Gap" project he was planning. On August 7—as Sarah, Blanche, and the rest of the family headed home to Lowell for what Sarah hoped would be a brief visit—Butler called for a "preliminary survey" of the canal, and three days later the digging began. "My canal is getting on famously," he wrote cheerfully to Sarah later that month, not long after he got word that his alma mater, Waterville College, would be renamed "Colby University" to honor its generous wartime donor. "Certainly the donation of Mr. Colby was a most munificent one," Butler wrote to one old schoolmate, Moses J. Kelley, with what seemed like a measure of bitterness, "which I wish I had the power to imitate."[41]

During the weeks the canal project was underway, Butler traveled briefly to Lowell to visit his family, to New York City to deal with more of his late brother's affairs, and to Washington to meet with various officials. Then, in early September, news of General Sherman's capture of Atlanta brought renewed hope to the war-weary North, dramatically improving Lincoln's chances for reelection. Soon came word of Gen. Philip Sheridan's successes against Confederate general Jubal Early in Virginia's Shenandoah Valley, and the end of the war once again seemed to draw near. "Grant gives me his unabated confidence," Butler informed Sarah with renewed self-assurance in late September, and two days later, he shared his plans for what he hoped would be a "very conclusive" move by his command. The operation was to begin with an assault on the Confederate defenses at a place known as Chaffin's Farm, or New Market Heights, located high on a bluff above the James River. Following the assault, the Army of the James would march the remaining less than twenty miles into Richmond and take control. "Prepare your Army," Grant ordered Butler on September 27, approving the plan. "The prize sought is either Richmond or Petersburg, or a position which will secure the fall of the latter" as a prelude to the capture of the Confederate capital.[42] Now free of the problematic Smith and Gillmore, Butler welcomed this new opportunity to demonstrate his own military value and that of his army.

In the offensive action that began on September 29, 1864, writes one historian, "movement against the enemy's left was intended to secure a permanent foothold along the southeastern approaches to Richmond, thereby expanding the siege" of Petersburg "to include a direct threat to the Confederate capital." As it actually played out, the plan produced "severe fighting," after which "Butler's forces were able to secure the desired foothold." As Butler explained to Sarah, "Gen. Ord's column [E. O. C. Ord was now commanding the Army of the James's Eighteenth Corps] was to attack the enemy's intrenched camp" at Chaffin's Farm, and "this was most gallantly done." Simultaneously, Gen. David Birney, now commanding the Tenth Corps, "with Paine's Division of colored troops, took the strong works of the enemy at New Market . . . a charge agreed to be the most gallant and dashing of the war." "The result of the movement now in inception is still undecided," reported the *Army and Navy Journal* cautiously on October 8, "but it promises to be momentous."[43]

Despite their early successes, however, Butler and the Army of the James were stymied again when "stiff enemy resistance" precluded any further advance on either Richmond or Petersburg. Instead, over the next several weeks, as the cold weather approached, the men could do little more than construct winter quarters for themselves "in preparation for the anticipated period of low-level activity that would continue until the commencement of the next spring's campaign." To be sure, Butler was disappointed. But he also came away from the events at New Market Heights more profoundly and indelibly impressed than he had been previously by the courage the Black soldiers had displayed and the quiet suffering they had endured. To Sarah, he poignantly described how it felt to witness the bodies of some 200 Black men who had given their lives in the recent assault. The dead, he wrote, "lay with their backs to the earth and their feet to the fore," their "sable faces made by death a ghastly, tawny blue," yet still marked with the "expression of determination" characteristic of those "who die instantly in a charge." "Poor fellows," he reflected with evident respect, even awe:

> they seem to have so little to fight for in this context, with the weight of prejudice loaded upon them, their lives given to a country which has given them not yet justice, not to say fostering care. To us, there is patriotism, fame, love of country, pride, ambition, all to spur us on, but to the negro, none of all these for his guerdon of honor. But there is one boon they love to fight for, freedom for themselves and their race forever, and may my "right hand forget her cunning" but they shall have that. The man who says the negro will not fight is a coward. . . . His soul is blacker than the dead faces of these dead negroes, upturned to heaven in solemn protest against him and his prejudices. I have not been so much moved during this war as I was by this sight.

Days later, when Secretary Stanton informed Butler that he would soon be placing 5,000 more Black soldiers from Kentucky under his command, Butler welcomed them. "I told you they would do well in my Department," he replied. "Their praises are in the mouth of every officer in this Army. Treated fairly and disciplined they have fought most heroically." Soon, too, Butler oversaw the awarding of the first Congressional Medal of Honor to a Black soldier, the Fourth USCT's Sgt. Maj. Christian Fleetwood, in recognition of Fleetwood's courageous conduct under heavy fire at Chaffin's Farm.[44]

Just a couple of weeks before Lincoln's reelection, Sarah, the children, and Harriet returned to Fort Monroe. Lincoln's victory had for a time seemed highly doubtful, given the terrible losses sustained by the Union army so far that spring and summer and the political machinations that resulted. "Politically, the chances are for McClellan," Sarah had written to Butler on August 13, "a strange thing when it was so clearly decided that his career was finished. Lincoln's hopes are less every day." "The present condition of public sentiment," wrote a correspondent from Rochester, New York, a few days later, "is most unfavorable to the President," who "has lost amazingly within a few weeks," and he predicted that "if the public sentiment here affords a fair indication of the public sentiment throughout the country, the popular suffrage to-day would be 'for a change.'" "I have seen and talked with nearly all the leading men in the city," wrote Colonel Shaffer from New York City, "and they all are of one opinion in regard to Lincoln. They consider him defeated." For his part, Shaffer—perhaps with Butler's tacit approval—had begun maneuvering toward a possible surprise nomination of Butler as a presidential candidate. "You can depend that work is begun, and a Call that will startle the country will come," Shaffer informed him. "Nearly all speak of you as the man, but I studiously avoid bringing your name in." The fall of Atlanta changed everything. "Will not this help Lincoln?" Sarah asked. "The good news from Atlanta has set the people wild," Butler agreed. "I think one more success and [McClellan's] chances vanish." Noting again that "Lincoln is gaining," and clearly aware of the interconnectedness of political and military affairs, Sarah now advised her husband to pursue Grant's favor in order to advance his own career. Should Lincoln be reelected, she counseled, "Grant will be the best friend you can have."[45]

Election Day was November 8. A week beforehand, Stanton requested that Grant send troops to New York City to help oversee the election there. Stanton's concern arose from the city's perennial political and racial divisions, which had erupted during the 1863 draft riots, as well as rumors of possible Confederate interference along the lines of the recent raid on St. Albans, Vermont, by Confederate operatives organizing in Canada. Grant selected Butler for this assignment. Because he and his troops would be placed under Gen. John A. Dix's authority, Butler was not keen on the job: "I think," he grumbled to Stanton, "I shall be of more use on the James." Once in New York, however, Butler took to the task with his usual vigor and administrative ability, immediately issuing his General Orders No. 1, in which he declared his determination to protect the right of all eligible voters and to "preserve the peace of the United States, to protect public property, to prevent and punish incursions into our borders, and to insure calm and quiet." Butler's order, reported the *Army and Navy Journal*, "was a characteristic and judicious document," which skillfully navigated between "the curt expression of arbitrary will and a profusion of apologetic explanation." For New Yorkers who might be "alarmed" by the arrival in the city of "a Major-General from the front," assuming it meant "something sinister and perilous," the newspaper insisted that Butler's order took precisely the right tone. "We rejoice," wrote New Yorker S. E. W. Dunham, "that you are in command here." Butler's presence, Dunham observed, "inspires universal confidence that the peace will be kept, which has been so openly threatened."[46]

"All is quiet here," declared Butler on Election Day. Two days later Grant observed that the election—a risky proposition indeed in wartime—had "passed off quietly," not just in New York but also "throughout the land," which he considered "a victory worth more to the country than a battle won." In the eyes of many New Yorkers, Butler deserved all the credit for having maintained calm there. "We attribute the preservation of the peace and good order of the city on the day of the election," noted the Nineteenth Ward's Loyal League Committee, "primarily if not exclusively and entirely to the presence of General Butler in command of this place." These citizens praised Lincoln "for his sagacity and promptness in sending to this post a General endowed with great executive and administrative abilities, energy, and force of character, unyielding firmness, and intensive sagacity, whose presence alone gave assurance of protection to the loyal and peaceable, and of retributive punishment to the disloyal and disorderly." Soon, and with their heads held high, Butler and his men headed back to Virginia, but not before he gave a public speech endorsing the election results and conveying his enthusiastic support for President Lincoln. It is entirely possible that as the war seemed to be drawing to a close, Butler was looking ahead and hoping Lincoln would reciprocate and offer him a cabinet appointment in his second term.[47]

In early December, even as the Dutch Gap project continued, Butler's attention turned to other things, including the recent reorganization of the army, which included combining the Black units of the Army of the James's Eighteenth Corps into an all-USCT Twenty-Fifth Corps under the command of Butler's friend Maj. Gen. Godfrey Weitzel, who had once refused to command Black soldiers at all. Also occupying Butler's mind was a plan to attack Fort Fisher in Wilmington, North Carolina, that he, Grant, and Adm. David Dixon Porter—with whom Butler had collaborated (and tangled) in connection with the capture of New Orleans—were attempting to devise. The successful reduction and capture of Fort Fisher would effectively end Confederate blockade-running by closing the South's last operating port, through which Lee was still drawing supplies for his shrinking, increasingly ragged and hungry army. To accomplish this goal, as Grant later explained it, Butler proposed a scheme that involved intentionally exploding a steamer "loaded heavily with powder" as close to shore as possible below the fort, which would in turn "create great havoc" onshore and thus make the army's work of capturing the fort "an easy matter." Although he himself was doubtful of success, Grant recalled that Admiral Porter "seemed to fall in with the idea." In a late December 1864 letter, Sarah suggested that Porter—whom she had thoroughly distrusted since New Orleans—also believed "the movement would prove a failure."[48]

In the end, Grant approved Butler's plan on the premise that even if it failed, the negative consequences would be minimal. By December 9, the details for the operation were in place, but bad weather and other complications delayed the attack for two more weeks. "What is the prospect of getting your expedition started?" Grant asked on December 14. Finally, late on December 23—two days after Sherman's army arrived in Savannah, Georgia, and a week after Gen. George Thomas completed the destruction of Confederate John Bell Hood's army in Tennessee—the steamer *Louisiana* carrying 235 tons of gunpowder maneuvered "to within about five hundred yards of the shore," timers were set, and the naval crew and all surrounding federal ships once again "put out to sea" for their own and the landing forces' safety. At 2 a.m. on December 24, there was an explosion or, as one historian describes it, "actually four explosions, for the timers did not work and the various powder compartments exploded separately, with the first explosion probably blowing some of the unexploded powder overboard. The force of the blast was thus much diminished, and the current had also dragged the insecurely anchored ship farther from the fort." The effect on the fort itself was negligible.[49]

All was not yet lost, however. In anticipation of landing the several thousand soldiers who still hoped to capture the fort, Admiral Porter's fleet now proceeded with a massive bombardment. How much damage they actually inflicted is contested; what mattered in the end is that although some troops did land safely at some distance from the fort and even captured a nearby Confederate garrison, once they actually began to approach the fort itself, they deemed it insufficiently damaged and determined not to proceed. Porter subsequently insisted that his fleet had weakened the fort more than enough to enable its capture. General Weitzel, however, disagreed, having concluded that the fort "was left substantially uninjured" by Porter's bombardment and therefore "could not be carried by assault." Concurring with Weitzel, Butler ordered the ground troops and their prisoners to withdraw to the transport vessels and return to Fort Monroe. Butler's decision on this particular occasion, writes one recent historian, represented "an unusual instance of military sagacity," taking the form of an unwillingness to subject his soldiers to what would likely be a bloodbath. For his part, however, although he admitted that uncontrollable delays and bad weather had contributed to the operation's failure, Grant believed that Butler had "made a fearful mistake" by ordering the retreat, which then allowed the Confederates to reinforce the fort and the surrounding area. "My instructions to him," Grant wrote later, "were explicit in the statement that to effect a landing would be of itself a great victory, and if one should be effected, the foothold must not be relinquished." Unfortunately, Grant continued, "General Butler seems to have lost sight of this part of his instructions."[50]

Porter, too, was angry, believing that his naval forces had completed their particular assignment and that responsibility for the failure to capture Fort Fisher was Butler's alone. "The record of the Wilmington expedition is now closed," the *Army and Navy Journal* soon reported, "and it is to be added to the list of failures for the year 1864." Taking the widest possible view, however, the paper advised that "this single and comparatively trifling dash of defeat comes in the midst of a great wave of triumph, and it can be borne with equanimity." The *Journal* then assigned blame to both Butler *and* Porter, who soon published his own self-serving account of the expedition. According to the *Journal*, echoing criticism that had followed the Big Bethel fiasco years earlier, Butler himself should have landed with the troops and personally examined the situation rather than relying on his subordinate, Weitzel. Still, the *Journal* insisted, it was wrong for Porter—a naval officer—to make claims about what the land forces could or could not have accomplished. Subsequently, Grant, Porter, and Maj. Gen. Alfred H. Terry organized a second assault on the fort, which proved successful but bloody. "I have the honor to report," Terry wrote on January 16, 1865, "that Fort Fisher was carried by assault this afternoon and evening," but, he added, "I regret to say our loss is severe, especially in officers." "Porter has caused a useless slaughter of life," Weitzel grumbled, "and it should be known to the people."[51]

As 1864 came to a close, Butler's Dutch Gap project, too, seemed destined to produce disappointing results and at considerable human cost. "At first," reported the *Army and Navy Journal*, "the detail was large," but over the months the number of men available and strong enough to undertake such heavy labor had varied widely. Moreover, those soldiers who were deployed—most of them Black—suffered severely from both illness and enemy fire, though many of them learned to carve protective "shelters and bomb-proofs" in the banks of the river to improve their chances of survival. At one point Butler sought to counteract some of the Confederates' cruelty, not just toward the men digging the canal but also toward the many Black

The Dutch Gap project, by Alfred R. Waud. Courtesy of the Prints and Photographs Division, Library of Congress, Washington, D.C.

soldiers being held in prison camps: in addition to publicly challenging Robert Ould to ensure that the Black men were treated fairly, in mid-October Butler briefly ordered that Confederate prisoners of war be detailed to labor on the canal project in the same numbers as the Black prisoners being forced into labor by the Confederate army.[52]

Butler had predicted the Dutch Gap project would take ten days; in fact it took almost four months of hard, debilitating labor to produce a canal "522 feet long, and about 120 feet wide at the top, and 40 feet wide at the bottom, and about 70 feet deep." And then, the *Army and Navy Journal* reported gloomily, "when the bulkheads holding back the river" were finally blown up on January 1, 1865, "the earth rose to a considerable height, but obstinately fell back into the canal," blocking any passage. Though later that month the canal was in fact finally opened, as the new year began Butler's engineering project, which had occupied so many men at such horrendous physical peril for months, seemed to have been "rendered useless," adding fuel to his opponents' claims that he was incompetent and should be sacked.[53]

"The New Year has come," wrote Sarah as 1865 dawned. "What does it bring to you and I?" In the wake of Lincoln's reelection, the failed Fort Fisher expedition, and the Dutch Gap flop, what the new year brought was the end of Butler's US Army career. "I am constrained to request the removal of Major General B. F. Butler from the command of the Department of Virginia and North Carolina," Grant informed Secretary Stanton on January 5. "I do this with reluctance, but the good of the service requires it." Grant further pointed to a "lack of confidence" in Butler's "military ability"— precisely whose lack of confidence, he did not specify—and, also without further elaboration, to the "objectionable" quality of his "administration of the affairs of his Department." Lincoln approved Grant's request, and on January 7, Halleck issued the order installing General Ord in Butler's place. The following day, embittered and convinced that his removal was a direct response to his unwillingness to sacrifice his soldiers unnecessarily at Fort Fisher (or elsewhere), Butler nevertheless gave the men of the Army of the James a rousing farewell address full of praise and encouragement and devoting specific attention to the USCT troops. "You brave black soldiers of the Army of the James," Butler declared with deep and sincere appreciation, have "shown yourselves worthy of the uniform you wear," "won the admiration even of those who would be your masters," "illustrated the best qualities of manhood," and "unlocked the iron-barred gates of prejudice, opening new fields of freedom, liberty, and equality of right to yourselves and your race forever." In the future, Butler promised, "your General's proudest memory will be to say with you, 'I, too, was of the Army of the James.'"[54]

"General Butler's star," observed the *Army and Navy Journal* a week later, "so lately in the zenith, has sunk below the horizon." For now, however, the paper chose not to amplify the abundant criticism Butler's foes gleefully heaped upon him, which Butler himself later referred to in his usual wry way as "the delightful stream of obloquy which is pouring upon me." Instead, the paper observed that many officers—regular army officers included—had been "glad to have him come among them" with his impressive administrative talents and his "remarkable energy, keen insight, and vigor," all of which they were pleased to see used to the country's advantage. Butler's struggles only came, the *Journal* theorized, when he was given responsibilities for which, as a civilian general, "experience had not fitted him," and which he unfortunately never saw fit to refuse. In any case, having made invaluable contributions to the Union's war effort, Butler could now enjoy "the consciousness of having played a distinguished role in our war, with whose history his name is inseparably connected." For, the paper insisted, "everybody must concede his excellence as an executive officer, as a man of shrewdness, vigor, administrative ability, and skill and practice in state-craft." The *Journal* then laid out the long list of Butler's wartime accomplishments, taking special note of the "world-wide significance" of the contraband policy he had initiated in May 1861 and observing, in connection with his disappointing performances on the field of battle, that in fact "most of our leading generals have committed quite as serious errors." In closing, the *Journal* reminded readers not to consider its "little sketch of General Butler's career" the equivalent of "an obituary." Rather, "we trust that he will yet be of use to the country," if not in the army, then "in a more congenial and appropriate sphere."[55]

Letters of support poured in. "If all the Generals had been of your patriotism, and courage, and stern spirit," wrote one friend, "the rebellion would have been swept away in 6 months." The ever-loyal James Parton angrily declared Butler's removal "the work of ill-wishers," all of whom—"Meade, Hooker, Burnside, Banks, Grant"—had "made prodigious and bloody failures," without being subjected to the same sort of punishment. "It was only because it was *you*," Parton insisted, "that they were in such a desperate hurry to strike." For his part, in a letter to Grant's chief of staff, Butler resisted the temptation to complain that he had been dismissed simply because he was not a West Point alumnus and professional officer, which some of his allies believed to be the case. "To put the removal on the ground that I was the last of the 'civilian generals,'" he wrote, "brings an issue between the regulars and volunteers, and I assure you that the person who penned that does not love the General [Grant] or else is as stupid as a Quartermaster who would let the horses of a whole army starve for want of forage when there is plenty in the country if he had a little energy to get it." Meanwhile, he gratefully welcomed the words of support he received. "I cannot describe my regret at your leaving the Dept.," wrote D. D. Bulman from the provost marshal's office at Fort Monroe. "I shall look forward to, and pray for the time to come, when you shall be reinstated with all the honor due your worth, and your enemies made to feel their meanness." "I suppose that your refusal to attack Fort Fisher was the noblest action of your life," wrote James Freeman Clarke, "and yet it is the one which will bring the most unpopularity to you." "The Powers were only waiting for a pretext to remove you," wrote Colonel Shaffer, and Fort Fisher provided it. "Give Mrs. Butler my compliments," he added, "and say to her that I have ordered your portrait by Antrobus sent to her, which I wish her to accept as a token of my regard for her and as an acknowledgment of her many kindnesses."[56]

Three weeks after its initial coverage of Butler's removal, the *Army and Navy Journal* adopted a different tone, now reporting with apparent surprise that back in Lowell, Butler had begun spreading the theory that his removal *had* been politically motivated, not because he was a civilian general but because he had acted to protect his troops from unnecessary bloodshed at Fort Fisher and thus made commanders who freely squandered their men's blood (including those who were drawn from the professional military class) look bad. On January 29, before a huge gathering at Lowell's Huntington

Hall, Butler vigorously defended his leadership in the Department of Virginia and North Carolina generally, and at Fort Fisher specifically, observing that in contrast with many of the West Point alumni, "when we of the volunteer army of the United States make failures, we do not make disasters." In this speech, Butler further drew attention to his work on behalf of the tens of thousands of desperate runaways from slavery for whom he had taken responsibility when he arrived in the department, creating a system that provided them with work as well as food, shelter, and educational opportunities, and brought thousands of the men into the US Army. Butler reminded listeners of his efforts to create a fair system of prisoner exchange, especially as the exchange related to Black soldiers. In conclusion, he expressed his ongoing willingness to serve the country however he was needed, while insisting that a "lasting peace" would come only "provided we deal justly by all men, white and black." Absent "fair play, justice, equality before the law, for black and white," peace "will never stand."[57]

Reporting on Butler's provocative speech, the *Army and Navy Journal* now predicted that the former commander of the Army of the James "will never again be permitted to assume a military position" and, moreover, that even Butler himself probably "never expects to do so" or he would have held his tongue. Apparently disgusted, the paper went so far as to characterize Butler's speech as "strongly savoring of insubordination," and backhandedly described Butler's deep commitment to his Black troops as evidence that "in the chess of politics, Butler evidently proposes to play always with the black pieces." Its patience exhausted, the *Journal* warned that "an officer who enters the Army gives up some of that privilege of broad and minute criticism which civil life in a free country permits," and that Butler had violated that principle. Others used the opportunity of Butler's Huntington Hall speech to launch new attacks on his character. "Butler," wrote one anonymous correspondent, "you are at heart a vagabond . . . coward . . . poltroon . . . jackass . . . viper . . . brazen, impudent bag of wind . . . an imposter and a damned scoundrel." Some, however, echoed Abram Ely of Oswego, New York, who read the published version of Butler's speech and then filled a letter with words of ardent support, which he closed with the statement: "You are my candidate for the next President."[58]

History will do substantially right by us all. We who have tried to do our duty with singleness of purpose, to the best of our abilities, will have that place which is accorded to conscientious patriotism. If in anything history fails, we shall have at least the approval of our own hearts and consciences, which after all is the greatest reward.
—BUTLER, DECEMBER 1865

I come to you, the successor of noble old Thad Stevens,
for assistance. . . . I am a colored man.
—EDWIN BELCHER TO BUTLER, APRIL 1869

Reconstruction Congressman
1865–1874

Benjamin Butler's return to Massachusetts did not end the robust debate over the reasons for his removal from command in the Department of Virginia and North Carolina, nor did another appearance before Congress's investigative Joint Committee on the Conduct of the War, before whom Butler vigorously—and, from the committee's perspective, successfully—defended his wartime performance. Meanwhile, as winter gave way to spring in 1865 and the war ground inexorably toward Union victory, Butler (along with his supporters and his foes) wondered what lay ahead for him professionally. Ideally, he would find a consequential outlet in the postwar world for his legal training and skills and for the experience, knowledge, and political insights he had gained during the war. Butler dearly hoped, furthermore, to find suitable ways to use his undeniable stature as a leader in the intertwined processes of emancipation, arming Black soldiers, and laying the foundation for Black Americans' claims to the full rights and responsibilities of citizenship. His enemies' harsh and enduring criticisms aside, inquiries such as the one he received in late January 1865 from Hiram Barney of New York—who sought guidance for establishing a "safe depository for the colored soldiers and laborers to place their surplus earnings upon interest," in other words, "a Trust Company of Savings Bank for the freed-men"—only heightened Butler's sense that he had a unique combination of skills and experiences to contribute as Reconstruction began in earnest.[1]

Even as his professional future remained unclear, in the early months of 1865 Butler welcomed numerous invitations to give speeches, in which he consistently and vigorously promoted the cause of Black Americans' civil and—for Black men and Black veterans especially—political rights. As part of a celebration of Congress's January 31, 1865, passage of the Thirteenth Amendment to the US Constitution abolishing slavery, Butler shared his thoughts in early February at the Music Hall in Boston. There he spoke about the future of the freedpeople and his vehement opposition to the idea that they should accept "colonization" outside of the United States. "What true citizenship is it," he demanded, "to be deprived of their equal rights in the land their arms have helped to save from the fiery furnace of rebellion?" Rather, Butler proposed that every Black man must be allowed to "enjoy the right of selecting his place of labor; the person for whom he will labor, if not for himself; to make his own contract for his labor," and "to deter-mine its length and its value." Butler also addressed the issue of government assistance for the formerly enslaved, which he considered an absolute—if temporary—obligation, a form of reparations for centuries of injustice that had left millions of Black Americans in a dependent state. Now was the time for the government to take action to develop the freedpeople's indepen-dence by establishing schools to prepare them for citizenship and providing them with "a fair share of the lands" they had already worked for genera-tions. Only in this way could the "freedman" (by which he usually meant the freedpeople generally) be "furnished" with "the means of beginning that life which justice, equal laws and equal rights have for the first time opened up to him and his children forever." Only after the freedpeople had access to the necessary tools to become truly independent could White Americans step back and hope "to receive the pardon of the Almighty for the sins we and our fathers have committed towards him."[2]

Black Americans did not fail to notice and express gratitude for Butler's speeches on their behalf, further enhancing his belief that he had a special role to play in the coming postwar period. Days after he addressed the Music Hall gathering, the Black chaplain of the First USCT Infantry Regiment, Henry McNeal Turner, expressed his appreciation. "There was never a man more beloved than you were by the colored troops," wrote Turner. "They not only regarded you as their invincible friend" and "one in whose hands their interests and rights were safe," but Black men who had served in the Army of the James also knew that Butler had "done more to raise them to man-hood than all the other Generals who have lived." Turner now boldly pre-dicted that Butler's name, "like Jesus of Nazareth," would "stand chiseled in the principles of justice and righteousness as long as God shall revolve this world." Soon Butler established a "Butler Scholarship" for the sons of wounded soldiers, White *and* Black, at Andover Academy in Massachusetts. In his letter of thanks, the school's treasurer promised, "We shall be glad to have you send in the 'contrabands,' or the 'sons of Erin,' or the lad of any other race and nationality, to enjoy its benefits."[3]

One of the possible futures Butler imagined for himself in this period was to fill a cabinet seat in Lincoln's second administration. Surely Lincoln would want representatives of the Republican Party's powerful Radical wing—who endorsed stern punishment for the rebels as well as real social and racial transformation in the South—in his new cabinet, if only to mollify them. Although he technically remained a Democrat, Butler's politics increasingly aligned with the goals of the Radical Republicans, not least their deter-mination to advance Black Americans' rights, so perhaps he could fill that slot? From such a post, Butler believed he could influence federal policy in effective and knowledgeable ways, and in early March he quietly suggested himself as a possible cabinet nominee to a key Radical leader, Ohio senator Benjamin Franklin Wade. "Of course I do not mean to have this made an open matter, evoking opposition," Butler advised Wade. "What I want is a quiet movement, which shall justify the President in doing that which will relieve him of having berated me unjustly [referring to Fort Fisher and But-ler's removal from command] if he should desire to do so, as I think he may."[4]

Butler waited in vain for an appointment, however, as Richmond fell, Lee surrendered his Army of Northern Virginia, and Lincoln was murdered. Days after the assassination Butler returned to Washington to press his case for a cabinet position with the new president, Andrew Johnson, whose early bluster toward the defeated Confederacy's leadership sounded much like the punitive rage Butler and the Radicals shared. Johnson did meet with Butler at least once, on April 28, and perhaps it was then that the new president encouraged him to "make suggestions of such thoughts as may strike [you] in relation to public affairs." For his part, Senator Wade was optimistic that Johnson would appoint Butler to replace the indefinitely incapacitated sec-retary of state, William Seward, still recovering from the grievous wounds he sustained when he was attacked on the night of Lincoln's assassination. "I have great faith in Mr. Johnson, and believe he is entirely sound on all these subjects," wrote Wade on May 9. "I know he holds you and your counsels in the highest estimation, and it seems to me while these great questions are pending you ought to reside near the throne." But as Butler's former chief of staff J. W. Shaffer soon wrote from D.C., "No one appears to have any idea what Johnson will do; as far as I can learn he has scarcely consulted anyone, and is waiting to see what will turn up."[5] Indeed, in late May Johnson stunned many observers by adopting a generous policy of conciliation and forgiveness toward the former Confederacy. The chances of him bringing anyone associated with Wade or the Radicals into his cabinet basically dropped to zero.

An alternative future Butler envisioned for himself as the war wound down was in some sort of leadership role connected with the Bureau of Refugees, Freedmen, and Abandoned Lands, created in March 1865 as an agency of the War Department to facilitate early postwar Reconstruction in the South, primarily but not exclusively relating to the freedpeople. Prominent figures among Butler's friends enthusiastically endorsed this idea, especially those who admired what the schools for the contraband near Fort Monroe and elsewhere had already achieved. Of the Normal School in Hampton— today, Hampton University—which Butler had initially staffed with "convalescent and disabled soldiers," Salmon P. Chase, now chief justice of the US Supreme Court, wrote, "the building is admirable, and the whole arrangement and management seem all that could be hoped for under the circumstances." Butler's interest in protecting the educational work he and various philanthropic agencies from the North had begun in the area only deepened as he learned that the federal government and relevant missionary societies were feuding over possible changes that might result in fewer Black children having access. At the same time, Butler also believed he had valuable insights to offer regarding the best economic and agricultural policies for the defeated South, not least because of his wartime creation in New Orleans of a wage labor system for producing sugar. Significantly for the future economic independence of the freedpeople, Butler recommended that Johnson issue an executive order declaring that "he who sows or plants shall also reap," and that "his right in the product of the soil produced by his labor and care shall appertain to him."[6] Johnson chose not to heed this advice.

Indeed, as Johnson raced toward conciliation, Butler's speeches consistently, eloquently, and uncompromisingly made clear that *he* was moving in the opposite direction, which thrilled those who were similarly troubled by Johnson's leniency. Even before Johnson officially revealed his policy of appeasement toward the former Confederacy, a standing-room-only crowd at the Union League Club in New York enthusiastically applauded Butler's stern proposals for Reconstruction. Although Butler still described himself as an "old-fashioned Democrat," much of his speech on this occasion could easily have been drafted by Pennsylvania's Thaddeus Stevens, perhaps the most radical of the Radicals in Congress. "Until some means are devised to enable the Southern people to govern themselves in the Union," Butler thundered, "disorder must be repressed, peace preserved, crimes punished, and the industrious and well-doing protected by the military powers of the United States." As Secretary of War Stanton had done during President Lincoln's final cabinet meeting, Butler urged the appointment of military governors for the states formerly in rebellion; perhaps he also hoped to be chosen for such a post. These military governors, he declared, "should be selected as much for their knowledge of civil affairs as of 'army regulations,'" and should be charged with ensuring that all new state constitutions explicitly and permanently forbade slavery, secession, the assumption of the Confederate debt, and the voting rights of Confederate military and political leaders. Until such principles were enshrined in their constitutions, Butler insisted, the states of the former Confederacy must be kept "under military rule as belligerent" entities. Eventually, he predicted, "the influx of Northern enterprise, capital and sentiment brought in by our brave soldiers coming there to settle, and by our school teachers educating the colored citizens of the United States therein dwelling" would alter the rebel states' cultures enough to fit them for readmission to the Union. And if it took a century for that to happen, he shrugged, so be it. Success depended on the complete destruction of "the landholding and slaveholding aristocracy of the South, which has brought so much of evil upon us," Butler insisted, along with establishment of permanent protections for the freedpeople's rights and welfare.[7]

Butler gave many such public speeches in the spring and summer of 1865, and he shared his views on Reconstruction and the future of the freedpeople extensively with his correspondents, too. "Have we liberated the negro to hate him; fought for his emancipation for four years only to deepen our dislike to him; called upon him to stand side by side with us in the shock of arms, our dead buried on the same battlefields with him in a common grave, only to intensify our pride of Race?" he asked rhetorically in one letter. "Have we broken up a social condition, which at least he found tolerable [sic], to put him in one where his existence is an impossibility?" Butler's bold persistence on issues of race relations brought numerous accolades. In July, the Massachusetts branch of the Army and Navy Union, a veterans' organization, elected him president. Surely more gratifying, however, was the early August resolution of the Colored Men's Convention of Virginia, expressing gratitude to "all true friends of their race," but especially to Butler, "who first decided the fate of slavery" at Fort Monroe and since then had earned "the greatest share" of Black Virginians' "love and respect." That same month, organizers of an Emancipation celebration involving Blacks from southern New York State and northern Pennsylvania invited Butler to address their gathering, calling him "our best friend." In his letter acknowledging the invitation, Butler reiterated his increasingly familiar views and offered encouragement. "Let the colored people maintain their rights as citizens with dignity [and] forbearance," he wrote, "under the wrongs which will be put upon them by prejudice and ignorance. Let them show by industry and frugality and obedience to the laws that they are worthy of those rights, and I am sure, as the sun shines on the just and the unjust, they shall attain every right which belongs to the citizens of the United States." That summer Butler commissioned the US Mint to strike the "Butler Medal" as a tribute to the USCT veterans of the Army of the James. "I wish very much to procure one of them," wrote Andrew Johnson's secretary, R. D. Mussey, although he admitted, "I am not a 'colored soldier,' nor have I 'ever shown conspicuous bravery.'"[8]

In early September, Sarah confided to a friend that neither his removal from army command nor even the end of the war had produced measurable leisure time for her husband of more than twenty years. Fortunately, she noted, he was able to find some relaxation each day playing billiards—"We have an exquisite table," she boasted—and in any case, Butler much preferred working to being on vacation. Good thing, too, as final preparations for the Massachusetts Republican Party's state convention, scheduled for September 14 in Worcester, were underway, and the Republican Caucus in Lowell had opted to nominate Butler as a "delegate at large." Still officially (if not philosophically) a member of the Democratic Party, Butler accepted the nomination and then took the opportunity at the convention to reiterate his vision for Reconstruction and declare Andrew Johnson's "experiment" in managing the process "a failure." "If we are to go on as we are now tending," he had informed Senator Wade some weeks earlier, "I certainly do not desire to take part in the Government. All is wrong—we are losing the just results of this four years' struggle." In Worcester, Butler pointed to the many "instances of ill treatment of the negroes and other outrages" that had taken place in the South on Johnson's watch, as well as the frequency and shamelessness with which former Confederates across the region were now openly demonstrating their disdain for federal authority, the occupation forces, the rule of law, and the basic rights of the freedpeople. Butler now even went so

Wife Sarah Hildreth Butler. Photographer unknown. Courtesy of the
Ames Family Papers, Sophia Smith Collection, SSC-MS-00003, Smith
College Special Collections, Northampton, Massachusetts.

far as to publicly endorse Black male suffrage "and the power of the general
government to establish it" as a counterweight to white supremacist resurgence in the South. Butler's convention remarks were well received by the
attendees, though the *Springfield (Mass.) Weekly Republican* complained that
he had "used up too much time" with his speech, leaving too little time for
the convention's "remaining work."[9]

Observers from Maine to Louisiana and west to California studied, and
frequently celebrated, Butler's current course as the logical extension of
Union victory in the war, and many sought his advice. In early October,

Butler heard from Gen. Harris Merrill Plaisted, a Waterville College alumnus (class of 1853) and future governor of Maine who had served with Butler in Virginia in 1864. Plaisted reported that their alma mater had decided to build "a *Memorial Hall*, in honor of her sons fallen in the war, and also to found a *Military Professorship* in connection with the college." The committee assigned to bring these plans to fruition, Plaisted explained, was eager above all for Butler's input. Butler thanked Plaisted for his confidence: "I am sure nothing can be a higher reward to a General for services done," he wrote, "than to possess the good will and respect of those gallant, brave, and deserving officers who have served with him. My greatest satisfaction is to believe that quite all of my good officers have given me their love and respect." With his usual humor, he added, "It is almost an equal delight to think that quite all the vicious ones hate me intensely."[10]

Butler surely derived great satisfaction, too, from a letter from Thomas W. Conway, directing Freedmen's Bureau affairs in Louisiana, informing him that "your name among the poor whites, and especially with all the colored people" in New Orleans "is spoken with a feeling which would make the impression upon the mind of a stranger that they regarded you as a God." Added Conway, "Were you to put your feet upon the streets of this city, fifty thousand people would desire to pave your pathway with rich flowers." Black New Orleanians especially, Conway reported, "esteem you as their deliverer." Butler also heard from Clara Barton, eventually the Civil War's most famous (but hardly only) woman nurse, who sought his advice in connection with her efforts to identify all 13,000 Federal soldiers, Black and White, who had died at Andersonville Prison. Barton reminded Butler that "I too was of the Army of the James," and thanked him profusely for his support, advice, and friendship. "You have comprehended me when others could not," she wrote, "and proffered me aid and sympathy when others would not, and I only know that when my arm grows weak, and my eye dim, the mention of your name must recall momentary strength to the one, and rekindle the fading light in the other."[11]

Butler officially resigned his army commission at the end of October, effective November 30. "I retained my commission from May till November," Butler explained to a correspondent months later, "at the request of President Johnson, so that I might be employed on the trial of [Jefferson] Davis if he was to be tried by Military Commission," which did not happen. Although Butler was no longer a US Army officer, his emotional and political ties to the military endured, especially when it came to the Black veterans of the Army of the James. Late in November, unable to attend a public reception honoring a Pennsylvania USCT regiment in Harrisburg, Butler sent a letter of tribute, fondly addressing the veterans as "my colored fellow-soldiers" and praising them richly for their "patience and discipline in the camp," their "bravery and good conduct on the battle-field," and, "above all, their devotion and unswerving loyalty to the flag and the Government." According to a reporter from *The Liberator*, when Butler's letter was read aloud at the gathering "the applause was deafening." With good reason, too, for Butler's efforts to influence government policy in favor of the freedpeople in the South, the veterans of the USCT, and Black Americans generally continued unabated. By the late fall he went on record supporting an amendment to the US Constitution that would guarantee Black Americans' equal rights as citizens, "overturn the lingering remains of the authority of the Dred Scott decision," and undermine the ghastly "Black Codes" that were being passed across the states of the former Confederacy. "The fact is," wrote J. W. Shaffer to his former boss during a visit to the South, "that if something is not done, the negroes will turn on the whites, and who can blame them? Use your influence," he urged, "and have something done."[12] Butler was trying.

On December 6, 1865—two days after the Thirty-Ninth Congress convened and refused to seat the newly elected representatives from the South—the Thirteenth Amendment to the US Constitution was ratified. That same month, Ulysses Grant's final report on the war appeared. While the amendment's ratification and Congress's rejection of the southern representatives pleased Butler greatly, Grant's report did not; instead, it temporarily reopened (and salted) the original wound Grant had inflicted by dismissing Butler from army command at the start of the year. "It is generally admitted," the *Army and Navy Journal* noted, "that General Butler receives the largest proportion of the adverse criticism of this Report." Convinced that Grant had once again treated him with undue harshness with respect to both the Bermuda Hundred campaign and the initial attempt on Fort Fisher, Butler promised a friend the report would be "met in due time by the inexorable truth of history," which he certainly meant to have a hand in crafting. Supporters encouraged Butler to write his own report of the events in question and remind the public again of everything he had achieved on the Union's behalf, often in the face of seemingly insurmountable obstacles. "If Gen. Butler had had the same chance at Washington City that Grant started with," wrote one advocate, "Butler would have captured Richmond six months before Grant started."[13]

One might suppose that Butler's efforts to defend his wartime performance while simultaneously analyzing and seeking solutions to the vexing problems of Reconstruction would amount to sufficient labor for a forty-seven-year-old with a family, a profession, and a variety of business investments to manage. A man of prodigious energy, however, Butler also found time in the early postwar period to establish the United States Bunting Company in Lowell, which eventually employed some 2,000 workers. The company's aim was to produce, for the first time in the United States, bunting fabric and related products, especially flags, which had previously always been imported from England. By December 1865 Butler's new company was fully up and running, at which time he proudly requested from the clerk of the US House of Representatives the dimensions of the American flags that traditionally flew at the Capitol. Within a few weeks, one of the company's agents delivered the first American-made flag—twenty-one by twelve feet in size—to be "hoisted to the Senatorial flag-staff, and unfurled to the breeze." Meanwhile, Butler also devoted time and energy to reviving his legal practice. The war, he told one aspiring lawyer and former soldier, had "broken up my business and position as a lawyer, and left me completely stranded." By early 1866, Butler's law firm was fully back in operation, and press reports show him appearing once more as an attorney before the Massachusetts Supreme Judicial Court.[14]

Indeed, that March, Butler's legal career got a high-profile boost from his involvement in the US Supreme Court's consideration of *Ex Parte Milligan*, which examined, as the *Boston Daily Advertiser* explained to its readers, "the whole question of the jurisdiction of military tribunals and martial law" during the war. In this case, Butler, Attorney General James Speed, and Henry Stanbery (who replaced Speed as attorney general later that year) appeared for the government, Butler offering what one historian has described as "breathtakingly broad positions in defense of military commissions" that centered the argument for the wartime powers of the federal government on the Emancipation Proclamation. Former attorney general Jeremiah Black, David Dudley Field, and James A. Garfield appeared for the plaintiff, Lambdin Milligan, who—with others—in the fall of 1864 had been tried and convicted by a military commission in Indiana of conspiracy against the federal government (as well as other disloyal practices), even though the civil courts were in operation there. Now the case had made its way to the Supreme Court, and in early April 1866 in his capacity as chief justice, Butler's old friend Salmon P. Chase handed down the court's ruling. Although the full majority opinion and the concurrences in the case did not become public until the end of the year, the decision constituted a ringing defeat of the government's (and Butler's) case, denying the legitimacy of the military commission's jurisdiction in 1864 Indiana and, by extension, anytime anywhere that civil courts were open. The Court further ordered that Milligan and his cohorts be freed from the Ohio penitentiary where they had been in custody.[15]

"I am vexed in spirit and weary beyond thought," Butler wrote gloomily to Sarah from Washington in the wake of the decision. As his willingness to execute William Mumford in New Orleans in 1862 demonstrated, Butler as a wartime military commander had generally adopted a stern and uncompromising stance when confronted with civilian opposition to the Federal cause. The end of the war had not altered his stance, and his low spirits in the spring of 1866 also reflected his deepening concern over the direction Reconstruction seemed to be heading, including what he considered Congress's refusal to adequately challenge Andrew Johnson's conciliatory vision for (White) national reunion with all of its concomitant perils for the freedpeople. "I fear all is lost in Congress," he told Sarah, observing that Congress's Joint Committee on Reconstruction now seemed unlikely even to consider the issue of Black male suffrage, which he had begun promoting months earlier. He was pleased and honored that spring, when the Massachusetts state senate elected him major general of the state militia, but what he really wanted was a way to have a significant impact on Reconstruction policy, even as he also yearned for more time at home with his family. Then came the call to serve on the board of managers of the newly created National Asylum (later National Homes) for Disabled Volunteer Soldiers (NHDVS), which had been created on paper at the same time as the Freedmen's Bureau but was only just becoming a reality. In mid-May 1866 the *Lowell Daily Citizen and News* reported that the specific sites for the future asylums remained to be determined, but they must be "situated in the loyal States," should be at least 200 acres in size, and be "in healthy locations" that were "easily accessible by railroad or otherwise." Over the next few weeks, all "proposals, specifications and estimates and plans" were to be sent to Butler, who quickly went from being a board member to being board president. In October, on Butler's recommendation, the former Togus Springs Hotel outside of Augusta, Maine—which continues today as the Togus Veterans Administration Medical Center—began operating as the first asylum in the system.[16]

Butler continued giving speeches throughout the spring and summer of 1866. These included another one at the Music Hall in Boston shortly before the deadly race massacre in Memphis, Tennessee, in which he declared that the federal government's core principles should be "justice to all men, equality of right, equality of protection, and equality of power under the government." From Butler's perspective, "those who would hinder the operation of these principles must be put aside," and he again decried Johnson's approach to Reconstruction, which could only have succeeded "if all the people in the South were loyal." To the contrary, "those who have been fighting us for four years don't love us and don't love the Union; and the fact that they have abolished slavery because they were forced to, doesn't make them love us any better." Butler advised "keeping the rebel states out of the Union until they have demonstrated their loyalty" and called for a federal constitutional amendment stipulating that "every citizen of the United States shall have equal powers and rights in the several States"; "representatives shall be apportioned among the several States according to their respective numbers"; "no rebel shall have the right to vote for members of Congress, and for electors for President and Vice-President of the United States" until 1870; and "neither the United States nor any State shall assume or pay any debt or obligation already incurred, or which may hereafter be incurred in aid of insurrection or of war against the United States, or any claim for compensation for loss of involuntary service or labor." Butler further recommended excluding Confederate military and political leaders from *ever* holding elected office, and called for the enactment of a series of measures designed, on the one hand, to destroy the power of those who had led the South into rebellion and, on the other, to ensure protections "for the rights of those men" who "have fought side by side with us" to defend the government. Among such protections Butler again highlighted the importance of granting Black men the right to vote. "When we gave the musket to the colored man," he explained, "we promised in the presence of high heaven to give him the ballot." He then added words that he would repeat many times in the decades ahead, and that were eventually carved on his gravestone: "Every man has a right, because he is a man, to be the equal of any other man if he can."[17] The following month the Thirty-Ninth Congress passed the Fourteenth Amendment, which incorporated many of the principles Butler had lifted up; the amendment then went out to the states for consideration and was ratified two years later.

By the end of the summer of 1866, which witnessed another eruption of racist violence in July—this time in New Orleans—Butler's views on Reconstruction and the need to guarantee the future welfare of the freedpeople were indelibly clear. Those who shared his perspective were thrilled to have such a prominent, eloquent, irrepressible figure in their corner, and many urged him to run for Congress as a Republican. In early September Butler further advanced his growing reputation as a solid ally for Black Americans by joining Frederick Douglass at an assembly of southern Unionists in Philadelphia, the Southern Loyalists' Convention. This gathering came hard on the heels of the August 1866 National Union Convention in the same city, where Andrew Johnson had launched his appalling "Swing around the Circle" lecture tour. According to the *Massachusetts Spy*, "the most noticeable feature, politically" of the convention Butler and Douglass attended, especially in contrast with the gathering the previous month, was the attendees' "intense radicalism" and commitment to social and racial transformation in the South. "Everywhere and under all circumstances," the *Spy* observed, "there was no strong word uttered, no radical thought or plan expressed or proposed . . . which was not greeted with the heartiest mark of approval." Moreover, the figure whose "distinctly radical sentiments" received the greatest praise and the "mightiest applause" was Butler, for reasons the *Spy* deemed "obvious": "New Orleans was fresh in the mind of all," and "they remembered the soldier-executive who of all others has best taught the nation how to conquer rebellious sentiments and govern those who hold them."[18]

With the congressional election looming in November, Massachusetts Republicans grew even more determined to put Butler forward as one of their candidates. On September 6, the *Salem Register* reported that "several hundred" Republican leaders in the state's Fifth District—which did not include Lowell, but did include Cape Ann, where the Butlers had their elegant summer residence, Bay View—signed a letter begging him to run under their banner for that district's House seat, believing he alone could "truly represent the prevailing sentiments" of the party "in this the severest trial of our country's existence." Butler agreed: his views on Reconstruction clearly echoed those of Radicals like Benjamin Wade and Thaddeus Stevens, so it made sense for him to join their party and run as a Republican, even if it meant abandoning the Democratic Party that had for so long been his political home. Less than two weeks later, Butler not only attended the Republican State Convention at Faneuil Hall in Boston but presided over it. Subsequently, Butler gave a series of speeches around the state reiterating his views on Reconstruction, Black Americans' rights, and his growing opposition to President Johnson. "May my right hand forget its cunning, and my tongue cleave to the roof of my mouth," Butler declared in Salem in late September, "before I will allow any of the rights of those glorious black men who stood my equals in arms, in the Army of the James, to be trampled on. I prefer," he added, "to have a black man by my side with a rifle pointed from me, rather than a reconstructed rebel with the muzzle of his gun pointing toward me." Once again Butler openly advocated Black male suffrage.[19]

Butler campaigned widely in Massachusetts; he also extended his reach by traveling west to meet with supporters there. In Cleveland, Ohio, in early October, Butler spoke at the elegant Kennard House, where Johnson had recently defended his controversial (and congressionally overridden) vetoes of the Freedmen's Bureau and civil rights bills and had gone on to provoke his audience with questions like, "Why don't you hang Thad. Stevens and Wendell Phillips?" and "What constitutional provisions have I violated?" When Butler visited Cleveland, reported the *Massachusetts Spy*, he joked, "If the President had asked, what constitutional provision have I NOT violated, his task would have been easy." Butler then presented what might easily have served as an early draft of the future articles of impeachment against the president, declaring that Johnson "had formed, and put into execution a deliberate plan to bring the Congress of the United States into public hatred, ridicule, and contempt"; "corruptly and wickedly used his constitutional power of removal and appointment to office"; "usurped the powers of Congress in establishing the basis of peace"; and "nullified its statute in regard to captured and confiscated property." The people of the country, Butler pointed out, knew "how to deal with a usurping President, a king or a dictator." And there is no question that he was already thinking explicitly about impeachment as the best and perhaps the only means—hopefully sooner rather than later—of "remove a stumbling block" (Johnson) that stood "in the way of the progress of this Nation." At least one newspaper reporter took Butler's comments as a clear sign that he was proimpeachment and also had "presidential aspirations" of his own. And in fact many of Butler's supporters hoped that he *would* run for president in 1868. "It seems to be quite extensively predicted," wrote one, "that you will be a candidate for the Presidency at the next election." This correspondent worried that Butler's significant philosophical and political development over the last few years might raise questions in the minds of some, but he remained convinced that America's "yeomanry, who have carried us triumphantly through the war," would stand behind him.[20]

Whatever his long-term aspirations were in the fall of 1866, for the time being Butler trained his sights on the US Congress. In early October, he accepted the unanimous nomination of the Fifth District's Republicans. Predictably, political enemies present and past—including wartime adjutant general of Massachusetts and former editor of the *Lowell Courier* William Schouler, who years earlier had opposed Butler's ten-hour legislation for factory workers—immediately sought to challenge the legitimacy of his candidacy on the premise that his primary residence lay outside the Fifth District. These efforts failed, however, and Butler won the seat. That November, Republicans in Massachusetts's Sixth District, where Lowell was situated, also sent his old rival Nathaniel Banks to Congress. Indeed, the election of 1866 sent so many Radicals to Washington, Butler felt certain that justice would soon triumph over Johnson's betrayal of "the principles of the party which elected him." He hoped the nation's gravest dangers were now in the past.[21]

In March 1867 Butler joined the landmark Fortieth Congress for the first of his four consecutive two-year terms in the US House of Representatives, which were followed, after a one-term hiatus, by a fifth term in the Forty-Fifth Congress from March 1877 to March 1879. It merits note that during his first four terms, which lasted from March 1867 to March 1875, Butler played a central role in most if not all of the legislation Congress advanced for the purposes of wresting control of Reconstruction from Johnson (and, in 1868, unsuccessfully impeaching him), defending Union victory over the Confederate rebellion, protecting the freedpeople and their allies, and extending the same rights of citizenship to Black Americans that White Americans already enjoyed. Butler's first eight years in Congress overlapped substantially with Ulysses S. Grant's years in the White House and witnessed—among other things—the ratification of the Fourteenth and Fifteenth Amendments to the US Constitution in July 1869 and February 1870, respectively; the election of the first Black US senator, Hiram Revels of Mississippi, in 1870; the (brief) opening up of West Point to Black cadets; the rise of the Ku Klux Klan and other white supremacist organizations in the South and Congress's efforts to squash them; the end of political Reconstruction (all of the states of the former Confederacy were readmitted to Congress by July 15, 1870, and between October 1869 and November 1874, seven of them were "redeemed" as state Democratic parties reasserted their authority);[22] the completion of the transcontinental railroad in May 1869; deepening concern among many White Americans about increasing competition from imported Chinese labor; the growth of the women's suffrage movement; powerful debates about the country's financial systems and currency practices; and the Panic of 1873 and the rise of the Greenback Party. Throughout these years Butler held his ground staunchly on the left wing of the Republican Party even as the party, Congress, and the nation as a whole changed and political alliances shifted in response to a host of cultural and economic stresses. The end of Butler's fourth term, and his defeat in the election of 1874, coincided with the Democratic Party's reclaiming its majority in the House of Representatives and asserting its power elsewhere as well, including in Massachusetts. Four years later, Democrats reclaimed the majority in the US Senate.

The defining feature of the Fortieth Congress—Butler's first term—was surely its relentless opposition to Presidential Reconstruction and the president himself, which took a variety of forms and culminated in Johnson's impeachment in the spring of 1868. Indeed, as soon as the legislators convened in March 1867 they began asserting control over Reconstruction with three encompassing and transformative Reconstruction Acts along with the Tenure of Office Act. The Reconstruction Acts echoed many of Butler's views on how to proceed: they broke the region occupied by the former Confederacy (except Tennessee, which had been successfully "reconstructed" in June 1866) into five military districts, assigned them military governors, and made their readmission to the Union contingent on congressional approval of their newly crafted state constitutions, which must abolish slavery, ratify the Fourteenth Amendment, and acknowledge the right of Black men to vote. Meanwhile, the Tenure of Office Act aimed to shield government officials who had been appointed by Lincoln but whom Johnson now seemed keen on removing, specifically Secretary of War Stanton who, like Butler, was determined to punish the former Confederacy for its rebellion and transform the South. Additionally, the Fortieth Congress very quickly began to consider impeaching the president, building on a conversation that had begun in January when Ohio representative James Ashley presented a series of resolutions for discussion that looked a good deal like the charges Butler had made against Johnson months earlier in his Cleveland speech. "I am glad to see the resolutions for the impeachment of the 'Vice President' are at length introduced in Congress," wrote one Massachusetts state senator. "I hope you will not falter or hesitate until the Traitor is removed."[23]

As the Fortieth Congress got underway, Butler took a seat on the Appropriations Committee, where, he later wrote, he focused on various financial questions, including "whether the bonds of the United States should be paid in gold and silver in preference to the other debts of the United States." Through his work on this committee, Butler began to carve out a well-deserved reputation as a strong supporter of allowing greenbacks— sometimes called the "rag-baby currency"—to become permanently "the lawful money of the United States." Indeed, throughout his time in Congress, currency and national finance questions remained an important focus of Butler's attention. But his first speech as an elected member of the House of Representatives, given less than a week after he was sworn in, was an eight-minute-long discourse on the topic of Johnson's impeachment. Having already put down a marker publicly on this issue prior to his election, Congressman Butler now reviewed the "grave charges made against the President of the United States" by Ashley in January and argued that Congress "would be false to itself—false to the country—false to the principles of the American government, did they shrink from the investigation."[24]

As it happens, whether or not they amounted to a sufficient case for impeachment, the legitimate and severe political criticisms Butler, Ashley, and others made of Johnson and his Reconstruction policies soon became entangled, problematically, with lingering issues associated with Lincoln's murder. In late February 1867, after nearly two years on the lam in Canada, Europe, and Egypt, John Surratt was captured and returned to the United States in chains. Surratt's mother and seven others had been convicted in July 1865 of conspiring with John Wilkes Booth to assassinate the president and other government and military leaders, and she and three others had been executed. Predictably, John Surratt's return to the United States rekindled much of the fury and confusion that had attended the assassination and the original conspiracy trial. Additionally, it was well known that Andrew Johnson had been one of the conspirators' targets the night Lincoln was killed, but the man tasked with killing him had failed to complete his assignment. Given how thoroughly Johnson now seemed to sympathize with the defeated Confederates, Butler and others among Johnson's fiercest opponents now wondered if perhaps he had actually collaborated with Lincoln's murderers, or even orchestrated the assassination, in order to create a path for himself to the presidency. "The complicity of Johnson" in the assassination plot, wrote one of Butler's shadier correspondents with considerable exaggeration, "is fully believed in by a majority of the people of the whole country," and he offered to help secure deponents to that effect. For their part, Johnson's allies decried such theories as absurd, and some argued—not without merit—that Ashley, Butler, Stanton, and even Judge Advocate General Joseph Holt, a Stanton ally who had clashed with Johnson repeatedly and very publicly since the trial of the original conspirators, meant to use the opportunity of John Surratt's upcoming trial to advance the case for Johnson's impeachment.[25]

Unlike the military commission that had convicted the original conspirators, Surratt's trial took place in civil court, beginning on June 10 and lasting about eight weeks. "The long-drawn out Surratt trial now narrows toward a close," observed the *Army and Navy Journal* with relief on August 3, adding that numerous witnesses had so completely contradicted one another during the testimony phase that it seemed impossible the jury could reach a verdict. They were right: the jury was hung, which allowed Surratt to walk free just as Jefferson Davis had recently done following two years of imprisonment at Fort Monroe, to the deep disappointment of many northerners and especially Butler and the Radicals. To them, the ambiguous end of Surratt's trial, combined with Davis's release *without* trial and Johnson's vetoes of the Reconstruction Acts (which Congress subsequently overrode), only reinforced the view that Johnson must have been involved in Lincoln's murder. Consequently, for some time after the trial ended Butler continued to chair a congressional committee whose sole purpose was "to investigate the facts & circumstances attending the assassination of President Lincoln." In response, Johnson's most fervent supporters north and south gleefully heaped invective on Butler and others who had suggested his complicity in the first place. In the end, even Butler was forced to conclude that "there was no reliable evidence at all to convince a prudent and responsible man that there was any ground for the suspicions entertained against Johnson" in connection with the Lincoln assassination.[26]

One happy distraction for Butler from the John Surratt trial and Congress's ongoing struggle with Johnson that summer was his receipt of an invitation from James Champlin, president of now-Colby University, in which he described Butler as the college's "most distinguished soldier." Champlin invited Butler to speak at the school's upcoming August 14 commencement, which would include dedication of the cornerstone for the proposed Memorial Hall to honor students who had died in the war. (Butler was unable to attend.) More pressingly, he received abundant reminders about the central issue that had propelled him into Congress in the first place: the rights of Black Americans, including veterans, to full citizenship and equal protection under the law. Such reminders included a letter from two Black veterans of the Seventh USCT who had served with Butler in the Army of the James, thanking him for his past kindnesses and urging him to do whatever he could in his new position of influence to bring the remuneration of Black enlisted men into line with that of Whites. Although "we slaves fought as hard, and did more hard work than free men," Edmund Bennett and Edward Hinson pointed out, Black soldiers like themselves had received only $100 in bounty upon enlistment, versus the $300 bounty White soldiers collected.[27]

This was neither the first nor the last plea Butler received from individuals who hoped his many speeches in favor of Black Americans' uplift had been sincere, and that he would now use his seat in Congress to realize the goals he had so often articulated. "We hold you ever our leader," USCT veteran Isaiah Mitchell wrote. "God [has] bless[ed] us by sending you to the halls of Congress. We believe that you are going to offer resolutions so as we may get that which we are entitle[d] to." "God bless you, my dear General," wrote another correspondent, after learning that Butler planned to nominate the first Black cadet to West Point, "in your endeavor to reconstruct our Govt, & our society, on the principle of 'intrinsic righteousness.'" Butler's proposed nominee for the cadetship, James Gregory, was then a senior at Oberlin College's preparatory school and was, according to one supporter, "rather small." Still, he was "quick in all intellectual movements" and by disposition "sensitive, ambitious, thoroughly generous, dignified and polite." In the end, Gregory proved ineligible on the basis of his age. Butler did not give up, however, on the idea of nominating a Black cadet and thereby taking an important step toward the transformation of the professional army's officer class. At the same time, he publicly endorsed the principle of electing Black men to serve not only in state legislatures but also in the US Congress, observing to one correspondent that Frederick Douglass "would make a better representative of people black or white" than many Whites as the "always patriotic and loyal" Douglass was "better fitted" both morally and politically for the post.[28]

The paper trail from Butler's years in Congress is replete with evidence that he was a reliable and powerful friend to the freedpeople and, as one group of Black Baltimoreans wrote in early 1868, "one of the able champions of the principles of equality of all men." Indeed, it will be recalled that Butler had a history of defending the rights of struggling Whites, too, and as a congressman he did not abandon his concern for them. Poor and laboring White women and men took note and expressed their appreciation, not least for his views on national finance and support for greenback currency. "A national league for the protection of American labor will be formed," Samuel Wilkinson advised Butler from Philadelphia in May 1867, and the organizers were considering nominating him for president. "Will you accept?" Meanwhile, however, although gritty determination to lift up and sustain all of the nation's most downtrodden citizens lay at the heart of Butler's work throughout his time in Congress, his immediate attention between late February and the end of May 1868 was focused on removing Andrew Johnson, whom he deemed the gravest obstacle to that goal.[29]

On February 21, 1868, Johnson knowingly and purposefully violated the Tenure of Office Act by attempting to fire Secretary Stanton. In response, the House of Representatives quickly passed eleven articles of impeachment and elected Butler one of the "managers" of the process. On March 4, Butler and the other House managers presented the articles to the Senate, where Johnson's trial would take place. The charges were read in the Senate chamber on March 13, and on March 30, after a series of delays, Butler opened the trial with a roughly three-hour-long speech, listing Johnson's many offenses. "The three days devoted to the preparation of this case were three of the hardest labor of my life," he later recalled. "Please accept my thanks for the copy of your great argument in the impeachment case," wrote Stanton the following day. "As an American citizen, and as your friend, I rejoice at the mighty blow you struck against the great enemy of the nation." "Your opening speech," wrote another correspondent, "has been received as a master-piece." In contrast, the (Washington, D.C.) *Daily National Intelligencer* characterized Butler's opening salvo as an argument with no basis in law that "utterly fails to make out even the semblance of a case in court." Of Butler himself, the *Intelligencer* added crudely that he was only "chosen for the occasion" because he was "peculiarly adapted to the duty, since having no reputation to lose, and being artful and unscrupulous as the champion and advocate of criminals, he was supposed to be the most fitting attorney for so desperate and unworthy a task."[30]

Although Representative John A. Bingham of Ohio officially served as the impeachment's lead manager, over the weeks that followed Butler assumed the greatest share of the managers' work. "Mr. Butler calls for the witnesses," mocked the *Boston Daily Advertiser*,

> Mr. Butler explains the purpose of testimony, Mr. Butler answers the objections of the counsel on the other side, Mr. Butler supplies the amusing retorts which enliven the occasion, Mr. Butler bullies the Chief Justice, Mr. Butler announces that the case is closed. . . . If Mr. Butler has not finished his oysters when the fifteen minutes' recess is over, the case waits for him. . . . In short, so far as appears to the looker-on from day to day, it is the people of the United States proceeding against an offending president through Benjamin F. Butler, their spokesman and prosecuting officer.

Brushing aside such all-too-familiar ridicule, Butler was initially confident. "I believe the impeachment sure," he told a correspondent on April 8. Warm words of support from friends and political allies encouraged him. "Permit a stranger to thank you with all the fervor of a warm heart," wrote Amos Hill in mid-April, "for the fidelity and unexampled skill with which you conduct the trial of the impeachment of the traitor and usurper, Andrew Johnson." Especially pleasing, one suspects, was the letter from USCT veteran William Forten of Philadelphia's prominent Black Forten family, thanking him for his efforts. Like Butler, Forten believed that Johnson's removal from office would have direct, positive consequences for the future of "my whole race." Butler's opening speech, he declared, "completely unmasks a *traitor* and his *hellish crew*," while at the same time it "opens wide the door to that fast dawning morn, when color shall cease to [be] a means available to every *cowardly scoundrel* by which he may under shadow of *law* and *usage disfranchise, outrage, degrade* and *insult* with impunity, the *loyal* and *brave defenders* of their *imperiled country*." When the time came for the Senate to vote, however, Johnson was spared by the smallest of margins being removed from office.[31]

It seems clear that Butler's own political ambitions, amplified by his complicated relationship with Ulysses Grant—who increasingly seemed likely to become the Republican nominee for president in 1868—played a part in his proimpeachment fervor. Butler resented Grant's public depiction of his performance during the war, and in the spring of 1868 he also objected vigorously (and publicly) to Grant's apparent willingness to try and bridge the gap between Johnson and the Radicals, as well as Grant's seemingly moderate, perhaps even reconciliationist views on Reconstruction. Friends Grant and Butler shared strove to mediate between the two men, if only for the sake of the Republican Party's future. "In a recent interview with General Grant," Republican journalist George Wilkes informed Butler in April, "I took the liberty of expressing my regret that any misunderstanding should continue to exist between himself and you; and particularly now, that public events required both of you to cooperate to the extent of your abilities in a common cause."[32] For the time being such efforts proved unsuccessful, and the men's mutual alienation persisted.

It would be wrong, nonetheless, to conclude that Butler was feckless or more committed to his own ambitions, as his opponents liked to claim, than to the party's, the freedpeople's, or the nation's welfare. "My enemies," Butler observed toward the end of the summer, "have told you that, because of personal differences" between himself and Grant, "I should swerve from that path of loyalty to the Republican Party and to the country which I had marked out for myself at the beginning." But, he insisted, "these slanderers mistake their man." Similarly, given Butler's views about what the US victory in the war should mean for the errant Confederacy, and particularly for the freedpeople, it would be wrong to assume that his determination to remove Johnson from office—and from any position of influence relative to the rebuilding of the nation after the war—was predominantly self-serving. Butler's challenges to Johnson, and to the reconciliationists who were eager to "have peace" without protecting the former bondspeople in any meaningful way, were hardly cost-free for him. And although he was impressively resilient in the face of constant attacks from his foes—in June 1868, one member of the Pennsylvania branch of the newly formed Ku Klux Klan explicitly warned that white supremacist allies in Lowell were preparing to kill him next time he went home—that does not mean those attacks brought him any pleasure.[33]

The impeachment trial ended in mid-May 1868. In the remaining months of the Fortieth Congress, Butler advanced a resolution to protect American fishing rights in the Gulf of St. Lawrence, engaged in discussions about proposals to reduce the size of the regular army, and dealt with countless requests for patronage. In addition, he continued his work developing the NHDVS system, which the grateful *Army and Navy Journal* called a "most beneficent and successful charity" marked by the "frugality and good sense" of its administrators, especially Butler. In the months that Congress was out of session, Butler tended to his private law practice. Then, in August, after the Republican Party unanimously nominated Grant for president, Butler began his own reelection campaign. As before, he gave numerous speeches, now addressing not only Reconstruction and the future of the freedpeople but also the nation's financial system, his reasons for supporting the failed impeachment effort, and the importance of supporting Grant and the Republicans generally in November. "Am I not justified in assuming," he declared on one occasion, "that the coming election is but a renewal of the strife at the ballot-box which we decided by the cartridge-box?"[34]

Throughout his reelection campaign Butler remained unflinching in the face of his political opposition's familiar invective: an early October article in the *Boston Daily Advertiser* described him as a man of "violent" temper, "bitter hatreds," and "extreme political opinions" who "represents no cause, no principles, no policy but the now obsolete policy of vengeance." At the same time, he was sustained by such accolades as those offered by a letter to the editor of the *Springfield Weekly Republican*. "No name of an American, not excepting the lamented Lincoln's, or the great general's"—Grant's— was "more familiar to the lips of his countrymen than Gen Butler's," this letter claimed. "In the West, and among southern union men, he enjoys a popularity second to no member of his party, while the mention of no other name will so instantly 'stir a fever in the blood' of the rebels and their sym-

RECONSTRUCTION CONGRESSMAN

pathizers." Butler was resoundingly reelected, and at year's end he began refurbishing the house he had purchased on the corner of 15th and I Streets NW with an eye toward a much longer residency in Washington than he had previously imagined. "The chamber carpets in our room and Blanche's are up," he informed Sarah, then in Lowell, in mid-December. "Have got an old washerwoman scrubbing and will try to be clean."[35]

In late February 1869, toward the end of its final session, the Fortieth Congress accomplished one of Butler's key goals, the passage of the Fifteenth Amendment to the Constitution authorizing Black men's right to vote throughout the United States; the amendment was ratified a year later. Then, on March 4, the same day Ulysses Grant took the oath of office as the nation's eighteenth president, the Forty-First Congress convened. Like the Fortieth, the Forty-First Congress had a Republican majority, though Thaddeus Stevens had died the previous August and other leading Radicals had lost their seats in the November election, including Butler's close allies James Ashley and Benjamin Wade. Congressional approval of the readmission of Tennessee, South Carolina, North Carolina, Florida, Alabama, Louisiana, and Arkansas, too, meant that these former Confederate states' representatives were now seated, further diminishing the Radicals' power. Meanwhile, many of the challenges of Reconstruction remained unresolved and were even exacerbated by the rise and fury of white supremacist organizations like the KKK, which relentlessly targeted both the freedpeople and their White Republican allies, including White northerners who had gone south to advance the cultural, economic, and political transformation Butler and others so eagerly sought. "I write to inquire," wrote Butler correspondent and former USCT chaplain Henry McNeal Turner, now a leading Black Republican in Macon, Georgia, in frustration,

> whether Congress is going to do anything for us here or not. If it is a fact that the party for whom we have sacrificed everything is going to desert us in the face of all the representations made to them . . . then it is time we knew it. We have been murdered by hundreds and thousands have been sent to prison, for our political principles. And even today white men swarm the country who gloat over the number of radical negroes they have shot. Our churches and school houses are fired and burnt to ashes for fun and past time. . . . If we are to be forsaken now in our distresses and troubles, then let us know the facts as they exist, so we can commence to leave the state, or declare ourselves no longer members of

the Republican party. The way Congress is doing, we will never be able to rally the colored people again. Thousands have already declared that the Republican party have led us in[to] the wilderness and deserted.[36]

As Turner explained, and Butler later recalled in his autobiography, former Confederates across the South and their allies elsewhere found the growing political power of the freedpeople intolerable. "To-day," noted one Black voter from Delaware in a January 1869 letter to Butler, even without the passage and ratification of the Fifteenth Amendment, "colored men are voting on equal terms with white men in Maine, New Hampshire, Vermont, Massachusetts and Rhode Island, of the New England States." The amendment, however, had provoked new efforts "to control the negro," Butler explained years later, "by a series of outrages and murders never equaled in a civilized country." White supremacists formed "large bands of organized marauders" who "dressed in fantastic uniforms" and, in terrifying night rides through predominantly Black communities, "inflicted unnumbered and horrible outrages upon the negro so that he should not dare to come to the polls," all because "they wanted to insure a white man's government." As the Forty-First Congress got underway, Butler's response to this grave and intensifying problem—including now as chairman of the House of Representatives' Committee on Reconstruction—was to push hard for enforceable laws which, "with their punishments and modes of execution" would prove "sufficiently severe" to "prevent those outrages entirely, or at least to punish them." Of particular interest to Butler were the situations in as-yet-unreconstructed states like Virginia and Georgia, where acts of political oppression and terrorism against the freedpeople were rampant.[37]

Even as he and his allies in the Forty-First Congress dug in to fight white supremacy and the steady rise of neo-Confederate Democratic political power in the South (and, by extension, in Congress itself), Butler devoted time to his many other responsibilities, including his ongoing leadership of the NHDVS. There his work ranged from making high-level decisions for the organization to explaining to individual applicants how the system might serve their particular needs, and to disorderly residents why they were being evicted. "You are a quarrelsome, fighting man, often troublesome when sober, and terribly so when drunk," he wrote to one New Yorker. "You are therefore dishonorably dismissed from the Asylum, with an assurance that you will never be readmitted." Butler also managed a robust correspondence with both Black and White patronage seekers as well as veterans of the USCT, who frequently sought his help getting the balance of their bounty payments or applying for pensions, a service he provided to Black veterans free of charge for the rest of his life. Correspondents also included advocates for Black southern candidates for elected and appointed office; women's rights activists such as Elizabeth Cady Stanton, who encouraged him to endorse the cause of women's suffrage; desperate people of all sorts appealing for financial assistance on the basis of his growing reputation as "the poor man's friend"; and furious opponents who hoped in vain to intimidate him. "If Hell claims its own you are a doomed sinner," wrote one adversary, "and if you do not go to Hell there is no use of having a Hell." Meanwhile, back home in Lowell, Butler established yet another business enterprise, the United States Cartridge Company, which went on to employ over a thousand workers and became a highly successful (and profitable) producer of ammunition, with sales not only in the United States but also Russia and Europe, until the company was sold after World War I.[38]

On December 6, 1869, the Forty-First Congress convened for its long second session, which ran for the next seven months. As the legislators gathered in Washington, friends and supporters celebrated Butler's return to his "sentinel post, on the watch towers of the country." Some expressed concern that a financial crisis was developing, which the Republicans must address soon in order to preserve the faith of "common people" across the country in the party's capacity to lead. Butler, too, worried about the nation's finances, but his central focus remained on the growth of reconciliationist sentiment in the North along with the violent anti-Black, neo-Confederate rebelliousness that was erupting across the South. In mid-December—shortly before Secretary Stanton died unexpectedly at the age of fifty-five—Butler issued a lengthy public reply to the prominent New York newspaper editor Horace Greeley, in which he condemned Greeley's recommendation for universal amnesty for the former Confederacy. "It is not the 'ex-rebel' to whom I am opposed," Butler wrote, "but the *present* rebel, who is only restrained by the strong arm of the Government from showing the intensity of his hate and the bitterness of his malignity toward the Union." Several days later, Butler gave a long speech in Congress calling for Georgia's return to military rule following the resurgence of white supremacist violence there, of which the so-called Camilla Riot in September 1868 was but one dramatic example. "Wrong and murder have gone on in the State of Georgia long enough," Butler thundered, "and it is our duty at the earliest possible hour to interpose." Butler denounced as an illusion the claim that Georgia had become "as quiet and peaceful" as "any northern State," a claim he attributed to those who colluded to "shield the men who there commit the foulest crimes." He further denounced any congressional representatives who obstructed the passage of vigorous anti-KKK legislation, which aimed to protect White and Black Republicans in Georgia and elsewhere whose lives, liberty, and property were in terrible danger.[39]

In part as a result of Butler's plea, Georgia's final readmission to the Union remained in limbo for several more months. But the readmission of Virginia at the end of January 1870 and of Mississippi and Texas shortly thereafter meant that ten of the eleven former Confederate states were now back in the Union, their elected representatives, in turn, increasingly empowered to shift the political balance both nationally and at the state level. Black Americans and their allies, like Butler, clearly recognized what this meant for their immediate safety and future welfare, and in the eyes of some, a good deal of the blame fell on the shoulders of increasingly timid, conciliatory Whites *within* the Republican Party who had seemingly abandoned the party's initial burst of commitment to the freedpeople. "Great dissatisfaction in the Republican party (the greater part of which are colored men)," wrote one of Butler's Black correspondents from Florida, "exists throughout the State, more on account of the rascality of those whom we have been electing to office without any benefit to ourselves than anything else. . . . We are becoming discouraged and hardly know whom to trust. . . . Do you think that we are asking too much when we demand some of our rights be attended to?"[40]

For his part, Butler continued to hold firm on the Radical end of the Republican Party, regularly repeating his urgent calls for federal intervention in the racial conflict and violence that plagued the politically, but by no means socially or culturally, "reconstructed" South. His many and wide-ranging correspondents kept him informed. "The Ku Kluxes are immigrating to this county in great numbers," wrote one desperate sheriff from Paris, Texas, having observed that "the juries of this state will never treat the colored people with humanity, and it is insanity to expect such a thing." "I have no doubt you are in possession of all the facts" in connection with the "driving away of the colored people from the well known 'Taylor Farm' situated in this country near Sewall's Point," wrote a friend in Norfolk, Virginia. "This has been done, and done in the very worst season of the year . . . and there looms up before them a dreary season of want and suffering." Meanwhile, in the spring of 1870 Butler continued his campaign to promote racial diversity and egalitarian ideas among the nation's military leaders by once again nominating a young Black man to West Point: Charles Sumner Wilson of Salem, Massachusetts, the son of a USCT soldier who had died during the war. "You have done several morally heroic things in your day," wrote one supporter upon hearing the news. "But, in my opinion, this is the boldest and grandest of them all!!!" Rufus Saxton, himself a West Point alumnus who as military governor of the wartime Department of the South had been actively involved in recruiting Black soldiers for the USCT, similarly praised the move. "If West Point shall fail in the future to represent those advanced opinions upon the equality of all men before the law which are the foundation of all the glory and success of the great party of which you are a recognized leader," he declared, "then it will be unworthy of the support of a government which respects the rights of all the governed." Saxton hoped Butler's nominee was blessed with "some of the brains of his illustrious namesakes," Charles Sumner and Henry Wilson, as he would surely "have many a hard battle to fight" if he became a cadet.[41]

As happened the first time Butler nominated a Black cadet, the War Department denied admission to Wilson, who was only seventeen, "on the ground that he is not of the requisite age." Later that spring, however, West Point finally admitted its first Black cadet, James Webster Smith of South Carolina. Smith's experiences of racism at the academy, however—which Butler observed with deepening concern—were brutal, and Smith did not graduate. On a happier note, the March 30, 1870, ratification of the Fifteenth Amendment brought Butler satisfaction, welcome praise (including from Frederick Douglass), and a measure of hope. So did the arrival in Washington of the first African American to serve in either branch of the US Congress: Senator Hiram Revels of Mississippi, freeborn in North Carolina and a veteran chaplain of the USCT. The passage of the anti-KKK Enforcement Act later that spring, for which Butler had campaigned so relentlessly as a way to protect Black men's voting rights and Black Americans' safety generally from white supremacist terrorism in the South, was also encouraging. Still, the intensification of White Americans' desire for their own sectional reconciliation—regardless (or in many cases *because*) of what that might mean for Black Americans—left Butler with less and less company on the Radical end of the Republican Party spectrum.[42]

As before, during the years of the Forty-First Congress, Butler's persistent concern about racial inequity and violence in the South did not occlude his awareness of the plight of poor farmers and laborers there and across the nation generally. Indeed, as time passed Butler became more and more sure that the country's economic system was failing White and Black citizens in similar and even interconnected ways; that the postwar struggles of poor White wage workers and farmers, in other words, were more similar to those of the freedpeople than they were different, and that all these problems were inextricable from—though perhaps not entirely explained by—the hard money, probusiness, and probanking financial policies that the so-called moderates *within* the Republican Party seemed increasingly inclined to pursue. Butler's economic analysis resonated with the experiences of his own impoverished youth and his early years as a lawyer in Lowell, and the more he publicized his views in speeches and in writing, the more his reputation grew as one who could be relied on to defend the weak whoever and wherever they were. "I read the announcement of your proposition to introduce a bill to tax fancy, & articles of luxury, & thus relieve the heavy burthen now borne by the laboring & poor class of community from heavy taxation," wrote one correspondent from New York City in the spring of 1870, with relief and optimism.[43]

True to the era, Butler's concern about poor Black and White American laborers—farmers as well as wageworkers—also inflected his thinking about Chinese immigration, which a number of his correspondents urged him to denounce. "The policy of importing such people with Asiatic habits and modes of life will be a disaster to the country," wrote one. Butler gave his first speech on this subject at a Fourth of July celebration in Connecticut in 1870, and in it he stressed his conviction that the Constitution "gives equality of right to all men before the law, and equality of power to every citizen born within the United States, or made so under the very beneficent provisions of our laws." He further and rather expansively predicted that by the end of the century the United States would have absorbed Canada, adding that he himself certainly welcomed Canadians into the US body politic. But in contrast with the egalitarian views he so readily espoused when it came to Black and White Americans, he deployed the disturbing and familiar racist and xenophobic language of his day to warn against efforts to incorporate "men unfitted by race, by nurture, or political, social, and industrial culture" who were "strangers to our civilization and subjects of another heretofore deemed semi-barbarous," in other words, the Chinese. Comments like these cannot help but recall his comments in Maryland at the start of the Civil War, regarding the possibility of a violent uprising by "savage" Black bondspeople, though Butler insisted that his intent was not so much to exclude Chinese immigrants because they were "semi-barbarous strangers to our civilization" but because they were not *free laborers*, or even *voluntary immigrants*. "All men" who came to America of their own volition and sought to "add their labor, their energies, and their industry in aid of our own" should be invited in, he declared, and in that way, American labor as a whole would be "neither degraded or enthralled."[44] How well his audience then or others later understood this nuance, and how much it actually distinguished his position on Chinese immigration from more explicitly bigoted views that were circulating, is debatable.

That November, amid rumors that he would run to replace Henry Wilson in the US Senate, Butler was returned again to his seat in Congress. Notably, a month before the election, he received an inquiry from a leading figure in the Massachusetts Labor Reform Party—whose members were primarily former Republicans distressed by the party's growing commitment to hard money policy—asking if he would accept their nomination as well. "As laboring men we vote for none but those who are identified with our principles and platform," wrote George Ober. "If you are with us we [will] rally all the sons of toil to your support." Butler sincerely welcomed the additional nomination, which both reflected and amplified his expanding appeal to laborers generally across the country. "I look upon your election to Congress standing upon the workingmen's platform as a glorious triumph of our principles," wrote another correspondent all the way from California. "I hope the day is not distant when the workingmen of this nation can place you upon their platform concerning the highest place within the gift of the people of this nation and the world," namely, the presidency.[45]

Working women, too, observed Butler's support for and deepening identification with American labor, and in December 1870, as the Forty-First Congress was settling into its third and final session, activist Aurora H. C. Phelps urged Butler to begin advocating explicitly for women's labor reform as well. Labor, wrote Phelps, was the cause of "the entire human race," not just of men; it was the cause of "the poor against the exactions of the rich; of the oppressed against their enslavers; of the toilers against the grinding monopolies of power." Moreover, labor reform and land reform were inseparable. Specifically, Phelps believed that increased access to "ownership of the soil" offered women the key to their future "earthly and eternal well-being." Like so many others who brought their concerns to his door, Phelps was confident that Butler would agree, not least "because of your lifelong reputation as the people's child and defender" and "because of the unforgotten, proudly remembered struggles of your youth" and "your mother's prayers, toils, and sacrifices for your prosperity and renown."[46]

Around this same time, former Civil War nurse Mary Morris Husband, too, addressed Butler as "a friend to women" and urged him to support laws that would enable women, who had sacrificed so much in the war, to "take up western lands" where they, like veteran soldiers and sailors, could "make comfortable homes for ourselves, & would probably benefit the country equally with the men." Also seeking Butler's support in late 1870 was "new departure" suffragist Victoria Woodhull, who requested that he engineer an invitation for her to appear before Congress. He did, enabling Woodhull to address the House Judiciary Committee on January 11, 1871, with Susan B. Anthony and Elizabeth Cady Stanton also in attendance. On that occasion Woodhull boldly defined the core principle of the "new departure" movement: that "women are entitled to vote under the Fifteenth Amendment without further legislation." "Permit me to say what I should have said days since," she wrote appreciatively to Butler afterward, "that I have no words by which to express my gratitude to you for the great kindness and courtesy you extended me in such a humble manner." Woodhull praised Butler's rare capacity for "treating women as something more than a mere animal, to be used for animal purposes," and insisted that she had "always regarded you as one of the nation's greatest men," and not just a great man, but a good one, too. The combined influences of his strong mother, strong wife, and strong daughter surely deserved much of the credit for shaping Butler's views on women's rights.[47]

When Butler introduced a bill the following year proposing a constitutional amendment to grant women the right to vote, his action elicited both the deep gratitude of suffragists like Woodhull and suggestions for ways he could advance the status of American women even further. "I wish," wrote one woman correspondent, "you would have the law made that the man shall take the woman's name when a marriage takes place instead of the woman being compelled to take the man's." Meanwhile, Butler's reputation among Black Americans as their foremost advocate in the federal government remained unsurpassed, yielding requests for help of all sorts from individuals seeking jobs or assistance filing their pension applications to groups urging that he push for additional federal policies to finally put the KKK out of business. There was, as well, the familiar stream of praise and thanks. "In you," wrote William D. Matthews, a veteran of the USCT now living in Leavenworth, Kansas, "the colored race has a true friend."[48]

The Forty-Second Congress ran from March 4, 1871, to March 4, 1873, and during those years Butler continued to strengthen his standing as a supporter of labor and of women's right to vote, even as he remained committed to advancing Black Americans' rights, welfare, and safety. On evidence gathered by the joint congressional committee established to undertake "a massive investigation of the activities" of the KKK and others like it, Butler led the successful charge for additional legislation to protect the freedpeople and their White allies in the South, including revisions to strengthen the Enforcement Acts' ability to crush white supremacist terrorism there. "Father made a grand speech on the Ku Klux Bill," Blanche wrote proudly to her mother on April 6, 1871, from Washington, where she was temporarily standing in as mistress of the house. "The bill for protection passed the House today—much to Father's relief—for he has carried the whole load and kept the members here in spite of their determination to adjourn." In the speech to which Blanche was referring, Butler bluntly argued that Congress's willingness to allow the advance of the Democratic Party in the supposedly reconstructed states of the South had produced nothing but "disorder, outrage, and murder." Moreover, the "unhappy and, in my judgment, mistaken policy" of rushing Reconstruction had led to a situation in which "the struggle for political power lost by the arbitrament of arms was therefore renewed in the rebel States" in other ways. Defeated in the shooting war, southern Whites now "resorted to their favorite and oft-tried means of political success," namely, "fraud, coercion, and force." Local courts could not possibly keep up, he continued, as "recent developments of lawlessness and crime show an extent of organization, a fixedness of purpose, and a ruthlessness in execution of that purpose which demonstrate that the ordinary machinery of judicial tribunals are entirely inadequate to meet the great emergency." It was time, Butler raged, to bring "the strong arm of military power" to bear on the South once again. Congress *must* intervene, and if it refused to do so, "an indignant people ought to hurl us from our seats." Should it renege on its promises to the freedpeople—"the only people in the South who were our friends during the war, save the soldiers that we sent to destroy the rebellion"—the Republican Party "ought to be disbanded."[49]

Butler surely felt like a voice crying out in what was becoming a wilderness. Even before the legislators gathered for the Forty-Second Congress's first session, the signs of his political isolation there were mounting. Sectional reconciliationists and probusiness/antilabor forces continued to gain ground within the Republican Party, though the functional reconciliation he managed to achieve with the party's leader, President Grant, did provide a small degree of consolation. Meanwhile, Butler's more progressive correspondents shared his feelings of frustration and alienation, and some now encouraged him to leave the party, which had seemingly abandoned its roots and original core principles. "The Republican party is fatally dismembered & deserves to die, in my judgment," woman suffragist Isabella Hooker had written as early as March 1871. Just over a year later, in May 1872, a longtime Republican mirrored Butler's urgent desire for a "radical change" in the party's focus, at least when it came to the needs of common people versus the financial elites. "While the great body of the party were battling for the destruction of chattel slavery," wrote D. Richey, "a few avaricious bankers and money changers & land grabbers were permitted to establish the present iniquitous banking system and to rob the people of a very large portion of the public domain, thus establishing a money oligarchy & land monopoly scarcely less unjust and oppressive than chattel slavery itself." Now, these oligarchs had become "so powerful" that "they control all legislation, state and municipal," provoking "the people" to rise in protest against their oppression. "If the Republican party would perpetuate its rule," Richey advised, "it must meet the hopes of its true friends by abolishing these cunningly devised schemes for enriching the few at the expense of the man—for oppressing and degrading the wealth producing classes and reducing them to a state of practical serfdom."[50]

Butler's complete estrangement from the Republican Party remained some years in the future, however, and in the fall of 1871, with the encouragement of his friends and supporters, including Victoria Woodhull, he ran under the party's banner for governor of Massachusetts. "Without a doubt you will be run for Mrs. Governor next fall," Blanche had jokingly warned her mother that spring. "I can see that Father has it strongly in his mind." While Congress was out of session, Butler campaigned across the state, giving speeches that struck familiar themes but also undeniably positioned him outside what had become the party's mainstream. Still, the speeches pleased Butler's faithful supporters, White and Black, who appreciated his willingness to stay the course ideologically as others in the party drifted away. Upon learning of Butler's candidacy for governor, one ally who described himself as "an old Democrat" captured the sources of Butler's ongoing support when he wrote, "There is no man in Massachusetts with the exception of [John A.] Andrew who has done more to protect the interest of the colored man than you," and "as it respects the poor laboring white man likewise." A Black correspondent from Boston agreed. "Sir," he wrote, "as you have done so much for the colored people, I can but advocate your election." Black activists in Washington, D.C., too, endorsed Butler's candidacy for governor, asserting their "implicit confidence" in his "integrity, sincerity, and pre-eminent fidelity to the principles of liberty and justice," and predicting that his election as the Bay State's chief executive would "go far towards strengthening the hands of radical men everywhere" as well as "preserving and making effectual that policy in national affairs . . . through which only our people in the South have any hope of deliverance from Ku Klux outrages and systematic, persistent persecution." From as far away as New Orleans, Black Americans similarly expressed their earnest support, recalling Butler's "prompt and practical espousal" of "the rights of our race in 1862," when he called on them to "button on the American soldier's jacket," and later, in the aftermath of the war, his "continuous fidelity in Congress in our behalf."[51]

Opposition to Butler among "old guard," rich, White, conservative Republicans in Massachusetts, however, ran deep and yielded new and fierce waves of accusations against him in the press, some of which even sought to revive tales about his supposedly disreputable behavior when he was a student at Waterville College. As one supporter from Lawrence explained in September, "Certain wealthy men, including bank officers, agents of mills, &c" in the state had even combined forces to launch an "anti-Butler movement," gathering information about his supporters, particularly among the state's "labor-reform men who are in full sympathy with you," in order to expose, embarrass, and threaten them, and discourage them from voting. These affluent opponents "say they shall spot every man that goes on to the platform with you as a friend of the labor reform movement and in the future treat them as the common enemy of the Republican party." Some remarked that opposition to Butler was directly related to his consistent public support for Black rights and Black voters. In the end, although he was initially optimistic, the state Republican convention did not nominate him, selecting instead William B. Washburn, who won the election in November with the ardent backing even of party leaders like Charles Sumner and Henry Wilson. Still, Butler's campaign had left many observers with the indelible impression that he was "the strongest man in the country" when it came to working for "the masses," be they "Labor Reformers, the Irish, the colored voters," or women. "Father has shown that he has immense strength in the state," Blanche observed after the convention, "and has gained more by this campaign. So it is not at all to be regretted that he made the trial."[52] Meanwhile, Butler retained his seat in Congress. Apparently Massachusetts Republicans were more comfortable having him represent the state in Washington than having him serve as the leader of the party back home.

Between the time Butler was first elected to Congress in the fall of 1866 and the start of his fourth consecutive term there in March 1873, the nation—including the Republican Party—had clearly undergone significant changes. The same was true of Butler's family. Among other things, in the fall of 1869 his two sons, Paul and Bennie (then seventeen and fourteen, respectively), began a two-year period of study in Frankfurt am Main, Germany, where they lived with his former law associate, William Prentiss Webster, who was serving as US consul-general there; his wife, Susan; and their children. The boys' initial departure for Europe left Sarah despondent. "They have gone, all gone," she wrote sadly in mid-October 1869, noting that when her husband was away too, there was "no one left" in Lowell "but me and the servants," as Blanche often stayed with her father in Washington. Sarah wondered about the wisdom of sending the boys away: "Will they learn enough in two years to pay us for the loss of their dear company?" she asked. Soon, however, as she had done when Blanche first started school in Georgetown, she began to fill her letters with words of maternal guidance. "Whenever you see Ben," she wrote to Paul in late November, "observe whether he is dressed with neatness, if his hands are clean and his clothes well brushed," and she begged Paul to be careful "in your attempts at fencing," for "we don't wish to see you maimed or disfigured." For his part, Butler—who had long promoted the opportunity to experience other cultures—urged the boys to make the most of their time abroad, write frequently (taking care "in spelling and the frame of your letters"), and keep a careful account of their expenses. He also offered more comfort in the face of their apparent homesickness than he had when Blanche first went away to school in 1860, perhaps having learned more about the feeling himself over the years. "Never be ashamed of home sickness, Boys," he wrote. "It shows that you had a good home and know how to prize it," and he added, "I did not think I loved you both so much until we parted." As requested, Paul and Bennie wrote on a regular basis, though perhaps not always willingly. "Ask Father if I must write to him every fortnight," Bennie complained to Sarah in December 1869, "for when I write to you I tell you everything that there is to be said."[53]

Over the next two years, the elder and younger Butlers exchanged newsy letters across the Atlantic filled with questions—"Tell us if you have grown half an inch taller and if you drink beer daily," Blanche inquired of her brothers on one occasion—as well as descriptions of their respective experiences, activities, and observations. "The chimney sweeps here are [the] funniest looking people you ever saw," Paul wrote in March 1870. "They are all rather tall and thin and always wear stove pipe hats." Butler and Sarah also received lively updates from Sarah's sister, Susan Webster, with accounts of their travels in and around Germany, including a visit with Mary Todd Lincoln and her son, Tad. In 1870 and again in 1871, Sarah spent about four months in Europe visiting and traveling with her sons and the Websters. As always, Butler missed her sorely when they were apart. "You have been away fifty-one days now and it seems months," he complained in one letter. "Call it what you will, use, habit, work, association, friendship, love. Twenty-seven years of intimacy cannot be broken off without wrenching the

Son Bennie at West Point. Photographer unknown. Courtesy of the
Ames Family Papers, Sophia Smith Collection, SSC-MS-00003, Smith
College Special Collections, Northampton, Massachusetts.

heart." After the boys returned from Germany in 1871, Paul began his studies at Harvard College, and in the spring of 1873 Bennie began his cadetship
at West Point as a classmate of Henry Ossian Flipper, the first Black cadet to
graduate from the academy. "I am proud to say," Flipper later commented in
an interview, "that among the three hundred cadets I hadn't a better friend
than the son of the Massachusetts statesman." Bennie shared his father's
egalitarian instincts but not his military aspirations. He struggled academi-
cally through all four years and had little interest in a life of military service.
"You seem to think that the only thing about which I care is whether I shall
get in the army or not," Bennie grumbled in February 1874. "To get in the
army is not what I want at all."[54]

As for Blanche, she had caught the attention of Gen. Adelbert Ames, a
native of Rockland, Maine, who was twelve years her senior and had served

Daughter Blanche. Photographer unknown. Courtesy of the Ames Family Papers, Sophia Smith Collection, SSC-MS-00003, Smith College Special Collections, Northampton, Massachusetts.

in the Army of the James before being sent to North Carolina with the Twenty-Fourth Corps near the end of the war. In 1868 Ames was appointed military governor of Mississippi and subsequently also commander of the Fourth Military District, which included Arkansas. By the time Blanche and Adelbert began courting in earnest he had become one of Mississippi's elected US senators. "We have a very pleasant acquaintance in Genl Ames the new senator from Mississippi," wrote Sarah to her sons in March 1870. "He is at the house daily and thinks that does not give him time enough." Soon Blanche and Adelbert were engaged. "I am very well pleased with him," Sarah informed the boys, and "I think your Father is satisfied decidedly better than with any person that she has met before."[55]

Blanche Butler and Adelbert Ames married on July 21, 1870. Blanche was twenty-three. "If I had known that Blanche would go and get married while

I was away I should not have gone," moaned Paul from Germany. Given her father's increasing support for women's rights, it comes as no surprise that the couple had discussed in very modern terms—for 1870, at least—the language they would use in their vows. "It is the style now," Blanche informed her fiancé, "to leave out the word 'obey' from the Marriage Service. I thought I had better write and ask you if you had any objection—at the same time to inform you that I have not the least intention of making that promise." "Well, Love, that does not frighten me," Ames replied cheerfully. "No, Blanche, I do not ask that you promise to *obey* me—I only ask that you love me." After the wedding the newlyweds spent a few weeks in Lowell before taking an extended fall honeymoon that included a visit to Ames's parents in Minnesota. During their Minnesota sojourn, Blanche's parents also traveled west to meet their new in-laws, Butler taking the opportunity to inspect the NHDVS's asylums in Milwaukee and Dayton, Ohio. Then the young couple headed south to Mississippi.[56]

In August 1871, Sarah and Benjamin Butler welcomed their first grandchild, Butler Ames, whose birth offered some emotional compensation for the death, in October 1870, of Butler's mother, Charlotte, following "a sharp sickness of about three days." When their grandmother died, Butler advised his sons not to "grieve too much." Charlotte was, after all, he wrote, "quite old as you know, being far advanced in her 79th year." Far more important, she had left her descendants with "an example how to do our duty to everybody." As for himself, he wanted them to know, "I owe all I am in the world to her exertions when I was young, and her care of me; and if in anything you are proud of me, you owe it to her." According to another member of the family, Charlotte Ellison Butler was "a remarkable woman" to whom "duty was a daily, constant habit, a second nature."[57] The influence she exerted on her son's life, ideas, and goals was immeasurable.

The birth of Blanche and Adelbert's first child brought new light and provided some welcome inspiration for Butler's sense of humor. "Is it determined that the poor creature shall be cursed with the name of Butler Ames, and nothing more?" he asked on Christmas Eve 1871, around the time the child was christened. Yes, Blanche replied, though she noted, "He will have to be a very smart boy to come up to the expectations his name will give rise to." Blanche took great pleasure, and perhaps experienced some surprise, as she observed how comfortable her father seemed to be with the child, whom she brought to Massachusetts in the summertime to escape the heat and fevers in Mississippi. In Lowell and at Bay View, little Butler Ames got plenty of attention, his grandfather allowing him play with his good watch and tug the cigars out of his mouth, all the while declaring the boy a strikingly well-behaved child.[58]

For Butler during this period, the satisfactions and joys in his own children's lives contrasted sharply with the keen disappointments that resulted from his nephew George's many struggles. Born to Andrew Jackson and Joanna L. Butler in Missouri in 1840, George H. Butler had served as an officer in the regular army during the war, first with the Fourteenth US Infantry Regiment and later on his uncle's staff. Afterward, George spent some time as a popular theater critic and journalist in New York City before receiving an appointment from President Grant—likely at Butler's request—to serve as a US consul in Alexandria, Egypt. It is unclear exactly when George's problems with alcohol began, but they followed him wherever he went, plunging him into one scandal after another and undermining his ability to enjoy a stable, healthy life or, for that matter, pay his mounting bills. His disease also produced the usual cycle of excuses, pleas for help, attempts to get sober, and heart-wrenching relapses. And although he repeatedly threatened to turn his back on George for his nephew's own sake, Butler never did. Eventually George lost his consulship and returned to the United States, where he struggled on for another decade and a half, sobering up occasionally but never for long. As one account described it, George "went down gradually for a time, and then made a headlong rush like a man who would throw himself into the sea."[59]

Even as he strove to help his troubled nephew, Butler also provided steady assistance to the widow of William Mumford, the firebrand rebel whose execution he had approved in New Orleans in 1862. Mary Mumford's financial difficulties came to Butler's attention in February 1870 when one of her friends contacted him to ask, "Could not the Government do something for this woman?" Although the inquirer admitted that William Mumford had "brought his own fate" upon himself "through his own hot-headed, impulsive, southern temper," she insisted that his widow—a Massachusetts native, she took care to note—was a "noble, high-minded, talented woman" now mired in poverty with three dependent children. Perhaps Butler could find her a government clerical position? He did, and for several years Butler and Mary Mumford exchanged letters directly. Sometimes he also sent her money.[60]

Yet another individual to whom Butler provided special attention—including both financial assistance and legal counsel—was the abolitionist and woman's rights lecturer Anna E. Dickinson; Butler even helped to find employment in the Internal Revenue Department of the Treasury for Dickinson's brother, Edwin. Eventually, as will be seen, their relationship became a source of much consternation for him, not to mention rumor. It began in the early 1870s, however, as a result of his susceptibility to pleas for help, based on his own youthful experiences of poverty and family suffering, not unlike his sympathy for the financial struggles of a multitude of others, now including even White southern farmers who just a few years earlier had taken up arms against the United States. "The Southern states are hopelessly insolvent," wrote one friend from Greensboro, North Carolina, in late 1871. "The despondency of the masses of the Southern people is owing to the fact that they can see no way out of their financial embarrassments." The postwar "financial embarrassments" Americans across the continent were experiencing, of course, became even more severe as the great depression known as the Panic of 1873 got underway in earnest following the stock market crash in September of that year.[61]

That fall, though he still held his seat in the Forty-Third Congress, Butler ran again for governor of Massachusetts, technically as a Republican and with the backing once again of the state's Labor Reform Association. Butler's allegiance to the Republican Party generally, and in Massachusetts particularly, however, had become seriously frayed, not because he was ideologically fickle, as his opponents liked to claim, but because the party had moved so far away from the ideological positions that originally drew him into it and that he still held. Leading Republicans increasingly sought to distance themselves from Butler, demonizing him as ridiculously, even dangerously out of step with the "sensible" agenda of the party's mainstream. In response, many of Butler's supporters urged him to abandon the party altogether. "It seems to me," one Boston correspondent wrote in May 1873, "that you have arrived at a period in your career in which you must make a break," for "if you tamely accept what the Republican party deals out to you, this is about the last of Ben Butler." Butler approached the fall 1873 campaign with optimism, despite the steady stream of fierce criticism from the state's Republican press, particularly in connection with a bill he had sponsored earlier that year—with exquisitely poor timing—and which opponents pejoratively nicknamed the "Salary Grab Act." In the bill, Butler had proposed higher salaries and back pay for the president, supreme court justices, and members of Congress in order to enable them all to hire sufficient staff to do their jobs and serve their constituents and the public more effectively. "It will be a lively fight," he told Blanche, referring to the upcoming election, "but I think I shall win."[62]

Butler was wrong. "At the primary meetings for the election of delegates" to the state's Republican convention, he later recalled, "more than a majority of the delegates elected were in my favor." But the state party's central committee and many of its leaders "were bitterly opposed to me." Consequently, they "organized the convention against me" by means of "fraud and deception" and succeeded in stopping his nomination. Upon learning the news, Adelbert Ames, who shared his father-in-law's views on most issues, expressed sharp disappointment heightened by raw anger over "the triumph" of Butler's adversaries in a contest the entire nation had been watching. Moreover, as Butler later insisted, it was apparently not enough for his opponents in the state Republican Party to undermine his candidacy for governor that one year; "they then declared that I never should be governor of Massachusetts." In rebuttal, Butler promised that he would indeed be governor of Massachusetts someday, but not as a Republican. Still, he gave a gracious concession speech, which one supporter described as a display of "nobility that ought to shame & silence your enemies." Weeks later in Mississippi, supported by White and Black Republican voters in the state, Adelbert Ames achieved what his father-in-law had not, and was elected governor. "Father is greatly pleased at your success," wrote Blanche from Lowell, where she had been staying since before their daughter Edith was born on March 4. "Butler left the table to call his grandfather out to supper. In his haste to get back, his foot slipped and he gave his head a hard bump. Father consoled him by saying 'never mind, my boy, your Father is Governor of Mississippi.'"[63]

In fact, prior to the nominating convention Blanche had worried that losing the race for governor would diminish her father's influence in Congress, "for it will be said that he cannot carry his own state." Regardless, Butler pressed on in Washington, delivering a major speech in January 1874—just a couple of weeks before Ames's inauguration in Mississippi—in support of the civil rights bill he and Charles Sumner had first cosponsored back in 1870. On this occasion, Butler began by addressing the racism that had shaped his own perspective in the past, and then explained how thoroughly his direct observations of the courage and other "high qualities" of the Black soldiers with whom he had served during the war had permanently altered his point of view. "From that hour," Butler insisted, "all prejudice was gone, and an old-time States-right democrat became a lover of the negro race." Henceforth, "as long as their rights are not equal to the rights of other men under this Government," Butler declared, "I am with them against all comers." He challenged opponents who argued that the goal of the bill was to "establish social equality" between Blacks and Whites. The goal, he explained, was to ensure that "every man has the right to be the equal of every other man if he can," and that "all constitutions, all laws, all enactments, all prejudices, all caste, all custom" that operated "in contravention of that right" were recognized once and for all as "unjust, wicked, impolite, and unchristian." Once again, Butler urged Federal intervention in cases where individual states failed to live up to this standard.[64]

"I believe that your speech on the 'Supplementary Civil Rights' bill delivered yesterday," wrote one admirer, "will do more toward eradicating the prejudice against the negro from the public mind than all the speeches that have been made by others during the past seven years." "We recognize you as one of the best friends of our race in this country," wrote the president of the Colored National Labor Union from Baltimore. "We feel under many obligations for the interest you have taken in our behalf." Similarly, the editor of the Black newspaper *The Progressive American* lauded Butler's speech and expressed his hope that "the day is not far distant when we the people may exercise our right of franchise in your behalf for the office of presidency of these United States." Indeed, after Charles Sumner died on March 11, 1874, Butler became, for many, the last remaining reliable friend of Black rights in Congress. Throughout what remained of his fourth term he continued to give speeches filled with details he gleaned, in part, from the many letters he received from Blacks across the South describing their ongoing oppression and the violence they still endured from white supremacists determined to force them back into virtual slavery. "On Monday night, April 24th, 1874," wrote one woman from Macon, Georgia,

> my front door was burst open by disguised men who had hoods or such over their faces. . . . They dragged me out of bed. . . . One knocked me over the head four or five times with a pistol, while others tried to tie my only garment I had on around my head. I was pulled out of my door and though I still fought them they forced my face down in the sand my nose now bleeding copiously from my terrible struggle as a woman with five men unknown to me. One sat on my head. One held my hands another my feet while two took switches already cut and whipped me. They cut my poor back all to pieces. . . . Now Sir, is it not possible still for the Government to protect us?

Blacks in the South and their allies across the country considered Butler a hero—their hero—and an increasingly rare source of hope.[65]

At the same time, as the ongoing financial panic gripped the nation, Butler's concern with questions of currency, national finances, banking, and labor generally continued to grow, not least in connection with the negative implications for debtors and the poor of the strict hard money policy the Republican Party seemed determined to pursue. On April 22, Grant vetoed Senate Bill No. 617, "An Act to fix the amount of United States notes and the circulation of national banks, and for other purposes," which had been designed to ease the effects of the Panic by increasing the money supply. Grant's veto discouraged Butler, who had favored the bill and had urged both an expansion of the money supply and a national policy of free banking. Was there any reason for a person of his views even to remain in politics? "I am a good deal disheartened," he wrote Sarah on April 24. "Why do I not go out of politics and quit?" And yet, he could not quit. Too many supporters, Black and White, men and women, had too much faith in his ability to steer the nation in a better direction. "We lack energetic & far-seeing men in our public affairs," wrote one correspondent. "You are the only live man, on the carpet, at the present time. Help us out."[66]

Convinced as they were that only Butler's leadership could bring order out of the nation's political and economic chaos and end the suffering of Black and laboring Americans, supporters pressured him to run for governor of Massachusetts again in 1874 and then for the presidency. "You have here and elsewhere 'national' and sincere friends," wrote one New Orleanian that spring, "who know but too well that had it not been for your extraordinary firmness, the streets of New Orleans would have been converted into the worst field of slaughter and destruction, in addition to the threatened calamity of starvation, which you happily averted." This correspondent reported that even in the South, former rebels "are by degrees recovering from their distempered passions" and "now smart keenly under the misrule and mismanagement of the states since reconstruction." Now they wanted him back in New Orleans, or in the presidency. "You may hear on the streets, out of the mouths of your bitterest enemies," he wrote, "Give us Butler!"[67]

In the midst of all this tumult, Butler fell quite ill with what some referred to as an "inflammation of the bowels." "Your Father has been sick for a week," Sarah informed Blanche on May 11. "Many think he broke down from too much work." News of Butler's illness brought a flood of letters of condolence, recommendations for cures, and sample medicines. "*Make him* stop hard work and take care of his health," demanded one supporter. "We cannot lose him." By late May, Butler was still not well; according to Sarah, the doctor had diagnosed him as suffering "renal colic," possibly kidney stones, as she noted that "several little gravel stones have passed with the water." Blanche suggested that her father dial back on his political engagements and ambitions, including abandoning the idea of running for governor again. She urged him instead to "play a great many games of billiards," go swimming "as often as the water is warm enough," and "sail constantly," presumably on the 109-ton racing yacht, *America*, that he and a friend had purchased for about $5,000 the previous summer. "This I am sure," Blanche wrote, "will effect a complete cure, and is not a very disagreeable prescription." As a consequence of his illness, Butler at least temporarily, and not for the first time, gave up smoking cigars.[68]

The illness eventually passed and in the fall of 1874 he ran again for Congress but not for governor. Predictably, some of his most earnest supporters in this campaign were southern Blacks who had reached the point of despair over Congress's (and the Republican Party's) steady rightward turn. "Gen[eral]," wrote one USCT veteran from Bournie, Mississippi, in September, "the Col people of the South is glad to see that you is a candidate for congressman. We can't see how we could get our Rights if you was out of Congress," and he encouraged Butler to run for president in 1876. That fall, however, for the first time in five consecutive outings, Butler received the Republican nomination in Massachusetts but lost the election, raising more clearly than ever the question of whether the Republican Party had truly ceased to be the most appropriate political home for him. "You are wise in sticking to party, in one sense," wrote B. Franklin Clark of Charlestown, "& foolish in another." Clark predicted that Butler's views on various matters would ultimately put him fully at odds with where the party was heading, and when that happened, he recommended, "let the party go to the D—l," but "don't you go down with it." Rather, "Come out for the people, the suffering people, independent of party, & lead them into a more prosperous & harmonious condition, & great will be your reward."[69]

In November 1874, Massachusetts elected not only a majority of Democratic congressmen—including one from Butler's district—but also a Democratic governor. "The battle is over," wrote one friend from Marblehead in dismay, "and by everything known to malignant men, you have been defeated," a result he characterized as a "thunderbolt." Soon, this correspondent predicted, "we shall hear the groans of the colored man, south of the old slavery line, reverberating through the land in consequence of your defeat," along with the bitter complaints "of the poor laborer and the small businessman who carries on his business on borrowed capital at enormous rates." A supporter from Pennsylvania described Butler's electoral loss as "a death blow to the Republican party," and another in Washington described his own response to the news as reminiscent of the "very profane teamster who when the end board of his cart came out, while hauling a load of potatoes up a very steep hill, was expected to give the fullest rein to his pro-fanity. Quietly surveying the catastrophe," however, the teamster "picked up the end of the board and replaced it, and started up his team, remarking to himself, '*that he could not do the subject justice*.'"[70]

"The full effect of the weak-knee'd policy of a Republican Congress tem-porizing with Rebels & Rebellion will soon be known & realized by the mis-guided people of the North, and they will then have as perfect an under-standing as I now do of the great loss that the cause of good Government has suffered by your defeat in the late Congressional election," wrote Rufus Bullock of Albion, New York. For the moment, however, Butler felt a mea-sure of liberation. "I need no condolence," he advised one friend. "Relieved of two years of profitless work in opposition to our overwhelming majority in the House, I feel as if emancipated from a task. I have sought to do my duty to the country and to my fellow-men, and await with confidence a just verdict to that effect." Meanwhile, Blanche observed to her husband, no one could know "what the future will bring in the way of political life for Father." Fortunately, he still had "his profession, and I think will prove sufficient." Moreover, she hoped, Butler would now be free to spend more time with his newest descendant, Blanche and Adelbert's third child, daughter Sarah Ames, who was born a month before the election.[71]

I have watched sir with pride and a feeling that I cannot express of your devotion and sacrifice for the cause of the oppressed and downtrodden since the traitors of my country rose in rebellion. . . . Whatever those dirty journals say about you I can assure you that the thinking people . . . are with you and admire with pride the way you lay your enemies prostrate at your feet in Congress as well as out of Congress.
—J. MAHONEY TO BUTLER, FEBRUARY 1875

Whatever comes of the party it behooves you and me and all good Republicans to stand firmly by the fundamental principles of the party which I understand to be equality of right, equality of power and equality of burden, of the government to all men under the law. Upon that platform I shall be found in the future as I have been in the past however parties or names may change.
—BUTLER, APRIL 1878

The Road to the Massachusetts State House
1875–1882

Benjamin Butler lost his reelection bid in November 1874. As the new year began, however, two full months remained before the Forty-Third Congress would give way to the Forty-Fourth, and Butler's efforts during those weeks centered on achieving passage of the Civil Rights Act, which many within and outside of Congress still considered essential, both for protecting Black Americans' fundamental rights and for preserving their loyalty to the Republican Party. "Pass the civil rights bill in some form this Congress," wrote a correspondent from Virginia on January 27, "or we will lose the colored vote of the South." On February 3, 1875, Butler gave a major speech in favor of the bill, which immediately drew stern rebuke from those who opposed it, including John Y. Brown, a Democratic representative from Kentucky. Such attacks only strengthened supporters' enthusiasm for the bill and for Butler himself. "I have just laid down the paper with the account of the shameful attack on Genl Butler in the House yesterday by Mr. Brown," wrote Phoebe Couzins from Missouri. Couzins was one of the first women attorneys in the United States and a fierce advocate of women's rights. Butler, she insisted, "must know that the venomous attacks are but the smouldering hatred of the rebellion, fanned again into expression through the late democratic victories." And in words Butler himself might have used, she added, "We have not done with the slave power yet, and if the Republican party does not stand firm to its principles, and pass the Civil Rights bill, we shall have the work all to go over again."[1]

Others agreed. "Thank you for the manly and consistent course you have pursued in connection with the civil rights bill," wrote a veteran from Kansas shortly after Butler's speech, noting that while "a great many republican papers over the country, west as well as east, join with the democracy in a shout of delight at your defeat last fall," such "is not the feeling of the people." "Give that scoundrel Brown your very best!" wrote another correspondent, from Ohio; "give those Southern traitors the same kind of treatment that you gave them at New Orleans and the North will back you." Allies in Georgia, too, offered support. "Threatening language and billingsgate can never harm you," wrote one, "while vindicating the truth and pleading for justice to a race that has been degraded almost beyond redemption by the God forsaken wretches who are still trying to oppress them. . . . Push ahead General." "Colored men all over this land from the Atlantic to the Pacific ocean have watched with intense anxiety," observed C. H. Tandy from St. Louis. "You have endeared yourself to every intelligent man & woman & child who is old enough to know right from wrong . . . and through the entire state of Missouri, you can't find a child that is not taught to revere the name of the late Charles Sumner & Hon. B. Butler."[2]

The House of Representatives passed the Civil Rights Act on February 4, the Senate followed suit on February 27, and President Grant signed it into law on March 1. Words of gratitude and relief flowed in. "Allow me in the name of the colored people of Cincinnati and of the whole country," wrote Robert Harlan on March 15, "to thank you for your noble effort in pushing the Civil Rights Bill through Congress." A few days later came a letter of appreciation from a group of Black residents of Portland, Maine. "Our thanks to the Hon. B. F. Butler," they wrote, "for his efforts in securing the passage of the Civil Rights Bill. That he may soon be returned to the National Council [Congress] as the guardian of civil rights is our sincere wish." In the years ahead, the Civil Rights Act was enforced unevenly at best, and a series of Supreme Court decisions soon began to chip away at its power. But in the spring of 1875 its passage, along with the Thirteenth, Fourteenth, and Fifteenth amendments to the US Constitution, seemed to offer yet another form of insurance for Black Americans in their quest to enjoy the benefits of full citizenship. "The civil rights bill," Butler explained to a correspondent in Oregon that spring, "gives to the colored man every right I have, no more, no less."[3]

Once the Forty-Third Congress adjourned at the beginning of March, Butler refocused a good deal of his attention, at least for the time being, on his business and legal work. "Father has gone to Washington again to try some cases in the Supreme Court," Blanche informed Adelbert. "He is looking remarkably well, and happy. I think it agrees with him to be out of politics." Although he surely welcomed a break from the Washington maelstrom, however, Butler could not tear his eyes away from national affairs or ignore his concerns about resurgent Democrats' ongoing "redemption" of the states of the former Confederacy, with its profoundly negative implications for the future of the country and, specifically, for Black advancement. Butler's old friend and mentor Caleb Cushing, now serving as US ambassador to Spain, urged patience, and suggested that soon Americans would actively be seeking Butler's return to the halls of power. "You have no cause, in my opinion, to regret not being in the House of Representatives," Cushing wrote. "Life in Congress, if anything, is essentially a combat with rivals or opponents, and of consequent invidiousness." Moreover, "temporary retirement" could have its benefits, including enabling "the people" to appreciate Butler's abundant accomplishments (in contrast with others' bland records) and mobilizing them to send him back to Washington.[4]

As he watched to see whether Cushing's prediction proved accurate, Butler's interest in matters relating to the national currency, the financial system, and the struggles of working people and the poor, Black and White, women and men, continued to grow. In March 1875, shortly after he left Congress, Butler addressed these concerns in a speech at New York's Cooper Union, which produced a host of requests for him to speak at Greenback conventions and labor gatherings all around the country. Three months later, he published an extended article in the *New York Arcadian* outlining his views. Here and elsewhere Butler boldly challenged the nation's economic system, which seemed purposely designed *not* to produce genuine equality and democracy but, rather, to benefit and protect the "robber barons" and even widen the gap between the wealthiest capitalists and the rest of the population. The problem, in other words, was systemic. "I do not blame Vanderbilt for having acquired his immense fortune by manipulating the prime necessities of life, to wit, the carriage of freight and passengers," Butler insisted.

"I only blame the laws which enable one man within the space of between 28 and 70 years to make such an immense fortune from and out of the necessaries of life." To a correspondent in New York's Finger Lakes region he described in detail the organized chicanery that financial elites engaged in—not unlike religious leaders, or scientists—to "control the people," in this case by obscuring any and all sources for understanding how the economy, or money, works in the first place. "Through all ages," Butler explained,

> religious beliefs have been enveloped in mystic symbols and clouds of superstitious imagery. For centuries the reading of the Bible, the foundation of our own religion, was kept from the people and confided to priests alone, so that they might be, as it were, the ruling class. In medicine even the prescriptions for drugs used to heal the sick were put in an unknown tongue by the doctors so that medicine might be a mystic art, and until later times the laws were printed in an unknown tongue, and even to this day they are enveloped in a technical phraseology so that the people may not understand the law.[5]

"Now," Butler continued, the nation's "monied class" were making a concerted effort to "envelop all the principles of finances, the uses which money performs on behalf of the people, the relation of money to value, the question of what is money, whether it must of itself have intrinsic value to be money," and so forth, in "mystery," until even highly intelligent people outside the circles of power came to believe that "nothing can be known about money or finance." This scheme ensured the perpetual grip on power of the nation's financial elites, along with their capacity to "live upon the labors of the producing classes," as if that was the natural and only possible arrangement. Butler noted, too, that by "purchas[ing] and manipulat[ing] the newspapers," the same group of capitalists guaranteed that "even a fair discussion of these questions" could never take place, though in truth, financial systems were actually quite simple and easy to comprehend. "There is no magic, witchery, mysticism, or obscurity in the laws which govern finance any more than in the law of gravitation," he wrote. And he hoped "that we shall soon have for the benefit of the people" a simple, clear, and equitable system of currency, "made for the people and not for the privileged class," which he would be pleased to help construct. "I am now out of political contests," Butler advised a correspondent in Chicago that summer, but he would gladly return to the fray if the nation's economically oppressed wanted him to, especially if he saw evidence "that the workingmen of the country will unite to claim their fair share of its protection"—including a democratized financial system—"through political organization."[6]

When he was not tending to his professional obligations, giving speeches, or debating the nation's future with his many correspondents, Butler found regular respite during his hiatus from Congress in sailing and even racing his beloved yacht, *America*, though racing, predictably, came with its own frustrations. "The *America* has returned," Sarah informed Blanche on one disappointing occasion in July. "The race was a failure." More troubling that the occasional racing defeat were Bennie's ongoing academic problems and persistent homesickness at West Point, where Butler served as a member of the board of visitors for the end-of-year examinations that June. Also unsettling was the lack of clarity about Paul's future following his graduation from Harvard in the spring. "Father wants Paul to go on to Washington this winter and study law for six months," Blanche wrote Adelbert in September. "Paul has not yet said whether he would prefer to do this, or go into the Cartridge Mills at once." Also disquieting was nephew George's steady downward spiral, his alcoholism and depression complicated by an apparent concussion received in a recent fall. Butler summed up his nephew's difficulties as "an affliction of the head which requires absolute rest and quiet, and careful attention to diet" and arranged to have George institutionalized (at his expense) at the Catholic Providence Hospital in Washington. Surely Butler's greatest source of personal anxiety during this period, however, was Sarah's health. Always vivacious in the past, Sarah now experienced regular bouts of exhaustion, which she and others chalked up to "overexertion in house fixing" at their various residences. But her often sore and hoarse throat suggested something more serious.[7]

Meanwhile, Blanche, Adelbert, and their growing family had begun Adelbert's term as governor of Mississippi in good cheer. "Gen'l Ames has purchased a place at Bay St. Louis," on the Gulf Coast, Blanche had written Paul in mid-January, "and we are going there in the course of a month or so" to enjoy "fine hunting and fishing," a good view of Ship Island, and the chance to "shoot alligators, and eat oranges." The Ames children were all healthy, though three-year-old Butler, the oldest, was growing rapidly and seemed hopelessly clumsy. "He can fall down in the middle of the room tripped up by his own feet twenty times a day," Blanche wrote, adding that the boy routinely asked, "When we are going to see Gram?" Edith, she noted, was "as fat as ever" and "growing more interesting daily," and baby Sarah was proving "as sweet as a peach," so much so, in fact, that "she is in danger of being neglected she is so patient and always ready to smile." In what little free time she had, Blanche enjoying painting. "I have nearly completed the head of Edith's portrait and am well pleased with it," she informed Sarah. "It is better than Butler's and will make a beautiful picture."[8]

By the fall of 1875, however, Blanche and Adelbert's upbeat mood had given way to anger and exasperation as a result of Democratic Party's fierce resurgence in Mississippi and the anti-Black agitation and violence that accompanied it, along with apparent northern indifference. "What I regret more than anything else," Ames confessed, "is that the north cannot and will not understand the rebellious and barbarous spirit which prevails among the whites here." Deeply disturbing, too, were the efforts of white supremacist organizations and corrupt Democratic Party politicians to unseat Ames, who was so closely associated with his father-in-law and what remained of the Radical Republican agenda. Their goal was a Democratic takeover of the state legislature in the fall election, which they planned to follow with Ames's impeachment and removal, and they were more than willing to employ terror as their method. The "redeemers," Adelbert warned Blanche, meant to carry the election "by violence and murder," get rid of him however they could, and then "turn the state over to the president of the Senate, one of their own men." Moreover, their scheme was making good headway. "Through the terror caused by murders and threats, the colored people are thoroughly intimidated," he observed in mid-October. "A *revolution* has taken place by force of arms, and a race are disfranchised." If Democrats continued to have their way, Black Mississippians would soon be "returned to a condition of serfdom—an era of second slavery." Meanwhile, the Mississippi "redeemers" attacked Ames for, among other things, having committed the heinous "crime" of allowing Black citizens to form militia units of their own. "The militia question is agitating the 'white-liners' very much," Adelbert explained. "I understand they are willing to promise almost anything if I will cease with my militia movements."[9]

As the situation in Mississippi deteriorated, it seemed that the federal government must intervene, at least to ensure a safe and legitimate fall election. "The President will come to the rescue, Del," Blanche wrote optimistically, and she urged her husband to stay the course while continuing to meet and strategize as usual with local Republicans. Still, she cautioned, "women and children should not attend the meetings," and "so far as possible the men should be armed for defense." Moreover, if the meetings were "disturbed" by those who meant to destroy the Republican Party and force Blacks back into virtual slavery, Republicans White and Black must be prepared to fight back, with violence if necessary. Having come of age during the Civil War and the early years of Reconstruction, and being her father's daughter through and through, Blanche believed that southern Blacks and their White allies must begin to practice "self-protection." If the time came, she declared, "it should be understood that there would not be a single house belonging to a white-liner left standing above the ground." Targeted acts of arson against the state's brutal white supremacists were surely "less reprehensible than murder" and were also "likely to prove far more efficacious."[10]

Butler, too, was prepared to encourage Black southerners' (and their White allies') violent self-defense if it became necessary. "Some colored men called on Father and asked him to subscribe for arms," Blanche reported as the crisis developed. In response, Butler offered "a package of Lucifer matches" with which, he told them, "if you cannot take care of yourselves . . . you are not worthy to be freemen." Butler then asked his visitors why, when they and their friends were "molested," they did not "burn the dwellings and cotton fields of your persecutors. Take it when there is a high wind," he advised, and "you will not have to burn more than four or five before they will be glad to let you alone.'" In a letter to a group of Republicans in Shreveport, Louisiana, Butler offered a similar recommendation. As long as Black southerners continued letting themselves be killed "by every marauding white man who will do so," he wrote, "so long there will be no help; nor do I believe there is any aid to be looked for" from the federal government. "All I can say to the colored men," he counseled, "is to help yourselves and Heaven will help you," and if it were up to him, "I should take to killing equally if I were a colored man," for "as soon as those marauders who ride at night and shoot colored men find it dangerous to do it they will stop it, and not till then."[11]

As the weeks passed, it seemed increasingly likely that the federal government actually would *not* intervene in Mississippi after all, despite the national attention the situation had garnered and despite Butler's repeated attempts to persuade President Grant to do something. Ames grew despondent. "I can but feel sore at the treatment I have received at the hands of the general government," he confessed to Blanche. "The national administration has acted in a selfish, cold-blooded spirit in this whole trouble. I am disgusted." So disgusted, in fact, that Ames had decided the family should leave Mississippi altogether. "When my term as Gov. shall end," he wrote, "we will bid good-by to politics here—if I do not resign before." Meanwhile, Blanche remained in steady contact with her father, funneling him information to support his attempts to embolden the president. "I enclose another letter from Gen'l. Ames," she wrote in late October. "By it you will see that all your efforts have been useless, unless the President will at once order the troops to report to Gen'l. Ames so that he can order them into action the moment there is any outbreak." In the end, the November election in Mississippi proved a "complete Republican rout," but it passed without overt violence, brazen intimidation of Black and White Republicans having done the trick of suppressing their votes. "So Ames has lost his state," Butler sighed. "Poor fellow. I sympathize with him." In the weeks that followed, Mississippi's new "redeemer"-controlled legislature launched the second phase of its plan: impeachment of the sitting governor. But the threat of assassination lingered. "A prominent Democrat said that Gen'l. Ames' life was not worth the snap of a finger," Blanche wrote to Sarah in December. "Nobody in the North can realize the condition of affairs."[12]

From December 1875 into the early months of the new year, Butler and Ames corresponded at length on the impeachment question. Ames had little confidence that the state's Democrats, having triumphed in the election, would stand down from their assault on his office. Butler urged him nevertheless to refute whatever charges they presented, and to provide—"in the most dignified way"—a detailed statement, in his upcoming annual gubernatorial address, about any irregularities associated with the recent election. "The facts," Butler recommended, "should be stated with some boldness." Butler also offered to send a trusted attorney to Mississippi to assist with Ames's defense, all the while expressing confidence that President Grant would eventually position himself publicly on Ames's side. "Be not cast down or worried," Butler wrote encouragingly. At the same time, he reached out to Mississippi's sole Black state senator, Blanche K. Bruce, with suggestions for a speech that Bruce could give on Ames's behalf when the seemingly inevitable impeachment trial began. Speak "for your race," Butler urged, and do so "strongly, spiritedly, defiantly." "It is time," he added, "that somebody spoke up loudly and clearly for the colored man," as he himself had been doing for more than a decade.[13]

In his early January 1876 annual address, Ames did as Butler recommended. "You will see," he observed later, "that I have very courteously and briefly told the story of the wrongs" inflicted upon "the colored people and their friends in this state." Predictably, Ames's speech failed to appease his opponents, who grew, if possible, even angrier and more determined than they had been before. To Butler, Ames emphasized the irony of the situation: that "a gang of law breakers"—legislators "elected" through the intimidation of and violence against Black citizens and their White allies—were now accusing *him* of breaking the law by allowing for Black militia units, which they claimed were designed to provoke a "war of the races." In reply, Butler continued to convey confidence—whether or not he actually felt it—that Grant would come to Ames's aid and that Mississippi's Democrats would eventually realize that impeaching him was a gamble they could not afford. Ames remained unconvinced.[14]

For her part, Blanche fumed, detailing to Sarah the hatefulness of the former Confederates who now dominated the state she had grown to love. "This lovely climate and fertile country," Blanche wrote bitterly in early March, "is inhabited by a race which seems to have lost all the heavenly fire of noble purpose." Rather, "in proportion as the Negro acquired under the lash docility, humility, and subservience to authority, the master gained ferocity, arrogance, and resistance to all law, human and Divine." Now this cruel dynamic was playing out in the most grotesque and personal manner. As expected, the Mississippi House of Representatives soon reported twenty-one articles of impeachment against Ames to the state senate, but in the end there was no trial. Instead, Butler's rather paradoxical but perhaps ideally selected law associate, Roger A. Pryor—a former Confederate general and Democrat who had moved with his family to New York after the war—negotiated an arrangement whereby the state legislature would dismiss the impeachment articles in exchange for Ames's honorable resignation as governor.[15] "Conviction was certain," Ames wrote shortly after he agreed to the deal. "There was but one question for me to consider—and that was *self*. The revolution last fall had destroyed our party. A contest could have resulted in no good to anyone." Soon he, Blanche, and the children were on their way to Minnesota for a visit with his parents unless, of course, "the health of Mrs. Butler should require Blanche's presence."[16]

As Ames's letter implied, Sarah's health had continued to decline. When Butler had mentioned Sarah's recurring sore throat to a correspondent in mid-January 1876, he still seemed hopeful that nothing more severe was developing. But by early February there was good reason for alarm. "I am sorry to say that Mrs. Butler is exceedingly ill," Butler wrote to Ames, adding, "she has lost flesh and is being pulled down." Blanche grew anxious. "Why did you not tell me?" she scolded her mother. Sarah tried to tamp down Blanche's fears, joking that her voice was "still hoarse" but she could easily "manage to get along without it," and insisting that in every other way her health was "very fair." In truth, Sarah's condition was becoming dire, her spirits were low, and she was now considering surgery to relieve the pain, though her physicians continued to insist that she was experiencing nothing more than a "slight inflammation" of her throat, brought on by the cold weather, and that recent difficulties with respect to her breathing were "but a nervous affection." Too readily persuaded by the doctors' confidence that all would yet turn out well, Butler took time away in early March to give a much-appreciated address at Lowell's semicentennial celebration. Thomas Wilson, who had first arrived in Lowell as "a little Scotch boy, seven years old" around the same time Butler did, found the speech particularly moving. Wilson had worked for many years in the local mills and, as a proud resident of the "Spindle City," was thrilled that in Benjamin Butler, Lowell "had one so competent to do her justice on the occasion of her first Jubilee."[17]

In the midst of Ames's struggle for his political life and Sarah's struggle for her very survival, in early 1876 Butler also found himself dealing with the final stages of a major scandal involving his woman's rights activist friend, Victoria Woodhull, the esteemed Congregational minister Rev. Henry Ward Beecher (brother of Catharine Beecher and Harriet Beecher Stowe), and Beecher's lover, Elizabeth Tilton, who was married to Theodore Tilton. After first learning of the affair between Beecher and Tilton in 1872, Woodhull had published an article decrying Beecher's hypocrisy, specifically his many public statements denouncing her and the principle of "free love": the freedom of both men and women to engage in sexual relations outside the bonds of marriage. Woodhull's explosive article, which appeared in the newspaper she and her sister edited, *Woodhull and Claflin's Weekly*, embroiled her in a series of trials over several years, all related to the original affair and her exposé. On several occasions, Woodhull had leaned on Butler for legal advice and counsel, which he meted out while also trying to keep a safe distance. "I am very glad [Father] had nothing to do with that old Beecher trial," Blanche had confessed to her mother in May 1875. The controversy took a long time to die down, and in early 1876 Butler briefly agreed to take the case of one of Theodore Tilton's friends, Francis D. Moulton, whom Beecher had accused of libel after Moulton publicly confirmed that Beecher and Elizabeth Tilton were indeed lovers. Moulton approached Butler to help him clear his name and hopefully bring the scandal as a whole to an end. As it turns out, although Butler considered Beecher guilty on all counts and was, as ever, hardly averse to involving himself in such a high-profile and controversial case, he found working with Moulton impossible, and in late February decided to resign as his attorney.[18]

A month later, as the Ameses were pulling up stakes in Mississippi and preparing for their trip to Minnesota, it became obvious to Butler that, regardless of what the doctors claimed, Sarah's suffering was genuine and dangerous. He decided to escort her home to Lowell, making the trip from Washington in gentle increments. On April 1, he advised the clerk of New

York City's elegant Fifth Avenue Hotel that he and Sarah would be arriving in a couple of days with a small entourage. "Please give me a parlor with a little sleeping room attached," he wrote. "Have fire in both when we arrive." That same day, Butler asked an associate in Boston to set up lodging at the equally luxurious Tremont House for the group of travelers on the next leg of their journey, and to arrange for Sarah to meet with a respected local physician. Butler shared these rapidly evolving plans with Adelbert and Blanche, further mentioning the possibility of Sarah's undergoing surgery if the doctor in Boston recommended it, which he probably would. Now for the first time, although he urged them not to worry unduly, Butler suggested Blanche might want to skip the trip to Minnesota in favor of a visit with her mother. "I do not conceal from you," he admitted privately to Adelbert, "that Mrs. Butler would be exceedingly gratified if Blanche could be with her and relieve her from the care of housekeeping during this painful and perhaps dangerous operation." Somewhat portentously he added, "If Blanche can come home and bring the children, I would not wait for warmer weather." "I know how much Mrs. Butler is to you & I have never known a more lovely woman or a more valuable life," wrote Butler's business associate in Lowell, Richard Fay, who had recently learned of Sarah's illness. "I pray with all my heart that she may be relieved from suffering & may long be spared to you."[19]

Soon, correspondence by means of conventional letters gave way to telegrams urging Blanche's speedy return, and on April 7, Adelbert wired from Tennessee that he, Blanche, and the children were on their way. Sadly, they arrived only in time for the funeral. In the early hours of April 8, Sarah Hildreth Butler died at Massachusetts General Hospital from a malignant cancerous thyroid tumor which, according to her death certificate, she had endured for a decade. She was fifty-nine. Within hours of her passing, Butler began the heartbreaking work of notifying family and friends and making arrangements for the disposition of his wife's remains. "Sarah died at one o'clock and thirty minutes this morning at Boston," he informed his half-sister, Betsey Stevens, in New Hampshire. "She will be buried Wednesday at the earliest, perhaps not until Thursday. Won't you and such of your family as can, come down?" To his troubled nephew George he wrote similarly, and to Rev. Theodore Edson, who had performed their wedding at St. Anne's Episcopal Church in Lowell thirty-two years earlier, Butler sent a request that Sarah's funeral also be held there.[20]

In the days and weeks that followed, letters poured in from friends, family, acquaintances, strangers, old rivals, and more, all filled with profound, affectionate, and respectful words of condolence as well as acknowledgment of the deep love that had bound Benjamin and Sarah together over more than three decades. "Her memory will bless all her dear ones, & linger like the perfume of flowers," wrote one friend. "We can but feel that her days of trial were ended, her mission fulfilled, & her reward was waiting her, in the summerland into which her bright spirit has melted from your home." "Knowing as I do how close was the bond," wrote another, "& knowing as I do, and as the world does not, how tender-hearted a man you are, how can I possibly speak a word that can assuage any degree of your grief?" "We are overwhelmed by the awful news," wrote a third. "We feel that our loss, too, is irreparable,—the noblest friend, the greatest woman, we have ever known." "I am very sorry for you in your sudden affliction," wrote Butler's nephew George, "and sympathize deeply with the children who are deprived of so good a mother and counselor." From Germany Butler received condolences from his brother-in-law, William Webster, who had watched over Bennie and Paul during their years of study there and whose own wife, Susan—Sarah's sister—had died two years earlier. Webster sent words of singular empathy and sorrow. "I received your telegram informing me that the Fates were pursuing you and inflicted upon you and yours the greatest of all calamities," he wrote. "Since we left Lowell, many of our connections have been taken from us. And now, after the loss of my own dear wife, to know that the sister, so dear to her, and the person above all others, on whom she knew that she could always rely to counsel and befriend her children, is now gone too, makes us all think that one place is like another to us." Sarah's April 14 funeral at St. Anne's brought together not just a host of local admirers and family members but also "distinguished people" from Boston, New York, Philadelphia, Washington, "and even farther west and south," observed the *Boston Evening Journal*, all of whom "came to do homage to one whose years were full of usefulness and goodness." Accompanied by hundreds of reverent mourners, Sarah was then buried in the family plot in Dracut. Following the service, Butler put his faith in Time to ease his grief. "There is no other palliative or soother," he wrote to one friend, "for such a pain." To Blanche he admitted, "I am well but very lonely at the table and when I am alone."[21]

Shortly after Sarah's funeral, Butler fell ill with a severe and unusually lingering cold. In late May, his health finally improved, he took a fishing trip with Paul to New Hampshire to help distract him from his terrible loss. Throughout the summer and into the fall Butler sailed on the *America* and kept busy with legal work as well as fielding the many requests for help that continued to come his way, including from Mary Mumford and other job seekers, whose inquiries he frequently answered in thoughtful detail.

When a Miss Lizzie N. Wheeler of Whitefield, Maine, for example, informed him that she was thinking of moving to Massachusetts to work in one of the mills, he wrote at length to discourage her. The mills, he explained, "are not what they were thirty or forty years ago." Nowadays, they were instead largely "filled up with foreign employees," who, though they were "as good as anybody else" at a fundamental level, nevertheless might not be "fit associates for a young girl like yourself." Butler then went on an extended, nostalgic riff about his experiences in Maine while studying at Waterville College. In closing, and perhaps thinking how he might have advised Blanche in similar circumstances, he recommended that Wheeler seek a position as a domestic servant at some "respectable farmer's house" there rather than subjecting herself to "the vicissitudes of trade and the temptations of city life without protection." As before, Butler also continued to advise veterans, Black and White, who sought guidance regarding their pension applications. "I have probably obtained and advocated a thousand cases of pension for disabled soldiers, their widows and children," he wrote irritably to one. "I have never taken a cent for my services and I do not mean to begin now." In June, Butler attended the impressive Centennial Exposition in Philadelphia, which had opened on May 10 and ran for six months. And around this time, during a sojourn in Washington, D.C., he hired a young Black "manservant" named Albert West, whom he called "West" and who became, for the duration of Butler's life, his constant trusted and devoted aide and companion. Then roughly thirty years old, West was a formerly enslaved veteran of the USCT who may well have served in Butler's Army of the James. According to one contemporary source, West's conscientiousness, self-reliance, and deference when the two men met—West was working at a local livery stable at the time—had "stormed the general's own imperial heart and quite captivated it."[22]

There were also the grandchildren to enjoy. "Father has a great fancy for Butler," Blanche wrote to Adelbert at the end of May from Massachusetts, where she had remained to assist her father and provide companionship while Adelbert visited his family out west. As proof of the bond between grandfather and grandson she described a recent encounter. "A few days ago," she wrote,

he and Butler were the first at breakfast. Butler said "I want some of that, Grandfayer." "Do you know what it is?" "No, but I want some." Father took a small piece of liver on the fork and was about to put it on Butler's plate, when the young man said "That is not big enough, I

Longtime "bodyman" Albert West (?). Photographer unknown. This image, the only photograph of a Black man in an album of personal and family photographs from Butler's later years, seems highly likely to be of West. Unfortunately, the image is not labeled in the album, so it is impossible to know for certain. Courtesy of Special Collections & Archives, Colby College Libraries, Waterville, Maine.

want more." Father put another piece on the plate. "No, I wants more." So a third piece was added. Butler tasted of it and did not like it, and called for fish balls. Father gave him the fish balls, but at the same time pointed out to him the fact that he would have appeared better to have been more moderate in his demands for liver.

"I speak of this," Blanche added, "to show how patiently Father attended to his whims," possibly in contrast with the way she recalled him "attending" to his own children's "whims" when they were small.[23]

"Butler has become his Grandfather's companion," Blanche wrote a few weeks later. "He goes to the depot for him and with him. Edith also went down so that Father is well received. It is an odd sight to see those two small mites riding in the barouche all alone." In late September Blanche related an incident involving her father, the children, and a dispute over some candy. "Father returned last night," she wrote, bringing candy "as usual." But whereas little Butler "was delighted to see him," Edith "refused to kiss him until he produced the candy from his pocket." The following morning Edith wanted more candy, and when her grandfather refused, she upped the ante instead of backing down, now asking him "to buy her a little wagon." Blanche found this all highly amusing and observed that the children provided "a good deal of company for Father." Still, she noted, his grief over Sarah's passing persisted, and sometimes she heard him at night talking to himself in his room. "Poor Sallie, poor Sallie, I wish you could be here," she overheard him muttering on one occasion, using his pet name for Sarah. "In two or three years I shall follow."[24]

Butler's friends' keen awareness of his grief did not prevent them from urging him to run again for Congress in the fall; it probably inspired some to do so in the hope that another term in Washington would help to fill the void Sarah's death had left behind. Some encouraged him to run for president, but for the time being he was not interested. "I have your very kind and appreciative note suggesting my name for a [presidential] candidate before the convention at Indianapolis of those who believe in relieving the distress of the country by a change of our financial policy," Butler informed his friend James Buchanan, editor of the *Indianapolis Sun* (and no relation to the former president). "I aspire to no honors of that sort; I am content to be a soldier in the ranks." In fact, Butler was more than willing to make another congressional run, but he warned supporters he would do so only on his own terms, refusing to compromise his principles or grovel before party elites simply in order to obtain the Republican nomination. When W. A. Simmons, whose appointment as the Boston Custom House collector he had helped engineer, suggested that Butler refrain from antagonizing party opponents on a particular issue, Butler's reply was firm: "I am not so desirous of an election to Congress as to give up my manhood to get it."[25]

In the end, Sarah's absence accelerated Butler's return to the fray, and in early August he agreed to run again for US Congress to represent Massachusetts's Seventh District, in which Lowell was now situated. "Gratefully sensible of your confidence in me," Butler told his supporters, and despite some lingering "reluctance to peril the quiet and independence of private life," he was prepared to "put myself in your hands and in those of the other voters of the district at the coming election." As the news of Butler's candidacy spread, words of encouragement came from far and wide. Many correspondents believed his return to Congress would have outsized benefits for the nation as a whole, serving, on the one hand, to tame the Redeemer Democrats and their "moderate" Republican allies in the national legislature and, on the other, to discourage further neo-Confederate resurgence in the South. "I am glad to see that you have buckled on your armor again for the fight," wrote an ally from North Carolina. "You are worth more to the party and the country and the House than a gross of those wishey-washey creatures who are in the present Congress, who deal with traitors with gloves on." "I am truly pleased that you have again been placed before the people by your numerous friends in the 7th Cong. Dist.," wrote another, from Boston. "I hope you will be elected by a large majority and I *know* you will." "General," wrote W. H. Clement of Lowell, "we have always regretted your removal from this District . . . where we claim that you belong," and "we rejoice that you are now to return to us to go away no more." More than ever before, Clement insisted, "the country needs your service." Blacks from across the country, too, expressed relief and joy that Butler might soon be back in Washington. "As a colored man," wrote Jefferson Martin of Dowagiac, Michigan, upon learning of Butler's candidacy, "I will vouch to you and to Massachusetts that every colored man in this broad land wishes you back to Congress."[26]

In early September, Blanche reported to Adelbert that Butler's return to politics had indeed buoyed his spirits, and the Republican Party's recent state convention at Worcester, where "his name called forth more applause than any other," had left him "full of the nomination, and oblivious to all else." Determined opponents within the Republican Party reacted to the news, too, organizing quickly to torpedo his candidacy. These foes included Butler's longtime nemesis (and, briefly, Grant's attorney general) Ebenezer Rockwood Hoar, who considered himself a moderate Republican and who had opposed both the impeachment of Andrew Johnson and federal intervention to protect the freedpeople after the war. Butler and his allies despised Hoar, and the feeling was mutual. "You will see by the papers," Blanche updated Adelbert a few weeks later, "that Judge Hoar has accepted the nomination on a bolting ticket. He has no hopes of being elected, but thinks he can take enough votes from Father" to ensure the victory of John K. Tarbox, the Democrat running in the same district. "It is as mean a position as ever a man took," Blanche declared angrily, "as he works not to

Washington D.c. Oct 14" 1876

Hon. B. F. Butler,
          Dear Sir:
               *I have been instruct-
ed by my father to inform you that he
would be pleased to serve you, and that
he would look upon it as a great calamity
if you are defeated and a great triumph if
you are successful.*
      *Mr. Eugene Welburn and Mr. Mr. Johnson
are the best speakers, and if I am successful
in getting a leave for them they will leave here
for Lowel Sunday night next. Mr. Clapp has
already given Consent for Johnson, and I am to
see Secy Chandler to day for Welburn.*
            Respectfully yours

                Fredk Douglass jr.
Lock Box 31

Letter from Frederick Douglass Jr. to Butler. Courtesy of the Butler
Papers, Manuscripts Division, Library of Congress, Washington, D.C.

advance his own interest (that is a proper ambition for anyone) but to defeat
another." Still, she noted, "Father is sanguine, as he always is."[27]

Indeed, if Butler was annoyed by Hoar's hijinks, he remained undeterred
by them and proceeded to campaign for the Seventh District seat with his
usual vigor, bolstered by reliable and powerful allies, including Frederick
Douglass. Douglass, the great man's son informed Butler in mid-October,
"would look upon it as a great calamity if you are defeated and a great

triumph if you are successful." One person who was *not* so keen on Butler's running for Congress again was Bennie, now twenty-one and in his final year at West Point. "What do you think of Father's chances?" Bennie asked Blanche. "I sometimes hope he will get in & then again I almost hope he won't for he will be so busy that he will be away all the time." Bennie did not bother to hide his ambivalence from his father, either. "I congratulate you on your success in the Seventh District," he wrote, "although I almost wish that you were not going back to Congress, for it will take up so much of your time after I get home." Still, he admitted reluctantly, "I suppose you enjoy it, so it is all right."[28]

Efforts by Hoar and other mainstream, hard money, "moderate" Republicans to thwart Butler's election to Congress grew intense. From Butler's perspective, his opponents within the party seemed to represent "the whole moneyed power of the United States" gathered together in "an emanation of personal malignity and spite" that, he explained to one supporter, might result in the destruction of the state Republican Party altogether, or at least Butler's abandonment of it. His friends agreed. In a letter to the editor of the *Boston Traveler*, George W. Putnam described Hoar's scheme as the manifestation of a "deep, strong, & remorseless" attempt to "utterly destroy" Butler's political career. Hoar's animus toward Butler, Putnam explained, arose quite simply from his elitist disdain for Butler's democratic impulses and determination to uplift and protect society's underdogs. For proof, Putnam pointed to the fact that "the mass of Butler voters in his District are poor workingmen" who were dependent "upon their daily toil for bread for themselves & their families" and to whom party "loyalty" meant little. In contrast, almost all of the poor laborers' employers were diehard anti-Butler Republicans who were actively threatening their employees with dismissal if they voted for him.[29]

In October, Butler published a lengthy retort to Hoar's many and frequent "imputations" against him. At the same time, he continued to build support among potential voters beyond his reliable base of White working-class Republicans and Black Republicans of all classes. Now Butler actively sought the endorsement of the Seventh District's White Democratic workingmen as well. Toward this end, in his campaign speeches and writings Butler emphasized his long-standing and unwavering defense of labor, greenback currency, civil rights, and equality more generally. He contrasted his views with the apparent commitment of *both* parties' leaders to hard money platforms that benefited wealthy capitalists at the expense of working people, as well as their shared refusal to respond forcefully to the growing and violent rebelliousness of the former Confederates, whom White workingmen in the North regardless of party had been instrumental in defeating as soldiers during the war. "If you Irish Democrats and laboring men will go with me and vote with me to put down this new spirit of rebellion in the South" as they and their predecessors had done during the war, he promised, "then I will attend to the question of currency in such way as I think would be best for the whole country." Indeed, even before he decided to run for office again, Butler had begun a conversation with others who similarly struggled with the major parties' platforms and believed the time might have come for the establishment of a third party, possibly led by Butler, that focused specifically on the needs of labor and the poor. "What must the working men of this country do to be saved?" an ally in Boston had asked Butler as early as February. Was Butler willing to meet—as soon as possible—with a gathering of "prominent labor reformers" to "publicly advise and counsel them" on this question?[30]

"We want greenbacks for circulation for money," declared Peter Parker of Groveland, Massachusetts, and Butler, long a supporter of greenback currency, now had "the power of doing a great deal of good" if he would only "strike out boldly for the people." The "great tidal wave is rolling in," Parker insisted. "Go for the people and you are all right." Labor organizations from around the country urged Butler to come speak to their members. "The Workingmen's Industrial Council of this City," wrote B. C. McCormack of Troy, New York, "knowing you to be a friend, desire that you address them in this city at an early date." "You should accept the invitation to speak at the Independent Greenback Convention in this city February 16th," advised James Buchanan from Indianapolis. "You are the only prominent man in New England who has made the greenback question an issue," observed Alex Troup of New Haven, Connecticut. "Your future is identical with its success, and the struggle we are entering upon is your struggle."[31]

Butler found the idea of a third party intriguing and suggested a gathering in Washington to discuss it and to begin identifying those "measures of relief" that might truly "aid the destitute who crowd our cities, to acquire homestead upon unoccupied lands" while at the same time stimulating industrial production. And as the campaign continued, he emphasized a simple message: that "the cause of equal rights and liberty" is "paramount to every other issue." Butler did not just mean the equal rights and liberty of men; he also meant women, whose support he cultivated—especially the support of women's rights activists—even though they could not vote. "I have long been known to be in favor of woman suffrage," he wrote to Henry

Blackwell, the husband of Lucy Stone, founder of the American Woman Suffrage Association. "We amuse the women every fall by resolutions as we pet children with sugar plums when they cry for roast beef which we think too strong for their stomachs." "I have never doubted upon the question of woman's right to the ballot," he declared to his friend Phoebe Couzins. "As nations have gradually emerged from barbarism, woman has been elevated from being the slave and puppet of men to equality of social position," and the United States, too, must follow this path.[32]

Although Democrats around the country dominated in the November elections, Butler won his seat. From far and near, letters of congratulation and relief rolled in. "While lamenting over our general defeat," wrote one Republican from St. Paul, Minnesota, "there is some consolation in knowing that we have saved something from the wreck. Your election is a blessing to the country. The rebels cannot march in triumph through that House while you are on the floor." Wrote a friend from Boston, "I am happy to know that there is one man going to Congress who does not, never did, & never will, fear the rebels." "This is a victory of the bone and sinew of Massachusetts," crowed L. C. Bateman of New Hampshire, "over blue blood and kid gloved aristocracy." A correspondent from Illinois confessed that he had just named his newborn son after Butler, whom he had admired "ever since you contrabanded the Negro." "I rejoice for the black man of the South," declared a supporter in Dayton, Ohio, "that you will be his mighty defender in high places." And a group of Republicans in South Carolina insisted that "no hearts were more thankful, no voices more jubilant" than Butler's many admirers there. "Your election here," they wrote, "is regarded as a God send, and the knowledge that liberty, loyalty and justice is to have a champion in Congressional combat equal to every emergency, has re-souled even the doubting ones."[33]

Black Americans, too, expressed their delight in Butler's reelection. Wrote Rev. S. P. Huskins of Brunswick, Georgia: "Please believe that we the colored Republicans of Georgia . . . was very glad when we seen your grand triumph over the Demo nominee from Mass. Therefore we shall pray for your success." And it is clear the appeal of Butler's "small d" democratic political agenda had crossed party lines, as he had hoped. "In common with a great many of my Irish fellow countrymen," wrote James O'Berne of Washington, D.C., "I have to congratulate you most sincerely." O'Berne added that "Irishmen" in New York as well as the nation's capital, "even tho' they be Democrats," were nevertheless "glad at yr election." But he cautioned, "Do not forget them when you have a chance to give them a lift." Wrote another Irish American supporter from Minnesota, "I send you the congratulations of myself and of, at least, two thousand Irish voters of this country who are proud of your victory over the crystallized bigotry of seven generations of a common enemy." From Indiana came a letter describing Butler broadly as "our great champion for human rights and progress."[34]

Butler won his November 1876 election handily, but with twenty Electoral College votes in dispute, the murky results of the presidential election between Ohio Republican Rutherford B. Hayes and New York Democrat Samuel Tilden required several months, a series of negotiations, and a controversial "compromise" before a resolution was reached on March 2, 1877. In the interim, Butler and his allies pondered the implications of the Hayes versus Tilden question, at least one correspondent warning that if Tilden, who had won the popular vote, became president, Butler might find himself involved in another impeachment proceeding. Like many observers, Butler worried that although "the country wants peace and quiet," handled poorly the quest for a resolution in the contested presidential election might lead to a renewal of armed conflict. This seemed especially likely if that resolution involved the removal of the remaining Federal troops from the South, where their limited presence nevertheless offered some protection to the beleaguered freedpeople.[35]

"The compromise bill has very few friends here except the rebels," wrote a friend from Baltimore, as precisely such a plan became more likely, "and they only accept it because it gives them another chance to swindle us." And he added, "If Tilden is declared President, it will scarcely be safe for some of us to live here." To a correspondent in Georgia, Butler tried, perhaps in vain, to explain the importance of the Federal troops' continued presence there. "You will not allow a negro to have equal political privilege in the Southern States which the Constitution guarantees to him," Butler wrote. Rather, "you insist upon coercing him to vote against what he believes to be his interest by threats of discharge from employment if he does not do so." Truth be told, Butler warned, "you may thank God that Grant sends down troops to your States," because as long as the Federal soldiers remained in the South, "the negroes look to them for protection, and do not undertake to protect themselves." Should the Federal soldiers be recalled, however, and the freedpeople realize they were on their own, well, "God help you and yours." Instead of objecting to the soldiers' presence, Butler urged his correspondent to commit to subduing fellow Whites across the South who persisted in stirring up racial trouble by "talking about the lost cause, and war, and appealing and organizing Southern riots." As for all the rabble-rousing southern journalists, "hang them," he advised, and "you will go far toward having peace."[36]

Butler also considered the implications of the Hayes-Tilden "compromise" for the survival of the Republican Party. "Our party is going through troublous times," he observed flatly in one letter. Even if the Republican Hayes became president, Democrats now held a majority in the House of Representatives, which meant that Hayes would be "powerless to carry out any Republican measures." Moreover, Democratic rage over Hayes's assumption of the presidency would ensure that the Republican candidates lost seats—perhaps many seats—in the 1878 midterm election. On the other hand, should Tilden become president, the Republican Party, as the opposition party, might paradoxically become "stronger and better than ever even if it should have to be re-organized." Regardless of *how* the presidential election mess got sorted out, the next Congress, and the party, would face severe challenges. "The public service when well done is not a bed of roses, nor always an assurance of safety," he wrote to Horace Maynard, the American ambassador to Turkey, "but we must take what comes as it comes." As for himself, Butler insisted, "I fear neither the bludgeon nor the horse-whip, as I can meet those, and I have some skill with the use of pistols as weapons of defence." He reassured New Hampshire newspaper editor William E. Chandler that in the midst of all this "hubbub," he was determined to stay focused on his long-standing and primary goal, namely, "that safety, freedom, peace and quiet shall come to the colored man in the South." And he added, "I shall address myself to that point very much regardless of everything else."[37]

In the end, the Compromise of 1877 made Hayes president in exchange for an end to what remained of Federal military occupation of the former Confederacy. "I have never seen an administration launched in the way our present one is," Butler observed to a friend in New Orleans. "On the whole the Republican party is in a very unfortunate condition." To his old friend James Parton he expressed disappointment that the new president seemed entirely uninterested in the advice of congressional Republicans, especially those who shared Butler's views on the question of the administration's "southern policy." Indeed, the split within the Republican Party on that issue was, as he put it, "wider than a church and deeper than a grave," and in the months between the Forty-Fifth Congress's brief first session and its reconvening in October, it became increasingly clear that most leading Republicans in Massachusetts and in Congress were lining up with Hayes's conciliatory approach. "The thing has happened, which I supposed would happen and which in my judgment was not best to oppose," Butler explained to a friend in Springfield, Massachusetts, following the annual state Republican convention that fall, "to wit, the endorsement of the policy of Mr. Hayes."[38]

From the moment Butler was elected by the Seventh District, Black Americans had not only congratulated him but had also been urgently appealing to him for help. "When you rode over the battle ground and saw the dead men of my color," wrote W. H. Moor of North Carolina, a veteran of the USCT and the Army of the James who was now a state senator, "you said that you would ever stand up for us so now Gen I appeal to you to stand by your sentiments and you will find that we the colored people will stand by the party." Butler's Black correspondents flooded him with reports of continued violence, and not just in the South. "We are sold out to the old slave oligarchy," wrote a black Vermonter in April. Some wondered whether the time had come for blacks to "self-segregate" and Butler, who had opposed colonization in the past, now agreed that the idea of "self-segregation" had some advantages. "Under existing circumstances," he admitted to a veteran of the Fifty-Fourth Massachusetts now living in Memphis, "I should advise the colored people if they find themselves oppressed at the South to quietly withdraw to some country where they will not be so oppressed." By "some country," however, Butler did not mean a foreign land, but somewhere else in the United States, which was Black Americans' rightful home as much as it was Whites'. "I have your note in regard to legislation to send the negroes to Liberia," Butler responded to J. W. Wilbourn of Tennessee. "I certainly shall not favor any such legislation. They were born here, have the same rights here under the Constitution that you have, and ought to stay here. There is no more reason why they should be sent to Liberia because their ancestors came from Africa, than that you should be sent back to England because your ancestors came from Cornwall." At one point Butler even considered establishing a settlement for Black Americans on land of his own, but he did not pursue the idea. During this period Butler also weighed in on the question of whether or not to continue allowing Black soldiers to serve in the so-called peacetime army, which was actively if intermittently engaged in war against the country's Native people. His answer was yes, putting him at odds with William T. Sherman, then serving as the army's commanding general. "I honestly think," Sherman declared, "the white race the best for this."[39] Based on his own experience with Black soldiers during the Civil War, Butler disagreed.

As Hayes's conciliatory southern policy took hold, the pressure built for Butler to take a bold, public stand against it. "The Republican party is in much need of some one in Congress to hold up the trailing flag of our party," wrote one New Yorker, "and to you more surely than to any other man do we look for aid." Still, Butler held his peace, at least in public, suggesting privately to some friends (though probably not very seriously) that there remained a remote possibility conciliation would actually bring about an end to sectional and racial tensions, in which case the Republican Party would have fulfilled its mission and could then be allowed to fade away entirely. Meanwhile, women's rights activists, including Susan B. Anthony, pressed Butler to use his influence in Congress on *their* behalf, Hayes having expressed himself as "non-committal" on the subject of women's suffrage. Banking on Butler's "unselfish interest in the cause of human liberty and progressive enterprise" for women as well as men, some even urged him to sponsor a bill to establish a "National University" for women in Washington, to be funded by the federal government.[40]

Currency reformers, too, pleaded with Butler to exploit party instability on both sides of the aisle and create a bipartisan coalition against the hard money hardliners—the so-called "Gold Bugs"—in favor of the "Rag Baby," paper money. "The repudiation of the Greenback," warned a correspondent from New York City, would pitch America's struggling laborers into "the dark valley of the shadow of death" even as it ensured the permanence of a "privileged and protected aristocracy." "Once I thought you a bad politician," wrote another from Skowhegan, Maine, "but this opinion I have had reason to change" as "your stand on 'the money question'" is "a stand for humanity." If the Republican Party had at one time been the "friend of the poor," observed a Californian, now it was turning into the "party of oppression," increasingly determined to "rob the poor man of his dearest rights by adding to his burthen." On behalf of "the labor element of this state," this correspondent begged Butler to "do now as you have ever done" and "prove yourself the champion of right, and the friend of the poor." In doing so, he promised, "you will receive the blessings of millions yet unborn." "Your name has become a household word in the Western states," declared a supporter in Iowa, where Butler was widely known as "the friend of humanity, the bold advocate of the people's rights, the terror of official rings and rogues," and a man who stood "always on the side of the underdog."[41]

During the months Congress was out of session, Butler maintained his robust correspondence while staying busy with his legal work, continuing his administrative leadership of the NHDVS, and fielding the usual requests for assistance of all sorts, including from Mary Mumford and, more recently, Elizabeth Van Lew, the former Union spy in Richmond. That summer he also celebrated Bennie's long-awaited graduation from West Point after months of encouraging him to try and improve his academic standing before leaving the academy. "Let me entreat you to do your best in the three months remaining," Butler had written in February, "to fetch up your own standard as high as possible." Bennie promised to try, but he was eager to be done. "Only seventy-three days to graduation," he wrote exuberantly on April 1; a week later he was dreaming about a postgraduate sailing adventure with some friends on his father's yacht.[42]

Bennie, Henry Flipper, and seventy-four other cadets graduated on June 14, 1877, after which both Bennie and Flipper were assigned to service with the all-Black Ninth Cavalry in Texas. From El Paso, Bennie still showed no sign of enjoying military life. "My present duties consist in copying affidavits," he wrote dully, "most of which are not worth the paper they are written on." Butler urged Bennie to press on despite his boredom, in preparation for a possible future career in the law and, even more important, so that he might eventually "leave the Army with honor, not to return to it again until the exigencies of war against somebody worth fighting shall call for the services of every true man of the nation." Likely Bennie's most dramatic experience while he was stationed in Texas was coming dangerously close in the spring of 1878 to being murdered by former Confederates determined to exact the most painful revenge possible against his father. "I saw by today's telegrams that two masked men made an attempt on Ben's life near El Paso," Adelbert wrote to Blanche. "Ben has been there long enough. He had better live in civilized New England and abandon a country where savages [by which he meant former Confederates rather than Native Americans] are still fighting the battles of the rebellion."[43]

For his part, Paul Butler was now to all intents and purposes running the US Cartridge Company, while also doing as much sailing as his leisure time allowed. "Paul has been elected President of the Vesper Boat Club of Lowell," Bennie informed his father enviously, "& I suppose feels very proud of himself." In the course of his work Paul did some traveling in Europe, including Russia, where, according to Blanche, he negotiated an order for "a million cartridges" and twenty "Lowell guns." "Paul has brought quite a number of little trinkets, as mementos of his travels," Blanche wrote to Adelbert following one of Paul's trips, adding, "He says the Russians are peculiar in this respect that you have to explain every little thing just as you would to children and that they ask the most absurd questions." As for Blanche, she spent her time managing her own family and the house in Lowell, with occasional trips to visit her in-laws (and so her husband could attend to some business ventures) in Minnesota. When she and her family traveled west, Blanche always made sure to let Butler know how much his grandchildren missed him. "Edith," she wrote on one occasion, "has a great deal to say of her 'grandfather in Lowell who has no hair in the middle.' She thinks she 'likes him the best.'" Butler doted on the grandchildren and frequently worried about their health, especially when they were away. On one occasion, learning that his namesake was suffering from the aftermath of a bout of diphtheria, he urged Blanche to bring the family back to Massachusetts as soon as possible, confessing that little Butler's illness had "given me more anxiety than I ever thought I should take about a young gentleman of his size." When he learned, a few days after the event, that Blanche had given birth to her fourth child, Blanche Ames Ames, Butler pretended to scold his son-in-law for not informing him sooner. "What do you think the telegraph was meant for?" he demanded, before resuming a more familiar tone. "Tell the children that Grandfather is coming," he wrote, "and we will have a frolic together."[44]

Even as his own children and grandchildren seemed to be thriving for the most part, Butler's nephew George continued his inexorable descent, reaching the point where his uncle considered him essentially beyond help. And yet, Butler did not give up, even offering to pay for Joanna to come east from California to stay with her son if she and George thought that would make a difference. To one friend he observed in frustration that George had "broken every pledge to me that he has ever made," and had even "disgraced me" by his inability to function effectively in the various government posts Butler had managed to wrangle for him. "He is forty years of age and thoroughly able to take care of himself if he will," Butler insisted, displaying his own failure to understand the consequences of alcoholism. "If he will not, nobody on earth can take care of him and there is the end."[45]

On the national level, the summer of 1877 witnessed what came to be known as the Great Railroad Strike, a violent upheaval of labor in response to wage cuts that only deepened Butler's determination to advance a legislative agenda, once Congress reconvened, that included both a firm response to ongoing white supremacist terrorism in the South and meaningful labor and currency reform. "You are well aware of the great labor troubles and the existence of general dissatisfaction throughout the whole of this large country," wrote Herman Thomes, a coal miner, in late August. "For the last two years almost every workingman in the United States was down to actual hard pan dry bread and old clothes." The previous year, the nation had celebrated the centennial of its independence, "but where is that great freedom now?" he asked, adding, "The eyes of hundreds of workingmen are anxiously awaiting your movements and your advice." In consultation with his friend James Buchanan in Indiana, where the idea of a Greenback/Labor Party continued to gain momentum, Butler considered pressuring the treasury secretary (then General Sherman's brother, John Sherman) to refrain from ordering a contraction of the currency and the "retiring" of paper money "until after consideration of the financial measures necessary for the relief of the country." Buchanan recommended a more radical effort, including a thorough restructuring of the nation's financial arrangements. "The banks," he declared, "have been our great enemies. They have held the people of the nation under their thumb and the only thing that will entirely break their power is to smash the banks."[46]

On October 15, the Forty-Fifth Congress, where Democrats now held a 52.6 percent majority, finally reconvened for its back-to-back second and third sessions, lasting until June 20 of the following year. The Forty-Fifth Congress ultimately produced three major pieces of legislation in which Butler had a strong and active interest: the Bland-Allison Coinage Act, introducing silver dollars into the national currency (Butler advocated paper money but he greatly preferred "bi-metallism" to a narrow reliance on the gold standard); the National Quarantine Act, establishing the sort of strict policies for preventing the importation of contagious diseases to the United States that Butler had favored in New Orleans; and the Posse Comitatus Act, limiting the federal government's capacity to deploy the US military to enforce domestic policies, which he vigorously opposed as yet another example of the North's abandonment of their obligations to the freedpeople. Among the other bills this Congress considered was "an act to relieve certain legal disabilities of women," which Butler strongly supported and on behalf of which he invited Belva Lockwood—like Phoebe Couzins, one of the first women attorneys in the United States—to address the House Judiciary Committee on which he served. The House voted soundly in favor of the bill (169 to 87 with 36 abstentions), which would have granted women lawyers the same rights as male lawyers, but it failed in the Senate.[47]

Throughout this period, Butler's steady prolabor, progreenback, anti–hard money views riled his opponents but thoroughly pleased his friends irrespective of their party affiliation. As Cornelius O'Donnell of Aiken, South Carolina, wrote shortly before the Coinage Act's passage, "You are a Republican and I am a Democrat but your ideas on the currency of the country are correct and I know they are the honest ideas of an honest man." A supporter in Illinois offered Butler similar praise as well as thanks. "We of the West are very much rejoiced to see you stand up boldly and manfully for the best interests of the toiling of the nation," he wrote, "when so many thousands of the moneyed tyrants of the East, by whom you are more immediately surrounded, are making such disparate efforts to close up the common avenues to general prosperity." Wrote one Indianan, "I am more than pleased to see you stand by the old Greenback," and he hoped a third party—the Greenback Party—would soon become a reality and "save this country."[48]

Meanwhile, Butler remained in touch with Black and White contacts across the South regarding the ongoing racial tensions and violence there that clearly indicated the former Confederates' determination to at least virtually re-enslave the freedpeople. Among his correspondents was Robert Hansen of Georgia, who reported being "arrested, tried, and convicted" for "aiding to protect the life and property" of another Black man like himself and who now begged to know "if there is any law of the United States under which a poor and oppressed citizen can be protected, and have an impartial trial in case of arrest." "The Southern States are doing away with their state prisons and say they are leasing out the prisoners to private parties, who are to have the sole control of the convicts," wrote another correspondent, advising Butler that the ultimate goal of this arrangement was clearly "to revive slavery." Appealing to Butler as "the most prominent officer in defending the poor colored people during the late war," A. B. Lind of Wilmington, North Carolina, begged him for money to help arm local Blacks who were forming militia companies for self-defense, as others had done in Mississippi under Governor Ames. "I am not appealing for myself," Lind insisted, "but for my men directly, and for the safety of my race." Still, for the time being and in contrast with his past practices, Butler remained unusually quiet in public on the president's policies toward the South, though he privately deplored them and continued to believe conciliation would ultimately destroy the Republican Party. He considered it unwise, he explained to a friend in Acton, Massachusetts, "for any Republican," himself included, "to do anything which might drive the President into the arms of the Democracy." So he stayed silent, though "I am certain you will credit me with love of country as well as love of party, if you knew how much I have repressed, both in feeling and in thought." And he promised, "When in my judgment it becomes necessary for the safety of the country or the protection of the true and loyal men of the South to speak out, then if I hold my peace the very stones will cry out."[49]

During his time in the Forty-Fifth Congress, Butler bit his tongue more often than he had in the past, but it bears noting that his opposition to an easy, undemanding reconciliation with former Confederates was already a matter of public record, like his ardent support for Black Americans' rights and his views on labor and financial reform. Such views faced powerful political resistance in Massachusetts and elsewhere, however, threatening his future in Congress or in any position of real influence, and like any politician, he weighed his options along with his ambition and his goals. At the same time, he refused to align himself with the mainstream of his party for his own benefit though he was certain that if at any point he had openly (if disingenuously) expressed "advocacy of the views of the bullionists and hard money people," he could have become "the dandled pet of the money changers and those that sold doves." Instead, the path he had chosen had produced "a large portion of the objection to me that has made itself apparent." Still, he sighed, "what am I to do?" In the end, he would always choose to "stand up in the fear of God and love of man, erect in his image, and do that which I believe to be for the best interests of my country and the good of the people."[50]

Of course, the views Butler held that provoked his opponents delighted his supporters, like the Boston laborer who described himself as a representative of workingmen in Massachusetts and across the country, who thanked Butler for being the sole member of Congress with "the moral courage to stand up & speak the great truths as you have done for the cause of labor." Such accolades were uplifting, as were the many invitations Butler continued to receive. "Will you come to our city and address a grand mass meeting of the people on Independence Day on the labor and currency reform questions?" asked James Springer of Chicago. "The laboring men and currency reformers of the West would delight to see and hear you who have been one of their most fearless champions." Calls for him to run for president at the next opportunity still came on a regular basis, including from California's Workingmen's Party. Writing from San Francisco, Henry Finnegas promised the support of laboring men up and down the West Coast, especially if Butler formed an alliance with the racist, virulently anti-Chinese labor leader Denis Kearney. Others wisely encouraged Butler to steer clear of Kearney, calling him an "ignorant brute" whom Butler must "renounce" immediately if he did not want Kearney to become "a millstone about your neck."[51]

Then, in April 1878, Butler's period of relative public reserve ended when he embroiled himself in a dispute over a seemingly minor government appointment: the next doorkeeper of the House of Representatives. Although Butler had largely muted his views over the past year on the related questions of sectional reconciliation and racial justice in the South, this "raucous debate" put him back in the spotlight on both issues. The argument began when Butler nominated Irish-born James Shields, who had served as a US senator from both Illinois and Minnesota and had commanded volunteer forces as a brigadier general in the Mexican-American War and again in the Civil War, in the course of which he sustained an injury. Shields's supporters, including Butler, considered him a hero and also believed the honorary position of doorkeeper should be filled by someone not associated with the Confederates' attempt between 1861 and 1865 to destroy the federal government. House Democrats—many of them former Confederates themselves—not only objected to Shields's nomination but also insisted that Butler had nominated him expressly in order to "exploit bitter and painful war memories" and thereby derail Hayes's reconciliation agenda. They then nominated Charles William Field of Kentucky, a former Confederate major general who had also been wounded in the war. In his opposition to Field's nomination, Butler emphasized the high irony of selecting as House doorkeeper a man who had spilled his own and others' blood in order to destroy the United States, but the Democratic majority prevailed, and Field was installed. Butler's "commitment to the memory of loyal Union men" in this instance did not go unnoticed, however. "Permit an old soldier to again congratulate you on your gallant fight for an old comrade for doorkeeper," wrote one supporter from Nebraska. "You have sent a bigger shell in the rebel lines than has been exploded in their ranks since you hoisted the American flag over the St. Charles in New Orleans." And, he added, "the Government never had a truer soldier upon the battlefield, or our dead and living comrades a better friend in and out of Congress, than Gen'l Benj. F. Butler."[52] Butler may have gone temporarily quiet on certain issues, but his loyalty to the victorious Union, and what he understood to be the responsibilities associated with that victory, had not been forgotten.

On Decoration Day in 1878, Butler raised his voice again as the "orator of the day" before a large gathering of Civil War veterans and others at Gettysburg, just shy of fifteen years after the great battle there. On this occasion Butler's topic was "The Private Soldiers in the War of the Rebellion," and his speech, delivered in a "blinding rain," reminded listeners that the soldiers' sacrifices, and especially their deaths, "make it a duty to remember not only our rights but our wrongs," even as the nation continued to move forward in peace. "In commemorating our dead, or in honoring our living soldiers," he insisted, "we neither reproach nor criticize those who fought against us. . . . We may not forget that they were good soldiers in a bad cause," and "no man ought to feel that we acted unjustly or unkindly toward any other class of citizens because we prefer loyalty to treason."[53] Reconciliationists were displeased.

Then, in July, Butler traveled to Atlantic City for some rest, to ponder his political future, and, it seems, in the hope of enjoying some female company—Anna Dickinson's company, to be precise—though it is unclear what degree of intimacy he sought with her. One of Dickinson's biographers describes Butler as "fascinated by Anna, with her wandering fame," and claims that from the moment they met years earlier—even while Sarah was still alive—Butler had sought out the much younger woman as a possible mistress. Another defines Butler's approach to Dickinson as a "courtship." The two had certainly been in some contact for a number of years, and on more than one occasion Butler had provided Dickinson, as he provided so many others, with financial support. Moreover, it is entirely plausible that Butler found Dickinson attractive and was drawn to her emotionally and otherwise, especially given the great loneliness he experienced after Sarah died. "I have no home life now; that has passed and gone," he wrote sadly to one friend, "although I have three loving children who are more than dutiful and kind to me." Less plausible, given the strength of his love for Sarah and his family, is the idea that even while his marriage endured he had been seriously considering taking Dickinson as a lover. Moreover, it is hard not to be struck by the depiction of Butler as a comical, pathetic suitor who never had a chance (a "bumbling old man," in the words of one historian), rather than as a generous if somewhat awkward, lonely, older friend. In any case, although he invited "Lizzie" Dickinson to join him on the Jersey shore in the summer of 1878, she did not go. Their relationship cooled somewhat as a result, but on the whole, he remained supportive for several years to come.[54]

By the time he returned from New Jersey, Butler had to decide whether or not to run for election again in the fall. He chose to do so, but not for reelection to Congress. Instead, he set his sights on the governorship of Massachusetts and also officially withdrew from the Republican Party, whose surrender to conciliation with the former Confederacy and whose antilabor, hard money agenda had become intolerable. Leading Massachusetts Republicans were glad to see Butler go, because they disagreed with his political views and also, it seems, because they feared that his election to the governorship as a Republican could set him up for a successful presidential run in 1880. "I recognize that there is to be an overturn of parties," Butler had observed to a correspondent in Salem earlier that year, "but come weal or woe I am going in one direction, which I have been going in for the last ten years." Instead, Butler accepted the nomination of the state's Independent Greenback Party. Hearing the news, a correspondent from Rome, New York, offered thanks, adding, "Though the papers say a great many things against you, none of them can say that you were not the poor man's friend." Butler also welcomed the enthusiastic support of many of the state's Democrats, over 50,000 of whom signed a petition endorsing his candidacy. "I suppose it would be possible to force a nomination from the Democratic Convention," Butler hinted to a friend in Springfield in early August. Claiming that he would not make the effort himself, or even actively try to arrange it, he would certainly accept the nomination if it somehow came to pass. In the meantime, he was content to run without the official support of either major party, instead aiming to maximize his appeal to labor. This required, among other things, performing a delicate balancing act with regard to the influential, racist, anti-Chinese labor leader, Denis Kearney, which Butler attempted to do by publicly disavowing his opponents' claim that he and Kearney had forged an alliance, while simultaneously acknowledging that not all of Kearney's ideas were completely objectionable. Kearney, he noted, certainly seemed uniquely able to engage and inspire "a class of men that have lain dormant in politics," which Butler considered commendable.[55] It was not Butler's finest moment.

Butler made a good showing but was defeated in his November 1878 bid for the governorship, earning 110,000 votes to the 135,000 received by the Republican, Thomas Talbot, who had previously served as lieutenant governor and acting governor. There were some reports of corruption in the voting process: Butler received numerous letters after the fact from voters saying they had been denied access to the ballot for spurious reasons. Most supporters, however, blamed his loss on the "ocean of lies, denunciation & slander" with which well-placed opponents, especially rich and powerful Republicans, had dogged his candidacy, especially through the press. "No man of great abilities," observed a friend from Marblehead, "ever undertook the cause of the millions without bringing upon him the sneers, threats, & persecutions of the rich & powerful part of the community," and such had been Butler's fate. As others had done before, this same friend compared Butler to Thaddeus Stevens and promised that things would turn out better next time around. Regardless of the outcome of the election, agreed a correspondent from Ohio, Butler had strengthened his already solid reputation around the country as the one true friend of "farmers and workingmen," which would not be forgotten. "I have voted the Republican ticket for quite a number of years," wrote a disappointed Bostonian, but "I shall vote it no longer." Rather, in any future matchup, Butler could count on him for support, even if Butler's opponents tried to suppress the vote by claiming that Butler was dead. "I had much rather vote for a dead Butler," he declared, "than for a living Talbot!"[56]

Butler completed his fifth and final term in Congress in March 1879, not long after the Specie Resumption Act, passed initially in 1875, took effect, restoring the gold standard and retiring the greenbacks. "I entertain the most unwavering faith," Butler wrote to one correspondent, "in the power of the government to coin money out of any material it sees fit, and with any means it sees fit," though he continued to hope that currency would eventually be produced in such a manner as to be "most cheap and convenient for the use of the people." That same year Butler stepped down as head of the board of managers of the NHDVS following thirteen years of successful leadership. He also gave numerous speeches on a wide variety of political topics, including the question of whether or not the federal government should continue to honor Southern claims for damages wrought by the war. "So long as war claims are presented," he opined in a major speech on the topic, "so long the wounds of the war will be kept open, and so long there will be misunderstanding between the several sections of the Union." Nevertheless, he continued, although "my friends on the other side desire 'by-gones to be by-gones,'" and while reconciliation in some form was certainly "desirable," northerners "never can or will forget," nor should they, the particular "valor and patriotism of the soldiers who fought for the Union in the hour of direst trial." Back in Lowell, Butler filled some of his new leisure time by looking over Paul's shoulder as Paul managed the Cartridge Company. "I hear complaints of the quality of the manufacture of your ammunition, especially that which went to the Russians," Butler grumbled. "I did not use to hear these complaints of the workmanship of the cartridge in past times. Why do I hear them now?" As before, for relaxation and pleasure he enjoyed playing billiards and sailing when he could, often inviting friends along. To at least one potential guest he issued the playful warning that an adventure on the *America* required each person onboard "to be able to eat and drink unlimitedly, not be sea-sick more than one half of the time and keep good natured under difficulties, if any occur, especially in drizzly weather."[57]

Even as supporters encouraged him to look ahead to the 1880 presidential race, in the fall of 1879 Butler ran again for governor of Massachusetts. "The people of Mass want Gen. Butler for Governor," wrote a friend from Jamaica Plain, just outside of Boston, "and the people also want Gen Butler for president of this nation." As always, Butler gave numerous speeches, accepting invitations from across the state as well as from beyond its borders, such as the one he received in August from a labor organization in Wilkes Barre,

Pennsylvania, asking him to address a "mammoth picnic" of "thousands of the united workingmen" there. "There is no man today in the United States," these laborers' representative claimed, "more endeared to their hearts than yourself." Having built a strong foundation of support among the state's Democratic voters on his previous outing, Butler ran this time around as the official nominee of the state's Greenback *and* Democratic parties. Indeed, it was John Tarbox—the Democrat whom Ebenezer Hoar and the state's "establishment" Republicans had pitted against Butler years earlier—who informed him of the party's nomination. In his letter, Tarbox addressed "the general desire of the people not bounded by the limits of national party divisions for a change of administration" that would, they hoped, lead to the "promotion of wholesome public reforms in the State government, not reasonably to be hoped for from the powers now in control." Massachusetts Democrats, he explained, were ready to endorse Butler for governor because they trusted his promise that if elected, he would restore to the state's government "the efficiency, economy, and justice to the people of all classes, which characterized the earlier days of the republic.'" As usual, Butler's supporters rejoiced while his opponents groused, many of the latter now mocking the Democrats for allowing Butler to "swallow" their party whole, purely, they were certain, for the sake of his own ambition.[58]

Once again Butler made a good showing but lost the election, earning 108,000 votes to Republican John D. Long's 121,000. For the next two years he did not put himself forward as a candidate. Indeed, asked by his sometimes law associate Roger Pryor the following summer what his views were on the upcoming presidential election, Butler replied that he was taking a break from politics. He would *not* vote for Republican James A. Garfield, whom he associated with the party's abdication of its postwar responsibility to the freedpeople. And although he felt "a great personal respect" for the Democratic candidate, Winfield S. Hancock, he disagreed with the national Democratic Party's conservative platform and therefore would not vote for Hancock or, indeed, do any campaigning for anyone. As it happens, that summer Butler was even at odds with the national Greenback Party, which he accused of "attaching itself to a socialist tail," by which he meant the internally fractured party's decision to welcome to its convention a delegation from the Socialist Labor Party. "I am no socialist," Butler declared, describing himself instead as "a radical Democrat." And anyway, "I want no office." Garfield's assassination soon brought Chester Arthur to the presidency, but Butler insisted to Blanche, "I have heard no news—not even who the Cabinet are—and care about as much as I know."[59]

Instead, Butler refocused his energy on his business and legal work, developed a correspondence he had begun a few years earlier with Thomas Edison regarding Edison's many inventions, took a six-week trip to California, testified before Congress on the dangers of corporate monopolies (specifically the emerging monopoly represented by Standard Oil), welcomed another grandchild, Adelbert Ames Jr, watched sadly as his nephew George continued to suffer, extended his hand to many who approached him for help, including, with increasing reluctance, Anna Dickinson, and rebuffed a request from Colby University for yet another donation. In his letter responding to the request, Butler hinted that the college should perhaps have been renamed after *him*, not Gardner Colby, and criticized the second part of the college's name too, noting that "the institution is not a University in any true sense of the term, so in my judgment the name is a misnomer." (Within about a decade the school changed its name again, to Colby College.) During these years Butler also half-heartedly swatted away a variety of rumors that resurfaced—to a great extent courtesy of the increasingly influential apologists of the "Lost Cause"—about his supposedly nefarious activities during the war. Butler considered the rumors a predictable consequence of his fame, too, as well as his complicated, outspoken character and political history, not to mention his looks. "I have never undertaken to enter into denials or explanations of the various slanders against me," he explained to a friend in New Jersey, "because the bitterness engendered naturally in the war made them very numerous and men possibly believing them to be true thought by pressing them upon me and circulating them as true, they could obtain money." Moreover, "If I had undertaken to answer them all I should have had time to do nothing else. . . . I have trusted that so far as I know a blameless business and social life would be the best answer. . . . I am content to leave such matters to the fair judgment of all honest men."[60]

In the late winter and spring of 1881, Butler, West, Paul, and Bennie—home from the army at last—took an extended sailing trip to the Bahamas, Cuba, and Florida. From Nassau, Butler informed Blanche—"the only person in the United States who I suppose cares very much whether I have got here right or wrong"—that he was hale and hearty but her brothers had been suffering from seasickness. From Havana, he described his impressions of the city, including its excellent cigars. Butler also observed the city's struggles dealing with yellow fever, which the Cubans, he said, referred to as "a visitation of God" but he considered "a visitation of nastiness" and a "scourge" that "six months of energetic administration" under his leadership could resolve. "I would contract to do it pay contingent upon success," he wrote,

but "I should want full military power." From Cuba the traveling party visited Palatka, Florida, and then made a nostalgic stop at Fort Monroe. "All
well," Butler informed Blanche on April 8. "Cargo: sundry empty wine bot-
tles, some full ones, sundry empty cigar boxes, some full ones, one alligator
skin 8 ft. long and sundry skins of birds."[61]

That summer, Butler sailed north to Nova Scotia with Paul, Adelbert,
grandson Butler, and West as companions. "I was amused yesterday," Adelbert informed Blanche in one letter, by a "scuffle between your Father and
Butler. The former had a cloth skull cap and a short blouse on and of the
two seemed the most boyish—a big, fat, jolly boy." Now a law student at
Columbia University in New York City, Bennie did not join them. And, in
fact, Butler never again saw his younger son alive. It appears that Bennie
suffered from Bright's disease, a kidney condition often associated with dia-
betes, and he succumbed to it quite unexpectedly on September 1, 1881, at
age twenty-six, before Blanche was able to summon the sailing party home
from their adventures. Subsequently, the Butlers' summer home at Bay View
was closed for the year; Bennie's funeral, like his mother's five years earlier,
took place in Lowell.[62]

Once again, Butler's mail filled with letters of condolence; once again, he
struggled to respond. To a law associate he admitted, "I am forcing myself
now into work, and have but little heart in what I'm doing." To a friend who
had recently lost his mother, he wrote, "We can mingle our griefs together,
you for the mother and I for the son." As before, he banked on the passage
of time to lighten the weight of sorrow. "Time, the all healer," he wrote, "is
the only cure." To Frank Blair Jr., one of Bennie's closest friends from West
Point, he expressed special thanks for the bond the two young men had
shared. "Had my feelings of regard not been quite sufficiently extended to
you before as Ben's classmate and chum, your very kind note of sympathy,"
he wrote, "would have as far as such a thing is possible, given you his place
in my regard." Blanche, too, mourned deeply. "Poor Ben!" she wrote to Adelbert, having just visited her brother's gravesite in the family cemetery. "The
turf is already taking root on his grave, and we all go on the same as if he
were still with us. It is hard to realize that we are to hear his happy laugh and
see his sunny handsome face no more." Meanwhile, and perhaps with fresh
determination, Butler renewed his efforts to help his nephew, even as he
announced to his sister-in-law Joanna and the nurses at the hospital where
George had most recently been receiving care that he was letting go.[63]

As the new year dawned, a return to more active political engagement
once again provided Butler with some relief from his heartache and loneli-

ness. Not surprisingly, for all his earlier bluster about abandoning politics altogether, Butler was unable to do so. In the spring of 1882, as the Chinese Exclusion Act—signed into law in early May—was still being debated in Congress, Butler's correspondents pressed him on his views even though he officially remained on the sidelines. In response, Butler typically referred inquirers to the stance he had taken in his 1870 speech on Chinese immigration, and specifically the point that forced immigration for the purposes of labor should not to be tolerated. To his discredit, however, he avoided confronting the bill's obvious racism. Then, by early September, he was clearly considering running for governor again in what would be his fifth attempt. "Everybody tells me that there is a fine chance to run," he mused to a friend in California, "but I have less ambition to be Governor of Massachusetts than I once had and I reluct at the turmoil and work and both of it all the more especially if I should happen to be elected." Within a couple of weeks, however, both the Greenback and Democratic parties had nominated Butler again. "I sincerely hope the gods will be propitious this time," wrote Phoebe Couzins, "and seat you in the gubernatorial chair. Then, ho! For the White House." Only half in jest, Couzins suggested that perhaps she and Susan B. Anthony should join his campaign "to help stump the State for you," and, should he win, they could then become members of his cabinet. Anthony, Couzins advised, would make "a good secretary of state and I might fill the Atty Genl's office with distinction."[64]

During the campaign, Butler faced concern and even scorn from those who questioned the meaning and sincerity of his return to the Democratic Party's banner. As he had done before, Butler insisted that over time not he but the *parties* had shifted their positions, ideals, and agendas. "I stand for the country and the Union now as I have always stood for them," he explained to a correspondent in Indiana, reminding him that Republicans and Democrats had fought together to save the Union, and that there were both Republicans and Democrats who shared his commitment to the enduring principles of "equality of right, equality of burdens, equality of power, equality of privileges to all men under the law." Now that "the issues of the war" had largely "passed away" and the Constitution had been altered to enshrine equal rights at least in theory, the key questions that remained unresolved had to do with "administration, taxation, economy and honesty in the public service" and their enforcement. Butler argued that in most things his views remained fundamentally "the principles and measures" of which "Jefferson, Madison, and Jackson stood as the exponents" (though he surely now excepted their support for slavery). "If the Democrats can forgive

Butler as governor of Massachusetts. Photographer unknown. Courtesy of the Ames Family Papers, Sophia Smith Collection, SSC-MS-00003, Smith College Special Collections, Northampton, Massachusetts.

me for my opinion of some of them during the war," he added with humor, "I certainly can forgive them all their ill opinion of me because of my acts during the war." At the same time, Butler courted the state's Black voters who, he hoped, would understand that if he became governor, his dedication to the poor and workingmen and workingwomen of Massachusetts would include them as well. "Your note conveying the information to me of the personal regard of yourself and the club of colored voters which you represent is gratefully received," he wrote to William B. Berry of Boston. "I know in my own conscience that I have never done any act and I certainly do not intend to do any act prejudicial to the colored race. Their rights are now assured by the Constitution and legal enactment," he declared with considerable, and arguably even callous, exaggeration. "That I have the confidence and regard of that class of fellow citizens, is very gratifying."[65]

On Tuesday, November 7, 1882, on a fusion Greenback-Democratic Party ticket, Butler was elected governor of Massachusetts by a margin of about 15,000 votes over his opponent, Republican Robert R. Bishop. Letters of congratulation poured in, including one from the Sisters of the Visitation in Georgetown, who ran the school Blanche had attended years earlier. "Among the hundreds of letters of congratulation upon my election," Butler replied, "no one has touched me with so deep sensibility as that I have had the honor and pleasure to receive from you," and he thanked the sisters for their "fostering and maternal care" of his beloved daughter while she studied there. Alas, neither his achievement of this long sought-after goal, nor the birth of yet another grandchild—his sixth, Blanche and Adelbert's daughter Jessie Ames Ames—could erase entirely the sadness that lingered from Bennie's death. In a letter to Frank Blair Jr., Butler noted that "the fact that Ben could not have lived to see it and share it" deprived his electoral "triumph" of "much the largest part of its gratification." Indeed, in an earlier letter Butler had described his heartache with striking eloquence. Near the first anniversary of Bennie's death, Blair had written that his own grief would never fade, to which Butler replied that pain from the loss of loved ones *must* fade, and thankfully so. For "if it were not so, surrounded as we are with loved ones, the accumulation of griefs unsoftened would make life a horror to men in advancing years." The "loss of friends," he continued, "is the sadness of old men. We see them drop around us day by day as we grow more recluse and lonely by their loss." And "if Time did not soften these afflictions as its covering hand softens all natural devastations, old age would indeed be miserable."[66]

God made me in only one way. I must be always with the under dog in the fight. I can't help it; I can't change, and upon the whole I don't want to.
—BUTLER, JULY 1883

The working man in the largest sense is the only foundation upon which society can quietly and firmly rest; and the prime question of statesmanship is how the producer . . . can be made happy and contented, and be elevated.
—BUTLER, JUNE 1884

He died as he wished. He wore out instead of rusting out.
—*BOSTON JOURNAL*, JANUARY 1893

It is always to be borne in mind that those nearest this man, who knew him through and through, knew his faults and virtues, believed in him, loved him.
—*BOSTON GLOBE*, JANUARY 1893

The Final Journey
1883–1893

On January 4, 1883, Benjamin Butler began his term as governor of Massachusetts with a two-and-a-half-hour-long inaugural address before the overwhelmingly Republican state legislature. If in recent years the Bay State's governor had indeed had "less administrative power than the governor of any other State," as he recalled in his autobiography, Butler's inaugural evinced his determination to invest the role with real power. "Gov. Butler being a man of strong common sense and indisputable courage," observed the *Albany (N.Y.) Evening Post*, "his message," which the paper described as "brilliant," was "full of ideas and wise suggestions." These included plans for rooting out corruption in state agencies so that the bulk of the money allocated to them went into the agencies' operations rather than the pockets of the bureaucrats who ran them. In addition, Butler wrote, "I advocated many democratic measures." Butler's law associate Roger Pryor described the speech as "a state paper of unsurpassed power" to which the press had given its "unanimous approval." "The 'Second Hero of New Orleans,'" declared the

Albany Evening Post, "has more brain power than all his predecessors put together."[1]

One of the first steps Governor Butler took to transform state institutions was to name Clara Barton, the highly respected Civil War nurse and founder of the American Red Cross, superintendent of the Massachusetts women's prison. Barton's appointment met with no obvious resistance, in sharp contrast with Butler's efforts to reform the Tewksbury Almshouse. Founded in the early 1850s as a "house of refuge" for the state's poor and mentally disabled, Tewksbury had been run by a Republican Party loyalist, Thomas J. Marsh, and various members of his family for the last quarter-century. At the time Butler arrived in the State House, Tewksbury housed several hundred needy residents, mostly of Irish descent. Lately some of the almshouse's practices had come under public scrutiny, yielding reports that the bodies of those who died there were frequently sold to Harvard College's medical school for study, or to other interested parties to be "skinned and the skins tanned" and then manufactured into bizarre curiosities for sale to collectors of the macabre. Other accusations pertained to the alleged "licentiousness of the assistant superintendent, killing of inmates by his sister, stealing property of the State by his mother, abuse of insane and other patients," and more.[2]

As governor, Butler demanded a thorough investigation of the institution, which unearthed substantial evidence of administrative malpractice, genuinely gruesome practices involving the residents who died within its walls, and what Butler considered the issue of greatest importance: the "cruel and abusive treatment of the living," including children and even babies. Butler's many years of administrative experience convinced him that such practices were by no means simply the inevitable result of a lack of financial resources. "Give me charge of them," he demanded. "I know how much such an institution will cost" to run both efficiently and decently. "We are interested and pleased," wrote Blanche later that spring, "with the Tewksbury investigation," whose revelations she declared "astonishing." Another correspondent congratulated Butler on his "investigation of the dark, and horrid deeds perpetrated by those miserable scamps, the Marshes," and urged him to "go on with your good work" despite the vigorous opposition of the Marshes' "long established ring" of Republican apologists and that of "the Press, the clergy, and the wealth of the country," who were eager to keep Tewksbury's ghastly secrets hidden.[3]

Although the investigation of Tewksbury exposed genuine abuses, it also clearly, immediately, and predictably became inseparable from the battles that were the hallmark of Butler's political life. Opponents accused Butler of using the almshouse scandal for his own political purposes without any actual concern for the victims he claimed to be defending. Butler, in turn, pointed out that most of the almshouse residents could not or did not vote, so his efforts on their behalf would never translate into electoral support. Opponents strove to produce a counternarrative that defended the Marshes' administration of the institution, including a pamphlet by a member of the state's Board of Health, Lunacy, and Charity, who claimed to have visited the asylum on numerous occasions and always found "scrupulous neatness everywhere," all the residents in "excellent condition," the wards "very cheerful and comfortable," and everyone well fed. Still, even she had to admit that "some violations of decency occur, of which I have had ocular demonstration," and while she spoke favorably of Thomas Marsh, she acknowledged that the institution was understaffed, a number of the attending physicians were "slipshod," and Tewksbury on the whole could benefit from certain "modern ideas and improvements" that a new, younger superintendent might spearhead. In the end, Butler was largely successful in his effort to bring about change there: the media attention surrounding the Tewksbury investigation produced a good deal of popular outrage, which resulted in the replacement of the Marsh clan with a new superintendent, C. Irving Fisher, and a sharp decline in complaints. More broadly, the investigation brought national attention to the problems of institutions like Tewksbury all over the country. "If General Butler were Governor of Texas," observed the *New York Tribune* later that year, "he might perhaps find a legitimate object of attack in the Dallas county poor-farm, the alleged brutal management of which is said to be creating intense excitement and indignation."[4]

Even as the Tewksbury investigation was underway, in June 1883, Butler drew opponents' fire for attending the graduation ceremony at Paul's alma mater, Harvard College. At the Williams College graduation that summer, Butler—who had previously received an honorary degree from Williams— enjoyed a warm welcome. At Harvard, however, the college's overseers unmistakably slighted him by denying him the honorary Doctor of Laws degree customarily awarded at commencement to the sitting governor. Some of the overseers' animosity was a response to the Tewksbury investigation, with its revelations about Harvard Medical School's grim connections to the almshouse. From the perspective of Butler and his allies, however, the bigger problem was that the president of the board of overseers was his long-standing political adversary and still one of the state's leading Republicans, Ebenezer Hoar. Supporters of the overseers rejected this explanation, the *Springfield Daily Republican* insisting that their decision to deny Butler the degree simply reflected a welcome "re-awakening" of the college's "care in the bestowal of honors." Butler, the paper declared, "has many attractive qualities" and "admirable private virtues," but "in political life" he was nothing more than "an unscrupulous demagog[ue], a humbug in his pretensions of reform," and a "deliberate and wanton defamer of the good name of his state by reckless statements to further his own private ends." To award him an honorary degree, the paper insisted, would have rightly exposed Harvard to the charge of being "grossly lacking in spirit and in self-respect as a seat of morality and learning."[5]

Despite being advised of the overseers' decision beforehand, and despite an additional warning that if he attended the ceremony he "would not be treated by the students with the respect due to his office," Butler attended the graduation ceremony anyway. "I thought it would be more proper and dignified conduct on my part," he later recalled, "to attend the commencement with all the state and escort with which any governor had ever attended." And with his usual resilience and ability to dismiss criticism, he still found the experience "enjoyable." Certainly Butler also enjoyed the many warm letters of support that flowed in afterward, praising his gracious and upbeat handling of the college's act of public disrespect. Harvard, wrote one alumnus, had not only insulted Butler but had also committed a grave and foolish affront to the state's electorate by declaring, in essence, that the voters were "not competent to elect a governor fit to receive this degree." Retribution would follow at the ballot box, he promised. "Your course will redound to your reputation," wrote another friend. "You were there to represent the Commonwealth and you have done it manfully and successfully." To Blanche, Butler good-naturedly described the whole affair as a meaningless kerfuffle, "only a little game of skill between self and brother Hoar" that was best "described in the old nursery rhyme: 'He digged a pit / He digged it deep / He digged it for his brother / But he fell in / And was drowned therein / And died instead of 'tother.'" Blanche was proud. "You seemed so far above the Harvard crowd, and they powerless to affect you, even to anger," she replied, "and that is some consolation."[6]

Because the Massachusetts governor's term lasted only a year and the parameters of the position were so constrained, and in spite of his own desire to make the position more meaningful in practical terms, Butler was unable to accomplish of much of lasting value before it was time to start focusing on reelection. One other important issue that engaged his attention and had a significant impact, however, emerged in the context of his official role in connection with state judicial nominations. Roughly four months after Butler assumed office, the death of the municipal court judge in Charlestown provided an opening for him to nominate a replacement. Initially, Butler nominated James O'Brien, a White Democrat of Irish descent. Republicans, however, dominated the eight-man executive council that was authorized to approve or reject the governor's nominations, and they turned O'Brien down. Next, Butler nominated a second White Democrat, Joseph H. Cotton; the council rejected him, too. Butler then recommended a highly regarded Black attorney, Edward G. Walker, a Democrat, a Butler supporter, and the son of the great Black abolitionist David Walker. Butler likely assumed the executive council would be more hesitant to reject a Black Democrat than a White one, but he was wrong. The council rejected Walker too.[7]

Having turned away all of Butler's Democratic selections, the executive council now took the interesting step of suggesting that Butler nominate Republican George Lewis Ruffin, a former barber and the first Black graduate of Harvard Law School (class of 1869). As it turns out, Ruffin was an excellent choice for the post and Butler knew it. An 1887 anthology of prominent Black Americans, *Men of Mark*—coedited by one of Butler's longtime Black correspondents, USCT veteran Henry R. Turner—described Ruffin as "a man of charitable, warm-hearted and generous impulses," of "sterling worth, exalted reputation, and legal ability," with a "distinguished, prepossessing appearance" and a "rich voice and charming manners," whose life "was a shining example of what can be done even in cultured Boston." Setting party rivalries aside, Butler quickly agreed to nominate him, probably surprising the council, which now had no choice but to approve Ruffin for the post. "There is no man in the U. States happier in the thought of your elevation to the honorable office you now hold," wrote Frederick Douglass to Ruffin upon hearing the good news. "Long life to your honor!" On November 19, 1884, Butler administered the oath of office, making Ruffin the first Black judge in the United States. At a dinner in Ruffin's honor two days later, Black USCT veteran and historian George W. Williams called Butler's appointment of Ruffin "another mile-post in our march toward that perfected and symmetrical manhood that has been our aim, as a race, since all legal barriers were thrown down by the shock of embattled arms." Ruffin presided over the Charlestown court until his death from Bright's disease—the same disease that had killed Butler's son Bennie—in November 1886.[8]

The struggle over the judicial nomination took several months to resolve, during which Butler's reelection effort also got underway. At least one historian has suggested that Butler eventually grew "tired of fighting" the

Republican-controlled executive council and really only reluctantly agreed to the Ruffin nomination after he came to the conclusion that "he would get some credit for the landmark appointment no matter which man took the bench." "Everybody in the Commonwealth knows," one cynical contemporary remarked, that Butler's willingness to nominate a Black man at all was nothing more than "the last staggering effort of a politician to catch the Negro vote" in favor of his reelection as governor. Among others, however, the biographical sketch of Ruffin in *Men of Mark* saw things differently, arguing that Butler was "a staunch friend of the race" and had "always shown his fidelity to it." Another contemporary source insisted that Butler "had always had a desire to see the colored people of the commonwealth represented in some of the honored positions," and after all, he had nominated Edward Walker first, before the council suggested Ruffin. Moreover, this source opined, when the council rejected Walker and suggested Ruffin, they actually did so out of spite, hoping that Butler would refuse to nominate a Republican, especially one who might even have actively campaigned against him in the past. And in any case, the election was already over when Butler called the council's bluff and agreed to nominate Ruffin, so his decision no longer offered him any immediate political benefit.[9] It would be wrong to deny Butler's political ambitions and his capacity for wily maneuvering. It would be at least as misguided, however, to treat his successful nomination of the first Black judge in the United States as somehow detached from his record of determined support for Black Americans' advancement.

In any case, by the late summer of 1883 Butler was running for governor again, having been greatly encouraged by the many friends and allies who urged him to throw his hat back in the ring. Fearful of the negative implications for their party's long-term survival should Butler be reelected, his Republican opponents once again came out in force during what became a "bitter and fatiguing" campaign. Though Butler ran again as the official nominee of the Greenback and Democratic parties, there were, as before, also some Democrats—"representatives of the old time blue blood democracy," as the *Essex Statesman* put it—who hoped he would lose. Indeed, according to the *Statesman*, Butler was "handicapped at the outset" by the collaboration of these wealthy, "blue blood" Democrats with "their old Republican foes" to bring about "the defeat of a man whom they both feared and hated" precisely because he had proven himself to be, above all, "a steadfast friend of the man who has to work for a livelihood" rather than of the rich and powerful. Friends reported that local opponents as well as adversaries from beyond the state's borders were pouring money into the campaign of his Republican opponent, George D. Robinson. "No decent party would let you remain in their ranks," wrote one harsh critic from Colorado. "You are only fit to be with repudiating Greenbackers," whom he defined as "men who would make money out of paper and dump it into the streets by the cartload for lazy tramps to gather."[10]

Butler lost the gubernatorial election by about 10,000 of the over 300,000 votes cast. Subsequently, he later joked, "having redeemed my promise to my enemies that I would be governor of Massachusetts," he did not run for governor again. Supporters were disappointed, but many also rejoiced that he was now, presumably, free to focus on seeking the presidency in 1884. Wrote one ally from Florida several weeks before the gubernatorial election took place, "As an American citizen and one who loves this country, I respectfully ask . . . that you use all honorable means to place *yourself* at the *head* of *this Government*." This correspondent shared Butler's view that "the true political issue before the country today is economical liberty for the *producers* of wealth." Furthermore, he expressed confidence that the core of Butler's enduring political strength lay "not in the machinery of either of the old parties, but in the *workshop, mill, and harvest field*." A month after the election, one life-long labor leader from Troy, New York, declared that the "wistful eyes" of "thousands upon thousands" of poor and working people, "not only in this state but all over the country," were looking to Butler "as their Savior."[11]

As a candidate for governor in 1882 and as governor in 1883, Butler had focused the bulk of his political attention on his state's most pressing issues, but he remained keenly attentive to national developments. At the same time, his national reputation had continued to grow. For in the eyes of supporters from coast to coast, Butler seemed a rare specimen, perhaps one of a kind: a major politician genuinely dedicated to addressing the needs of labor, the poor, and the underdog in all forms, a man of uncommon wisdom, savvy, experience, and influence determined to challenge "jobbery, corruption, and monopolies" and all other types of undue power that wealthy elites so shamelessly exerted. From Minneapolis, one correspondent reported a general feeling among the city's laborers that Butler would prove their "deliverer from a danger constantly encroaching upon the rights of the people, a deliverer from the government of monopoly by, of, & for monopoly." Even in the South, wrote another, the "old bitter feeling" that had once prevailed toward him was subsiding as he proved himself to be someone who reliably "works for the country and not for party," for the people and not for the powerful. Notably, leading suffragists, who appreciated Butler's friendship and his history of public support for women's rights, still numbered among his most earnest supporters. In the words of his friend Phoebe Couzins, Butler, like his outspoken women's rights allies and unlike so many other politicians, clearly had "backbone enough" at least "to say 'Boo' to a goose!"[12]

The steady expansion of Butler's national appeal and influence, amplified by his brashness, unapologetic ambition, and refusal to heed demands for party loyalty when they came into conflict with his own political agenda, only further riled his opponents. In turn, their antipathy, combined with his easy-to-caricature physical appearance, produced an uptick in the ridicule he endured during this period from the popular press in both articles and images. "We are ever on the lookout for funny men," observed the weekly humor magazine, *Puck*, in May 1883, "and you are the funniest man we know." "We have always had a vague idea that Mr. Benjamin F. Butler has missed his vocation," the same magazine declared that July. "As a circus advance agent, he would have held a proud preeminence that would have made him the wonder of centuries to come." That December, the magazine pointedly compared Butler's supposed lack of physical beauty with that of one of the most outspoken and radical women's rights and dress reform activists of the day, Dr. Mary Walker, known for wearing trousers under her shortened skirts and sometimes even a man's top coat with tails. Later that month, as Butler was preparing to leave office, *Puck* mocked him as a "defeated prophet of reform" willing to accept the support of any one or any party simply in order to advance his own personal ambitions.[13] For his part Butler remained unsurprised and undaunted by the scorn.

Early in his term as governor Butler had written to a friend in Chicago denying his interest in the presidency. Once he left the governorship behind on January 3, 1884, however, the pressure supporters exerted tapped into his deep well of political ambition. It stirred, too, his profound desire to accomplish the sweeping political agenda he defined, again, with deceptive but appealing simplicity: "equal rights, equal powers, equal duties, and equal burdens to all men under the law." That January, the *American Sentry* confidently predicted that if Butler ran for president in the fall, he would be swept into office by the nation's workingmen, starting with the factory operatives of Massachusetts, "who can cite countless cases where he has taken up their cause often without hope of reward except that only which comes of doing good." Indeed, it was "Butler's defense of those unable to defend themselves," observed the *Sentry*, "that has given him such a deep hold in the hearts of the people." Butler was "a people's candidate," and his supporters were now rising from coast to coast as a "people's movement" that was no

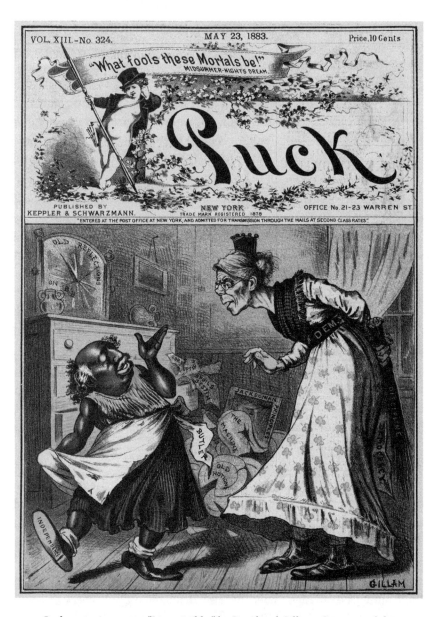

Puck magazine cover, "Incorrigible," by Bernhard Gillam. Courtesy of the Prints and Photographs Division, Library of Congress, Washington, D.C.

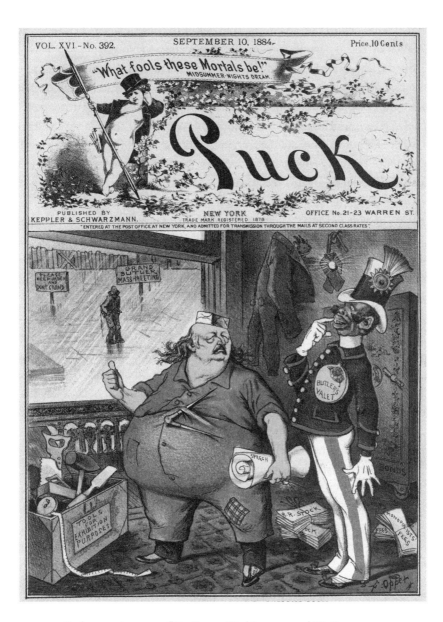

Puck magazine cover, "The Bogus Workingman and His Lonesome Boom," by Frederick Burr Opper. Courtesy of Special Collections & Archives, Colby College Libraries, Waterville, Maine.

longer beholden to the old political parties or to "intimidation, bribery," and "fraud" by those parties' leaders. Butler's correspondence from this period is filled with letters from struggling Americans, men and women, Black and White, convinced that he truly cared about their needs and would do what he could to help them. "You are so good to all who need help," wrote one. "I know," wrote another, "that I am addressing a friend of the poor." "You have always been the Union soldier's friend, and are noted for getting after all manner of rascality with success," wrote a third. "I believe you to be the colored man's friend," wrote Fred Tower.[14]

One indication of the geographic spread of Butler's popularity was the formation of "Butler Clubs" all across the country; according to one correspondent, the clubs were popping up "at the rate of one hundred per day." Like the Butler Clubs, workers' associations, including some state branches of the Knights of Labor, saw Butler as the best and perhaps only viable candidate against entrenched corporations and financial elites, and they, too, urged him to run. Using official Knights of Labor stationery, a writer from Topeka promised that if Butler ran for president, "the industrial classes of Kansas" would give him "a rousing majority." Most voters in Kansas, he explained, were "farmers, mechanics, and laborers," many of whom once belonged to the Republican Party but who no longer had faith in "either of the old political parties" with their "corrupt vicious and unprincipled political regimes." They believed in Butler, however, had organized a Butler Club, and were prepared to join other "workingmen, Greenbackers, and Anti-Monopolists" in casting their ballots for him even as similar coalitions were forming in Nebraska, Iowa, Colorado, and Missouri. "The patriotic, honest, industrious, unselfish, and liberty-loving elements of this section of the Country," this Topeka labor organizer explained, "are looking with hopeful eyes to you, as their political 'Moses' who can and will save them and this nation from the avarice, greed, and enslaving aristocracy that has become so thoroughly entrenched in the political, social, and commercial structure of the government." Butler, he concluded grandly, was "the Lincoln of this epoch."[15]

Black Americans stung by the accelerating backlash against Black freedom and citizenship, too, earnestly hoped their longtime and steadfast friend Butler would now run for president. Most recently, the backlash included the Supreme Court's October 1883 decision—in what came to be known as the Civil Rights Cases—which, in essence, declared the Civil Rights Act of 1875 unconstitutional. Butler had been instrumental in getting the law passed shortly before he completed his fourth term in Congress. Now the Court argued that the federal government could *not* intervene in the states to defend the promises of the Thirteenth, Fourteenth, and Fifteenth Amendments. "The colored people," observed one of Butler's Black correspondents, W. J. S. Bowe from Richmond, Virginia, "have been held in political bondage upon unreasonable ground" since the Civil War. Now, he observed, White Americans and particularly Republican Party reconciliationists, "who hold it to be patriotic to erase all memory of war and civil discord between the white people by the fraternal kiss of peace," seemed to expect Blacks to vote for them and maintain them in power, though they no longer demonstrated a sincere and reliable commitment to Black rights. "Tired of sowing for others to reap," and "surrounded with many antagonistic forces," Bowe informed Butler that Blacks in droves were leaving the Republican Party and its core of "monopolists of the North whose corporate interests must first be assured." They sought instead *true* allies in the quest for justice and full citizenship, wherever those allies might be. Bowe urged Butler to put himself forward as the candidate whom Blacks could actually trust "to help save a country from further disgrace and a people from further tribulations." "The colored men know me," Butler wrote proudly to a friend in New York City, and he speculated that his election could well "wipe out the colored line at the South by bringing the two races together under one political head," though he might need to run as a new kind of Democrat, or under some new party's banner, to achieve that result. If he succeeded, it "would be the greatest service to the country" he could offer, and probably also the last.[16]

As Butler pondered a future where the nation's White and Black poor and laboring people came together under his leadership, some supporters expressed concern about the corrosive potential of the lingering bitterness felt by some southern Whites, who still resented his actions as a Union general and particularly his occupation of New Orleans. Butler was unconcerned. "I note what you say about the prejudice that exists in the South in regard to myself," he observed to a correspondent in Texas. "The people in the South remember that I carried on war against them when they were my enemies and the enemies of my country," and they were right to remember. "When I am called upon to make war," Butler explained, "I kill, slay, and destroy my enemies in every way I can," and furthermore, "I am sorry I did not do it better, and more of it, because that would have brought the war sooner to a close and saved a great many valuable lives on both sides." Now, however, those same southerners should understand that "I make peace in the same way that I make war." In other words, "When I am at peace, I am at peace all over, and I don't have any sleeping prejudices against those with whom I make peace because they were once my enemies." If some

White southerners considered him "very strenuous against them" during the war, might they not now anticipate "the same strenuous exertion in their behalf, in behalf of the Country, and in behalf of good government and honest and faithful administration"? If so, Butler promised, "they can have it," and if not, "they can remain in their prejudices and probably be governed by some sneak who pretended to be a friend of theirs when he ought to have been their enemy, and will be an enemy of theirs in fact when he pretends to be their friend." To friends who worried specifically about the persistent rumors of his corruption and self-dealing in Louisiana, Butler offered the reminder that "there is no account of mine in the Treasury of the transactions in the war which [has] not been closed more than 10 years and there is no account of the transactions of mine in the Treasury that has not been closed more than 6 years, and as I know that I have accounted honestly for all the money that has come into my hands and can show it, I defy any republican or democrat, or the devil himself to touch me successfully." People should remember, he added wryly, that as far as corruption was concerned, "hell has been raked with a fine-tooth comb to find out something to say against me," all without success.[17]

According to the editor of the *Wymore (Neb.) Eagle*, as early as February 1884 nearly 5,000 newspapers around the country had indicated they would endorse Butler's candidacy should he run for president, and by mid-March, he had begun letting friends know that he was willing. "While I do not deem it proper for me to take any part in putting my name before any body of men as a candidate for any office," he wrote with not particularly credible humility, "I shall gratefully appreciate any action of the people, or any portion of the people of the Country who think I am fit to serve them in any office." When an artist acquaintance asked if perhaps he wanted a new engraving to be used for campaign purposes, Butler—well aware of the wildly unflattering depictions of him that so often appeared in the press—replied good naturedly, "I am very much obliged to you for your kind offer; but as every illustrated paper in the United States has made the people acquainted with my features through caricatures, I do not think it would be of any advantage to them or to me to have a new engraving made of them, as they grow worse every year."[18]

Butler had decided to run for president, but for a time he remained unsure if he should run as a Democrat, given his many doubts about even that party's willingness to stand reliably for the basic principles he asserted repeatedly: "equal rights, equal powers, equal duties, and equal burdens to all men under the law." As with the Republican Party, the most powerful leading

Democrats, he was certain, stood first and foremost not for the people but for the maintenance and expansion of their own and their party's dominance, as well as that of the nation's financial elites. "I begin to doubt whether anybody can be President, of either party, who is not a slave of the same ring," Butler confessed to one friend. "Associated capital brought in contact with the Government by the war naturally affiliated with the Republican party then being in power, not because of any principle of the Republican party, but because the Republican party was in power." Now he feared that "as soon as it is apparent that the Democratic party is to be in power, the same associated capital will become connected with that power, and will control its action."[19] Still, it seemed impossible to win the presidency without the backing of one of the major parties, even if—and it was a big if—Butler managed to draw together a large constituency of voters who were bound by their alienation from both.

In mid-May, the fleeting Anti-Monopoly Party gathered in Chicago and nominated Butler for president. "You have been nominated as the presidential standard-bearer of the Anti-Monopolists of the United States," wrote an excited supporter from San Francisco soon after, adding that California's Anti-Monopolists were with him. "We are right in this fight and so will surely succeed sooner or later," declared Butler upon learning the news. "We desire only to restrict and curtail the exercise of any powers by any body of men which tend to injure the mass of men." Moreover, he opined, labor and capital need not be enemies; rather, "we hold him the enemy of both who endeavors to use capital so as to oppress labor, or to use labor so as to oppress capital," although "in the nature of things," the latter could "rarely happen."[20]

"It was a foregone conclusion that Butler would turn up somewhere," grumbled one opposition newspaper following the Anti-Monopoly Party's convention, going on to predict that Butler would also surely manage to "force his nomination on the Democratic party." In late May, the National Greenback Party, meeting in Indianapolis, also nominated Butler. "You are the working man's choice for President," wrote a Greenbacker from Illinois, who hoped that a Butler presidency would "lift up the banner of human liberty and human justice," "strike off the chains of wage slavery," and provide relief to labor's "groaning, struggling and plundered millions." "I am a Republican, died in the wool, and all my people are of the same faith," confessed a woman correspondent from New York City. "But I shall coax them all to vote for you because it is a certainty that you would work for the country's best good if elected." "The future historian will write your name in the brightest characters that adorn his pages," declared a supporter from Nebraska, "as the Leader of the Great Greenback Party and the Defender of the people and their money."[21]

In early June, the Republican Party nominated James G. Blaine of Maine, "the strongest man in the Republican party," according to one newspaper. Although he praised the party's platform for being "sensible, progressive, and in many things, to the point," one of Butler's correspondents observed that the Republicans had failed entirely at the convention to consider labor, the working class, or the growing problem of wealth inequality. "The million-aires were there," he wrote, "with palace cards, champagne, and fruit," but as usual, "the poor were not there, with their despair and misery—and so they were forgotten." And unless politicians finally began paying attention to the poor, to labor, and to the desperate unemployed, "these struggling, starving masses will only need a leader to inaugurate anarchy and bloodshed." Butler must do what he could to avert such a terrifying future. Lincoln freed the millions of Black Americans who had been enslaved in the South. It was now time for Butler—and, he hoped, the Democratic Party—to save the country's "white slaves" from "poverty and starvation."[22]

In the wake of Blaine's nomination, some friends suggested that Butler defer his formal acceptance of the Greenback and Anti-Monopoly Party nominations until after the Democrats met in July, as Greenbackers and Anti-Monopolists (as well as southern Blacks) would surely vote for him in any case, but "practical men" in the Democratic Party might also offer support so long as Butler resisted trumpeting the more radical nominations he had already received. Democratic Party leaders, one correspondent cautioned, were troubled by Butler's persistence in challenging "the business elements of the whole country," whose allegiance they, too, were desperately trying to secure. Meanwhile, others pressured the Democratic leadership to ensure his selection as the party's candidate. "Butler is the most popular man in the country today," declared a late June letter to the editor of the *Boston Globe*, and should the Democratic Party nominate him, "it would create an enthusiasm throughout the nation such as has never been seen or heard of before." Butler, this letter insisted, "is right on all the great questions of the day" and his administrative ability and experience were beyond dispute. "He is the man for the people and the man the people want."[23]

Having been selected by his state's Democratic Party to serve as delegate at large, Butler felt optimistic when he traveled to the national convention in Chicago in July. "You will occupy the most marked & prominent position of anyone in the Convention," wrote one friend upon hearing the news. "I have confidence that you will use it with skill." "In the name of the toiling millions," wrote a supporter from Louisiana, "I bid you God-speed at the Convention." The outcome of the convention was hardly clear, and opposition to Butler's nomination was stiff. "Whether Butler shall get the Democratic nomination or not," reported the *Dover (N.H.) Daily Republican* as the delegates gathered, "he is certainly giving that party a great deal of uneasiness."[24] Whatever "uneasiness" Butler may have been causing some people, when he arrived in Chicago he recalled being "very kindly received by the multitude" and was quickly chosen to serve on the platform committee.

Butler's political weight at the convention, as well as the resistance many Democrats had to some of his key ideas, became clearer still when the platform committee began to discuss the political lightning rod of protective tariffs. On one side were those, like Butler, who considered tariffs necessary to protect American industry and labor and raise money for internal improvements. "We can not have Free Trade in this country, however desirable theoretically it would be," Butler had written back in May. "Our country is so large, our interests so vast, and so much is to be done by the General Government that for a series of years we must raise hundreds of millions of dollars by taxation of some kind." And while direct taxation was certainly constitutional, indirect taxation was preferable. "I favor the raising of a sufficient amount of revenue for the economical administration of the Government [from "duties on imports" of "articles of luxury"] and no more." On the opposite side were the party's free traders who, to Butler and his allies, seemed virtually indistinguishable from those in the mainstream of the opposition party. These so-called Democrats were, as one friend put it, "as blind as they could be" on the importance of imposing tariffs to protect American labor, and acted as if "they were the hired agents of the Republican party to keep it in power." Over the course of three days the platform committee managed to find areas of common ground, but on tariffs, Butler later recalled, "we divided nearly in the middle." In the end, the committee voted down everything Butler and his allies had proposed "in favor of the laboring men, in favor of protection to American citizens on foreign soil, against monopolies, against land grabbing by a British aristocracy," and "against corporations discriminating in rates of fare and freight against the producer and the people." Instead, the committee produced what Butler described as "some mongrel resolution" that "meant anything or nothing" depending on how "one chose to construe it." And then, heavily influenced by the large, pro–free trade New York delegation, the convention nominated Grover Cleveland for president, and dispersed.[25]

Following the convention, some supporters encouraged Butler to endorse Cleveland, in the hope that doing so publicly would guarantee Cleveland's victory and ensure Butler a seat in his cabinet. Butler declined. For one thing, endorsing Cleveland would give the appearance of agreement with precisely the same Republicans whose "anti-Democratic sentiments and monarchial tendencies" had driven him from the Republican Party years earlier and who, he further believed, had actively conspired with their Democratic cohorts to engineer Cleveland's nomination in the first place. Even more important, Butler had no faith whatsoever in Cleveland's ability or willingness to form an administration that would pursue fair policies toward labor and the nation's neediest citizens. After all, Cleveland had received the nomination only "because he was backed by three of the worst monopolies in the United States," namely, "the New York Central Railroad, the Standard Oil Company, and the Southern employers who monopolize the labor of the negroes at half price" and then cruelly pitted them against White labor. Indeed, Butler considered Cleveland's nomination a disheartening guarantee that racial tensions in the South would only continue to escalate as northern capitalists joined former Confederates in stoking them for profit. "To the patriot and statesman," he sighed, "it is a sad subject of contemplation."[26]

Instead, "for better or worse," Butler decided to run for president as the Greenback and Anti-Monopoly candidate while also gathering whatever independent support he could elsewhere. As he explained to a friend in Connecticut, "I believe the exigency is now upon us to settle the question about the rights of labor and ameliorate the condition of labor," including, it seems, even Chinese labor, though the Chinese Exclusion Act had passed two years earlier. Now when he was asked about the Exclusion Act, he reiterated his opposition to forced labor, domestic or imported, but insisted more explicitly than in the past that he welcomed "every man" who had "energy enough and love of our institutions enough to bring him here." In the months remaining before the election, Butler strove to create and lead a fusion movement made up of Greenbackers, Anti-Monopolists, farmers and laborers, anti-Cleveland Democrats, alienated Black Republicans, and even women's rights advocates. "I hope that our people will all join together and organize a People's Party," he wrote; "our proposition is to fuse with the minorities everywhere." From Columbus, Ohio, one exuberant supporter promised that the 3,000 members of his Knights of Labor local would "rush to your standard like a prairie fire"; another from Illinois requested a portrait of Butler to hang at his local Butler Club, "not on the account of its rare beauty, but because it represents the man of our choice."[27]

As always, some of Butler's correspondents raised important questions and challenges, which he strove to satisfy. To one who intimated that Butler's own employment of laborers in the mills in which he had a financial interest contravened his claims of support for working people, he replied, "Did it ever occur to you that perhaps the very reason that I have invested my property very considerably in manufacturing industries was because I had the interest of the laboring men at heart and wished to furnish remunerative and fair employment for them?" A corporation, he added, "is not necessarily an oppressive machine," but if it became one, as the extortionist railroads had done, "it should be regulated by law and not set up above and beyond the law." To another inquirer, perhaps harkening back to conversations with protesting Lowell mill operatives back in the 1840s, Butler indicated that he did not believe labor strikes should ever be necessary, so long as "honest and fair-minded dealing was always had between the capitalist and the laboring-men, because their interests do not naturally clash." And he pointed out that the mills in which he held a "considerable interest" financially had never been subjected to a strike.[28]

Invitations came from across the country, a Maine supporter characteristically imploring Butler to come and give even just one speech, which, he promised, "would have more effect than all the hired speakers who could be sent here." Now sixty-five, Butler campaigned widely but not quite as tirelessly as he had done in the past, observing to Blanche that these days he sometimes felt weary on the stump. Still, he added gamely, "I trust you will think the old dog has not lost all his teeth, so he cannot bite at all," and in any case, "at least he can growl." At one point Butler took Adelbert, grandson Butler, and West on a campaign trip to Michigan and the surrounding states. "We have had a rather tiresome journey thus far," Adelbert complained to Blanche, though he clarified his comment by saying that "your Father flourishes like a green bay tree through it all" and was "very enthusiastically received" wherever they went. "Last night at Detroit," wrote a wide-eyed Butler Ames to his mother, "I was nearly crushed to death by the crowd who went to hear Grandfather speak. There was over 15,000 people there." Some days later Adelbert observed that while candidate Butler might not actually expect to be elected president, he nevertheless seemed "sanguine" about having begun to establish "a good foundation for a future party," a people's party, which would "need some nursing yet."[29]

How West experienced this trip or future excursions with Butler cannot be known—the paper trail is excruciatingly thin—but it is certain that he stayed close by at all times. Years later, the *Boston Globe* printed a touching story about the relationship West and Butler shared, which was warmly professional, inflected by Butler's increasing dependence on West as he grew older. "West always came after him in the evening to the State House" when Butler was governor," the paper recalled, "and assisted him downstairs to his carriage." Butler's eyesight was poor, and "there was a rise in the floor of the outer room leading to the extensive chamber" where Butler always stumbled "unless West was with him." Indeed, the *Globe* claimed, Butler half suspected that West "was as indispensable to him by reason of some occult influence" as "by the physical aid that he offered." Butler relied on West for basic companionship, support, and to help him keep track of his always abundant paperwork. According to the *Globe*, on one occasion when Butler took a hired public carriage alone from his State House office to his lodgings, he left a stack of "enacted and unsigned bills which he intended to look over" in the carriage. A few days later when the driver returned the papers unharmed, a relieved Butler declared that he would never again leave the office without West at his side.[30] And it seems he kept his word. One has to wonder how much if at all the two men discussed political and other matters during the uncountable hours they spent together. What a gift it would be to know.

As the election drew closer, wild accusations arose among some anti-Butler Democrats that he and Blaine were actively contriving to split the Democratic ticket and thereby deny Grover Cleveland the presidency. After all, the likelihood of Butler's own election was remote, so why else would he possibly be running? Popular illustrated periodicals pushed their mockery and denigration into overdrive, and in the end, despite the anti-Butler conspiracy theories and some two weeks of delay in determining which candidate had won the pivotal state of New York, the election went to Cleveland after all, making him the first Democrat to assume the presidency since James Buchanan back in 1856. As for Butler, he received an even smaller fraction of the vote than he had expected—just over 1 percent—leading him and others to wonder if the election had been corrupted.[31]

Butler's opponents were delighted by his defeat, of course, one "independent Republican" now generously advising him to "crawl into some hole & pull the hole in after you & quietly give up the ghost." Wrote a gleeful Minnesotan, "If your personal vanity has been gratified in posing as a candidate for the presidency, as the 'people's candidate,' it may not be so gratifying in looking over the return. 'The People' were not very numerous." This same correspondent declared Butler's latest electoral outing "the most foolish and ridiculous" of his career and echoed the theory that Butler had accepted a bribe from Blaine's people to help undermine Cleveland, albeit unsuccessfully. Butler, who rarely replied directly to what he called "abusing letters," nevertheless replied archly to this one. "You say that I desire only to rule or ruin," he retorted. In fact, "I planned to do neither, but I did endeavor to put before the country a platform of principles, and to inaugurate an organization, which will sooner or later, succeed in crushing our monopolies, and speculators in the necessaries of life such as grain, by whom the farmer, the producer and the laboring men, the consumers are alike robbed." Butler sharply denied the accusation that he had engaged in dirty dealing to win the election, an allegation, he argued, that revealed far more about the corrupt nature of the one who made it than it did about himself. "You, feeling conscious that you would have sold yourself for a consideration, suspect that I must have done so," he wrote. "The mole can never comprehend the beauties of the landscape but supposes the whole world is as dark as his world is to him."[32]

Crestfallen supporters struggled to understand why voters had not cast more ballots for Butler, as well as candidates further down the Anti-Monopoly/Greenback Party ticket. "This great city," wrote one frustrated fan from Chicago, "which a few months ago turned out thirty thousand people to bid you welcome, and marched ten thousand working men in line with their emblems, and mottos of welcome, could only rally on election day 502 votes for the head of their ticket, and left good men and true to stay at home, and sent men who belong to the criminal class, and trade scabs to the legislature." How was this possible? "I feel somewhat disgusted with men who complain of wrongs," he added, "and have not the nerve to attempt to right them." Some suspected outright fraud. Some placed at least some of the blame at Butler's own feet, like the New Yorker who wondered privately if Butler's loss was the result of his having "compelled the Democratic party to show its true colors at Chicago" but then not having moved quickly enough afterward to organize the disaffected into a new party under his own leadership. "More than three millions of voters were ready to rush to his standard," he wrote, but they soon "settled back into their old parties, not because they believed in them, but because the Butler movement appeared so tame, and started so slow." Those voters ultimately cast their ballots either for Blaine or for Cleveland, "but they do not expect relief from either." In fact, "their faith and hope is still in Gen. Butler" whom they now hoped would "lead them to victory in 1888." "The thought of the election gives me a mental sensation," wrote Blanche vividly, echoing the feelings of many, "which may quite properly be compared to the physical one experienced when eating unripe persimmons."[33]

Butler's year as governor of Massachusetts was his last in elected office and his 1884 quest for the presidency was his last campaign. "*I am most deeply disappointed,*" wrote a friend from Glens Falls, New York, on November 5, the day after the election and Butler's sixty-sixth birthday. It was a feeling Butler's supporters across the nation shared: "There must be a meaning in the discipline that seems to be given us, which you can more fully comprehend and explain." "You have been able to put forth such exertion in behalf of the People and of the cause of Liberty and Truth," wrote another grateful friend from New York City the same day, and he urged Butler to have faith that "men capable of thinking and acting for themselves" were even now poised to build a movement of the "masses of citizens" that would transform the American economy and financial system "in regard to wages, labor, currency, monopoly, and cooperation" and make it more equitable for all. Butler agreed that the "people's movement" had begun and must continue. "There is no cause for our being disheartened by the result of the election," he consoled one correspondent in late November. "As I said in every place where I spoke we were sowing the seeds of a new party" whose time would come, "whether you or I live or not." At sixty-six, however, Butler was ready step back and let others take the lead.[34]

Supporters were not yet ready to let him go. Some pleaded with him to run again for Congress in 1886, the next possible opportunity. Having ceased to believe that Congress was committed to, or even capable of resolving "the great questions now pending between labor and capital," Butler was not interested. "I have had enough," he declared. Friends continued to push. "Is it not about time you again appeared in the political field?" nudged one Bostonian in May 1887. "Is there any other man in the country that can bring together or hold together so large a body of 'Democratic Republican' voters, now ready to form an overwhelming third party?" And "could any other man do more to check the growth of ruinous 'monopolies' or secure a better system of 'finance' to relieve the masses of 'middle men' now floundering in despair?" Many still earnestly hoped Butler would one day be president. Again, Butler was no longer interested, having reached the conclusion that even the president "has so little power to do good and so much power to do harm that it is a dangerous place to be in." Two decades earlier, Butler admitted to one correspondent, "I might have entertained that ambition," but the intervening years had "taught me fully and truly what the President's office is," and he no longer had the energy or interest to pursue it.[35]

THE FINAL JOURNEY

Women's rights activists, too, hoped Butler would return to electoral politics; short of that, they hoped he would use his still significant influence to advance the cause. Soon after he was elected governor, Susan B. Anthony had implored Butler to address the Massachusetts state legislature on the "great principle of equality of rights to all citizens" and "the duty of the National government to protect" women *and* men "in the enjoyment of such equality of rights in whatsoever state or territory they may reside." At that time, Anthony had hoped (in vain) Butler could persuade the legislature to endorse the National Woman Suffrage Association's proposed Sixteenth Amendment to the US Constitution granting women the right to vote. Now that Butler seemed to have abandoned electoral politics completely, she urged him nevertheless to deploy his influence in other ways. In January 1889 Anthony invited Butler to speak to the annual women's rights convention in Washington and "make for us your solid pronunciamento for woman's full & equal possession of political rights." At the time she issued the invitation, Anthony herself was nearly seventy-nine; Butler was seventy. "It may be the last time I shall be on terra firma to invite you," she reminded him, "or the last time you'll be here to accept!"[36] Butler, however, continued to disengage.

The usual abundance of invitations to give speeches still made its way to his door, some of which he cheerfully accepted, like the August 1888 invitation that brought him before a crowd of about 5,000 at Boston's Tremont Temple, where he spoke for over two hours. He also continued to receive the familiar steady stream of letters asking for help. "I have heard you are the poor person's friend. I am old, and in trouble," began one 1889 supplication that was interchangeable with so many others. Given his reputation as "the poor person's friend," it is perhaps unsurprising that among those whose requests he either could not or simply did not satisfy, some responded with towering rage. "You are an old man and you will soon be summoned hence," wrote one correspondent, angry that Butler would not tap into his "millions" to offer him the "paltry sum" he had requested. "I leave my case to God: He will deal with you." As always, many correspondents sought advice only, not financial assistance. To one young man who wondered which profession to pursue, Butler replied that law and ministry had once offered the greatest opportunities, but in recent years, medicine and civil engineering seemed more promising.[37]

Increasingly, Butler refocused his attention on his numerous landholdings, which now included a cattle ranch in Colorado and some timber land in West Virginia, and his business interests: his investments in Lowell's mills and the Cartridge and Bunting companies and, more recently—in partnership with Adelbert Ames's father—some Minnesota lumber mills. Never one to allow his mind or investment portfolio to lie fallow, Butler also chased some business opportunities associated with new forms of technology, such as the development of elevated rapid transit systems in cities like Boston and New York. Butler considered these amazing new types of urban mass transportation essential for providing laborers—who often spent much of their time in dark and confined spaces—with a "means of reaching home expeditiously and cheaply" while also enjoying "light, air, and space, at least during the hours of recreation." Elevated railroads, he explained to one potential investor, "can be put up without any obscurity of light or interference with the air or vision. It can be run by any motive power, preferably electricity if that will be cheap enough." Indeed, for a time Butler even served as president of the Meigs Elevated Railway Construction Company, which built a prototype near Boston in East Cambridge. Butler took an interest in building canals and enhancing natural waterways, too, both of which he believed would provide the monopolistic railroad industry with meaningful competition and bring prices down for producers and consumers. For similar reasons he supported federal regulation of the developing telephone industry. "The telephone companies," he explained, "seem to forget that they are the servants of the public doing a public business for hire, gain and reward. They may stop doing the business, but as long as they do it they must do it when, how, where, and for what the law prescribes, like every other like business."[38] That Butler expanded his financial investments in this period of his life certainly shows he was an ambitious and intelligent businessman, which some might argue reflected his greed for wealth. But the enterprises in which he invested, and the reasons he chose for investing in them, can at least equally be read as an effort to marry his personal business and financial ambitions with a commitment to the public good.

Meanwhile, Butler attended to his legal practice in Lowell, Boston, New York, and Washington. "Practicing law is my amusement," he wrote to a professional friend in June 1887, "not labor, in the fatiguing sense of the word," though he admitted that the natural consequences of aging meant that he "must soon be driven from this class of relaxation" for fear he might inadvertently "do injustice" to a client. Butler accepted cases both large and small, including some that offered little or no financial recompense. Surely the highest-profile case in which he took part during these latter years involved two of the eight anarchists tried and convicted in conjunction with the 1886 Haymarket bombing in Chicago. Agnes Van Zandt, the mother of a woman who had become involved with one of the defendants, contacted Butler in early 1887, as the case was heading to appeal before the Illinois Supreme Court. Butler initially responded that he was ideologically supportive of the defendants but reluctant to take the assignment; his calendar was full.[39]

Later that year, however, with the case now poised for appeal before the US Supreme Court, Butler informed Van Zandt that he was willing to "take a retainer in behalf of the anarchists" provided he could be "reasonably satisfied that there are Federal points on which a writ of error can rest." Some of the anarchists' supporters were certain that with Butler on the job, the defendants would soon be exonerated. Butler, however, cautioned against "delusive" optimism, and in the end, the Court rejected the appeal on what amounted to a technicality. "A great wrong, in my judgment, has been done to the true course of justice in the United States Court as well as to our clients," Butler wrote to one of the other lawyers after learning the news, but there was nothing left to do now but "bow to the authoritative exposition of the law of the land." Butler's preparations for the case were substantial, time consuming, and required considerable travel between Lowell and Washington; his bill came to nearly $3,000.[40]

As the years passed, Butler increasingly said "no" more often than "yes" to the requests of various sorts he still received. "I am busying myself at my age in closing out those [endeavors] I am already engaged in," he informed one correspondent. "I have given up politics and political discussion," he explained to another, "and therefore do not feel myself at liberty, with pressing professional engagements, to examine into so important a matter as that referred to in your note." "I think I have given as much of my time and strength to the country as I am called upon to do," he wrote to a third. As he withdrew from the public sphere, the relentless ridicule that had dogged him for decades faded, too. Still, even in August 1890, *Puck* reserved some space in its columns to disparage him. "He had his period of usefulness, in the time of the civil war," the magazine declared, but more recently he had become little more than the "butt for cruel and heartless jests," not unlike Dr. Mary Walker, the radical women's rights activist and dress reformer to whom *Puck* had compared him in the past.[41]

Butler maintained a residence in Washington and occasionally practiced law in the city, but he spent less and less time there and gradually gave his lodgings over primarily to the use of his nieces Charlotte Stevens (his half-sister Betsey Stevens's daughter) and Harriet Hildreth Dunn (Sarah's sister's daughter), along with Harriet's husband Lanier Dunn, whose father, William McKee Dunn, was then judge advocate general of the army and

Butler's friend. By early 1891, Charlotte, Harriet, and Lanier had moved to a new, somewhat smaller house near the capitol, at 220 New Jersey Avenue SE, that Butler purchased to replace the larger one, and he, too, stayed there when he came to town. "I shall not feel at home, or as if I am to remain here," Charlotte wrote fondly to her uncle, "until you have made us a visit." Meanwhile, Butler engaged in a more regular correspondence with Charlotte's mother, Betsey, who still lived in New Hampshire, their letters revolving around family matters and the fine quality of the homemade sausages Betsey sent him at least once a year. "I need not say I am very much obliged to you," Butler wrote on one occasion. "You and I are all that are left of the old stock and the exchange of courtesies between us is perhaps one of the few pleasures remaining to us." After a particularly delicious batch of sausages arrived, he positively gushed with pleasure. "You cannot appreciate how much I have been pleased with your sausages," which, he observed, "I take from home to my office every day." At one point, Butler also selected one of his horses to give to Betsey, now in her eighties, which her son Thomas came from New Hampshire to collect and which Butler asked West to help deliver. When it came to horses, Butler observed, West "has the best judgment . . . as anyone I know of."[42]

Butler's ties to Betsey and her family were a source of great pleasure, in sharp contrast to his nephew George, who spent his final years in and out of the hospital, mostly in Washington and largely supported by his uncle. "It is utterly useless to attempt to do anything else with him," Butler had written to a friend years earlier, describing George as "an insane man" utterly incapable of controlling his self-destructive impulses. George's mother, too, gradually lost hope: "His brain is diseased," she wrote on one occasion. "God help him." Near the end, Joanna—to whom Butler periodically also sent money—came east to spend time with her son in the hope that her presence "might have an influence." It did not. In May 1886, at the age of forty-six, George left the hospital against his uncle's and the hospital staff's advice, and died soon after at a Washington, D.C., hotel. Subsequently, Butler escorted his nephew's remains to Lowell for a "proper burial" in the family cemetery, next to his father. "We cannot but mourn the loss," Butler wrote to Joanna, "of one of the finest intellects that I have ever known; but alas, we have to soften the reflection upon that loss by the fact that it had gone substantially long since."[43]

Of all his family members, Butler was surely closest to Blanche and her family, with whom he enjoyed warm and affectionate relationships and who now largely divided their time between a home in New York City and an ele-

Nephew George H. Butler. Photograph by Mathew Brady. Courtesy of Special Collections & Archives, Colby College Libraries, Waterville, Maine.

gant place on the New Jersey shore, to which they invited him for summer holidays. "We shall expect to see you down when the weather is warmer," she wrote one spring, "and the boats are running." Butler loved his daughter and grandchildren so much that one fall he offered to "buy a covered wagon, so that the children might have something in which to go to school in stormy weather," though Blanche wondered if perhaps West, who also thoroughly enjoyed spending time with the children, had "put him up to this." On occasion Butler grumbled about the children's noisy laughter, but as soon as they departed he recalled "how much comfort" they provided when they were around. For her part, Blanche increasingly worried about her father's health, and strove from a distance to assist him in whatever ways she could, including ordering clothes for him from a London shop he favored. "The address of the firm is on a small piece of tape sewed to the drawers," she reminded

Blanche, Adelbert Ames, and their children. Photographer unknown.
Courtesy of the Ames Family Papers, Sophia Smith Collection, SSC-MS-00003,
Smith College Special Collections, Northampton, Massachusetts.

him on one occasion. "West will know all about it." Blanche also regularly sought her father's advice about the children's education. "We think of sending Butler to Exeter," she wrote one summer. Soon, however, she and Adelbert decided on West Point, though no doubt with her late brother Bennie in mind, she did not press young Butler to pursue a career in the army. Rather, she insisted, he should decide for himself "whether he will prefer a military or civil life." In the summer of 1889, Butler Ames became a West Point cadet, his uncle having duly (and proudly) warned at least one old wartime colleague who was now a professor there that his grandson enjoyed playing tricks, "and he may be so disrespectful as to do the same to you."[44]

Butler's relationship with his son Paul, who still lived in the family home at Lowell when he was not traveling for business, seems to have been more cordial than openly affectionate. The two men consulted frequently about business matters and especially the Cartridge Company. They also found a pleasant source of connection in their shared love of sailing, Paul racing the *America* when the opportunity arose and developing an additional interest in what was known as "canoe sailing." Meanwhile, even as his business, professional, and other public activities wound down, Butler maintained an

Son Paul. Photographer unknown. Courtesy of the Ames Family
Papers, Sophia Smith Collection, SSC-MS-00003, Smith College
Special Collections, Northampton, Massachusetts.

array of personal contacts outside the family, many of which were tinged
with nostalgia. Not so his relationship with Anna Dickinson, whose determination to continue benefiting from his financial generosity—which her
sister Susan vigorously encouraged—was a source of mounting tension
between them and, eventually, rupture. "Dickinson and her sister were
pursuing a delicate strategy," writes one historian, which toward the end
included her producing a newspaper "exposé" that accused Butler of having
made romantic overtures toward her and then reneged on his promises. In
vain, Butler demanded a retraction of the story, which he considered black-
mail, and by the early 1890s, the relationship disintegrated into a series of
angry exchanges, demands, denials, and, finally, silence.[45]

Having been invited yet again to speak at his alma mater's commencement ceremony, in the summer of 1889 Butler made one last trip up to Waterville, Maine. Word of his impending visit appeared in the college newspaper as early as February: "Nothing has happened for some time so pleasing to the majority of the students," declared the *Colby Echo* on February 8, "than the announcement that Hon. Benj. F. Butler will deliver the oration next Commencement." In June the newspaper reported that Butler would be traveling to Waterville along the Kennebec River on the *America*. At the ceremony, Butler gave a speech that would hardly be welcome at a commencement ceremony in the twenty-first century, endorsing the annexation of Canada by the United States. He also delivered to the college's permanent collection the massive portrait John Antrobus had painted of him in uniform at Dutch Gap in 1864.[46]

As he settled into spending more and more of his time in Lowell, Butler joined the local post of the Union veterans' organization, the Grand Army of the Republic (GAR), which was named in his honor. With the years, many of Butler's former comrades (and adversaries) passed away: Ulysses Grant in July 1885, George McClellan that fall, Philip Sheridan in August 1888, Jefferson Davis in December 1889, and William T. Sherman in February 1891. Still, the war remained a powerful touchstone, and opportunities to weigh in on the commemoration and conflicted memorialization of the war did not diminish. During his final years Butler received numerous invitations to share his thoughts with a range of audiences (including a Decoration Day gathering at the NHDVS site at Togus, near Augusta, Maine), and a variety of other veterans' associations, Fourth of July celebrations, and gatherings of Black Americans, who remained intensely mindful of his many contributions to Black freedom and progress. "Our *colored people* all in the South," wrote an African Methodist Episcopal pastor in New Orleans thirty years after Butler's occupation of that city, "remember you as their deliverer," and "thank God for the day you put your foot on the streets of N.O." In reply, Butler expressed his deep gratitude for having been able to serve in any way as an "instrument" of Black freedom. "It is a great blessing to me," he wrote, "to have been brought in a slight degree to take part in this great work."[47]

Butler continued to speak up especially when he felt the Union cause, Union victory, or his own war record had been slighted. When tensions arose during the first gathering of Union and Confederate veterans at Gettysburg in the spring of 1887 over the question of whether Confederate flags captured by the Union should be returned "as a gesture of reconciliation," Butler flatly said no. The flags, he argued were "evidence of victory" by the United States and should remain in the hands of those who had captured them. When David Dixon Porter's memoir praised Butler for protecting New Orleans from pestilence but then gave most of the credit for subduing Louisiana's rebels to the military governor, George Shepley, and, further, accused Butler of being unpopular, inordinately "energetic in inflicting punishment," "lacking in tact" when it came to the city's women residents, and, by the way, an abject failure during the first attempt on Fort Fisher, Butler published a lengthy, point-by-point rebuttal and, for good measure, basically called Porter a coward. "These two old men," the *Wheeling (W.Va.) Register* observed wryly, "each with one foot in the grave, are fighting away just as if the safety of the country depended on the settlement" of their dispute.[48]

Perhaps because it fed the emerging Lost Cause explanation for the South's defeat and also contrasted so thoroughly with the reconciliationist impulses that had taken hold in recent years among White Americans north and south, Butler's occupation of New Orleans remained for many a focus of particular interest. Some correspondents urged him to publish his own account of the events there; others simply asked privately to know more about it, including a correspondent from Michigan who wondered whether Butler would still handle New Orleans in the same way if he had the chance to go back in time. In response, Butler declared unequivocally that he had in fact been "altogether too lenient" in New Orleans, and given the chance, knowing what he now knew about postwar southern resistance to federal authority, "I would drive every man woman and child that was in rebellion against the United States out of the limits of my Department and sell their property under the hammer in the marketplace and pay my soldiers with the proceeds, and give bounties to people in the North to come down and occupy the places that were vacant." Then and only then would America have enjoyed true peace between the sections, which instead remained elusive.[49]

On another occasion, two little girls from West Virginia asked Butler if he really did come away from New Orleans with a stash of stolen silver spoons. Recognizing the girls' youth, Butler replied with a mix of frustration and kindness. "If I were not convinced of the thorough good faith honesty of purpose and fairness of your letter," he gently scolded the girls, "I should not reply to it, but should receive it as an insult." Instead, confident that the girls bore him no ill will and were simply ignorant—"Who could have told you that foolish story?" he inquired—Butler pointed out that during the occupation, "I could command and did command money to be sent hither and thither by the millions." As such, "do you really suppose that with money under my order to that amount I would have busied myself in picking up spoons?" Not for the first time, he suggested that such rumors and "foolish stories" were the work of people who "know that if they had the chance to have stolen the spoons they would have done it, and therefore they suppose that I did as they would have done."[50]

Butler entertained a variety of other war-related questions in his correspondence: What ever happened to General Twiggs's swords? Was it true that Butler had helped to sustain the widow of William Mumford financially after the war and that he had even become friends with her and her children? He also replied to curious strangers whose questions had no connection to the war, such as the man who simply wanted to know how long Butler slept in every twenty-four-hour period. Indeed, the abundance of both benign inquiries and nettling challenges to his war record that filled his correspondence, along with the effect on his awareness of his own mortality that the steady passing of other Civil War luminaries imposed, finally persuaded Butler to begin writing his massive autobiography. "When do you propose to begin that book which you alone can write?" Blanche had asked back in November 1888, and others had floated the idea even earlier. Certain that his autobiography would sell, Butler had long thought of writing it but had never found the time.[51] Now that his various other responsibilities were winding down, the time had come.

And so Butler finally signed a contract for his thousand-page tome, arranging with his longtime friend and ally James Parton that Parton would finish the book if Butler died before it was done. (As it happens, Parton died first, in October 1891.) Eager above all "to be sure that the narrative of all I had done in the war should be set forth by my own hand," convinced that "nobody could make it complete but myself," and that "it was due to my own reputation and my children and friends that that should be done at all hazards, if life lasted so long," Butler focused by far the majority of his attention on the war years, vigorously defending his often-maligned record. "My publishers and myself are in the closing hours of my book," he informed a friend cheerfully in January 1892. "The printer is driving the publisher and he is driving me, so that I have not had an hour to myself anywhere which I have not been obliged to devote to that." As he explained to another inquirer, the entire manuscript had to be dictated by him to an assistant and later read back to him for corrections, because his vision had become so poor. "Between my own defective hearing and not too clear speech," he admitted, the book would, regrettably, contain a number of editorial mistakes in addition to errors arising from his own "ignorance." As soon as the book appeared, his correspondence overflowed with responses. To those who sent their compliments, Butler replied with gratitude, and to his critics, with polite disdain.

He had decided, he explained, after decades of being "the target of a few ignorant, irresponsible, mercenary news writers"—including *The Nation*'s founder, E. L. Godkin, "whose malevolence has exhausted the vocabulary of vituperation"—that he would let *Butler's Book* "make its own way with the reading public" and "take care of itself as well as it may do." As far as he was concerned, the "kindliness" with which the book had "been noticed by the leading press of the country" had quickly exceeded his expectations and that was good enough.[52]

"I am taking no part in politics," he reminded a friend during the 1892 political season that resulted in Grover Cleveland's return to the presidency, "save that of a looker on." Instead, that fall Butler participated in a "grand review" of some 70,000 aging Civil War veterans on Pennsylvania Avenue in Washington, D.C. "The General," reported *Harper's Weekly*, appearing in the parade in a carriage at the head of the members of his Lowell-based GAR post, was treated to the same "mead of cheers awarded to all the generals" who were present that day, including Oliver Otis Howard, Daniel Sickles, and others. "Somewhere above the White House reviewing stand," Butler then turned his carriage around and passed back along the line of Massachusetts veterans, and as he did so, "the men, who as boys had gone to war with perhaps more of the old Roundhead [anti-elitist] spirit than any other men who went, leaned with their hands on their bamboo canes or the staves of their battered battle-flags, and waved their slouch-hats and blue flannel kepis in their left hands." It was, the popular illustrated journal insisted, "the climax of Butler's career" and "a fitting climax" indeed, for although Butler may not have been "a great or even a good soldier," he was, without a doubt, "the highest type of the political soldier, with all the merits and most of the demerits of the class." Butler was in fact "by far the ablest of the lot who leaped from the stump to the saddle," in contrast with some of the West Point–trained professional officers of the regular army. He deserved to be remembered, too, as "a highly successful, perhaps a great lawyer, by the standard of to-day, a generous giver, a stout friend and bitter foe, a thriving manufacturer, and an enthusiastic yachtsman." Butler, *Harper's Weekly* concluded, was "an extraordinarily able man" and a devoted leader. "I would have come on to see the boys," the *Philadelphia Inquirer* quoted him as saying on the day of the grand review, even "if I knew I would draw my last breath here."[53]

When Butler turned seventy-four that November, his final breaths were, in fact, only a few weeks away. In recent years he had experienced a number of health challenges, including a painful injury at age sixty-nine sustained

when he slipped and fell while racing through the railroad station in Philadelphia. "My ankle turned," he explained to Betsey, "and I fell on a smooth
surface and threw out my arm to save myself instead of falling like a bag of
wool," dislocating his right arm and shoulder. "I sincerely hope the injury,"
wrote his old friend Phoebe Couzins upon hearing the news, "is not of a serious nature." A year later Butler suffered through a particularly bad, lingering
cold. Then, at seventy-one, he underwent an operation on one of his congen-
itally drooping eyelids in order to improve, he hoped, his failing eyesight. "I
have just been told," wrote Couzins fondly on that occasion, "that you had a
difficult and serious operation performed on your eyelid, that you may see
better. May the Lord have mercy upon your enemies and the lesser fry, if we
smaller members of the race are now to be subjected to the full visual gaze
of Genl Butler's unobstructed eye!" Butler joked in reply that he had "seen
too much of sin and sorrow in this world already" to be eager to see more of
it. Still, he would be pleased if the surgery "gives opportunity to see more of
the good and beautiful in the world and also specially to more crucially look
upon the faces of dear and long established friends." To those who suggested
that he had perhaps undertaken the procedure for some "cosmetic purpose,"
he replied with humor. "My looks," he wrote, "are beyond improvement in
any regard as I view them." To Blanche he explained the details, reassuring her good-naturedly that once the swelling went down, "the face will be
somewhat changed, but not enough so that I shall lose my eye-dentity," and
while the procedure had failed to make him better-looking, "I know it has
improved my sight, and the strength of my eye."[54]

Despite Butler's recent health problems, his death in January 1893 was
both sudden and unexpected. "I have just finished reading your book,"
wrote a friend from New Hampshire on New Year's Day, "and I feel frank
to say that it is the most interesting biography that I ever read in my life.
I read every word of it excepting the index." Two days later, Butler wrote a
newsy letter to his niece Charlotte in Washington and also ordered flowers
from a Boston shop for an old friend's funeral in Lowell, advising the shop
that West would pick the flowers up and deliver them personally to their
recipient. Butler continued to set up appointments, deal with his business
concerns, answer questions about how to apply for a pension, turn down
invitations to take new cases or give speeches, and thank fans for their compliments on his book. On January 4 he sent Betsey another paean to her
sausages, declaring the most recent batch "simply elegant" and as delicious
"as sausages used to taste to me years ago." He would soon be on his way to
Washington, he informed her, where he looked forward to spending time

with her daughter Charlotte. And from Washington on January 7 he advised Paul that he expected to remain in the capital for about a week, dealing with an important and time-consuming legal case.[55]

Then, around 11 p.m. on Tuesday, January 10, before settling in for the night in his own adjoining room, West gently helped Butler to bed. That afternoon, West had accompanied Butler to the War Department, the pair traveling the two miles by carriage through what one newspaper described as "the coldest weather that Washington has known for years." There Butler met for about an hour with Secretary of War Stephen Benton Elkins before he and West returned to the New Jersey Avenue house, arriving home chilled. Over the course of the evening Butler warmed up by the fire with hot drinks, joking sociably with members of the household as well as visitors, including one longtime legal associate, Judge O. D. Barrett, all the while insisting that he did not mind the cold weather nor would it prevent him from enjoying a good supper. Meanwhile, West likely went to stable the horses and carriage, have a meal of his own, and perform other familiar chores while he waited for Butler to call for his usual bedtime assistance.[56]

A couple of hours after the two men finally retired, West awoke suddenly to the sound of Butler coughing violently in the next room and, racing to his aid, soon realized the gravity of the situation. Butler had hauled himself to a nearby bathroom, hobbled by his only slightly improved eyesight as well as excessive weight and discomfort from an earlier ankle injury. Soon he was coughing up blood. West escorted Butler back to bed, positioned the pillows for optimal comfort, and anxiously acknowledged the old man's feeble attempt to comfort him: "You can do nothing more for me." Back in his own room, West's concern about Butler's labored breathing deepened, and he soon alerted the other members of the household. Lanier Dunn immediately went to summon the doctor; by the time he returned, the end was only minutes away. Some days earlier, Butler had told a friend that when the time came, "I want to do my day's work and die" quickly. And so he did, at around 1:30 on the morning of January 11, apparently of heart failure "superinduced by an attack of pneumonia," though a subsequent autopsy indicated that his intense coughing had caused a blood vessel to burst, precipitating his abrupt demise. Soon telegrams announcing Butler's death were on their way to Paul in Lowell and Blanche and Adelbert in New Jersey. All of them started right away for Washington.[57]

The news of Butler's sudden passing quickly spread beyond the confines of the family. Newspapers as far away as California took note, commenting on his many accomplishments, his fame, and his presumed wealth, which the *Boston Globe* estimated at $7 million—almost $200 million today—in combined savings, real estate, and business investments. "Ben Butler Dead," read the blunt headline in Chicago's *Daily Inter Ocean* later that day. "The old veteran dies suddenly at his home in Washington," reported the *Boise Statesman*. "The news of General Butler's unexpected death at Washington came as a startling surprise to his associates as well as to his wide circle of friends in Boston," declared the *Boston Daily Journal*, and the *Jackson (Mich.) Daily Citizen* compared the abruptness of Butler's demise to "an electric shock." "One by one," observed the *Aberdeen (S.D.) Daily News*, "the brave generals who did much good service during the Rebellion, are entering 'the low green tent that never outwards swings,' and only the memory of their valor and its results remain with us." "He died with the 'harness on his back,'" commented the *Kansas City Star*.[58]

Black newspapers expressed particular dismay over Butler's death, eulogizing him consistently as a "friend of the colored race," "a staunch and enthusiastic advocate" of Black progress, and "one of the few American statesmen who have stood as a wall of defense in favor of equal rights for all American citizens." "The Negro," declared the *Indianapolis Freeman*, "never had a braver or more outspoken friend than Benjamin Butler was the last thirty years of his life, and by his death another name is added to that band of high-souled, philanthropic friends that when the Negro counts his jewels, should not be forgotten." "Among men who believe in the elevation of the masses, who believe that there is no cause more ennobling than that of striving to uplift his fellows," opined the *Detroit Plaindealer*, "Benjamin F. Butler will be considered as fit to rank with those men who have made such a cause their lifework." The *New England Torchlight* put it simply: "The white South hated him. The black South loved him." The *Parsons (Kans.) Weekly Blade* agreed, declaring that "no class of people could love more dearly this man than did the colored people of the South." Butler's "love for us," the paper wrote sadly, "was that of a brother." Reporting on the autopsy conducted to determine the actual cause of Butler's death, the African American *Washington Bee* informed readers that their friend Butler's brain "weighed four ounces more than that of Daniel Webster," which had previously been "one of the largest on record."[59]

In anticipation of the imminent return of the deceased's remains, Lowell's mayor ordered municipal flags lowered to half-mast and called a special meeting of the city council. Local businesses and schools hung crepe. Painters were dispatched to blacken the fence around the old Hildreth family cemetery north of the town center where Sarah, her parents, her sister

Susan, her first-born child Paul, her last-born child Bennie, as well as Butler's brother Jackson, nephew George, parents, and many other family members had been laid to rest. City employees labored to clear deep snow at the appointed cemetery plot and along the routes Butler's remains would travel: between the Merrimack Street train depot and the family home on Andover Street, and between St. Anne's Episcopal Church on Kirk Street and the cemetery. At the Massachusetts State House in Boston the flag was lowered to honor the former governor.[60]

On Thursday morning, January 12, President Benjamin Harrison appeared at Butler's Washington, D.C., home for a brief, intimate service with the gathered family. Then, some 500 US Army veterans, representing all twenty of the GAR posts in the nation's capital, escorted his casket to the Pennsylvania Railroad Station. About seventy-five of these men were USCT veterans who had served under Butler in the Army of the James. They included Charles Remond Douglass of the Fifty-Fourth Massachusetts, the youngest son of Frederick Douglass, who would die just two years later. Also present was the Fourth USCT's Christian A. Fleetwood, to whom Butler had awarded the first Congressional Medal of Honor received by a Black soldier. At the train station the veterans from the District of Columbia handed the casket off to others from Lowell's Benjamin F. Butler GAR Post, who had come to bring his body home. "Our beloved Comrade, Gen. B. F. Butler, was mustered out . . . on the morning of January 11, at 1.30 o'clock," wrote the post's commander, Col. Charles Dimon—who had commanded some of Butler's "galvanized Yankees" during the war—in an official notice. With four men standing guard at all times, bayonets fixed, they placed the casket aboard a special train. Also onboard were Paul; Blanche and Adelbert; Lanier and Harriet Dunn; the well-known artist John B. Bachelder, who was married to another Butler niece, Elizabeth Barber Stevens; Charlotte; Judge Barrett; and, of course, West.[61]

From Washington, Butler's remains traveled to New York; South Framingham, Massachusetts; and finally to Lowell. Delayed several hours by the bitter weather, the train arrived in Lowell shortly before 1 p.m. on January 13, showing clear signs of the "hard passage" it had endured over more than 400 wintry miles. As one observer noted, "Snow and ice were heavy upon all parts of the train, and the engine puffed and moaned after its work." Hordes of Lowell residents, including still more military veterans, came to the Merrimack Street depot to pay tribute, some having shivered in the cold and wind since early morning. Draped with the stars and stripes, bearing a wreath of roses presented by President Harrison, and with most of the grieving traveling party of family and friends trailing behind, the casket was then respectfully transported by the Post 42 veterans to Butler's Belvidere home, passing through a dense, continuous, and mostly silent crowd of onlookers that stretched all the way to the house's gates. For his part, West had gone on ahead with Edward H. Gannon, a recently naturalized Irish immigrant who also worked for Butler. At the house, "his face full of care and grief," West joined in receiving the remains.[62]

On Saturday, Butler's loved ones mourned privately, but the following day his embalmed remains were made available for public viewing at Huntington Hall, adjacent to the train station, where he had given so many rousing speeches over the course of his career. Now the hall was shrouded in black cloth. Among the decorations relieving the gloom, however, was an elegant and colorful flower arrangement sent by Frederick Douglass, which the press described as "a General's broken sword in immortelles, roses and carnations upon a tablet of ferns." Over the course of the ensuing day and a half, tens of thousands pressed into the hall to bid farewell, some coming great distances for the opportunity. Reporters observed individuals from "all ranks of life" among the crowds, including "here and there a war veteran with his medals for gallant service pinned upon his breast." They described as well seeing many young children, "who scarcely knew or realized the solemnity of the occasion, or could understand what it all meant," and watching an "elderly Irish woman" who "kissed her hand several times toward the casket and then passed on, weeping." Indeed, the numbers who came to Huntington Hall far exceeded initial expectations, forcing local police to move the line more quickly past the canopied black catafalque than many viewers would have liked, perhaps as many as seventy per minute. Hundreds were turned away, but those who entered the hall found Butler's moustache neatly trimmed and waxed, his hair brushed back, his head resting on a satin pillow, his hands crossed over his chest, and "a suspicion of a smile" on his face. In recognition of his forty-year-long practice of never going into public without a fresh flower in his lapel—a practice begun while his wife, Sarah, was still alive and that was often reflected in the illustrated magazines' Butler caricatures—a single red rose brightened the deceased's clean, dark dress suit. At Butler's head and feet stood two solemn sentries "at rest on arms," their rifles inverted, each presiding over a stack of guns and the state and national flags. Across the casket at his feet lay Butler's complete military uniform.[63]

The public funeral took place at St. Anne's on Monday afternoon, January 16. Still decorated with boughs of evergreen and holly from the Christmas holidays, the church where Butler and Sarah had married in 1844 was full to its 850-person capacity with many additional mourners wishing to come in. As the casket proceeded down the center aisle, congregants heard the organist playing Chopin's "Funeral March" while the city's fire alarm bells tolled once for each of Butler's seventy-four years; a battery of guns fired a salute. After the traditional service, a mile-long cortège in three divisions escorted the casket back through the snowy streets to the cemetery for burial. Hundreds of representatives from the many components of Butler's multifaceted life—civil, political, military, personal—participated in this final procession, newspapers noting that West joined the "relatives and friends in carriages" at the front of the procession, and that a group of Black New Englanders who had come "to manifest their esteem" marched somewhere in the middle. "We write to inform you that a delegation of representative colored citizens headed by the Hon. George T. Downing . . . and Hon. Edwin [*sic*] Garrison Walker"—David Walker's son and the man Butler had nominated for the judicial post eventually held by George Ruffin—"will attend the funeral," wrote Edward Everett Brown on January 13, requesting a place in the ceremonies for a dozen men "who feel deeply the affliction the colored people have sustained in the loss of their distinguished friend," the "faithful" and "lamented" Butler. "Our deceased friend," declared a group of Black Rhode Islanders in a letter to the Butler family, "vowed with a sacred oath . . . that he would stand by and defend the much abused colored people of the United States," and "as a General, a Governor, as a Legislator and as a civilian he was true to his vow." For block after block the town's buildings were hung with crepe and bedecked with flowers and other signs of collective grief, local schools as well as city offices and businesses remained shuttered for the day, and gun salutes continued all along the route. When the grand funeral and procession ended, the sound of "Taps" "floated out upon the clear, cold air," performed by chief bugler of the Sixth Massachusetts Regiment, which Butler had commanded at the start of the war. "Not again in this day and generation," declared one newspaper, "will Lowell see in her streets a spectacle so impressive, nor a pageant appealing more strongly to the hearts of the people." Truly, it was a monumental event, befitting a man whose range of labor, influence, and commitment had been so vast over so many years.[64]

Two months later, on March 15, 1893, the city of Boston conducted a service of tribute to Butler at Tremont Temple, a Baptist church with a racially integrated congregation and a historical commitment to social justice. At the time, Tremont's pastor was Rev. George C. Lorimer, whose son, George Horace Lorimer, had also attended Waterville College (class of 1898). On

Butler's funeral procession in Lowell. Photographer unknown. Courtesy of the Ames Family Papers, Sophia Smith Collection, SSC-MS-00003, Smith College Special Collections, Northampton, Massachusetts.

this occasion Frederick T. Greenhalge, a former mayor of Lowell and former member of the US House of Representatives who later became governor of Massachusetts, eulogized Butler for almost ninety minutes. Greenhalge began his remarks with the advisory that he had often disagreed with Butler on public matters, so he should not be expected to provide anything but the unvarnished truth about the man now. He then went on to describe Butler as "distinct in type," someone who "tower[ed] above ordinary men like a mountain peak," not in a gentle way, but rather "piercing the sky with sharp, jagged lines." Butler, Greenhalge seemed to say, was highly accomplished but also rough around the edges: scornful of convention, propriety, and institutions for their own sake. He was, Greenhalge explained, a disrupter of the "peace and comfort" of "comfortable men," a man who unfailingly "stretch[ed] out a friendly hand to the exile and the stranger, when it is difficult to see how he could gain thereby," and who stood resolutely and at all times on the principle that "every citizen of the republic," regardless of "creed or condition" or "race or party," should "wear the crown of his full, just, and equal civic rights as boldly and as proudly as king or emperor could wear the royal diadem." Greenhalge summed up Butler's life and work as an unceasing battle "waged against power, against wealth, against station." And so, he predicted, while others might condemn him as a troublemaker, Butler's memory would forever be "cherished by the sons of poverty; by the oppressed, the friendless, the unfortunate of every type."[65] No wonder Black Americans were so eager to express their thanks.

Notes

1. Ames, *Chronicles from the Nineteenth Century*, 2:594. Images of the gravestone are readily available online.

2. *Boston Globe*, January 11, 1893; *Washington Star*, January 13, 1893; *Literary Digest*, March 23, 1918; *New York Times Book Review*, March 18, 1918; *Boston Sunday Herald*, June 2, 1918; *New York Evening Post*, February 16, 1918; untitled, undated document in the Benjamin F. Butler Papers, Archives and Special Collections, Colby College, Waterville, Maine (hereafter BP-C). Numerous biographies deploy these nicknames in their titles or subtitles. See, for example, Werlich, *"Beast" Butler*; Trefousse, *Ben Butler*; Nolan, *Benjamin Franklin Butler*; Hearn, *When the Devil Came Down to Dixie*; and Nash, *Stormy Petrel*.

3. Butler, *Butler's Book*; *Boston Daily Journal*, January 11 and 16, 1893; *Boston Globe*, January 11, 1893.

4. *Boston Daily Journal*, January 11 and 16, 1893; *Washington Star*, January 13, 1893; *Boston Globe*, January 11, 1893.

5. *Boston Globe*, January 11, 1893; *A Memorial of Benjamin F. Butler*, 13, 15; *Colby Echo*, February 25, 1893.

6. *Colby Library Quarterly* 6 (September 1964); Marriner, *The History of Colby College*; Butler, *Private and Official*, 2:263; Raymond, "Ben Butler," 479. The late Harold "Hal" Raymond, who earned his PhD at Harvard and was a World War II veteran, began teaching in the History Department at Colby in 1952 and retired in 1994.

7. Raymond, "Ben Butler," 445. Raymond was referring to Holzman, *Stormy Ben Butler*; Trefousse, *Ben Butler*; and Werlich, *"Beast" Butler*.

For a number of years, beginning in 1965, Colby hosted what were known as the "Ben Butler Debates," a debate competition among students from Colby, Bates, Bowdoin, some campuses of the University of Maine, and the University of New Hampshire. Winners in various categories received silver spoons as awards.

8. *Colby Echo*, June 14 and 28, 1889; Whittemore, *Colby College*, 95. Butler's commencement speech, "Should There Be a Union of the English-Speaking Peoples of the Earth?," is available in pamphlet form in BP-C.

9. *Colby Echo*, February 8, 1889; "Remembrance of Colby Days, and of Subsequent Related Events," enclosure in a letter from Clarence LaVerne Judkins to G.

Cecil Goddard, February 7, 1940, in BP-C. The author of this item misremembered the year of Butler's visit as 1891.

It is interesting to note that Frederick Douglass visited Waterville in January 1855 (*Frederick Douglass's Paper*, February 2, 1855), where he spoke at the Baptist Meeting House, which was then closely affiliated with the college, whose roots were Baptist. He visited again in April 1864 (*Maine Cultivator and Hallowell Gazette*, April 2, 1864).

10. Butler, *Private and Official*, 5:665–67; Duerk, "Elijah P. Lovejoy"; Raymond, "The 'Beast' at the Top of the Stairs." "Should Colby then take down 'the beast's' portrait or at least remove it to a relatively infrequented place like the Chapel," Raymond asked. "It should do no such thing."

11. Raymond, "The 'Beast' at the Top of the Stairs." In the interest of full disclosure: I am the author of the new legend.

12. Kendi, *How to Be an Antiracist*, 230.

CHAPTER 1

1. *Farmer's Cabinet* (Amherst, N.H.), November 7, 1818. Butler's mother was born in February 1792.

2. New Hampshire Birth Index, 1659–1900; Patent of John Butler, 1810, box 257, Benjamin F. Butler Papers, Library of Congress, Washington, D.C. (hereafter BP-LC); Butler, *Butler's Book*, 41; Pierce, *Batchelder, Batcheller Genealogy*, 187; New Hampshire Marriage Records Index, 1637–1947; Massachusetts Town Birth Records, 1620–1850. *Butler's Book* says they married in July, but the official records indicate that the marriage took place in August.

3. Butler, *Butler's Book*, 40, 44; New Hampshire, Wills and Probate Records, 1643–1982; New Hampshire Births and Christenings Index, 1714–1904; "General Butler's Boyhood," Benjamin F. Butler Papers, Archives and Special Collections, Colby College, Waterville, Maine (hereafter BP-C); *Boston Globe*, January 11, 1893; Pierce, *Batchelder, Batcheller Genealogy*, 187; *Harper's Weekly*, June 1, 1861; Charlotte Ellison to John Butler, November 22, 1810, BP-C. In *Butler's Book* Butler claims that Richard Ellison and his wife immigrated to New Hampshire from Great Britain after Richard received a monetary award for military service to King William, but Charlotte's death record indicates that her father was born in New Hampshire (Massachusetts Death Records, 1841–1915). It is unclear which record is accurate. Also, there is some disagreement in the sources over the rank Joseph Cilley achieved. Elliott Cogswell says he was a captain. See Cogswell, *History of Nottingham, Deerfield, and Northwood*, 195. There is also a General Joseph Cilley in the record, but this seems to be a different person (180–81).

4. John Butler to W. Eustis, Esq., March 24, 1812; John Butler to unknown, August 1, 1812; and John Butler to A. Smyth, August 8, 1812, all in Letters Received by the Adjutant General, 1805–1821; *New Hampshire Patriot and State Gazette*, April 14 and June 23, 1812; Butler, *Butler's Book*, 40, 44; New Hampshire, Wills and Probate Records, 1643–1982; New Hampshire Births and Christenings Index, 1714–

1904; "General Butler's Boyhood," BP-C; *Boston Globe*, January 11, 1893; Pierce, *Batchelder, Batcheller Genealogy*, 187; *Harper's Weekly*, June 1, 1861; Charlotte Ellison to John Butler, November 22, 1810, BP-C.

5. John Butler to Charlotte Ellison Butler, March 23, April 27, May 16, July 4, July 10, August 19, October 2, and December 12, 1813, BP-C; 1790 US Census record for Zephaniah Butler.

6. John Butler to Adjutant General Colonel J. B. Walbach, April 18, 1814, in Letters Received by the Adjutant General, 1805–1821; John Butler to Charlotte Butler, January 5, 1814, BP-C; "General Butler's Boyhood," BP-C; Coburn, *History of Lowell and Its People*, 1:295; Nolan, *Benjamin Franklin Butler*, 2; Werlich, *"Beast" Butler*, 1–2; Nash, *Stormy Petrel*, 20–21; West, *Lincoln's Scapegoat General*, 8–9; Bland, *Life of Benjamin Butler*, 7–8; Butler, *Butler's Book*, 41–42; Parton, *General Butler in New Orleans*, 5; *Boston Globe*, January 11, 1893; *Portsmouth Oracle*, January 28, 1815.

7. 1845 Lowell City Directory; "Gen. Butler's Boyhood"; New Hampshire Marriage Records Index, 1637–1947; 1830, 1840, 1850 US Federal Census; Butler, *Butler's Book*, 44, 45, 49–50; *Repository and Observer* (Concord, N.H.), October 21, 1826; *New Hampshire Patriot and State Gazette*, November 5, 1827; Pierce, *Batchelder, Batcheller Genealogy*, 187. Butler's stepsister Betsey similarly recalled that he was "very small for his age" and a great lover of books ("General Butler's Boyhood," BP-C).

Butler distinctly remembered learning about the horrors of yellow fever from his mother after his father died, recalling that what she described "made so indelible an impression on my memory that it impelled me, when I was older, to investigate that scourge to such extent as I might, and this investigation had some effect upon my conduct of affairs in later life" (Butler, *Butler's Book*, 43).

8. An article in the *Colby Echo* of June 17, 1887, says of Charlotte Butler, "She stamped upon him her own excellent traits of character and her indomitable courage. She instilled into his mind principles of truth and manliness, and high ambition, which laid the foundation of his future eminent career."

9. *Farmer's Cabinet*, May 24, 1828; 1850 US Census; Butler, *Butler's Book*, 46–49; New Hampshire Wills and Probate Records, 1643–1982.

10. See relevant documents from 1828 and 1835 for Charlotte Butler in the New Hampshire Wills and Probate Records; "General Butler's Boyhood," BP-C; *Boston Star*, January 14, 1893; Butler, *Butler's Book*, 52; *Essex Register* (Salem, Mass.), March 16, 1826; US City Directories, 1822–1995, for Charlotte Butler in Lowell, Massachusetts.

Hersey's favorable description of Butler as a young boy is very much at odds with that offered in 1868—completely devoid of any supporting evidence—by a Wisconsin journalist and former copperhead, Mark Pomeroy, who clearly despised his subject. Butler himself noted Pomeroy's description in his autobiography and other writers subsequently replicated it in other forms. According to Pomeroy, when he was little Butler "was known as the dirtiest, sauciest, lyingest child on the road," an urchin who was both "tricky and wanton" and who "took delight in insulting little girls and beating smaller boys than himself." See Pomeroy, *Life and*

Public Services of Benjamin F. Butler, 8–9. See also Hearn, *When the Devil Came Down to Dixie*, 7. Both Pomeroy and Hearn, along with other hostile biographers, make a major point of Butler's crossed eyes and droopy eyelids, which Hearn identifies as a "severe case of strabism" that made Butler physically unattractive and gave him a "peculiar appearance" (Hearn, *When the Devil Came Down to Dixie*, 7–8). Perhaps reaching for an unkind pun, Pomeroy describes Butler as an "eye sore" (Pomeroy, *Life and Public Services of Benjamin F. Butler*, 9).

11. Coburn, *History of Lowell and Its People*, 1:6.

12. Coburn, 1:8, 21, 131, 138, 151, 152, 162, 191–92; Coolidge, *Mill and Mansion*, 22; Butler, *Butler's Book*, 52–53; Larcom, *A New England Girlhood*, 145; *Boston Commercial Gazette*, March 6, 1826; *Essex Register*, March 16, 1826. For a thorough study of the Lowell mills during this period and beyond, see Dublin, *Women at Work*. See also 1832 Lowell City Directory.

According to Coburn, "An enumeration of 1828," the year Charlotte Butler arrived, "showed 1,342 males, 2,190 females" in Lowell. Two years later, the count was "2,392 males and 4,085 females," and in 1836 "6,345 males, 11,288 females." By 1826 the company was "using cotton at the rate of 450,000 pounds annually" (162). The amount of slave labor that went into the production of that much cotton annually is staggering to consider.

13. Butler, *Butler's Book*, 51; *Proceedings in the City of Lowell at the Semi-centennial Celebration*, 37–40.

14. Butler, *Butler's Book*, 52, 55, 56; US High School Student Lists, 1821–1923; Coburn, *History of Lowell and Its People*, 1:193, 323; 1850 US Census; 1830 Catalogue for the Academical and Theological Institution of New Hampton, New Hampshire, 18, in US High School Student Lists, 1821–1923.

The BP-LC contain a charming, if historically questionable, essay by Butler, dated 1831, when he was twelve or thirteen, on the topic of "the discovery of America." It begins, "America had reposed in obscurity for more than 5000 years and mankind had not dreamed that it existed" (folder 1, box 3, BP-LC).

For what it's worth, I do not plan to draw attention to every discrepancy between the autobiography and the rest of the historical record. I also do not believe that many (if any) of the errors in the autobiography, such as they are, were intended to mislead readers. Rather, most of the mistakes arose from Butler's having written the book at speed, as an old yet still very busy man. Where I see errors that may have significant consequences, I will point them out.

15. Butler, *Butler's Book*, 55, 57; George L. Balcom to Benjamin Franklin Butler (hereafter BFB), September 29, 1836, in folder 2, box 3, BP-LC; James M. Flagg to BFB, April 17, 1861, in folder 9, box 3, BP-LC.

The BP-LC contain an essay written by Butler in July 1832, comparing the state of the country then to the same date in 1776 but also reflecting on the fact that while the Fourth of July should be a day to "awaken patriotic feelings," instead "how often is it a day of drunken revelry" (see folder 1, box 3, BP-LC).

According to Coburn, there were only eight students in the first class that entered Lowell High School with Butler in December 1831 (Coburn, *History of Low-*

ell and Its People, 1:193). It would not have been difficult to make friends, and enemies, in a group that size.

Waterville College became Colby University in 1867, in recognition of the generous contribution of Gardner Colby, who helped save the college from the financial ruin that threatened with drastically declining enrollments during the Civil War. A purely undergraduate institution, the school became known as Colby College in 1899.

16. Butler, *Butler's Book*, 57; Isaac Hill to Charlotte Butler, September 30, 1835, in folder 1, box 3, BP-LC.

17. Theodore Edson to To Whom It May Concern, January 26, 1836; S. R. Hanscom to the State of Massachusetts, January 25, 1836; William Graves to To Whom It May Concern; Caleb Cushing to Charlotte Butler, February 17, 1836, all in folder 2, box 3, BP-LC.

18. Marriner, *The History of Colby College*, 33, 122; Charlotte B. Hilton to BFB, August 5, 1842, in folder 2, box 3, BP-LC; Butler, *Butler's Book*, 57, 65; Whittemore, *Colby College*, 66; *Boston Globe*, January 11, 1893; *Colby Echo*, April 20, 1921, and June 17, 1887. In 1824, ten years before Butler matriculated, tuition, board, and miscellaneous expenses amounted to about $84 per year (Marriner, *The History of Colby College*, 62).

19. Marriner, *The History of Colby College*, 39, 47, 59, 60–61, 69–70, 85, 88, 93; *American Advocate* (Hallowell, Me.), October 22, 1834; Whittemore, *Colby College*, 1. A 1919 article in the *Colby Echo* observed that as a student Butler lived, at least for part of his time at the college, "in the northwest corner of the parlors of the Lambda Chi Alpha" fraternity, which was situated in North College (*Colby Echo*, January 17, 1919; see also Marriner, *The History of Colby College*, 336). Colby admitted its first woman student, Mary Low (Carver), in 1871. Smith also taught modern languages at the college.

20. Butler, *Butler's Book*, 58, 60, 62; Marriner, *The History of Colby College*, 126.

In April 1835, Butler also requested permission to be absent from the college for a time in order to attend to "business" in Cornville (BFB to "The Honorable Faculty of Waterville College," April 29, 1835, in BP-C).

According to Marriner there is "no record" of Butler "being disciplined, reprimanded, fined, or suspended" (Marriner, *The History of Colby College*, 127). Nevertheless, that Butler remembered his formative years at Waterville College as years of character-building resistance says a good deal about how he understood his own personality, behavior, and motivations in adult life.

21. *General Catalogue of the Officers*, 250; Joseph W. Russell to BFB, April 19, 1836, in BP-C; Butler, *Butler's Book*, 62. Like Butler, Russell went on to become a lawyer. Rufus Babcock left the presidency of the college for a church in Pennsylvania in the summer of 1836.

22. Butler, *Butler's Book*, 58; Marriner, *The History of Colby College*, 644, 75; Whittemore, *Colby College*, 47, 74. Over his four years at Waterville College Butler's professors also included Phinehas Barnes (Greek and Latin), Justin Loomis (chemistry and natural history), Calvin Newton (rhetoric and Hebrew), Stephen B. Page

(elocution), and Robert E. Pattison (philosophy), who followed Babcock into the college presidency (Whittemore, *Colby College*, 639–50, 630). Throughout his auto-biography, Butler depicts himself as a man of reason, logic, and education, rather than faith.

23. Coburn, *History of Lowell and Its People*, 1:204; Whittemore, *Colby College*, 40–41, 49; Marriner, *The History of Colby College*, 71–82, 630. According to Coburn, the British antislavery activist George Thompson came to speak at Lowell that fall. Indeed, Thompson apparently came to Lowell a couple of times in this period, but he was not warmly received. The town's leaders may have expressed some anti-slavery sentiments in principle, but at the same time Lowell's economic vigor and growth was utterly dependent on the institution, which the leaders clearly recognized.

24. Wongsrichanalai, *Northern Character*; Marriner, *The History of Colby College*, 128.

In his autobiography, Butler does not mention Lovejoy's murder. The BP-LC contain many essays he wrote while a student at Waterville College; only one of them, written two years before Lovejoy's murder and titled "The Abolitionists," deals with the slavery question. In it, Butler criticizes the abolitionists for having "created an excitement which has tended more to the destructions of the peace and harmony . . . of the United States (the only sure foundation of our liberties) than other causes combined" (folder 1, box 3, BP-LC). Of course, given how central the practice of recitation was to college education in this period, it is impossible to know how much this essay reflected Butler's own views, and how much it represented the views of his instructors.

25. Marriner, *The History of Colby College*, 123, 129; *Boston Globe*, January 11, 1893, and January 4, 1925; *Colby Echo*, March 19, 1924; unidentified clipping, "A True Story of General Butler," September 29, 1871, and unidentified clipping, "The Boy Makes the Man," March 1883, in BP-C.

Other sources, supposedly including a *Boston Globe* article from 1900 (cited in Marriner, *The History of Colby College*, 127), take delight in observing—in error—that Butler yearned for the post but failed to earn it. I have searched for this article but have been unable to locate it.

26. Marriner, *The History of Colby College*, 129; F. G. Cook to BFB, September 10, 1839; Enoch Merrill to BFB, October 19, 1839; Eben Freeman to BFB, December 11, 1839; all in folder 2, box 3, BP-LC.

27. *Colby Echo*, June 17, 1887, April 20, 1921, and March 19, 1924; *Boston Globe*, January 11, 1893.

28. *General Catalogue of the Officers*, 44; Arthur F. Drinkwater to BFB, July 25, 1839, and November 26, 1839, in folder 2, box 3, BP-LC.

29. *General Catalogue of the Officers*, 39, 41, 249; Moses J. Kelly to BFB, May 24, 1861, in folder 2, box 5, BP-LC; Edgar Harkness Gray to BFB, May 31, 1861, in folder 3, box 5, BP-LC; Lucius L. Scammell to BFB, June 26, 1868, and BFB to Lucius L. Scammell, July 6, 1868, both in folder 9, box 45, BP-LC. Whittemore, *History of Colby College*, 96.

In his letter, Kelly jokingly suggested "that next to being General in Chief of the U.S. Army or President of the U. States, you might prefer to be President of the General Society of the *Erosophian Adelphi*. I happen to have that position now & could easily secure it for you in 1862 if you will accept it." After the war Kelly took a position as chaplain at Togus, in Augusta, Maine, the first veterans' facility in what became a network run by the National Homes for Disabled Volunteer Soldiers, of whose board Butler became president.

30. *Portland Weekly Advertiser*, August 14, 1838; Missouri Marriage Records, 1793–1983 and 1805–2002; Butler, *Butler's Book*, 69.

Only twelve of those who entered Waterville College with Butler earned the BA in 1838. An entertaining story about Butler leading up to graduation—whose accuracy cannot be evaluated—appeared in a *Colby Echo* article in June 1887. It reads, in part, "He was returning to Waterville from Cornville,—where he had spent a part of his Senior recess before graduating,—on horseback, and in crossing a bridge near Waterville his horse stumbled, and threw him forward, with such force, upon the plate of the bridle on the horse's head, as to break out some of his front teeth. It was then Saturday before Commencement, the next Wednesday. It was no easy undertaking, at that time, to go to Portland, the nearest place where such a job could be done, get his teeth repaired, and get back to Waterville by Commencement morning; and yet he did it. There was no railroad then. Travel to Portland was by stage and steamboat, and all were astonished to see Butler returned in season to take part with his class in Commencement exercises, with damages repaired, and as cool as if nothing unusual had happened." Butler's "quick thought," added the author, "carried him through many college dilemmas" (*Colby Echo*, June 17, 1887).

Although the historical record is not absolutely clear, it appears that Butler's sister bore two children in 1839, the year she died: Isabella T. Holton and Francis Butler Holton (1840 US Census; see also 1850 US Census). It is not known whether Francis and Isabella were twins or born nine months apart; either would have been a difficult and likely even fatal scenario for Charlotte. Horace remarried in September 1840 (to Lucia A. Huggins) and again in 1844 (to Clara Harlow) (see Missouri Marriage Records, 1805–2002).

The US Census indicates that Andrew Jackson Butler and Johanna Butler remained in Missouri at least through 1850, when they were living in Hannibal with their children. In 1860, they were living in Sonoma, California, with mother Charlotte Butler and six servants. In that census Andrew Jackson Butler is listed as a real estate broker.

31. Butler, *Butler's Book*, 69–71; *Boston Globe*, January 11, 1893.

32. Coburn, *History of Lowell and Its People*, 1:218; *Proceedings in Massachusetts and New Hampshire on the Death of the Hon. Jeremiah Mason*, 3–4; Butler, *Butler's Book*, 63–64.

33. Butler, *Butler's Book*, 71–72, 74. See also 1840 Lowell City Directory, which shows Butler as a "student at law with William Smith." According to at least one source, Smith was the father of the founder of Wellesley College, Henry Welles

Smith, who changed his name to Henry F. Durant following a religious conversion. See *Lowell, A City of Spindles*, 151.

34. BFB to J. M. Damon, November 15, 1839, folder 2, box 3, BP-LC; Document titled "The weather is blue without," dated December 1836, in folder 2, box 3, BP-LC; Butler, *Butler's Book*, 73.

35. Butler, *Butler's Book*, 75–76; Warner, *Generals in Blue*, 60; Coburn, *History of Lowell and Its People*, 1:219–20.

36. Butler, *Butler's Book*, 77; *Boston Globe*, January 11, 1893. I have been unable to locate a record of this speech. It bears noting that Van Buren's attorney general (1837–38) was also named Benjamin Franklin Butler, which can be a source of confusion for researchers, at least until this "other" Benjamin Butler died in 1858.

37. Butler, *Butler's Book*, 78; Reade, *Origin and Genealogy*, 4, 54, 64, 66.

38. Butler, *Butler's Book*, 123–24; Coburn, *History of Lowell and Its People*, 1:296.

CHAPTER 2

1. Butler, *Butler's Book*, 985–86; Lowell, Massachusetts, City Directory, 1844; *Boston Daily Atlas*, January 16 and December 19, 1845. See also the certificate acknowledging Butler's admission as an attorney to the US Supreme Court, dated December 16, 1845, in Benjamin F. Butler Papers, Library of Congress, Washington, D.C. (hereafter BP-LC), folder 2, box 1. In his autobiography Butler notes that his admission to the bar of the Supreme Court came the same term as that of William Henry Seward and Abraham Lincoln, and when he was only twenty-seven years old (Butler, *Butler's Book*, 1007).

2. Reade, *Origin and Genealogy*, 63–64.

3. Coolidge, *Mill and Mansion*, 66, 202; *Boston Globe*, January 11, 1893; West, *Lincoln's Scapegoat General*, 21–23. See also Butler, *Butler's Book*, 986–1007, for his recollections of these early years in practice.

4. Dublin, *Women at Work*, 86–87; *Boston Globe*, January 11, 1893; Butler, *Butler's Book*, 90; Dickens, *American Notes for General Circulation*, 152–64. See also Hearn, *When the Devil Came Down to Dixie*, 14. Hearn's sketch of Butler's time in New Orleans is extremely critical, as the title of the book suggests. Nevertheless, even he gives Butler credit for taking on the cases of the factory girls "who scraped together a few dollars to press charges against the employment practices of the Lowell Mills" (14).

5. Benjamin Franklin Butler (hereafter BFB) to Charlotte E. Butler, September 15, 1844, Benjamin F. Butler Papers, Archives and Special Collections, Colby College, Waterville, Maine (hereafter BP-C); Butler, *Butler's Book*, 86.

6. Ames, *Chronicles from the Nineteenth Century*, 1:45–46; Reade, *Origin and Genealogy*, 59; Butler, *Butler's Book*, 78–79; *Boston Globe*, January 11, 1893.

The year given for Sarah's birth varies in the historical record, the *Boston Globe* at the time of Benjamin Butler's death reporting that she was born as late as 1821 (*Boston Globe*, January 11, 1893). The Massachusetts Town and Vital Records,

1620–1988, clearly indicate that she was born on August 17, 1816, making her more than two years older than her husband, which at the time may have caused her some embarrassment, amplified by the fact that she married "late," relatively speaking, at almost twenty-eight.

7. Lowell, Massachusetts, City Directory, 1844; Massachusetts Town and Vital Records, 1620–1988; Ames, *Chronicles from the Nineteenth Century*, 1:46; BFB to Charlotte E. Butler, September 15, 1844, BP-C. In this letter, Butler urged Charlotte to come home, insisting that both he and Sarah were eager for her company. He also wrote at considerable length, and in ways that indicate their close mother-son relationship, about a recent ankle injury. "Well I have very slightly sprained my ankle," he wrote, "just enough to give me a slight limp. I did it yesterday in precisely the same way that I cut my leg before only it was the other end of the same axle tree that broke this time and tumbled me out and no great harm done. They tell me down at the Barbers this morning when I got shaved that it was considered a hair breadth escape but then so is one's whole life. Now do not be fidgety and think this strain is anything more than I have represented because it is not. . . . You need not come home one moment sooner on that account."

The 1840 and 1850 US Censuses show Andrew Jackson Butler in Liberty and then Hannibal, Missouri. The 1860 census record shows him in Sonoma, California, now a "real estate broker" with six servants, including one who was listed as an "Indian." A newspaper article many years later says that "he spent 11 years in California after the gold excitement of '49" (*Boston Globe*, January 11, 1893). Charlotte remained with Andrew Jackson Butler's family in Missouri, and then in California, until the war. Joanna had a second child, Charlie, in 1850, but he died in 1853.

8. 1855, 1858, and 1859 Lowell City Directories; Ames, *Chronicles from the Nineteenth Century*, 1:46; *Catalogue of the Officers and Students of Dartmouth College*, 16; Reade, *Origin and Genealogy*, 56, 59–60; Certificate acknowledging Butler's admission to the Pentucket Lodge on September 17, 1846, and certificate acknowledging Butler's advancement to the degree of "Royal Arch Mason" in Lowell's Mount Horeb Royal Arch Chapter, February 12, 1855, both in folder 2, box 1, BP-LC; Massachusetts Mason Membership Cards, 1733–1990; *Boston Globe*, January 11, 1893.

Butler opened his Boston office in 1849 or 1850.

Hearn adds that Butler also "invested wisely" (in real estate and in stock in the Middlesex Mills in Lowell), all of which combined to make him a wealthy man (Hearn, *When the Devil Came Down to Dixie*, 17–19). See also Coburn, *History of Lowell and Its People*, 2:5.

William and Susan married in August 1850. Sarah's brother Fisher had married Lauretta Coburn of Dracut in 1846 (Reade, *Origin and Genealogy*, 59; Massachusetts Marriages, 1633–1850). There is some disagreement regarding when Fisher and Lauretta's marriage actually took place that year. Reade says they wed on Butler's birthday, November 5, but the public record says September 26. Perhaps there was a celebration in November, following the official marriage in September.

9. Trefousse, *Ben Butler*, 52; Butler, *Butler's Book*, 89.

10. Coburn, *History of Lowell and Its People*, 1:496; *Boston Daily Atlas*, September 15, 1847; writ issued for the arrest of BFB, September 10, 1847, and the subsequent statement from the court, dated September 15, 1847, both in folder 3, box 3, BP-LC; Trefousse, *Ben Butler*, 26.

11. Butler, *Butler's Book*, 91; Dublin, *Women at Work*, 113; Lazerow, "Religion and the New England Mill Girl": 436; *Berkshire County Whig*, June 19, 1845.

12. Hearn, *When the Devil Came Down to Dixie*, 14; Dublin, *Women at Work*, 108–9, 113, 118, 138; *Voice of Industry*, May 7 and July 2, 1847.

By way of example with regard to the changing Lowell workforce in this period, Dublin notes that whereas in 1836 only 3.7 percent of workers at the Hamilton Company were foreign-born, by 1850, almost 40 percent were immigrants—mostly Irish (Dublin, *Women at Work*, 138). Among the changes that went along with the increase in the number of immigrant workers was the decline of the boardinghouse system (143). It was fortunate for Charlotte Butler that her years of needing to support her children as a boardinghouse matron had come to an end by this point.

13. Butler, *Butler's Book*, 91–93.

14. Rice, *Reminiscences of Abraham Lincoln*, 139. In his 1888 compendium, Rice erroneously claimed to quote Benjamin Butler as saying that he (Butler) first saw Abraham Lincoln in Lowell in 1840, when the future president was supposedly campaigning for presidential candidate William Henry Harrison. In fact, Butler does not mention meeting Lincoln at *any* time before the Civil War, which he surely would have done had the encounter occurred. Moreover, Lincoln's visit to the Spindle City actually took place in September 1848, just a few months after Butler traveled to Baltimore as a delegate to the Democratic National Convention, which nominated Lewis Cass for president.

15. Mitgang, *Abraham Lincoln*, 65; Coburn, *History of Lowell and Its People*, 1:235.

16. Butler, *Butler's Book*, 79, 986; US Census Mortality Schedules, 1850–1885; *Boston Daily Atlas*, July 27, 1850; certificate of promotion, dated October 25, 1852, in folder 1, box 1, BP-LC; *Boston Courier*, March 30, 1854; West, *Lincoln's Scapegoat General*, 25; BFB to Sarah H. Butler (hereafter SHB), December 25, 1854, BP-C.

For an example of a typical Butler case during this period, see the case of accused murderer Daniel H. Pierson, "formerly a porter at several hotels and waiter in private families" in Cambridge, charged with killing his estranged wife and two children upon learning that the children were not his own (*Emancipator & Republican* [Boston], March 7, 1850; *Boston Daily Evening Transcript*, February 27 and March 2, 1850).

Benjamin and Sarah's granddaughter, Jessie Ames Marshall, notes that "after the birth of her youngest child Mrs. Butler did not entirely regain her former health and while never an invalid, the lack of perfect physical vigor and its consequent mental depression is shown from time to time in her letters" (Ames, *Chronicles from the Nineteenth Century*, 1:45–47).

17. BFB Will, in folder 6, box 2, BP-LC.

18. Charlotte E. Butler to BFB, September 5, 1846 or 1847 (internal evidence suggests 1847), in folder 3, box 1, BP-LC; Butler, *Butler's Book*, 93; Reade, *Origins and Genealogy*, 64–65.

There exists a single service card for an Andrew J. Butler from Missouri, enrolled as a private in Company I of the "Separate Battalion, Missouri Mounted Infantry." This is probably Benjamin Butler's brother, but I have not found other corroborative records.

19. Butler, *Butler's Book*, 93.

20. Butler, 97; Reade, *Origins and Genealogy*, 54, 64–65; Lowell, Massachusetts, City Directory, 1853. According Reade, Fisher Hildreth's "editorial labors" slowed after his appointment as high sheriff in 1850, and came to a virtual halt when he became Lowell's postmaster, although he continued to inspire others to write "political articles on important subjects" (Reade, *Origins and Genealogy*, 64).

21. Butler, *Butler's Book*, 98–99, 102; *Boston Semi-weekly Courier*, February 21, 1853. One notes again Butler's understanding of the oppressed wage laborers of his community as like enslaved Blacks in the South.

22. *Boston Daily Atlas*, March 6 and 9, 1852; Butler, *Butler's Book*, 109; Dublin, *Women at Work*, 202. A subsequent article in the *Boston Daily Atlas* claimed that coalition advocates like Butler (and maybe Butler himself) had stirred the mill operatives' passions by telling them that the factory owners in Boston had, among other things, "*fattened and kept their mistresses long enough out of the hard earnings of the hands employed in the mills*," and that "one of the *distinguished* Coalition leaders [meaning Butler?] had the *honor* of perambulating our streets, night after night, with a squad of noisy, ragged, drunken Irish boys at his heels for a body guard" (*Boston Daily Atlas*, April 2, 1852).

Nelson Lankford describes Butler as "the balding attorney whose jowls and hooded eyes suggested something other than probity" (Lankford, *Cry Havoc!*, 210).

In 1869, Hoar became President Ulysses S. Grant's attorney general.

23. *Boston Daily Atlas*, October 9, 1852, and May 11, 1853; Butler, *Butler's Book*, 110–14; *Salem (Mass.) Register*, February 10, 1853; *Pittsfield (Mass.) Sun*, April 14, 1853.

Biographer Hans L. Trefousse notes that by 1853, Butler had solid bank savings of $143,000, which probably included Sarah's dowry (Trefousse, *Ben Butler*, 27).

Not all of the "clamor" was religious: one legislator who opposed compensating the nuns for their loss argued that it made more sense "to indemnify William Lloyd Garrison . . . for the loss of property sustained by him, as well as serious inconvenience and jeopardy of his life, occasioned by a lawless mob" in Boston in 1835 (*Pittsfield [Mass.] Sun*, February 17, 1853).

24. *Boston Daily Atlas*, May 11 and June 24, 1853; Certificate from Waterville College, dated August 10, 1853, in folder 2, box 1, BP-LC; *Salem (Mass.) Register*, May 12, 1853; *National Aegis* (Worcester, Mass.), March 16, 1853; Butler, *Butler's Book*, 118–20.

25. Butler, *Butler's Book*, 120–21; *Lowell (Mass.) Daily Citizen and News*, October 29, 1856.

"I thank God," Butler added, "that upon my political escutcheon there is no tarnish of its brightness, in the form of adherence to any doctrine which would deprive of his equal rights with others a man of foreign birth, who comes to this country in accordance with the law of nations, and takes part in its government under its laws. I respected my great-grandfathers too much for that" (Butler, *Butler's Book*, 122).

26. Butler, *Butler's Book*, 125; *Boston Daily Atlas*, January 25, 1855. See also *Boston Courier*, January 25, 1855. Ben-Israel Butler was born on June 6, 1855.

27. *Boston Daily Atlas*, February 5, 1855; *Boston Courier*, February 5, 1855; *Salem (Mass.) Register*, February 5, 1855.

28. Butler, *Butler's Book*, 126–27; *Salem (Mass.) Register*, May 28, 1857; certificate from Gardner dated May 26, 1857, and Butler's sworn oath on June 16, 1857, and Jefferson Davis to BFB, February 21, 1857, both in folder 1, box 1, BP-LC. Gardner also recertified Butler as a justice of the peace for Middlesex County on March 3, 1857 (see certificate in folder 1, box 1, BP-LC). In 1859 Butler was authorized to serve as a justice of the peace for the entire state.

29. Butler, *Butler's Book*, 98; *Pittsfield (Mass.) Sun*, September 13, 1855, May 29, 1856, and November 4, 1858; BFB to SHB, May 30, 1856, in folder 3, box 1, BP-LC.

30. A. J. Cass to BFB, May 15, 1856, and J. L. Bartlett to BFB, October 24, 1856, both in folder 5, box 3, BP-LC. *Boston Press and Post*, June 19, 1856; Lossing, *Pictorial History*, 21. "I have always believed," Butler wrote later, that Buchanan "owed his election to a fraudulent return or count in the State of Pennsylvania" (Butler, *Butler's Book*, 133).

31. *Lowell (Mass.) Daily Citizen and News*, June 18, 1856; *Boston Press and Post*, December 4, 1856; *Boston Daily Atlas*, April 2, 1852; Butler, *Butler's Book*, 128–29. The *New York Evening Post* of October 21, 1858, quoted Butler as saying, "The people of every community, who associate themselves upon the territory of the United States and obtain sufficient numbers so as to be organized into a territorial government, have the right, by their legislation, under the constitution, to manage all their domestic institutions in their own way." With respect to the enslaved people, Butler still felt bound by the supreme law of the land including, apparently, the *Dred Scott* decision. "Slaves," the paper quoted him as saying, "being decided to be property by the Supreme Court in the states where slavery exists by local law, are protected as such in the territories," but he added, "more than this the South ought not to ask; more than this the North ought not to grant." The paper described Butler's position as an untenable "middle course between those who deny that the property of man in his fellow man exists in the territories under the constitution, and those who maintain that the people of a territory have no power over the question of slavery until they frame their state constitution and pass into a more independent form of political existence." In this speech, and not for the first time, Butler also expressed support for the annexation of Cuba.

32. *Lowell (Mass.) Daily Citizen and News*, October 31 and November 4, 1857, and August 28, 1858; *National Aegis*, October 31, 1857; Trefousse, *Ben Butler*, 52; *Boston Press and Post*, August 30, September 6, and November 4, 1858; *Daily National Intel-

ligencer (Washington, D.C.), October 16, 1858; *Charleston (S.C.) Mercury*, October 18, 1858; Certificate acknowledging Butler's election as state senator, November 30, 1858, in folder 1, box 1, BP-LC; *Hartford Daily Courant*, October 23, 1858; A. J. Cass to BFB, January 25, 1859, in folder 6, box 3, BP-LC; BFB to SHB, January 2, 1859, in folder 3, box 1, BP-LC.

As always, the *Lowell (Mass.) Daily Citizen and News* expressed its abundance of disdain for Butler upon his loss to Beach, calling Butler "the 'little joker'" who "appears when he isn't expected and discomfits those who thought they had him fast." Admitting that Butler had moved quickly to make Beach's nomination unanimous, the paper claimed that Butler had also gone on to complain about various comments opponents had made about him, including branding him a "[Stephen] Douglas man" (*Lowell [Mass.] Daily Citizen and News*, September 3, 1858).

33. *Lowell (Mass.) Daily Citizen and News*, January 12, 1859; *Pittsfield (Mass.) Sun*, January 13 and February 17, 1859; *Massachusetts Spy*, January 26 and February 2, 1859; *New York Daily Tribune*, February 5, 1859; *Salem (Mass.) Register*, February 21, 1859; *Boston Semi-weekly Courier*, March 14, 1859.

The *New York Daily Tribune* article, otherwise quite favorable to Butler, echoed the theme of Butler's appearance, saying that his "physiognomy, when in a state of lamb-like repose, does not resemble that of the Apollo."

34. *Pittsfield (Mass.) Sun*, September 8, 1859; *Boston Press and Post*, September 19, 1859; *Lowell (Mass.) Daily Citizen and News*, September 16, 1859; *Constitution* (Washington, D.C.), September 17, 1859; *Barre (Mass.) Gazette*, October 14, 1859; *Massachusetts Spy*, October 19, 1859.

The *Constitution* praised the convention's rejection of the extended naturalization period proposal but called the original proposal, shamefully, "a gross insult to the white men who are thus attempted to be placed below the negro in the scale of being and human rights." Meanwhile, the *Salem (Mass.) Register*, no friend to Butler, called the convention a "sham" and the nominating process for Butler a "farce" (September 19, 1859).

35. *Salem (Mass.) Register*, December 1, 1859; *Richmond Whig*, October 28, 1859; *New Hampshire Patriot and State Gazette*, November 2, 1859. In this same article, the paper recalled favorably how Butler had responded to Governor Gardner's order that he disband the Jackson Musketeers back in 1855.

36. *New Albany (Ind.) Daily Ledger*, November 7, 1859; Butler, *Butler's Book*, 134; *Lowell (Mass.) Daily Citizen and News*, January 11 and 18, 1860. Massachusetts newspapers from this period contain many references to cases Butler was arguing locally and in Boston in early 1860, and his papers also contain numerous letters home from Boston informing Sarah of his commuting schedule.

37. *Boston Courier*, April 16, 1860; Butler, *Private and Official*, 1:2–3.

38. *Lowell (Mass.) Daily Citizen and News*, April 26, 1860; Butler, *Butler's Book*, 134; *Boston Courier*, April 30, 1860; *Boston Recorder*, May 3, 1860.

Decades later, a newspaper article recalled that simply by virtue of being a northern Democrat in 1860, Butler was assumed by many to be proslavery, but "he did not accept the appellation," and his "willingness to support and perpetuate slavery came from no liking of the institution but from persuasion that the national constitution guaranteed it as a matter of state rights and that the union could be perpetuated in no other way," though the paper speculated that at the time, in keeping with his peers, Butler may well have felt "something of contempt for the black race" as well (*Boston Globe*, January 11, 1893).

39. Butler, *Butler's Book*, 135; *Boston Recorder*, May 3, 1860. The article added, "The unwarrantable demands of the slave-holding States may compel [northern delegates like Butler] to take this stand. We have never wished politically to interfere with their domestic institutions. They have created and are responsible for them. But they have no right to tyrannize over the free States and make us accessory to the guilt of slavery."

40. Butler, *Butler's Book*, 136, 140; *Lowell (Mass.) Daily Citizen and News*, May 16, 1860; *Massachusetts Spy*, May 9, 1860. Butler claimed to have voted for Douglas "seven times consecutively" (Butler, *Butler's Book*, 138). The *Boston Courier* (May 7, 1860) claimed that Butler did not vote for Douglas at all, but the *Boston Daily Advertiser* (May 9, 1860) confirmed that Butler voted for Douglas "on the first half dozen ballots."

41. Butler, *Butler's Book*, 138–40. Butler added, "If I had happened to vote for Horace Greeley, who was afterwards Democratic candidate for the presidency, my loyalty to the Union would have been highly praised for bringing forward the name of such a thorough-going, stanch, uncompromising Union man as that Abolition chief." But, he noted, in late 1860 Greeley wrote a number of editorials showing himself to be an anticoercionist relative to secession, and in at least one case, tolerant of the idea that states could secede and form a new nation if they chose (140–42).

42. Lossing, *Pictorial History*, 21–23; Butler, *Butler's Book*, 146; *Boston Courier*, May 7, 1860; BFB to SHB, May 6, 1860, in folder 2, box 1, BP-LC; William Locke to BFB, May 5, 1860, in folder 6, box 3, BP-LC.

43. *Lowell (Mass.) Daily Citizen and News*, May 16, 1860; *Boston Courier*, May 17, 1860; *Boston Daily Advertiser*, May 18, 1860.

44. *Salem (Mass.) Register*, June 25, 1860; *Lowell (Mass.) Daily Citizen and News*, June 25, 1860; Butler, *Butler's Book*, 144, 148.

45. *Boston Herald* article, reprinted in *The Liberator*, June 29, 1860; *Richmond Whig*, July 13, 1860; Butler, *Butler's Book*, 149; *New York Herald*, August 15, 1860; Isaac I. Stephens to BFB, August 9, 1860, in folder 6, box 3, BP-LC.

46. *Salem (Mass.) Observer*, September 15, 1860; *San Francisco Daily Evening Bulletin*, October 16, 1860; *Boston Press and Post*, August 27, 1860; *Boston Courier*, August 30, 1860; *Lowell (Mass.) Daily Citizen and News*, August 30, 1860; *The Liberator*, November 16, 1860; *Salem (Mass.) Register*, December 10, 1860.

47. *The Liberator*, November 16, 1860; *Lowell (Mass.) Daily Citizen and News*, December 8, 1860.

CHAPTER 3

1. "Memoranda of Estate & Liabilities of Benj. F. Butler, January 1, 1860," Benjamin F. Butler Papers, Archives and Special Collections, Colby College, Waterville, Maine (hereafter BP-C).

2. Sarah H. Butler (hereafter SHB) to Blanche Butler (hereafter BB), September 29 and October 15, 1860, and BB to SHB, undated, BP-C.

It bears noting that opportunities and expectations for the higher education for girls of Blanche's socioeconomic status were on the rise in this period, but hardly a given. Both her parents strongly believed in educating their daughter as well as their sons.

3. Benjamin Franklin Butler (hereafter BFB) to BB, October 8, 1860, in Benjamin F. Butler Papers, Library of Congress, Washington, D.C. (hereafter BP-LC), folder 3, box 1. See also the letter from Butler to the head of the Academy following the Charleston convention, in Ames, *Chronicles*, 1:47; and Butler, *Private and Official*, 1:2–4.

4. *Council Bluffs (Iowa) Bugle*, January 2, 1861; *Massachusetts Weekly Spy*, January 2, 1861; Butler, *Butler's Book*, 152–56, 159; Butler, *Private and Official*, 1:7. "I believed that secession was certain," Butler wrote, "and that war would inevitably follow" (Butler, *Butler's Book*, 145).

5. Leonard, *Lincoln's Forgotten Ally*, 117–22; BB to SHB, January 14, 1861, in *Chronicles*, 1:63–64.

6. Writes historian David Work, Lincoln's "political generals were not the failures often depicted in the historical literature and popular culture, but instead compiled mixed records. . . . Lincoln's decision to use them was wise, though he did not always employ them effectively. . . . The overall impact of political generals, however, benefited the Federal cause" (Work, *Lincoln's Political Generals*, 5).

7. *Lowell (Mass.) Daily Citizen and News*, January 22, 1861; Butler, *Private and Official*, 1:5–6.

8. Butler, *Private and Official*, 1:11; Butler, *Butler's Book*, 166; Werlich, *"Beast" Butler*, 15; Hale, *The Story of the States*, 327–28.

9. BB to SHB, February 11, 1861, in Ames, *Chronicles from the Nineteenth Century*, 1:65. See also Butler, *Private and Official*, 1:14, and BFB to BB, March 25, 1861, in folder 2, box 1, BP-LC; *Massachusetts Spy*, April 17, 1861.

10. Butler, *Private and Official*, 1:11–12, 15–16; James M. Flagg to BFB, folder 9, box 3, BP-LC. Carney then worked with other banks to increase the funding that was available (Butler, *Butler's Book*, 171).

11. Butler, *Butler's Book*, 174, 178, 183, 229, 241; *Massachusetts Spy*, April 17, 1861; Henry A. French to BFB, April 23, 1861, in folder 10, box 3, BP-LC; *Boston Daily Advertiser*, April 19, 1861.

12. Nevins, *The War for the Union: The Improvised War*, 81; Butler, *Private and Official*, 1:17; *Boston Post*, May 2, 1861; *Pittsfield (Mass.) Sun*, May 2, 1861.

13. Butler, *Butler's Book*, 176; McGinty, *The Body of John Merryman*. Union army superintendent of women nurses Dorothea Dix claimed that events in Baltimore

had spurred her to seek to create the federal nursing corps of which she became leader, and thousands of other women sprang into action at a local level to provision and care for the soldiers. See Leonard, *Yankee Women*.

14. Butler, *Private and Official*, 1:18, 22.

15. Butler, 1:19, 20, 24–28, 32; G. S. Blake to BFB, April 25, 1861, in folder 10, box 3, BP-LC.

16. Grimsley, *The Hard Hand of War*; Butler, *Private and Official*, 1:26–27, 35; Butler, *Butler's Book*, 210.

17. Butler, *Private and Official*, 1:37–38.

18. Butler, 1:38–41; Foner, *The Life and Writings of Frederick Douglass*, 3:95; "A Border State Matron" to BFB, May 16, 1861, and "An Elector of Washington County, New York," to BFB, May 17, 1861, both in folder 1, box 5, BP-LC.

See also H. J. Smith to BFB, June 20, 1861, in folder 2, box 8, BP-LC, which discusses "numerous outrages committed by General Butler's men in the neighborhood of Hampton," including the theft of human property, the destruction of crop fields, and the rape of women. The source for this information was local Virginia newspapers, which may raise questions about the veracity of the accusations.

It bears noting that in his *Private and Official Correspondence*, Butler's granddaughter did not shy away from publishing documents that displayed his worst instincts, such as this May 9, 1861, letter to Governor Andrew.

19. Butler, *Private and Official*, 1:26, 30, 60, 62; Lankford, *Cry Havoc!*, 216.

20. Butler, *Private and Official*, 1:36–37, 51–52, 64; Smith, *Mayflower Hill*, 23.

21. Butler, *Private and Official*, 1:51–53; BB to SHB, May 3, 1861, in Ames, *Chronicles from the Nineteenth Century*, 1:69.

22. Butler, *Butler's Book*, 226.

23. Butler, 225–27.

24. Butler, 227–28, 233; *Albany Journal*, May 15, 1861; *New York Herald*, May 15, 1861; *Baltimore Exchange*, May 15, 1861, reprinted in *Boston Daily Advertiser*, May 17, 1861.

Reverdy Johnson, who had represented the slave owner John Sandford in the 1857 *Dred Scott* case, and whom Butler describes as a "rank and bitter secessionist, and worse than others because he concealed it," successfully lobbied for Winans's release (Butler, *Butler's Book*, 234).

25. Butler, 235–37.

26. Butler, 235; and copy of Banks's official appointment in folder 4, box 5; copy of Dix's official appointment in folder 6, box 5; John Ryan to BFB, May 17, 1861, in folder 1, box 5; M. J. Kelly to BFB, May 24, 1861, in folder 2, box 5; and E. H. Gray to Benjamin F. Butler, May 31, 1861, in folder 3, box 5, all in BP-LC.

27. Butler, *Butler's Book*, 240; Butler, *Private and Official*, 1:92, 95–97; Ames, *Chronicles from the Nineteenth Century*, 1:71.

28. Butler, *Butler's Book*, 245–49; Butler, *Private and Official*, 1:101. See also Russell, *My Diary*, 409.

For a detailed description of the fort by an Irish journalist who visited in July 1861, see Russell, *My Diary*, 405–6.

In mid-December 1861, George wrote from Washington asking for money and explaining that he was "under arrest for knocking a man in the head who insulted me at the National Hotel" (George H. Butler [hereafter GHB] to BFB, December 11, 1861, in folder 1, box 9, BP-LC). Many more such incidents followed.

29. Butler, *Butler's Book*, 256; Butler, *Private and Official*, 1:103, 105. I would encourage those who have not yet had the opportunity to do so to see Richard Strand's play *Butler*, which deals with this particular moment in Butler's Civil War career. I also wish here to thank Strand for his generosity in sending me the script before the play was staged, so that I could examine his treatment of the events in question.

30. Butler, *Butler's Book*, 257–59; Butler, *Private and Official*, 1:106–7.

31. Butler, *Private and Official*, 1:110–11; *Lowell (Mass.) Daily Citizen and News*, June 5, 1861. Butler was prompted by letters such as the one from Hampton resident Elizabeth Devine, in which she informed him that "some of the troops have broken into my house. . . . They have destroyed and taken everything. I am a poor woman. . . . You may imagine my feelings when I saw the wreck. Every thing broken and taken. Doors knocked down; locks broken; glass jars scattered broken over the floor. What I had worked for through many a long and weary year, living by the hardest labor and the most rigid economy, destroyed, broken up before my eyes" (Elizabeth Devine to BFB, June 1, 1861, in folder 4, box 5, BP-LC). Notably, Devine wrote her letter a week after Butler ordered his troops to stop molesting private property.

James McPherson notes that by August, "a thousand contrabands were in Butler's camps, and abolitionists were making plans to establish schools and send missionary teachers to them." See McPherson, *Ordeal by Fire*, 289–90. See also Jackson, "The Origin of Hampton Institute," 133.

32. Butler, *Butler's Book*, 258, 261; Jackson, "The Origin of Hampton Institute," 134; *Massachusetts Spy*, May 29 and June 5, 1861; *Hartford Daily Courant*, June 5, 1861; Foner, *The Life and Writings of Frederick Douglass*, 3:109; *Boston Post*, May 27, 1861; *Pittsfield (Mass.) Sun*, May 30, 1861; *Centinel of Freedom* (Newark, N.J.), June 4, 1861; *New York Commercial Advertiser*, June 4, 1861; Cornelius Baker to BFB, May 28, 1861, and George Morey to BFB, May 31, 1861, both in folder 3, box 5, BP-LC.

On June 4, 1861, the *New London (Conn.) Daily Chronicle* commented that a "fair average" price for the slaves arriving in Fort Monroe—which it estimated at about 450 at that time—was $1,000 (*New London Daily Chronicle*, June 4, 1861). The *Daily Chronicle* also reported that one slave owner had come to the fort recently requesting the return of some thirty of his slaves, now sheltering at the fort. "The General," the paper reported, "said they came there of their own accord, and could go back with him if they desired to. They were asked if they desired to return with their master. They quickly decided that they preferred to remain with the soldiers."

33. Butler, *Private and Official*, 1:117, 119; Butler, *Butler's Book*, 256, 258–59; *Massachusetts Spy*, June 5, 1861; Downs, *Sick from Freedom*, 48; Carnahan, *Act of Justice*, 84, 86.

34. Belz, *Abraham Lincoln, Constitutionalism, and Equal Rights*, 103–4.

35. Oakes, *Freedom National*, 97, 103, 106–7; J. W. Perry to BFB, June 9, 1861, in folder 5, box 5, BP-LC; Cecelski, *The Fire of Freedom*, 48; *Springfield (Mass.) Republican*, June 15, 1861; *Augusta (Ga.) Chronicle*, June 5, 1861; *The Liberator*, quoting the *Charleston (S.C.) Courier*, June 7, 1861; *Augusta (Ga.) Daily Constitutionalist*, June 5, 1861; *Centinel of Freedom*, June 4, 1861; Jackson, "The Origin of Hampton Institute," 137.

David Cecelski also notes that Butler deployed some of the contraband as spies and scouts, including Abraham Galloway, who went on to have "a uniquely valuable role in Union intelligence-gathering in Tidewater Virginia" (50).

At least one document in the Butler Papers at the Library of Congress attests to Butler's use of the fugitives for getting information about Confederate movements in the area. See "Statement of a Negro Man, Giving Himself Up This Day," May 31, 1861, in folder 3, box 5, BP-LC, and the accompanying letter from G. K. Warren to Colonel A. Dwyer in the same folder.

The *Charleston (S.C.) Courier* article reprinted in *The Liberator* of June 7, which was written by the *Courier*'s Baltimore correspondent, ranted at length about Butler. "Fancy the old mush-head seated upon a charger, armed with sword and pistols, a cigar in his mouth and half tight, surrounded by his staff and body-guard, riding the streets in open day, blustering like a swelled frog, assuming importance much beyond what that reptile did when it swelled to bursting at beholding the ox. Thank fortune, 'Picayune Butler' has gone from town, as is well understood, at the bidding of his master, and left a gentleman—Gen. Cadwallader—to adorn the position he encumbered with a mountebank" (*The Liberator*, June 7, 1861). Contrasting Butler with a man who could be considered a true "gentleman" seems like a particularly telling aspect of the attack.

According to Barbara Tomblin, the day that Congress passed the First Confiscation Act, Butler "issued a special order stating" that if "vessels were found conveying away negroes for the purposes of aiding or comforting the rebellion, such negroes, if they desire, will be permitted to come to Fortress Monroe, where they will be employed or cared for.'" See Tomblin, *Bluejackets and Contrabands*, 16; and Butler, *Private and Official*, 1:201–3, regarding the implications of the First Confiscation Act.

36. Butler, *Private and Official*, 1:115, 122, 128.

Blanche clearly yearned to be reunited with her parents at Fort Monroe. On May 26 she wrote to Sarah, "Kiss Father four dozen times for me and tell him that I am afraid that I shall have to disband the company if he does not send for us soon" (Ames, *Chronicles from the Nineteenth Century*, 1:72).

37. *New York Commercial Advertiser*, June 6, 1861; Butler, *Private and Official*, 1:129. In the same letter, Blair—who had defended Dred Scott's claim to freedom in 1857—recommended that the fugitive slaves at Fort Monroe be sent "straight to Hayti."

38. *New Haven (Conn.) Columbian Register*, June 8, 1861; Nevins, *The War for the Union: The Improvised War*, 212. The Battle of Philippi in what is now West Virginia actually preceded Big Bethel by a week.

39. Butler, *Butler's Book*, 267, 269, 275; Butler, *Private and Official*, 1:132–34; Nevins, *The War for the Union: The Improvised War*, 211–12; Reardon, *With a Sword in One Hand & Jomini in the Other*, 60; *New York Evening Journal* (Albany), June 11, 1861; *New York Commercial Advertiser*, June 11, 1861; *Boston Daily Advertiser*, June 12, 1861.

When he wrote to Winthrop's mother about the death of her son, Butler told her that "his last thoughts were with his mother, his last acts were for his Country and her cause" (Butler, *Private and Official*, 1:138). Later, Butler also sent Winthrop's watch home to his family. See W. W. Winthrop to BFB, July 11, 1861, in folder 6, box 6, BP-LC.

40. Butler, *Butler's Book*, 269; Butler, *Private and Official*, 1:141; *New York Commercial Advertiser*, June 12, 1861; *Hartford Daily Courant*, June 12, 1861. See also *Senate Report 108*, part 3, *Report of the Joint Committee, 1863*, 37th Cong., 3rd Sess., 280–82.

41. Butler, *Private and Official*, 1:147–49, 155, 165, 177, 185–87; Butler, *Butler's Book*, 277. To Cameron, Butler added, "I confess that my own mind is compelled . . . to look upon them as men and women. If not free born, yet free, manumitted, sent forth from the hand that held them, never to be reclaimed" (Butler, *Private and Official*, 1:187).

"The favor you have shown the poor colored fugitives," wrote abolitionist Lewis Tappan in early August, "has filled the hearts of many friends of freedom with thankfulness. . . . The liberty-loving people of the North are unanimous in awarding to you great praise for all you have done on behalf of the down-trodden and oppressed who have fled to you for succor" (Butler, *Private and Official*, 1:199).

42. Butler, *Private and Official*, 1:132, 161, 162, 181, 189–90, 194, 203–4.

43. Butler, 1:172, 185, 195–98, 199, 206, 208, 215; Nathaniel P. Banks to BFB, June 15, 1861, in folder 6, box 4, BP-LC; Butler, *Butler's Book*, 279; "Major General Butler, Lowell Massachusetts, Rebel Conspiracy against the Union, Status of Slavery in the United States, 1861," July 23, 1861, in folder 1, box 7, BP-LC. Erastus Wright to BFB, August 8, 1861, in folder 3, box 7, and J. N. Mars to BFB, August 14, 1861, in folder 4, box 7, BP-LC.

Butler later claimed that "I told all my friends that I did not feel aggrieved at all; that I would beat Scott at his own game, as indeed I was already prepared to do; that he had sent Wool down without any instructions; that Wool could not go anywhere or do anything; that Wool did not like Scott any better than Scott did me; that Wool wanted all the work done by some one else while he had a nice place in the camp, and I wanted to do all the work I could do and have somebody else take the responsibility" (Butler, *Butler's Book*, 281).

44. Butler, *Private and Official*, 1:218, 219, 222; McPherson, *Ordeal by Fire*, 196. McPherson says this was the "first joint army-navy expedition for this purpose."

45. Butler, *Private and Official*, 1:228, 234–35; Nevins, *The War for the Union: The Improvised War*, 286; James S. Whitney to BFB, September 3, 1861, in folder 1, box 8, BP-LC; Butler, *Butler's Book*, 285.

46. Butler, *Butler's Book*, 287, 297; McPherson, *Ordeal by Fire*, 181; Butler, *Private and Official*, 1:239, 335–36; General Orders No. 1, October 6, 1861, in folder 3, box

8, BP-LC; Harris, *Lincoln and the Union Governors*, 32–33; James Whitney to BFB, September 24, 1861, in folder 2, box 8, BP-LC; Edward G. Hyde to BFB, October 27, 1861, in folder 4, box 8, BP-LC.

"I had opened the way through Annapolis for the troops to save the capital; I had fulfilled my mission at Fortress Monroe; and by taking Hatteras I had atoned for capturing Baltimore and wiped out Big Bethel, all in a campaign of four months and fifteen days, besides showing the administration and the country the best way out of the slavery question. In all this time nobody else had done anything except to get soundly thrashed at Bull Run" (Butler, *Butler's Book*, 288).

During this period Butler also strove to make peace with some of his former partisan opponents. See Butler, *Butler's Book*, 294; W. Griswold to BFB, September 17, 1861, in folder 2, box 8, BP-LC.

47. General Order No. 1, February 10, 1862, in folder 4, box 10, BP-LC; Benjamin F. Butler to Simon Cameron, October 29, 1861, in folder 4, box 8, BP-LC; Butler, *Private and Official*, 1:251–53, 262, 263, 315; A. G. Browne to George C. Strong, December 20, 1861, in *OR*, ser. 3, 1:847–50; Mr. Hine to "Dear Thomas," February 2, 1862, in folder 4, box 10, BP-LC.

Butler wrote, "In the matter of the so-called State aid to the families of the volunteers under your command, I wish to repeat here, most distinctly, the declaration heretofore made to you. I will personally, and from my private means, guarantee to the family of each soldier the aid which ought to be furnished to him by his town, to the same extent and amount that the State would be bound to afford to other enlisted men, from and after this date, if the same is not paid by the Commonwealth to them as to other Massachusetts soldiers; and all soldiers enlisting in your regiment may do so upon the strength of this guarantee" (Butler, *Private and Official*, 1:315).

48. *Boston Journal*, October 28, 1861; Butler, *Private and Official*, 1:277, 278, 286, 308–10, 316.

49. Butler, *Private and Official*, 1:274, 299, 344, 359–60; J. B. Salla to "Mr. Richardson," January 11, 1862, in folder 2, box 10, BP-LC; John W. Phelps to BFB, December 5, 1861, in folder 1, box 9, BP-LC; Frederick Holbrook to BFB, December 24, 1861, in folder 2, box 9, BP-LC; Butler, *Butler's Book*, 324.

For one individual soldier's impression of being deployed to Ship Island in early 1862, see B. B. Smith Diary. In his diary, on February 7, 1862, New Englander Smith described his curiosity, upon entering the Gulf Stream, of having "the company of a lot of porpoises at the side of the ship jumping and frolicking like a lot of puppies." On January 21, 1862, he also mentioned seeing, during a stop at Hampton Roads, "a large lot of negroes" who "were once slaves."

50. Butler, *Private and Official*, 1:323, 330–31, 359, 360–62; Ames, *Chronicles from the Nineteenth Century*, 1:78.

51. Butler, *Private and Official*, 1:363–67, 370, 373–74. Fulton repeatedly protested his arrest and claimed that Butler had ruined his reputation. See A. H. Fulton to BFB, March 24, 1862, in folder 8, box 10, BP-LC; A. H. Fulton to BFB, April 10, 1862, in folder 2, box 11, BP-LC.

52. B. B. Smith Diary, April 9, 1862; Alfred A. Parmenter to his parents, March 8, 1862, in folder 8, Alfred A. Parmenter Papers; Butler, *Private and Official*, 1:380, 382–85.

53. B. B. Smith Diary, April 9, 1862; Alfred A. Parmenter to his parents, April 10, 1862, in folder 8, Alfred A. Parmenter Papers; Butler, *Butler's Book*, 352–53; BFB, Circular, April 15, 1862, in folder 3, box 11, BP-LC; Butler, *Private and Official*, 1:385–86.

54. McPherson, *Ordeal by Fire*, 253–54; Butler, *Private and Official*, 1:386, 387–91, 401–5, 414, 416.

55. Nevins, *The War for the Union: War Becomes Revolution*, 97–99; Butler, *Private and Official*, 1:420–22, 425–28; B. B. Smith Diary, April 18, April 21, and April 30, 1862.

56. Butler, *Private and Official*, 1:425–29; Foreman, *A World on Fire*, 248–49; Nelson and Sheriff, *A People at War*, 91; Hess, *The Civil War in the West*, 84; Nevins, *The War for the Union: War Becomes Revolution*, 101; Addison Gage & others to BFB, May 3, 1862, in folder 4, box 11, BP-LC.

With New Orleans, Nevins writes, "the South lost a great deal of wealth, manpower, and manufacturing capacity, for its energetic people were already making an impressive amount of war material. . . . Still more important was the fact that the lower segment of the Mississippi was gone. . . . And [so] the 145,000 proud people of New Orleans, conscious of their rich history and cultural heritage, now entered upon their most tragic years" (Nevins, *The War for the Union: War Becomes Revolution*, 103).

CHAPTER 4

1. McPherson, *Ordeal by Fire*, 414; Hess, *The Civil War in the West*, 85. For the two ends of the spectrum, I think in particular of Chester Hearn's revealingly titled *When the Devil Came Down to Dixie* and James Parton's adulatory, 650-page *General Butler in New Orleans*.

2. Butler, *Private and Official*, 1:631–32. Indeed, disagreement over the very details of how New Orleans was captured, and who deserved the most credit, began almost immediately. On June 1, Butler wrote to Secretary of War Stanton challenging David Dixon Porter's account of the surrender of the forts during the expedition to New Orleans: "Permit me," he wrote, "for the sake of my brave and enduring soldiers of the 26th Mass. and 4th Wisconsin Regiments, who waded in the swamps in the rear of Fort St. Philip up to their armpits in water, in order to cut off its garrison and get ready to assault the enemy's works, to put the truth of history right before the War Department and the country, by the simple enumeration of the fact that it was due to their efforts and that of their comrades, and to those alone, that Forts Jackson and St. Philip surrendered when they did. No naval vessel or one of the Mortar fleet had fired a shot at the forts for three days before the surrender, and not one of the Mortar fleet was within twenty-five miles at that time. . . . I will not permit too great greed of praise on the part of any one to

take away the merit fairly due my brave soldiers, who endured as much hardship and showed as much bravery as 'the most gallant Tar of them all'" (Butler, 538–39). Porter countered Butler's claims: "I was very much surprised to hear . . . that you had accused me of making misstatements" (David Dixon Porter to Benjamin Franklin Butler [hereafter BFB], July 5, 1862, in folder 4, box 13, Benjamin F. Butler Papers, Library of Congress, Washington, D.C. [hereafter BP-LC]). The disagreement between the two men that began here grew into a full-blown feud later in the wake of other conflicts.

3. Butler, *Private and Official*, 1:433–40, 453; Hess, *The Civil War in the West*, 84–85, 87. Hess writes, "Years of experience currying favor with the working class of Lowell, Massachusetts, before the war had taught Butler many tricks he used to good effect in New Orleans. He understood how to take advantage of class tensions and how to sway the public mood" (85). I find Hess's suggestion—that Butler's good deeds on behalf of those in need in New Orleans were solely about "currying favor"—curious and dismissive of the possibility that Butler, for all his showmanship and bluster, genuinely meant to help the city's less fortunate residents.

Butler's confiscation of Confederate property in New Orleans, Hess also notes, "was probably the most extensive, systematic application of the Second Confiscation Act within a single military department in the country, and it likely had more to do with quieting anti-Federal activities than any of Butler's other policies" (87).

See also Foreman, *A World on Fire*, 249, and Abbott, *For Free Press and Equal Rights*, 13.

4. Butler, *Private and Official*, 1:455; Robert K. Smith to BFB, May 5, 1862, in folder 4, box 11, BP-LC; Downs, *Sick from Freedom*, 56; Butler, *Butler's Book*, 396.

5. William Marvin to BFB, May 20, 1862, in folder 2, box 12, BP-LC; Butler, *Private and Official*, 1:456; Erastus Everett to BFB, July 19, 1862, in folder 1, box 14, BP-LC.

6. Butler, *Private and Official*, 1:442, 457–59. See also Hess, *The Civil War in the West*, 88–89; B. B. Smith Diary, May 11, 1862.

7. Butler, *Private and Official*, 2:152–53, 242–43.

8. Butler, 1:554–55; Hess, *The Civil War in the West*, 88–89; Downs, *Sick from Freedom*, 56–57; "A Union Man" to BFB, June 26, 1862, in folder 3, box 13, BP-LC; P. Haggerty to Captain Page, May 27, 1862, in folder 3, box 12, BP-LC.

9. Hess, *The Civil War in the West*, 88; Butler, *Private and Official*, 1:486, 581–83; Marten and Foster, *More than a Contest between Armies*, 130–31; Campbell, "The Unmeaning Twaddle about Order 28": 11–30; Whites and Long, *Occupied Women*, 17–32; B. W. Richmond to BFB, July 4, 1862, in folder 4, box 13, BP-LC.

10. Hess, *The Civil War in the West*, 87; Butler, *Private and Official*, 1:497–98; Manning, *What This Cruel War Was Over*, 62–63; Von Drehle, *Rise to Greatness*, 192.

11. Manning, *What This Cruel War Was Over*, 63; Hess, *The Civil War in the West*, 87; Butler, *Private and Official*, 1:581–83 and 2:35–37, 292; Butler, *Butler's Book*, 421.

12. Butler, *Private and Official*, 1:482–83; Cisco, *War Crimes against Southern Civilians*, 66; Nelson and Sheriff, *A People at War*, 91; See S. H. Stafford to BFB, June 7, 1862, in folder 5, box 12, BP-LC.

Of Mumford, Butler wrote, "He was at the head of the gamblers of New Orleans and was a man of considerable education, some property, and much influence with the lower class" (Butler, *Butler's Book*, 439).

13. Hess, *The Civil War in the West*, 84; Butler, *Private and Official*, 1:577.

14. Nelson and Sheriff, *A People at War*, 91; Hess, *The Civil War in the West*, 87; Butler, *Private and Official*, 1:431–32; Butler, *Butler's Book*, 446ff.

Historian Christian McWhirter writes about the ways Butler even tried to control music in the city by ordering fines—and threatening arrest—against anyone who "sang, whistled, or played" the secessionist anthem "The Bonnie Blue Flag" (McWhirter, *Battle Hymns*, 109–10).

15. Cisco, *War Crimes against Southern Civilians*, 66; Butler, *Private and Official*, 1:448–49.

16. Butler, *Private and Official*, 1:459–63 and 2:16–24.

17. Butler, 1:486–87; Joseph B. Quinby to BFB, July 26, 1862, in folder 3, box 14, BP-LC; invoice of funds paid to Dr. William L. Miller, July 30, 1862, in folder 3, box 14, BP-LC; Thomas McKean Buchanan to BFB, September 9, 1862, in folder 2, box 15, BP-LC; C. Weigel to C. C. Morgan, September 9, 1862, in folder 2, box 15, BP-LC; Lieutenant Colonel Bullock to BFB, September 21, 1862, in folder 5, box 15, BP-LC.

18. Hess, *The Civil War in the West*, 86–88. He notes, "A Federal officer reported that fewer than 20,000 of the city's 170,000 residents took the oath."

19. Grimsley, *The Hard Hand of War*; Butler, *Private and Official*, 2:15; Mountcastle, *Punitive War*, 68–69.

20. Butler, *Private and Official*, 2:158–61, 186, 332–33; Frazier, *Fire in the Cane Field*, 88–90.

21. Butler, *Private and Official*, 1:450, 470–71.

22. Butler, 1:473, 490–91.

23. Butler, 1:553, 556–59, 581, and 2:16, 59.

24. George Coppell to BFB, June 14, 1862, in folder 6, box 12, BP-LC; Butler, *Private and Official*, 1:597–607 and 2:10–11.

25. Butler, *Private and Official*, 2:12, 70–71.

26. Butler, 2:188–89.

27. M. M. White to BFB, July 4, 1862, in folder 4, box 13, BP-LC; Theodore Laussade to BFB, May 10, 1862, in folder 4, box 11, BP-LC; Polycarpe Fortier to BFB, May 22, 1862, in folder 2, box 12, BP-LC; and Thomas Waterman to BFB, June 2, 1862; W. R. Bell to BFB, June 3, 1862; R. W. James to BFB, June 3, 1862; A. Delavigne to BFB, June 4, 1862; all in folder 4, box 12, BP-LC; Butler, *Private and Official*, 1:509–10.

28. "List of Persons White & Black in Camp Parapet," May 22, 1862, in folder 2, box 12, BP-LC; E. Adams to F. S. Nickerson, June 21, 1862, and G. W. Bartlett to BFB, June 21, 1862, both in folder 2, box 13, BP-LC.

29. Carnahan, *Act of Justice*, 118–20; Butler, *Private and Official*, 1:514.

30. Butler, *Private and Official*, 1:524–26.

31. Butler, 1:516–21. In this long letter, Butler revealed that he still held some truly unsavory views about Blacks' capacity for military service, claiming that "the negro here by long habit and training has acquired a great horror of fire-arms,

sometimes ludicrous in the extreme when the weapon is in his own hand. I am inclined to the opinion that 'John Brown was right' in his idea of arming the negro with a pike or spear instead of a musket, if they are to be armed at all" (519). Butler insisted that he had been "reared in the full belief that slavery is a curse," and that his antipathy for the institution had grown stronger the more he saw of it firsthand. But he still seemed to think that the worst feature of slavery was "its baleful effect upon the master, because, as under it he cannot lift the negro up in the scale of humanity, therefore the negro drags him down" (520). See also Oakes, *Freedom National*, 221–22.

32. Butler, *Private and Official*, 1:633 and 2:9–10, 41–42.

33. Hess, *The Civil War in the West*, 90; Benjamin F. Butler to Edwin M. Stanton, May 25, 1862, in Butler, *Private and Official*, 1:520 and 2:109.

34. Glatthaar, *Forged in Battle*, 7–9; Butler, *Private and Official*, 2:125–26.

As Glatthaar notes, "What made this entire event so peculiar was that within a few weeks, Butler made a 100 percent turnaround on the issue of Blacks in the military. Encouragement from Secretary of the Treasury Salmon P. Chase and military necessity convinced Butler to accept free Black militiamen for federal service a scant three weeks later, and the War Department supported the decision" (Glatthaar, *Forged in Battle*, 9).

35. Butler, *Private and Official*, 2:126, 143–46.

36. Butler, 2:147–48, 154, 164, 263, 270; Jeremiah T. Champlin to BFB, August 16, 1862, and John Gibbon to BFB, August 15, 1862, both in folder 5, box 14, BP-LC.

37. Butler, *Private and Official*, 2:132–34.

38. Butler, 2:156–57.

39. Butler, 2:186, 191–92.

40. Butler, 1:627 and 2:66, 209–11, 228.

41. Nevins, *The War for the Union: War Becomes Revolution*, 514; Glatthaar, *Forged in Battle*, 8–9; Hollandsworth, *The Louisiana Native Guards*; Burkhardt, *Confederate Rage, Yankee Wrath*, 15; Butler, *Private and Official*, 2:228–29, 270; Butler, *Butler's Book*, 493–94.

42. Butler, *Private and Official*, 2:328, 428.

43. Butler, *Butler's Book*, 495; Butler, *Private and Official*, 2:455; C. C. Antoine to Col. Stafford, October 22, 1862, in folder 3, box 16, BP-LC.

44. Butler, *Private and Official*, 2:328.

45. Butler, 2:397.

46. Butler, 2:426, 447–50.

47. Butler, 2:79, 115.

48. Butler, 1:532 and 2:115.

49. Butler, 1:610, 625, and 2:76–78, 110, 164–65.

50. Butler, 2:333–36.

51. Hess, *The Civil War in the West*, 91; McPherson, *Ordeal by Fire*, 414; Frazier, *Fire in the Cane Field*, 61–62, 83–84.

For many years in the twentieth century, Butler's alma mater hosted an annual debate competition for students from Maine colleges, and the winner of the competition received a "Butler Spoon."

52. Hess, *The Civil War in the West*, 88; Butler, *Private and Official*, 1:492, 612–13, 634–35.

53. Butler, *Private and Official*, 1:609, 625, and 2:1, 3, 5–6, 55. It is interesting that Butler's taking of Twiggs's property has endured as a greater scandal than Twiggs's betrayal of his oath.

54. Benjamin F. Butler to Reverdy Johnson, July 21, 1862, in Butler, 2:89, 94, 229–30. Andrew Jackson Butler had no official military rank and was sometimes referred to as "Captain Butler" as well. An undated memorandum in folder 3, box 9, BP-LC—which refers to troubling financial matters he was tangled up with elsewhere—reads in part, "Capt Butler, brother of the Maj. Gen'l, and commissary of subsistence on his staff, is implicated in the alleged forgery of the Broderick Will in San Francisco, where he formerly lived, the allegation being that it was he who perpetrated the forgery, and that he was to receive $15,000 from the proceeds of the estate, in compensation for his crime. The matter is now a subject of judicial investigation in San Francisco." On February 2, 1862, Lorenzo Thomas expressly informed Andrew Jackson Butler that he was not an officer in the US Army, the US Senate having "negative" his appointment. See Lorenzo Thomas to Andrew Jackson Butler, February 2, 1862, in folder 4, box 10, BP-LC.

55. Butler, *Private and Official*, 2:270–71, 328–29.

56. Butler, 2:320.

57. Butler, 2:355–60, 378–79, 413.

58. Butler, 2:423–25.

59. Ames, *Chronicles from the Nineteenth Century*, 1:85; Butler, *Private and Official*, 2:426, 427, 503–4.

In another, much earlier (May), letter to Harriet, she wrote, "Jackson will go as soon as he can gather his golden harvest, which will take but a short time longer. He is in the flush of successful operation, and has lost no flesh. Mr. Butler is thin and so am I. But it is in the nature of things that care and anxiety fall upon some few, and the prodigal reaps the fruit of their labour. I have reason to hope if I live to get home, that he is not hereafter to be a 'directing power in his brother's affairs'" (Butler, *Private and Official*, 1:531–32).

60. Ames, *Chronicles from the Nineteenth Century*, 1:81–83; Butler, *Private and Official*, 2:380–81, 393, 453.

61. Butler, *Private and Official*, 2:243, 248.

62. Butler, 2:258, 283, 320.

63. Butler, 2:461, 469.

64. Butler, 2:512–13.

65. Butler, 2:520, 541–42.

66. Butler, 2:545–48, 549. Writes Hess, "Butler's administration of the Department of the Gulf had created many enemies," and he had also created, out of necessity, "the most extensive military government of the war," involving "the

assessment of taxes, fines, punishments, charities, trade, regulation of churches, confiscation of estates and the working of plantations." Very quickly Banks began to initiate reforms, including reducing the number of families and individuals (both Black and White) Butler had been feeding, cutting the funding of relief programs in half, struggling to put former slaves to work on local farms and plantations, reorganizing the Black military forces (including dismissing Black officers), and adopting a more conciliatory approach to Whites who had supported the Confederacy (and in some cases still did). "A controversial administrator," Banks's administration also opened the gates, albeit inadvertently, to "a wave of Northern speculators," all of them expecting "'to be a millionaire in six months' and possessing 'few scruples about the means of satisfying their cupidity.'" Within weeks, "there were loud calls for Butler's return" (Hess, *The Civil War in the West*, 168–69). See also McPherson, *Ordeal by Fire*, 334; and Glatthaar, *Forged in Battle*, 8–9.

Among the changes Banks brought to the department, Butler recalled being most disappointed with his treatment of the Black regiments. "After I left New Orleans," he wrote in his autobiography, "General Banks enlisted many more of them, but was weak enough to take away from them the great object of their ambition, under the spur of which they were ready to fight to the death, namely, *equality* with the white soldiers. He was also unmanly enough to add injustice to that folly by taking the commissions from their line officers . . . and to brand their organizations with the stigma of a designation as a 'Corps d'afrique.' Yet, in spite of his unwisdom, they did equal service and laid down their lives at Port Hudson in equal numbers comparatively with their white brothers in arms" (Butler, *Butler's Book*, 495).

67. Butler, *Private and Official*, 2:547, 554–57.

68. Pickenpaugh, *Captives in Gray*, 63–64; Butler, *Private and Official*, 2:563.

69. Axelrod, *The Horrid Pit*, 15; Raymond, "Ben Butler," 445, 458, 461; McPherson, *Ordeal by Fire*, 414; Hess, *The Civil War in the West*, 90.

CHAPTER 5

1. Thaddeus Sherman to Benjamin Franklin Butler (hereafter BFB), January 4, 1863, in Benjamin F. Butler Papers, Archives and Special Collections, Colby College, Waterville, Maine (hereafter BP-C); Butler, *Private and Official*, 2:565–67, 569. In contrast to his critics, Hannah Lovering of Boston wrote that she and her husband had recently named their son after him—"Benjamin Butler Lovering"—in recognition of "your many and noble deeds performed in the service of your country" (Butler, 2:598).

2. Butler, 2:570–71, 582–83. Parton produced a glowing 650-page account, *General Butler in New Orleans*, a draft of which he sent to Butler in November (Butler, 3:150), and that was published in 1864. The two men also went on to be lifelong friends.

3. Butler, *Private and Official*, 2:553, 571, 573, 584, 587, 589–90, 593; Simpson, *Ulysses S. Grant*, 179.

4. Butler, *Private and Official*, 3:4, 15, 17, 20. "The happiest day of my life," Denison added, "will be the day when a steamer arrives with you on board." "The sooner Gen. Butler comes back the better it will be," he wrote to Chase two days later (Butler, 3:9).

5. Butler, 3:21–27, 57–58; Butler, *Butler's Book*, 570; Sarah H. Butler (hereafter SHB) to Blanche Butler (hereafter BB), March 5 and 11, 1863, in BP-C.

6. Butler, *Private and Official*, 2:568 and 3:40; Butler, *Butler's Book*, 562–65, 570; Butler, *Character and Results of the War*, 4–21.

7. Butler, *Private and Official*, 3:49, 55.

8. Butler, 3:59–64, 66; Trefousse, *Ben Butler*, 137.

9. Butler, *Private and Official*, 3:71, 72–73, 78, 81, 90, 96, 98, 106, 119, 120; SHB to BB, June 21, 1863, in BP-C.

10. McPherson, *Ordeal by Fire*, 388; Bernstein, *The New York City Draft Riots*, 55; Butler, *Private and Official*, 3:97, 103, 123; *Army and Navy Journal*, September 19, 1863.

11. *Army and Navy Journal*, November 7 and 14, 1863; Butler, *Private and Official*, 3:135, 138–39, 227; McPherson, *War on the Waters*, 198; Work, *Lincoln's Political Generals*, 144.

12. Butler, *Private and Official*, 3:139–41, 143, 145–49, 194. "The murder and abuse of black prisoners of war by Confederate troops . . . loomed large for Butler . . . that fall," writes David Cecelski in his study of Abraham Galloway, a Black Union spy who worked with Butler in Virginia. "Stories of Rebel soldiers killing black prisoners in the field and tales of atrocities against black inmates inside Confederate prison camps, reported by Union spies and Confederate deserters, infuriated both men. As a deadly smallpox epidemic swept Confederate prison camps that winter, the black leaders who counseled Butler underlined the importance of negotiating a prisoner exchange so that the black prisoners could get free of both their white tormentors and smallpox. Butler eventually attempted to negotiate with Confederate leadership via a 'flag of truce boat' that plied regularly back and forth across the James River, a move that black soldiers and contrabands applauded. But the Lincoln administration's policies toward black troops still fell far short of real equality and severely damaged recruiting throughout 1863 and beyond" (Cecelski, *The Fire of Freedom*, 93–94).

13. Butler, *Butler's Book*, 579; Butler, *Private and Official*, 3:174, 180–83.

14. Butler, *Private and Official*, 3:183–85, 187. "The law of Congress is imperative," Butler wrote to David Kelly on December 20; "I do not think it is just" (Butler, 3:232). Black Union spy Abraham Galloway, writes Cecelski, "beseeched [Butler] to demand from the War Department fairness and equality for black soldiers. Hearing similar complaints from all his black regiments, Butler pushed the secretary of war to pay black recruits salaries and enlistment bounties equal to those of their white counterparts, but his pleas fell on deaf ears" (Cecelski, *The Fire of Freedom*, 93).

15. Butler, *Private and Official*, 3:185–90, 197, 198, 227.

16. Cecelski, *The Fire of Freedom*, 95–96; Butler, *Private and Official*, 3:239–40.

17. Butler, *Butler's Book*, 618; Butler, *Private and Official*, 3:269–70, 281–82, 315; Myers, *Executing Daniel Bright*, 96–98, 108–10; Burkhardt, *Confederate Rage, Yankee Wrath*, 82.

18. Cecelski, *The Fire of Freedom*, 95–96; Butler, *Private and Official*, 3:298–300, 311–12, 315–16, 341–42.

19. Butler, *Private and Official*, 3:214–15.

20. *Army and Navy Journal*, December 19 and 26, 1863, and January 2, 1864; Butler, *Private and Official*, 3:248.

21. Butler, *Private and Official*, 3:255, 277, 543; Brown, *The Galvanized Yankees*, 9, 12, 65–68.

22. Butler, *Private and Official*, 3:334, 344, 352, 379–80, 407; SHB to BB, January 13 and 20, and February [date unknown] and 29, 1864, BP-C; BB to SHB, January 7, 1864, BP-C.

23. Butler, *Private and Official*, 3:373–74, 407, 408–10, 479–81; *Army and Navy Journal*, February 13, 1864.

24. Butler, *Private and Official*, 3:400, 410–12, 421–23, 447–48, 515, 575.

25. Varon, *Southern Lady, Yankee Spy*; Butler, *Private and Official*, 3:228, 319, 331–32, 380–83, 509, 516, and 4:94; Downing, *A South Divided*, 201.

26. Butler, *Private and Official*, 3:518; Nevins, *The War for the Union: The Organized War to Victory*, 14; Hess, *Trench Warfare under Grant & Lee*, 99–100.

27. Simpson, *Ulysses S. Grant*, 270; *Army and Navy Journal*, April 9, 1864; Grant, *Personal Memoirs*, 389–90; Butler, *Private and Official*, 4:7–9, 29, 56–57; Nevins, *The War for the Union: The Organized War to Victory*, 14.

According to historian David Work, the basic outlines of the plan for Butler's part of the campaign were devised by Butler himself, and then approved by Grant, but their conception of the overall goal of Butler's movement was different (Work, *Lincoln's Political Generals*, 145).

28. SHB to BB, April 13 and 25, 1864, in BB-C; Butler, *Private and Official*, 4:74.

29. Butler, *Private and Official*, 4:76–84, 140, 163–66; McPherson, *Ordeal by Fire*, 491; *Army and Navy Journal*, April 30, 1864.

30. BB to SHB, May 8, 1864, and SHB to BB, May [date unknown], May 8, 15, and 23, 1864, all in BP-C.

31. Butler, *Private and Official*, 4:171–72, 177, 181–82, 189, 191, 192.

32. Butler, 4:219, 227; *Army and Navy Journal*, May 14 and 21, 1864.

33. *Army and Navy Journal*, May 28, 1864; Butler, *Private and Official*, 4:227–28, 231.

34. Butler, *Private and Official*, 4:245, 257, 262, 264; *Army and Navy Journal*, June 14, 1864; SHB to BB, June 7, 1864, in BP-C.

35. Butler, *Private and Official*, 4:171, 183–85, 258, 315–18.

Brooks Simpson writes, "Grant erred in deciding to leave Baldy Smith with Butler: Smith disliked his superior and had a reputation for being disagreeable and contentious. These qualities had cost him a previous field command, and apparently he had not profited from his experiences. He did not yet know that Butler would be a worthy foe in the struggle for control of the operation" (Simpson, *Ulysses S. Grant*, 271).

36. Grant, *Personal Memoirs*, 396–99. See also *Army and Navy Journal*, July 27, 1878; and Butler, *Private and Official*, 4:285.

37. Beringer et al., *Why the South Lost the Civil War*, 317–18; Borritt, *Why the Confederacy Lost*, 92; Grant, *Personal Memoirs*, 399.

38. SHB to BB, May 31, 1864; BB to SHB, June 1 and 13, 1864, all in BP-C; Butler, *Private and Official*, 4:289, 328, 337; Simpson, *Ulysses S. Grant*, 335; *Army and Navy Journal*, June 18, 1864.

39. Butler, *Private and Official*, 4:325, 374, 457, 534–36, 546–47; Simpson, *Ulysses S. Grant*, 346–50; Brands, *The Man Who Saved the Union*, 316.

For his part, Halleck considered Butler useless for "command in the field," and additionally problematic because of his "general quarrelsome character." He did not think a western command would suit him and felt that Butler and Sherman would have difficulty getting along (Butler, *Private and Official*, 4:458–59).

Some have suggested that Lincoln's first choice for vice president in 1864 was Butler (*Colby Echo*, November 14, 1969), but I have not seen persuasive evidence that this was the case.

Had Sarah been able to vote, indications were that in June, at least, she would not have voted for Lincoln's reelection. Among Republicans, she favored Seward. Above all, she favored her husband. "I do not often praise you," she wrote on June 11, "but it is my firm belief that there is but *one man* now known to the people who can save this country in its present critical state from utter loss and confusion irremediable; and that is yourself. Not that in time of peace and plenty you would be the best or only man; but I have seen, nor heard, of no man but you with broad and comprehensive views, and also a determined will and grasp of power . . . to carry them into effect. I think the country is doomed if Lincoln is again elected" (Butler, *Private and Official*, 4:342–43).

40. Simpson, *Ulysses S. Grant*, 351; Butler, *Private and Official*, 4:374, 400, 426, 514, 548, and 5:2, 39.

41. Butler, *Private and Official*, 4:552 and 5:28–29, 80–81, 109; SHB to BFB, August 7, 10, and 14, 1864, in folder 5, box 1, BP-LC. "The difficulty is that I get credit for wealth I do not possess," Butler wrote to one friend regarding the college's name change. "The almost fabulous amount attributed to me by the newspapers is simply fabulous, and could only have been accumulated by that peculation and mal-administration which has been attributed to me. My sworn income returns are on file, my oath as to my brother's estate is also on record, and I need not assure you that they represent the true state of affairs. A donation to my Alma Mater such as you suggest would to any reflecting mind be proof positive of the truth of the allegations. No man not a merchant and most fortunate in mercantile speculations at that, at forty-five ought to be in condition to make such donations as you suggest, and as Mr. Colby has made from the fortunate gains of a long mercantile life. Repeating that I have no such wealth as would enable me to do it, yet if I had I should hardly make a public exhibition of that amount, to convict myself of the

accusations of my enemies, yet at a proper time, in aid of the accumulation of the fund, I shall be willing to give such reasonable amount as a private gentleman with a competence ought to give to such an object" (Butler, *Private and Official*, 5:80–81).

42. Butler, *Private and Official*, 5:119, 138, 144, 146, 153, 168, 171–73.

43. Frassanito, *Grant and Lee*, 295–96; Butler, *Private and Official*, 5:191–92; *Army and Navy Journal*, October 8, 1864.

44. Frassanito, *Grant and Lee*, 295–96; Butler, *Private and Official*, 5:192, 214, 215; Leonard, *Men of Color to Arms!*, 13–14.

45. Butler, *Private and Official*, 5:47, 54–55, 67–68, 125; SHB to BFB, September 3 and 7, 1864, in folder 5, box 1, BP-LC.

46. Butler, *Private and Official*, 5:306, 307, 310, 315–16, 324; *Army and Navy Journal*, November 12, 1864.

47. Butler, *Private and Official*, 5:331, 336, 347, 356. "I had a long conversation with the President on the subject of the Cabinet," wrote James W. White on December 29. "He was very non-committal, or rather reticent as to his purposes; but very friendly personally in his mention of you, although I could discern that an idea had taken possession of him that he would no longer be *master* if you were in the Cabinet" (Butler, 5:450).

48. McPherson, *Ordeal by Fire*, 505; Butler, *Private and Official*, 5:436. "You know how Porter behaved at N. Orleans," Sarah added. "He is the same man still."

49. Butler, *Private and Official*, 5:428, 430; McPherson, *War on the Waters*, 215; Grant, *Personal Memoirs*, 544–45.

50. Butler, *Private and Official*, 5:438, 442; Beringer et al., *Why the South Lost the Civil War*, 196–97; Grant, *Personal Memoirs*, 574–75.

51. Grant, *Personal Memoirs*, 546–47; Butler, *Private and Official*, 5:449–50, 458, 497, 513; *Army and Navy Journal*, January 7, 1865; Beringer et al., *Why the South Lost the Civil War*, 196–97. "The malign bluster of that incomparable ass who commanded the fleet has harmed no one but himself," wrote the always faithful James Parton (Butler, *Private and Official*, 5:465).

52. See *Army and Navy Journal*, September 17, 1864; Butler, *Private and Official*, 5:124, 250, 263–64. See my detailed discussion of Black soldiers and the Dutch Gap Canal project in Leonard, *Slaves, Slaveholders*.

53. *Army and Navy Journal*, January 7 and August 27, 1865; Butler, *Private and Official*, 5:483.

54. SHB to BFB, January 1, 1865, in folder 6, box 1, BP-LC; *Army and Navy Journal*, January 21, 1865; Simpson, *Let Us Have Peace*, 70; Butler, *Private and Official*, 5:468–69, 471, 472, 475–76.

55. Butler, *Private and Official*, 5:512; *Army and Navy Journal*, January 14, 1865.

56. Butler, *Private and Official*, 5:481, 485, 498, 501, 505, 511–12. The portrait Shaffer referred to is the one that now hangs so prominently in Colby College's alumni building.

57. Butler, 5:515; Butler, *Speech of Maj.-Gen Benj. F. Butler*.

The Dodd Family Papers contain some nice letters from Helen Dodd, a missionary who served in Butler's department as a teacher in 1863–64. Of Butler, she once commented, "He is a fatty" (Helen Dodd to Mother, December 10, 1863). She also described disciplining her Black students with a rawhide strap, adding, troublingly, "I do love them, and have no objection to kissing them, but the colored children do not seem to be as fond of kissing as the white, and we teachers do not think it best among so many dirty children to establish the practice" (Helen Dodd to Mother, December 25, 1863, Dodd Family Papers).

58. *Army and Navy Journal*, February 4, 1865; Butler, *Private and Official*, 5:529, 530.

CHAPTER 6

1. Wrote Godfrey Weitzel, who also met with the committee, "I have found the entire committee strongly in your favor," but he also noted that Grant "understood that you had declared war against him, and accepted the challenge" (Butler, *Private and Official*, 5:548). Butler, 5:525. The Freedman's Savings Bank was established in March 1865 and continued until 1874.

In books published twenty years apart, historian Brooks Simpson offers two very different views of how Butler handled his removal from command relative to the role Grant had played in it. In *Let Us Have Peace* (1991), he writes that Butler did not take "dismissal quietly" and soon "broke off all relations with Grant and set out to destroy him" by drawing much negative attention to Grant's "refusal to exchange prisoners freely as needlessly cruel," trading in rumors about Grant's drinking problems, and alleging that the lieutenant general was "a man without a head or a heart, indifferent to human suffering and impotent to govern" (210). As a result, Simpson notes, "Radical members of the Committee on the Conduct of the War" soon "launched an investigation touching on several aspects of Grant's generalship in order to vindicate their fallen idol," Butler (93–94). In *Ulysses S. Grant* (2000), however, Simpson writes that at the time "Butler left" the army, "if he had any dirt on Grant, one might think that now was the time to divulge it." He did not. "So off went Butler to Lowell" (401). I am at a loss to reconcile these two interpretations.

2. Butler, *Private and Official*, 5:544: *The Liberator*, February 10, 1865. Notably, in this speech at least, Butler seemed to suggest that the freedpeople would and perhaps should remain in the South.

3. Butler, *Private and Official*, 5:546–48.

4. Butler, 5:559–60.

5. Butler, 5:584–85, 595, 610, 614, 617–19; *Boston Daily Advertiser*, April 28, 1865.

6. Butler, *Private and Official*, 5:610–15.

7. *The Liberator*, May 12, 1865; Butler, *Private and Official*, 5:616.

8. *Boston Daily Advertiser*, June 29, 1865; Butler, *Private and Official*, 5:621–23, 646, 648; *Springfield (Mass.) Weekly Republican*, July 22, 1865; *National Aegis*, August 12, 1865.

9. Sarah H. Butler (hereafter SHB) to Dr. McCormack, September [date unknown], 1865, in folder 6, box 1, Benjamin F. Butler Papers, Library of Congress,

Washington, D.C. (hereafter BP-LC); *Lowell (Mass.) Daily Citizen and News*, September 12, 1865; Butler, *Private and Official*, 5:634, 642; *Springfield (Mass.) Weekly Republican*, September 16, 1865; *Boston Press and Post*, September 18, 1865.

In a letter to F. A. Angell a few weeks earlier, on the question of Black male suffrage, Butler wrote, "It is said that the Negro will vote as his late master directs, and thus increase his master's political power. Be it so. As the master will have control of all the voting, as he had before the war, if the negro does not vote, I do not see how he or we are worse off if the negro votes with him. If the master votes right, let the negro vote wrong. If the master votes wrong, then we gain the chance that the negro may not vote with the master. That chance is worth something. Thus we gain and can lose nothing by giving the negro the right of suffrage" (Butler, *Private and Official*, 5:639). A letter from Butler to Alex H. Bullock suggests that he had already committed to the idea of Black male suffrage by mid-June (Butler, 5:631).

10. Butler, 5:665–67.

11. Butler, 5:660, 670; Clara Barton to BFB, October 2, October 3, November 16, December 1, 1865, box 66, Clara Barton Papers, LC.

12. Butler, *Private and Official*, 5:678, 679–80, 684, 689; *Salem (Mass.) Observer*, November 18, 1865; *The Liberator*, November 24, 1865. No such trial by military commission—and no civilian trial of Davis either, for that matter—took place, and the former president was released from prison in May 1867.

13. *Army and Navy Journal*, January 14, 1866; Butler, *Private and Official*, 5:691–92, 694, 696–97, 699.

14. *Boston Globe*, January 11, 1893; Butler, *Private and Official*, 5:681, 685; *Lowell (Mass.) Daily Citizen and News*, February 16, 1866; *Boston Daily Journal*, February 20, 1866. See also *Springfield (Mass.) Republican*, April 7, 1866.

15. *Boston Daily Advertiser*, March 5, 1866; Witt, *Lincoln's Code*, 310; *Boston Daily Journal*, April 4, 1866; *Daily Constitutional Union* (Washington, D.C.), April 4, 1866.

16. *Salem (Mass.) Register*, May 24, 1866; Butler, *Private and Official*, 5:704, 705; *Springfield (Mass.) Republican*, April 21, 1866; *Lowell (Mass.) Daily Citizen and News*, May 19, 1866;

The NHDVS, writes Donald Shaffer, "consisted of a network of asylums scattered mostly across the North and supported by the federal government. Their initial purpose was to provide a refuge for disabled soldiers who were unable to earn a living after the war and had no family willing or able to care for them. Over time, however, the NHDVS network and other veterans' homes evolved into retirement facilities for impoverished elderly veterans with no better place to go" (Shaffer, *After the Glory*, 137; *Army and Navy Journal*, May 6, 1866).

17. *National Aegis*, May 19, 1866.

18. *Massachusetts Weekly Spy*, September 14, 1866; Foner, *The Life and Writings of Frederick Douglass*, 4:25. "When the delegates assembled at Independence Hall . . . to march to National Hall where the convention was to be held," Foner writes, "General Butler was the only one to remain near Douglass" (26).

19. *Salem (Mass.) Register*, September 6 and 20, 1866; *Boston Daily Advertiser*, September 14, 1866.

20. *Cleveland Plain Dealer*, September 4, 1866; *Massachusetts Weekly Spy*, October 5, 1866; Butler, *Private and Official*, 5:716; *Boston Daily Advertiser*, August 10, 1868; *Pittsfield (Mass.) Sun*, December 20, 1866; Lewis Tower to BFB, February 14, 1867, in folder 2, box 42, BP-LC.

21. *Boston Daily Advertiser*, October 12, 1866; Butler, *Private and Official*, 5:711–12; *Salem (Mass.) Register*, November 8, 1866.

22. These seven were Tennessee (October 1869), Virginia (October 1869), North Carolina (November 1870), Georgia (November 1871), Texas (January 1873), Alabama (November 1874), and Arkansas (November 1874). Mississippi followed in January 1876 and Louisiana, Florida, and South Carolina in the first months of 1877.

23. B. F. Pratt to BFB, January 8, 1867, in folder 1, box 42, BP-LC.

24. Butler, *Butler's Book*, 920–21; *Boston Daily Journal*, March 8, 1867; *Lowell (Mass.) Daily Citizen and News*, February 15, 1867.

25. Leonard, *Lincoln's Avengers*; George C. Moore to BFB, March 8, 1867, in folder 3, box 42, BP-LC; *Army and Navy Journal*, May 25, 1867; *Daily National Intelligencer* (Washington, D.C.), August 24, 1867; *Daily Ohio Statesman*, August 15, 1867. Questions about Johnson's complicity in the assassination were heightened by the discovery that the government had in its possession a diary that Booth had been carrying with him during his two weeks on the run after the murder. In particular, questions arose about the pages that seemed to be missing from the diary, how they had gone missing, and what pertinent information they originally contained.

26. *Army and Navy Journal*, August 3, 1867; Butler et al., *Remarks of Hons. G. S. Boutwell, B. F. Butler, and Thomas Williams*; BFB to John Pope, September 10, 1867, in folder 6, box 43, BP-LC; Butler, *Butler's Book*, 930. One person who may well have sympathized with Butler's experience of being the subject of political invective was James Longstreet, who wrote in late June thanking Butler for a recent letter and for his "sentiments of high appreciation and magnanimity expressed therein" (James Longstreet to BFB, June 27, 1867, in folder 13, box 42, BP-LC).

27. James T. Champlin to BFB, July 1, 1867, in folder 1, box 43; James T. Champlin to BFB, May 1, 1869, in folder 1, box 49; Edmund Bennett and Edward Hinson to BFB, July 22, 1867, in folder 3, box 43; all in BP-LC.

28. See also Robert Thompson to BFB, March 15, 1867, in folder 4, box 42; G. W. Shurtleff to BFB, May 15, 1867, in folder 9, box 42; BFB to A. J. Ransier, endorsement on a February 11, 1868, letter from Ransier in folder 9, box 44; all in BP-LC.

29. "The colored citizens of Baltimore" to BFB, February 1, 1868, in folder 8, box 44, BP-LC. See also various related letters in folder 6, box 44, BP-LC; Butler, *Private and Official*, 5:718; and *Massachusetts Weekly Spy*, February 28, 1868.

In a letter to his friend James Parton's wife, Fanny (the journalist known as Fanny Fern), Butler described a recent visit to Richmond, where Black residents showered him with appreciative attention. "No monarch ever had such a body guard so true, so faithful, and so loving," he wrote. "It is worth the war to have liberated a race so kindly and so grateful. Infamous, most infamous will the Republican party collectively and individually be if for one moment or in one jot or tittle we abate the protection thrown around that people to save them and their children from a worse fate than that to which slavery had doomed them if we desert them now" (Butler, *Private and Official*, 5:720).

30. Butler, *Butler's Book*, 926–28; *Lowell (Mass.) Daily Citizen and News*, March 3 and 14, 1868; Butler, *Private and Official*, 5:721; G. St. George to BFB, April 1, 1868, in folder 1, box 45, BP-LC; *Daily National Intelligencer* (Washington, D.C.), April 1 and 8, 1868.

31. *Boston Daily Advertiser*, April 8, 1868; BFB to unknown, April 8, 1868, in folder 1; Amos G. Hill to BFB, April 13, 1868, and William D. Forten to BFB, April 20, 1868, in folder 2, all in box 45, BP-LC. For a thorough study of the impeachment process, see Trefousse, *Impeachment of a President*.

32. George Wilkes to BFB, April 12, 1868, in folder 2; BFB to George Wilkes, May 2, 1868, in folder 4, both in box 45, BP-LC. According to McFeely, Grant "stood clear of the passionate battles over impeachment" (McFeely, *Grant*, 274). In *Let Us Have Peace*, Simpson notes that some people—including Butler—pointed to Grant's presence with Andrew Johnson during part of his Swing around the Circle tour in the fall of 1866 "as proof of the general's support for the president's policy" (152).

33. *Boston Daily Advertiser*, August 10, 1868; James Scibsen to BFB, June 22, 1868, in folder 9, box 45, BP-LC.

34. *Army and Navy Journal*, May 16 and July 18, 1868; *Boston Daily Advertiser*, August 10 and September 19, 1868; *Boston Daily Journal*, August 7, 1868.

35. *Boston Daily Advertiser*, October 3, 1868; *Springfield (Mass.) Weekly Republican*, October 3, 1868; *Lowell (Mass.) Daily Citizen and News*, November 4, 1868; 1868 Washington, D.C., City Directory; BFB to SHB, December 15 and 23, 1868, in folder 7, box 1, BP-LC.

36. Henry M. Turner to BFB, February 19, 1869, in folder 5, box 47, BP-LC. Turner continued, "And the Democrats are daily taunting us with it, by saying, *Now where is your damned Radical party? Why don't Beast Butler, and old Sumner, come to your aid, &c.*"

37. William Howard Day to BFB, January 6, 1869, in folder 1, box 47, BP-LC; Butler, *Butler's Book*, 961; Thomas M. Brown to BFB, July 10, 1869, and Rufus Babcock to BFB, July 8, 1869, both in folder 6, box 49; and Caroline Putnam to BFB, November 14, 1869, in folder 8, box 50, all in BP-LC.

38. BFB to James Kelley, May 13, 1869, in folder 3, box 48; Peter S. Blake to BFB, April 21, 1869, in folder 6, box 48; Alexander Richardson to BFB, April 11, 1869, in folder 5, box 48; Elizabeth Cady Stanton to BFB, May 4, 1869, in folder 1, box 49; Eleanor Ketchum to BFB, September 6, 1869, in folder 1, box 50; M. H. Bellamy to BFB, September 8, 1869, in folder 1, box 50; Anonymous to BFB, November 12, 1869, in folder 8, box 50; all in BP-LC; *Boston Globe*, January 11, 1893.

39. John Barr to BFB, December 7, 1869, in folder 10, box 50, BP-LC; *Boston Daily Journal*, December 17, 1869; Butler, *Reconstruction of Georgia*.

40. Frank Swaris to BFB, September 17, 1870, in folder 5, box 54, BP-LC. Georgia was finally readmitted on July 15, 1870. Mississippi was readmitted on February 23, 1870, and Texas on March 30, 1870.

41. James W. Stephenson to BFB, February 26, 1870, in folder 6, box 51; Anthony M. Dignowitz to BFB, July 18, 1870, in folder 8, box 53; A. W. McWhorter to BFB, July 1, 1870, in folder 7, box 53; Charles E. St. Clair to BFB, March 9, 1870, in folder 1, box 52; Rufus Saxton to BFB, March 28, 1870, in folder 3, box 52; all in BP-LC; *Portland (Me.) Daily Eastern Argus*, March 9, 1870; *Michigan Weekly Citizen* (Jackson, Mich.), March 15, 1870.

42. *New York Evening Journal* (Albany), March 28, 1870; C. A. Woodruff to BFB, July 14, 1870, in folder 8, box 53; James M. Deems to BFB, July 9, 1870, in folder 7, box 53; R. E. Hathaway to BFB, April 4, 1870, in folder 4, box 52; all in BP-LC; Foner, *The Life and Writings of Frederick Douglass*, 4:46. See also Flipper, *The Colored Cadet*, and Leonard, *Men of Color to Arms!*, for more on Smith's story.

43. Ang. H. Heyer to BFB, February 17, 1870, in folder 5, box 51; Mrs. E. Davis to BFB, February 24, 1870, in folder 6, box 51; Jonathan T. Hildreth to BFB, April 21, 1870, in folder 6, box 52; all in BP-LC.

44. David K. Hitchcock to BFB, June 24, 1870, in folder 6; George A. Potter to BFB, July 5, 1870, in folder 7; both in box 53, BP-LC. Two weeks earlier, Butler gave a speech in the House of Representatives advocating the US annexation of Cuba (Butler, *Independence of Cuba*). See also Butler, *Suggestions of the Effect of an Imported Laboring Class upon American Institutions*, 4–8.

45. Ames, *Chronicles from the Nineteenth Century*, 1:199; George Ober to BFB, October 4, 1870, in folder 7, box 54; A. E. Redstone to BFB, November 13, 1870, in folder 2, box 55; both in BP-LC.

46. Aurora H. C. Phelps to BFB, December 23, 1870, in folder 6, box 55, BP-LC. McFeely writes that Butler was "a rich man who had made his own money" and who "championed the down-and-out members of society in order that, in perfectly logical fashion, he himself might reach higher personal goals" (McFeely, *Grant*, 363). I tend to think this is a distortion of Butler's motivations. True, he was abundantly ambitious. But my read of the historical record of his life is that his concern for the downtrodden was deeply rooted and profoundly sincere.

47. Mary Morris Husband to BFB, March 13, 1871, in folder 2, box 58, BP-LC; Norgren, *Belva Lockwood*, 56; Underhill, *The Woman Who Ran for President*, 96–100; Victoria Woodhull to BFB, December 29, 1870, in folder 6, box 55, BP-LC; *Cleveland Plain Dealer*, January 12, 1871; Goldsmith, *Other Powers*, 248–53; Victoria Woodhull to BFB, February 26, 1871, in folder 4, box 57, BP-LC.

My own research suggests that rumors of Butler's romantic relationship with Woodhull (and other women) have been blown out of proportion.

48. Marie Ellen Sanders to BFB, March 16, 1872, in folder 2, box 67, BP-LC; Ames, *Chronicles from the Nineteenth Century*, 1:384–85; Victoria Woodhull to BFB, January 8, 1873, in folder 2, box 70, BP-LC; Underhill, *The Woman Who Ran for President*, 236–37; Goldsmith, *Other Powers*, 368; Madison Lewis to BFB, December 5, 1870, in folder 4, box 55, BP-LC; William D. Matthews to BFB, March 23, 1871, in folder 4, box 58, BP-LC.

An example of the sort of request for individual assistance Butler frequently received during this period is the letter from Thomas H. B. Reed of New York, in

May 1872, in which he asked Butler to send a letter on his behalf to his employer, the Pullman Company, to have him reinstated as a porter following his suspension "upon the false charge of uncourtesy to my passengers." Reed claimed that the charge came from a particular conductor, who had "always had a total dislike for me owing to my not [being] of that class of Colored men, that can be 'shown off' for the amusement of men who delight in seeing a Black man make a 'Nigger' of himself." He insisted that he had always been "mannerly and respectful to all," as "anyone that has ridden with me knows," and he was convinced that a supportive letter from Butler would effect his reinstatement (Thomas H. B. Reed to BFB, May 6, 1872, in folder 1, box 68, BP-LC). Butler wrote the letter and Reed was reinstated (Thomas H. B. Reed to BFB, May 11, 1872, in folder 2, box 68, BP-LC).

"Our whole county is ruled by the ku-klux," wrote a group of Black citizens from Jackson County, Florida, in June 1872. "The ku-klux all whipping women and men with full whips and paddles. . . . In May they gave a woman fifty lashes with a paddle and then the blisters they had made on her feet with the paddle they split them open by giving her seventy-five lashes with a bull whip. They tell us that our representative of this county must leave here before the election comes off in November and if they do not go they will kill them. Our governor is doing us no good and he says he can not protect us. Then our only hope is in the congress and the president. If the loyal people of the north could only see and know the outrages all being committed in Jackson county and the rebellious spirit of these rebel ku klux there would be a general uprising of them and they would not hesitate to come to our relief" ("235 Citizens" of Jackson County, Florida, to BFB, June [date unknown], 1872, in folder 3, box 68, BP-LC).

49. Mrs. Abel C. Thomas to BFB, January 16, 1871, and Isabella Hooker to BFB, January 17, 1871; both in folder 4, box 56; Elizabeth Cady Stanton to BFB, February 20, 1871, in folder 3, box 57; all in BP-LC; McFeely, *Grant*, 368; Smith, *Grant*, 545; *Boston Daily Journal*, March 1, 1871; Ames, *Chronicles from the Nineteenth Century*, 1:243; Butler, *Ku-Klux Outrages in the South*, 3–4, 17, 21.

The three sessions of the Forty-Second Congress were March 4–April 20, 1871; December 4, 1871–June 10, 1872; and December 2, 1872–March 4, 1873.

50. Ulysses S. Grant to BFB, January 14, 1871, in folder 3, box 56, BP-LC; McFeely, *Grant*, 363–64; Isabella Hooker to BFB, March 18, 1871, in folder 3, box 58; D. Richey to BFB, May 10, 1872, in folder 2, box 68; both in BP-LC.

51. E. J. Sherman to BFB, January 15, 1871, in folder 3, box 56; Victoria Woodhull to BFB, May 1, 1871, in folder 1, box 60; both in BP-LC. *Pittsfield (Mass.) Sun*, July 20, 1871; Ames, *Chronicles from the Nineteenth Century*, 1:243; "An Old Democrat" to BFB, September 13, 1871; G. M. Brown to BFB, September 15, 1871; Statement of Resolutions of the Radical Republican Workingmen's Association of the District of Columbia to BFB, September 15, 1871; in folder 3; and "Colored Citizens of New Orleans" to BFB, undated, in folder 6; all in box 63, BP-LC.

The DC Radical Republican Workingmen's Association went on to thank Butler for "his continuous struggles in our behalf, for his unceasing interest in our safety and welfare, and for the heroic endurance with which he bears the mountain load of contumely, falsehood, and reproach which rebel malignity and disappointed conservative hatred unite to heap upon him, and under which a less brave spirit or a less devoted purpose would shrink and waver."

The "Colored Citizens of New Orleans" added, "You asked the black man to stand by you and maintain his inch of Union soil. You enabled him to assert himself, to earn his title to that soil and to call the men of the North in your command his brethren. And you have done much for him since by zealously assisting to engraft his civil guarantees upon the same national charter that assures the defences of the white citizen."

Writes historian Stephen Kantrowitz, "Boston's black leadership occupied a curious and often uncomfortable position in the Republican party. The Massachusetts Republican establishment was composed of industrialists, entrepreneurs, urban elites, and useful men whom the power brokers came to trust. The party enabled them to protect their own interest, encourage economic development, and most of all prevent the reins of government from being seized by laborers, Democrats, or others with wild ideas about inflation, taxation, or expenditures. Black activists stood well outside this establishment. Their heroes were the Republican radicals," and by the early 1870s, they "yearned to embrace a champion more interested in protecting freedpeople than restraining public spending." They "found that champion in Benjamin Butler." In contrast, the Republican establishment in Massachusetts viewed Butler as "beneath them and unworthy of the high offices he sought." And as a result, "Butler's decision to seek the governorship in 1871 set black Bostonians and their elite coalition partners at odds." Then, "when Butler began his campaign by addressing black Bostonians at a Ward Six church, they responded to the gesture with affection and enthusiasm. . . . But the party establishment united against him" (Kantrowitz, *More than Freedom*, 367–69).

52. Richardson, *West from Appomattox*, 105; M. J. Kelly to "Mr. Editor," November 24, 1871, in folder 6, box 64; W. H. Laugre to BFB, September 18, 1871, in folder 3, box 63; Undated clipping from October 1871, in folder 3, box 64; John Burns to BFB, September 28, 1871, in folder 6, box 63, all in BP-LC. Ames, *Chronicles from the Nineteenth Century*, 1:319, 324, 326.

53. *Lowell (Mass.) Daily Citizen*, April 4, 1877; SHB to BFB, October 14, 1869; SHB to Paul Butler (hereafter PB), November 29, 1869; BFB to PB and Ben-Israel Butler (hereafter BIB), November 15 and 29, 1869, and May 7, 1870; all in Benjamin F. Butler Papers, Archives and Special Collections, Colby College, Waterville, Maine (hereafter BP-C); BIB to SHB, December 14, 1869, in folder 11, box 50, BP-LC.

54. Blanche Butler (hereafter BB) and SHB to PB and BIB, February 21, 1870; BIB to BFB, July 18, 1870; PB to BFB, March 4, 1870, all in BP-C; BFB to SHB, April 17, 1870, in folder 7, box 1, BP-LC; SHB to PB and BIB, May 1, 1870; SHB to PB, October 18 and November 6, 1870, in BP-C; Theodore Edson to BFB, February 12, 1871, in folder 2, box 57, BP-LC; PB to BFB, February 9, 1871, in BP-C; Ames, *Chronicles from the Nineteenth Century*, 1:231–32; SHB to BFB, March 7, 1871, in BP-C; BFB to SHB, March 23, 1871, in folder 8, box 1, BP-LC; Ames, *Chronicles from the Nineteenth Century*, 1:319, 324, 425, 454–55, 480–81, 583, 601, 667; Flipper, *The Colored Cadet*, 265;

BIB to BFB, February 12, 1874, in folder 3, box 73, BP-LC; BIB to BFB, January 22 and February 20, 1874, in BP-C.

Among the more interesting letters from the boys to their parents are those that include their observations of the Franco-Prussian War. See PB to BFB, August 1 and 16, and October 9, 1870, in BP-C; Susan Hildreth Webster to SHB, December 1, 1869, in folder 7, box 1, BP-LC.

55. SHB to PB and BIB, November 29, 1869, and March 13 and May 1, 1870, in BP-C; Ames, *Chronicles from the Nineteenth Century*, 1:42, 43.

56. PB to BFB, April 15, 1870, in folder 7, box 1, BP-LC; Ames, *Chronicles from the Nineteenth Century*, 1:177, 180, 190, 206, 209–10; SHB to PB, October 18 and November 5, 1870, in BP-C; *Army and Navy Journal*, March 25, 1871.

"Both Father and Mother seemed a little sad at parting from me," Blanche wrote in her diary after they left. "Father said to me, as he kissed me, 'Poor Blanche, poor girl.' 'Poor yourself,' I retorted. 'That is true,' and he kissed me again. . . . I do not know why he pitied me. Perhaps because he felt that I had passed a very happy and careless girlhood, and that now the troubles and experience of a married woman were before me. We seem much nearer, and fonder of each other than ever before. This may partly be owing to the fact that I no longer feel the least fear of him, as I did when a child" (Ames, *Chronicles from the Nineteenth Century*, 1:211).

57. BFB to PB and BIB, October 5, 1870, in BP-C; George H. Butler (hereafter GHB) to BFB, November 5, 1870, in folder 1, box 55, BP-LC.

58. Ames, *Chronicles from the Nineteenth Century*, 1:349, 352, 367. Blanche offered another charming story from the summer of 1873, at Bay View, involving her father and his grandson. "The other day he [little Butler Ames] set up a great noise about something which did not please him. Father took him up and told him to stop, which he did at once, but his little soul was full of resentment and he would not go near Father for two or three hours. It seemed to trouble Father, and after one or two ineffectual attempts at reconciliation he bethought himself of the hot-house grapes, armed himself with a bunch, called the boy's attention to them, and led the way to a sofa. Butler followed, climbed up, seated himself beside of father, and looking up into his face with a smile helped himself to grapes. Father was happy and felt that he held the trump card" (Ames, 1:511–12).

59. *Daily Critic* (Washington, D.C.), May 12, 1886; *New York Herald*, May 12, 1886; *Cincinnati Daily Gazette*, March 5, 1870; *Rhode Island Evening Press* (Providence), December 17, 1869; *Flake's Bulletin* (Galveston, Tex.), November 5, 1868; *New York Evening Post*, June 2, 1869; J. Becker to BFB, April 4, 1870, in folder 4, box 52; Hamilton Fish to BFB, July 23, 1872, BFB to Hamilton Fish, July 26, 1872; GHB to BFB, July 24, 1872, all in folder 5, box 68, BP-LC. *Daily Critic* (Washington, D.C.), May 12, 1886.

When he died in early 1864, Andrew Jackson Butler had left his family insolvent, which may well have contributed to George's problems. See *Portland (Me.) Daily Eastern Argus*, August 24, 1869.

60. Mrs. C. M. Currier to BFB, February 15, 1870, in folder 5, box 51; Thomas Dean to BFB, April 20, 1870, in folder 5, box 52; C. S. Currier to BFB, May 20, 1870,

in folder 3, box 53; Mary Mumford to BFB, January 10, 1871, in folder 2, box 56; all in BP-LC.

61. Anna E. Dickinson to BFB, September 14, 1871, in folder 1, box 59; Anna E. Dickinson to BFB, August 25, 1874, in folder 1, box 74; Susan Dickinson to BFB, August 9, 1874, in folder 5, box 80; Edwin Dickinson to BFB, August 12, 1874, in folder 5, box 80; all in BP-LC. Chester, *Embattled Maiden*, 145–46; Gallman, *America's Joan of Arc*; Thomas B. Keogh to BFB, November 25, 1871, in folder 6, box 64, BP-LC; Ames, *Chronicles from the Nineteenth Century*, 1:632.

I thank Gallman for sending me his detailed timeline of Dickinson's life, with communications with Butler highlighted clearly, early on in my research for this biography. Gallman argues that "by 1874 it was clear that Butler hoped to play a larger role in Dickinson's life" and "he was not above using Dickinson's brother to further these goals" (Gallman, *America's Joan of Arc*, 132). At the same time, it is clear to me that Butler and Sarah were still deeply bonded. On April 24, 1874, he wrote, using his pet name for her, "Sally, thirty years of married life have brought us too near together to be easily parted in person or heart and we shall be far more happy together than any way else. Is it not so? I feel very much as I sit lonely here tonight in my room . . . like writing you a *love* letter, if I only knew how to do it, but it is a species of composition in which I do not excel" (BFB to SHB, April 24, 1874, in folder 8, box 1, BP-LC).

62. William H. Hicks to BFB, May 30, 1873, in folder 5, box 70, BP-LC; Robinson, *The Salary Grab*; Ames, *Chronicles from the Nineteenth Century*, 1:485, 526, 544, 548, BFB to S. B. Gregory, March 7, 1878, in box 219, BP-LC.

63. Ames, *Chronicles from the Nineteenth Century*, 1:558, 630; Butler, *Butler's Book*, 967–68; C. L. Woodworth to BFB, September 11, 1873, in folder 3, box 71, BP-LC. When Ames was nominated by the Mississippi Republican Party in late August, Blanche wrote, "Father came home quite unexpectedly last night and brought the news of your nomination. He called your boy [Butler Ames] his young Excellency and asked me if I was not ashamed to get that position before my Mother" (Ames, *Chronicles from the Nineteenth Century*, 1:542). Butler also developed a loving relationship with baby Edith. "Father came downstairs about dinner time with Edith in his arms," Blanche wrote to Ames from Bay View in August 1874. "He was talking to her and she was coquetting in the most engaging way. As he passed the door he heard her voice, and looked in. She had just awakened, and put out her arms to be taken up. Of course he could not resist such an invitation" (Ames, *Chronicles* 2:2–3).

64. Ames, *Chronicles from the Nineteenth Century*, 1:539; Butler, *Civil Rights*, 5–12. In his powerful and inspiring inaugural speech on January 22, Ames boldly displayed his Radical Republican views and agenda, which had much in common with those of his father-in-law. See *Bound Correspondence*, vol. 1, BP-C. Mississippi saw a strong resurgence of white supremacist violence in 1874, which Ames struggled in vain to combat (Ames, *Chronicles from the Nineteenth Century*, 2:69–70).

65. C. H. Pollock to BFB, January 8, 1874; Isaac Myers to BFB, January 8, 1874; John J. Freeman to BFB, January 9, 1874; all in folder 1, box 72, BP-LC; "Citizens" to BFB, January 12, 1874, in folder 1, box 74, BP-LC; Ames, *Chronicles from the Nine-*

teenth Century, 1:661; G. Haven to BFB, March 18, 1874, in folder 1, box 76; Emma Hammack to BFB, May 2, 1874, in folder 1, box 78; P. B. Barrow to BFB, September [date unknown], 1874, in folder 1, box 81; all in BP-LC.

66. Oliver S. Dimmick to BFB, May 5, 1874, in folder 1, box 78; BFB to SHB, April 24, 1874, in folder 8, box 1; Peter Parker to BFB, May 17, 1874, in folder 3, box 78; all in BP-LC.

67. Burnham Wardwell to BFB, September 12, 1874, in folder 1, box 81; Burnham Wardwell to BFB, July 23, 1874, in folder 3, box 80; H. Bonzano to BFB, May 7, 1874, in folder 1, box 78; all in BP-LC.

68. Ames, *Chronicles from the Nineteenth Century,* 1:464, 485, 678, 682, 685–86; Edgar J. Sherman to unknown, May 22, 1874, in folder 3, box 78; PB to BFB, July 2, 1873, in folder 1, box 71; both in BP-LC.

69. Ames, *Chronicles from the Nineteenth Century,* 1:653, 654; P. B. Barrow to BFB, September [date unknown], 1874, in folder 1; Franklin Clark to BFB, October 15, 1874, in folder 5; both in box 81, BP-LC.

70. Duncan Blanton to BFB, November 4, 1874, in folder 1, box 82, BP-LC; Ames, *Chronicles from the Nineteenth Century,* 2:51; Knott V. Martin to BFB, November 4, 1874; "A Republican" to BFB, November 5, 1874; and John A. Grow to BFB, November 7, 1874; all in folder 1, box 82, BP-LC.

71. Rufus Bullock to BFB, November 9, 1874, and BFB to N. Dumont, November 8, 1874; both in folder 1, box 82, BP-LC. Ames, *Chronicles from the Nineteenth Century,* 2:58; Blanche Butler Ames to Adelbert Ames, October 8, 1874, in *Bound Correspondence,* vol. 1, BP-C.

CHAPTER 7

1. W. G. Riley to Benjamin Franklin Butler (hereafter BFB), January 27, 1875, and Phoebe Couzins to "My dear Mr. Clancey," February 5, 1875, both in folder 1, box 84, Benjamin F. Butler Papers, Library of Congress, Washington, D.C. (hereafter BP-LC). Couzins added, "Pray convey to Gen'l Butler my warmest sympathies and say to him that he must not forget that it is not personal enmity to him alone that provokes these attacks but the cruel hatred of a power striking at the freedom which he so grandly and nobly vindicated at New Orleans when in power." Subsequently, Couzins and Butler began corresponding directly, and they went on to enjoy a warm and mutually supportive friendship for the duration of his life.

2. M. R. Moore to BFB, February 10, 1875, in folder 2, and "Your Friend" to BFB, February 5, 1875, in folder 1; James Fitzpatrick to BFB, February 8, 1875, in folder 1; all in box 84; C. H. Tandy to BFB, February 13, 1875, in folder 4, box 85; all in BP-LC.

3. Robert Harlan to BFB, March 15, 1875; "Colored Citizens of Portland, Maine," to BFB, March 19, 1875; and printed tribute from Black citizens of Worcester, Massachusetts, March 22, 1875; all in folder 2, box 84; and Pauline Thomas to BFB, February 9, 1875, in folder 4, box 85 and BFB to C. H. Mercier, May 12, 1875, in box 214, BP-LC.

4. Ames, *Chronicles from the Nineteenth Century*, 2:249; BFB to George H. Butler (hereafter GHB), May 15, 1875, and BFB to John Lynch, September 22, 1875, in box 214; Caleb Cushing to BFB, September 28, 1875, in folder 2, box 85; all in BP-LC.

5. James Buchanan to BFB, December 16, 1875, and Edward Daniels to BFB, March 12, 1875, both in folder 1; James Buchanan to BFB, November 22, 1875, in folder 3; all in box 85; Butler, article for the *New York Arcadian*, June 30, 1875; BFB to James Parton, September 25, 1875; and BFB to R. H. Williams, November 4, 1875; all in box 214; all in BP-LC.

6. BFB to R. H. Williams, November 4, 1875, and BFB to Arthur DeLar, August 30, 1875; both in box 214, BP-LC.

7. Ames, *Chronicles from the Nineteenth Century*, 2:110, 122, 199, 227; BIB to BFB, January 8, 1875, in Benjamin F. Butler Papers, Archives and Special Collections, Colby College, Waterville, Maine (hereafter BP-C); William Belknap to BFB, March 3, 1875, in folder 3, box 84, BP-LC; Paul Butler (hereafter PB) to Sarah H. Butler (hereafter SHB), March 7, 1876, in series 3, box 52, Ames Family Papers; BFB to Sisters of Charity, December 18, 1875, and BFB to Rose E. Butler, December 18, 1875; both in box 214; Blanche Butler Ames (hereafter BBA) to SHB, February 1, 1875, in folder 3, box 85; all in BP-LC.

Notes on Paul Butler in the *Harvard College Class of 1875 Secretary's Report*, no. 8, *1875–1905*, read, "Since March, 1876, has been Treasurer of the United States Cartridge Company. Is Treasurer of the Wanesit Power Company, President of the Heinze Electric Company and of the Vesper Country Club. He has taken great interest in canoeing, winning many prizes in races for sailing canoes." The entry also notes that Paul was "married at Lucerne, Switzerland, July 21, 1905, to Joanna Handy Barstow."

8. BBA to PB, January 18 and 19, and February 9 and 21, 1875, all in folder 3, box 85, BP-LC.

9. Adelbert Ames (hereafter AA) to BBA, September 19 and 24, 1875, in *Bound Correspondence*, vol. 1, BP-C; Ames, *Chronicles from the Nineteenth Century*, 2:216–17, 223–24.

10. Ames, *Chronicles from the Nineteenth Century*, 2:181–82. See also AA to BBA, September 5, 1875, in *Bound Correspondence*, vol. 1, BP-C.

11. Ames, *Chronicles from the Nineteenth Century*, 2:244–45; BFB to H. Adams and others, November 28, 1875, in box 214, BP-LC.

12. Ames, *Chronicles from the Nineteenth Century*, 2:213, 215, 224, 227–29, 244, 254, 257; McFeely, *Grant*, 422, 424; BFB to BBA, January 12, 1875, in *Bound Correspondence*, vol. 1, BP-C.

13. AA to BFB, December 10, 1875, in folder 1, box 84; BFB to AA, December 23, 1875, in box 214; BFB to Blanche K. Bruce, January 1, 1876, in box 215; all in BP-LC.

14. AA to BFB, January 24 and 27, 1876, in folder 2; AA to BFB, January 8, 1876, in folder 1; both in box 86; BFB to AA, February 2, 1876, in box 215; all in BP-LC.

15. Ames, *Chronicles from the Nineteenth Century*, 2:210–11; AA to BFB, March 14, 1876, in folder 1 and Roger A. Pryor to BFB, March 29, 1876, in folder 2; both in box 87, BP-LC. As Pryor explained it, "I opened negotiations with the leading

men against us, with many of whom I had old and intimate associations, and, after a strenuous struggle, it was arranged that they should dismiss the charges, and then the Governor should resign." Pryor added that "throughout the trying crisis [Ames] bore himself as a brave and honorable gentleman" (Roger A. Pryor to BFB, April 3, 1876, in folder 3, box 87, BP-LC).

16. AA to BFB, April 2, 1876, in folder 3, box 87, BP-LC.

17. BFB to Philip Read, January 30, 1876, and BFB to AA, February 2 and 25, 1876, all in box 215, BP-LC; Ames, *Chronicles from the Nineteenth Century*, 2:283, 306, 307, 311, 345; Thomas Wilson to BFB, March 10, 1876, in folder 1, box 87, BP-LC.

18. Victoria Woodhull to BFB, January 12, 1875, in folder 1, box 84; see also BFB to Victoria Woodhull, April 28, 1875, in box 214; both in BP-LC. Ames, *Chronicles from the Nineteenth Century*, 2:106; BFB to F. D. Moulton, January 8, 1876, in box 215; F. D. Moulton to BFB, January 10, 1876, in folder 1, box 86; J. H. Martindale to BFB, March 2, 1876, and Benjamin D. Godfrey to BFB, March 12, 1876, both in folder 1, box 87; BFB to F. D. Moulton, February 24, 1876, and BFB to AA, February 25, 1876; both in box 215; all in BP-LC.

19. BFB to E. L. Barney, March 30, 1876; BFB to clerk of the Fifth Avenue Hotel in NYC, April 1, 1876; BFB to J. J. McDavitt, April 1, 1876; BFB to AA, April 1, 1876; all in box 215; Thomas J. Durant to BFB, April 3, 1876, and Richard S. Fay to BFB, April 7, 1876, both in folder 3, box 87; all in BP-LC.

20. PB to BFB, April 6, 1876, in folder 3; PB to BFB, March 16, 1876, in folder 1; PB to BFB, March 22, 1876, in folder 2; AA to BFB, April 7, 1876, in folder 3; all in box 87, BP-LC; Ames, *Chronicles from the Nineteenth Century*, 2:355–56; death certificate of SHB, April 8, 1876, in folder 3, box 87, BP-LC; *Boston Evening Journal*, April 8, 1876; BFB to Betsy M. Stevens, April 9, 1876, in box 215; GHB to BFB, February 1, 1876, in folder 3, box 86; BFB to GHB, February 2 and April 9, 1876; BFB to Joanna Butler, December 29, 1876; and BFB to Theodore Edson, April 10, 1876; all in box 215, BP-LC.

21. Mrs. H. S. Kimball to BFB, March 10, 1876 [clearly dated wrong], folder 1; Sidney DeKay to BFB, April 8, 1876, and Harriet Spofford to BFB, April 8, 1876, both in folder 3; all in box 87; BFB to Harriet Spofford, April 22, 1876, in box 215; GHB to BFB, April 13, 1876, and William P. Webster to BFB, April 25, 1876; both in folder 5, box 87; all in BP-LC; *Boston Evening Journal*, April 14, 1876; BFB to E. J. Sherman, April 22, 1876, and BFB to BBA, April 23, 1876, both in box 215, BP-LC.

22. BFB to AA, April 25, 1876, in Ames Family Papers; BBA to BFB, April 27, 1876, in folder 5, box 87, and May 6, 1876, in folder 1, box 88, BP-LC; Ames, *Chronicles from the Nineteenth Century*, 2:383, 394; BFB to Thomas J. Durant, September 1, 1876, and BFB to Lizzie N. Wheeler, September 3, 1876, both in box 216; BFB to W. S. McFarlane, April 18, 1876, and BFB to William Belknap, June 19, 1876; both in box 215; all in BP-LC.

In Benjamin Butler's papers the man referred to here appears virtually exclusively as "West." The 1880 US Census record identifies him as "Richard West" but also gives the name "Albert West," which appears on other official documents, such as the 1930 US Census record. For the most part, I, too, will simply call him

"West." West first appears in a letter from Blanche to Adelbert on September 9, 1876: "Butler is such a man that he is out with Jimmy or West the greater portion of the time" (Ames, *Chronicles from the Nineteenth Century*, 2:407). See also US Civil War Draft Registration Records, 1863–65. The 1830 US Census record for Albert West says he was born in Virginia, but other records say Kentucky. West himself may not have been certain about his place or date of birth.

23. Ames, *Chronicles from the Nineteenth Century*, 2:383–84.

24. Ames, 2:396, 407, 433–34.

25. BFB to James Buchanan, May 12, 1876, and BFB to W. A. Simmons, March 18, 1876, both in box 215; W. A. Simmons to BFB, March 16, 1876, in folder 1; and W. A. Simmons to BFB, March 20, 1876, in folder 2, both in box 87; all in BP-LC.

26. BFB to W. H. P. Wright, March 31, 1876 in box 215; BFB to Various Citizens, August 5, 1876, in box 216; T. F. Lee to BFB, August 21, 1876, and John Newell to BFB, September 21, 1876, both in folder 2, box 88; W. H. Clement to BFB, August 9, 1876, in folder 3, box 89; Jefferson Martin to BFB, August 26, 1876, in folder 4, box 89; all in BP-LC.

27. Ames, *Chronicles from the Nineteenth Century*, 2:401, 407, 438; Shugerman, "The Creation of the Department of Justice," 158.

28. BFB to Frederick Douglass Jr., October 11, 1876, in box 216; Frederick Douglass Jr. to BFB, October 14, 1876, in folder 1, box 91; BIB to BFB, May 1, 1876, in folder 1, box 88; BIB to BFB, July 24, 1876, in folder 2, box 89; BIB to BBA, August 21, 1876, in folder 3, box 89; all in BP-LC; Ames, *Chronicles from the Nineteenth Century*, 2:427.

29. John B. Demis to BFB, October 13, 1876, and George W. Putnam to BFB, October 11, 1876, both in folder 1, box 91; BFB to James E. Fuller, October 2, 1876; BFB to Phoebe Couzins, October 8, 1876; and BFB to T. B. Ross, October 10, 1876; all in box 216; all in BP-LC.

30. Butler, *Letter of General Benj. F. Butler to Hon. E. R. Hoar*; BFB to Reuben McFindley, October 11, 1876, in box 216; N. E. Chase to BFB, February 4, 1876, in folder 3, box 86; both in BP-LC.

31. Peter Parker to BFB, January 13, 1876, in folder 1; B. C. McCormack to BFB, January 15, 1876, and James Buchanan to BFB, January 26, 1876; both in folder 2; all in box 86; Alex Troup to BFB, March 11, 1876, in folder 1; and Charles Atwater to BFB, March 21, 1876, and Alex Troup to BFB, March 21, 1876, both in folder 2; all in box 87; all in BP-LC.

32. BFB to James Buchanan, February 2, 1876, in box 215; and BFB to Reuben McFindley, October 11, 1876, BFB to Henry T. Blackwell, September 7, 1876, and BFB to Phoebe Couzins, October 8, 1876; all in box 216; all in BP-LC.

33. Jonathan T. Averill to BFB, November 8, 1876; Henry A. Coffin to BFB, November 8, 1876; L. C. Bateman to BFB, November 8, 1876; C. L. Davis to BFB, November 8, 1876; and William Earnshaw to BFB, November 8, 1876 in folder 3; and Various to BFB, November 9, 1876, in folder 4; all in box 91, BP-LC.

34. S. P. Huskins to BFB, March 8, 1877, in folder 2, box 94; James O'Berne to BFB, November 8, 1876, in folder 3, box 91; James O'Brien to BFB, February 7, 1877,

in folder 5, box 93; N. N. Boydston to BFB, March 8, 1877, in folder 2, box 94; all in BP-LC.

35. James Brady to BFB, November 8, 1876, in folder 3, box 91, BP-LC.

36. B. F. Matthews to BFB, January 30, 1877, in folder 5, box 93; BFB to P. A. Summery, December 3, 1876, in box 216; both in BP-LC.

37. BFB to J. M. Stewart, February 14, 1877; BFB to Horace Maynard, January 3, 1877; BFB to William E. Chandler, January 4, 1877; all in box 217, BP-LC.

38. BFB to J. M. G. Parker, March 8, 1877, and BFB to James Parton, March 8, 1877, both in box 217; BFB to C. C. Merritt, October 9, 1877, and BFB to S. G. Wood, November 27, 1877; both in box 218; all in BP-LC.

39. W. H. Moor to BFB, January 10, 1877, and P. Merrill to BFB, April 12, 1877; both in folder 4, box 94; BFB to P. Merrill, April 24, 1877, in box 217; Joseph Hallowell to BFB, April 2, 1877, in folder 4, box 94; BFB to Joseph Hallowell, April 6, 1877, in box 217; Henry Adams to BFB, May 22, 1877, in folder 3, box 95; BFB to Henry Adams, October 17, 1877, in box 218; BFB to John L. Ruffin, July 14, 1878, in box 220; BFB to J. W. Wilbourn, December 15, 1877, and BFB to Richard S. Fay, November 25, 1877; both in box 218; William T. Sherman enclosed in J. Donald Cameron to BFB, February 21, 1877, in folder 1, box 94; all in BP-LC.

40. Joseph S. Norton to BFB, April 19, 1877, in folder 1, box 95; BFB to Roscoe Conkling, April 26, 1877, and BFB to Phoebe Couzins, May 1, 1877, both in box 217; Susan B. Anthony to BFB, January 1, 1877, in folder 4, box 93; Phoebe Couzins to BFB, May 19, 1877, in folder 3, box 95; E. Johnson et al. to BFB, March 13, 1877, in folder 2, box 94; all in BP-LC.

41. James Buchanan to BFB, March 7, 1877, in folder 2, box 94; James Buchanan to BFB, March 21, 1877, in folder 3, box 94; Joseph Breck to BFB, April 25, 1877, in folder 1, box 95; R. McAdam to BFB, May 7, 1877, in folder 2, box 95; H. C. Munson to BFB, October 12, 1877, in folder 1, box 97; George J. Campbell to BFB, October 15, 1877, in folder 2, box 97; George Crilly to BFB, May 3, 1877, in folder 1, box 95; all in BP-LC.

42. Elizabeth Van Lew to BFB, March 1, 1877, in folder 1, box 94; Mary Mumford to BFB, March 9, 1877, in folder 2, box 94; Mary Mumford to BFB, August 5, 1877, in folder 3, box 95; John M. Langston to BFB, March 6, 1877, in folder 2, box 94; and BFB to the widow of William Wallace Chisholm, January 2, 1878, in box 219; BFB to BIB, February 14, 1877, in box 217; BIB to BFB, February 18, 1877, in folder 1, box 94; BIB to BFB, April 1 and 8, 1877, in folder 4, box 94; all in BP-LC.

It bears noting that in *After the Glory*, historian Donald Shaffer suggests that Butler's "sympathy for African-American veterans" did not always play out in decisions he made for the service (139–40).

43. Flipper, *The Colored Cadet*, 251; BIB to BFB, January 14 and 19, 1878, in folder 1, box 104; BFB to BIB, February 6 and March 21, 1878, in box 219; BIB to BFB, April 8, 1878, in folder 4, box 106; all in BP-LC; Ames, *Chronicles from the Nineteenth Century*, 2:498.

Butler's own views on West Point are difficult to characterize or pin down. At times his bitterness over having been denied the opportunity to attend as a youth, and then having felt the sting of prejudice from West Pointers toward volunteer officers during the Civil War, seemed dominant. But he also sent his beloved son to the academy, used his seat in Congress to appoint others to attend, and enjoyed participating on the board of visitors when invited to do so. At best, one could argue that he saw the academy as a training ground for leaders who could bridge the gap between civic and military life. In February 1878, the *Army and Navy Journal* quoted him as saying that "West Point should stand between this country and a large standing Army; that in this way we should be training as great a number as possible of intelligent officers to the art of war, who would go into the business of life, after they got their training, outside of the Army, would acquire business habits, business thought, business energy and enterprise, and would be ready to spring to arms and form the nucleus of instruction of the volunteer force of the country whenever the country should need their services." Asked why he had sent Bennie to the academy, he replied, "Simply because it seems to me that in the next generation there will be war, as there has been in all past generations, and I want to stamp him with the patent of nobility, so that when he steps into war he shall not be looked down upon as a civil general or officer" (*Army and Navy Journal*, February 16 and 23, and May 25, 1878).

44. PB to BFB, February 1, 1877, in folder 5, box 93; PB to BFB, February 9, 1877, in folder 4, box 93; PB to BFB, February 22, 1877, in folder 1, box 94; BIB to BFB, April 8, 1877, in folder 4, box 94; BBA to BFB, June 19, 1878, in folder 5, box 108; BFB to AA, March 30 and April 24, 1877, in box 217; all in BP-LC; Ames, *Chronicles from the Nineteenth Century*, 2:447–48, 473, 489, 497.

In February 1878 some sort of accident occurred at the company, and it must be said that Benjamin Butler's response to the accident did not reflect him at his best. "I am sorry to hear of the sad accident at the Cartridge Company," he wrote to Charles A. Dimon, "but am glad to hear that it was no worse, and also that it was due to the carelessness of the operatives themselves. But see until they get well that they have the best care taken of them although the hurt was their own fault. Yet, being young people they are not so much to be blamed. I would make it imperative on your overseers to see to it that that cannot happen again" (BFB to Charles A. Dimon, February 13, 1878, in box 219, BP-LC).

45. BFB to GHB, October 10, 1877, in box 218; Joanna L. Butler to BFB, March 27, 1878, in folder 2, box 106; BFB to B. D. Whitney, March 1, 1878, in box 219; BFB to Joanna L. Butler, May 16, 1878, and BFB to GHB, June 30, both in box 220; all in BP-LC.

46. Herman Thomes to BFB, August 27, 1877, in folder 3, box 96; BFB to James Buchanan, October 17, 1877, in box 218; James Buchanan to BFB, October 19, 1877, in folder 2, box 97; all in BP-LC.

It is difficult to know what to make of Butler's July 23, 1877, letter to railroad magnate Jay Gould, whom he seemed to be trying to protect from the consequences of the uprising. "I telegraphed you this morning early in the hope that your whole troubles would be over," Butler wrote to Gould on July 23. "But assuming they are not I have been thinking that a gentleman with as many and various interests as you have better not come into personal conflict with these discontented men, and that therefore you had better be away in case of trouble. . . . Your lieutenants and executive officers can do anything required. . . . Hadn't you better be away if there is a row?" (BFB to Jay Gould, July 23, 1877, in box 218, BP-LC.)

47. Norgren, *Belva Lockwood*, 76.

48. Cornelius O'Donnell to BFB, January 17, 1878; T. J. Moore to BFB, January 18, 1878; William G. Kyte to BFB, January 22, 1878; all in folder 1, box 104; Various to BFB, February 7, 1878, in folder 3, box 104; and BFB to David Wilder, February 22, 1878, in box 219; all in BP-LC.

49. Robert Hansen to BFB, February 1, 1878, and William T. Biddle to BFB, February 4, 1878, both in folder 3, box 104; A. B. Lind to BFB, June 21, 1878, in folder 5, box 108; BFB to F. P. Wood, February 6, 1878, in box 219; all in BP-LC.

50. BFB to F. P. Wood, February 25, 1878, and BFB to James M. Caller, February 5, 1878, both in box 219, BP-LC.

51. C. A. Trundy to BFB, May 27, 1878, and A. H. Dooley to BFB, May 28, 1878, in folder 1; N. A. Plympton to BFB, June 7, 1878, in folder 3; James Springer to BFB, June 18, 1878, in folder 5; Henry Finnegas to BFB, June 21, 1878, in folder 5; all in box 108; BFB to L. R. Train, March 23, 1878, in box 219; N. L. Pratt to BFB, October 18, 1878, in folder 2, box 112; all in BP-LC.

52. Janney, *Remembering the Civil War*, 128; J. W. Pearman to BFB, April 14, 1878, in folder 4, box 106; BFB to AA, April 15, 1878, and BFB to J. C. Hemphill, April 24, 1878; both in box 219; all in BP-LC.

53. Butler, *Honors Due the Private Soldier*, 10; *Cleveland Plain Dealer*, May 30, 1878; *Boston Daily Advertiser*, May 31, 1878.

54. Ames, *Chronicles from the Nineteenth Century*, 2:499; BFB to R. M. Balch, March 8, 1879, in box 221, in BP-LC; Goldsmith, *Other Powers*, 432; Gallman, *America's Joan of Arc*, 150; Chester, *Embattled Maiden*, 194–97.

55. *Boston Globe*, January 11, 1893; BFB to William D. Northend, January 29, 1878; BFB to C. C. Merritt, April 1, 1878; and BFB to E. A. Olleman, March 18, 1878, all in box 219; BFB to J. A. Tower, June 4, 1878, in box 220; BFB to Eli Terry, December 15, 1877, in box 218; Peter Finnegan to BFB, October 21, 1878, in folder 2, box 112; BFB to C. C. Merritt, August 1, 1878; BFB to John J. Moore, August 14, 1878; BFB to Sumner I. Parker, August 17, 1878; BFB to Editor, *Boston Herald*, August 1, 1878; BFB to Henry M. Cross, August 21, 1878; BFB to T. C Gilman, November 27, 1878; all in box 220; all in BP-LC.

In truth, Butler's enduring concerns about the rights of Black Americans did not seem to extend quite so reliably to the Chinese, either in the United States or at home in China. When a correspondent in March 1878 requested that he use his influence to get Congress to help those who were suffering from famine in China, he offered sympathy but noted that Americans' suffering was his primary concern (BFB to L. Holmes, March 20, 1878, in box 219, BP-LC). In March 1879, however, Butler wrote to a Mrs. H. S. Dickerman of Holyoke, Massachusetts, "My proposition in this regard is this, that this country should be the home and recipient of every man from every nation who by his own volition enterprise and love of our institutions and civilization makes his home here; that such men are the source of our greatest power, prosperity and future wealth; that all imported labor of every description where men are brought here by contract or sent here by their government to get rid of them for their crime, are a source of weakness, against the policy of our institutions, and their importation under contract of any description whatever may and does to the extent it is permitted nullify all our tariff for the protection of labor upon which alone can a tariff or protection be defended" (BFB to Mrs. H. S. Dickerman, March 10, 1879, in box 221, in BP-LC). Notably, when Dickerman contacted Butler again in January 1881 asking him if he was willing to take a young Chinese man into his office as a law student, he agreed to do so (Mrs. H. R. Dickerman to BFB, January 26, 1881, in folder 1, box 127, BP-LC).

56. *Lowell (Mass.) Daily Citizen and News*, November 5, 1879; William P. Buckley to BFB, November 6, 1878; Frederick Robinson to BFB, November [date unknown], 1878; Charles A. Linn to BFB, November 1, 1878; Charles O. Swift to BFB, November 4, 1878; and Eugene Beebe to BFB, November 6, 1878, all in folder 4, box 112, BP-LC.

57. BFB to S. B. Chittenden, February 13, 1879, in box 221, BP-LC; Butler, *Remarks of the Honorable Benjamin F. Butler*, 3; BFB to PB, February 13, 1879, in box 221, and BFB to Sidney Webster, June 26, 1879, both in box 221, BP-LC.

58. Burnham Wardwell to BFB, May 30, 1879, and W. H. Hines to BFB, August 1, 1879, both in folder 2; John K. Tarbox to BFB, September 23, 1879, in folder 4; all in box 120, BP-LC. One particularly negative pamphlet that appeared during this campaign promised to expose the "incorrigible candidate" for "what he is, and not for what he claims to be." See *Butler's Record* (1879), BP-C.

59. BFB to Roger A. Pryor, August 3, 1880, in box 222, BP-LC; Ames, *Chronicles from the Nineteenth Century*, 2:520.

60. BFB to Thomas Edison, July 8, 1880, in box 222, BP-LC; Butler, *Argument of Benjamin F. Butler*; Ames, *Chronicles from the Nineteenth Century*, 2:503; BFB to Joanna L. Butler, November 20, 1880, box 222; BFB to Elizabeth Van Lew, April 4, 1882, in box 223; Susan Dickinson to BFB, October 1, 1882, in folder 1, box 127; BFB to T. E. Balch, December 6, 1880, in box 222; all in BP-LC.

"I have yours containing a request for a donation for the benefit of Colby University," Butler wrote to T. E. Balch in December 1880. "I was educated at Waterville College and I held my Alma Mater in as much reverence as any alumnus could. Within two years after I graduated I subscribed towards the wants of the College a sum equal to one-fifth of my entire income, although that was not a large one. I made some other small donations to the College. Some years afterwards the management sold for a very insignificant sum the college, so far as its name was concerned, for a subscription of an insignificant amount which served as an advertisement for the gentleman who gave the money who was not a graduate, while many of its poorer graduates had given the college a much larger sum in proportion to their means. From that time to the present my interest has ceased in Colby University" (BFB to T. E. Balch, December 6, 1880, in box 222, BP-LC). Less than a decade later, in 1889, as will be seen, Butler seems to have softened on his stance, returning to Colby to give the graduation address and deliver his massive portrait to its keeping.

Adelbert Ames Jr. was born on August 19, 1880.

61. Ames, *Chronicles from the Nineteenth Century*, 2:516–17, 522–23, 525–26; BFB to Simon Cameron, January 18, 1881, and BFB to Jay Gould, January 28, 1881, in box 222, in BP-LC. At the time of his death in 1893, the *Boston Globe* reported that Butler finally gave up smoking in the fall of 1882, after he "confided to his private secretary that he thought the habit of smoking had grown on him too strongly, and he was beginning to think that his will might be weakening" (*Boston Globe*, January 11, 1893).

62. Ames, *Chronicles from the Nineteenth Century*, 2:527, 529.

63. BFB to Sidney Webster, September 3, 1881; BFB to Wilson Strong, September 9, 1881; BFB to Frank Blair, September 23, 1881; BFB to Miss Josephine Chestney, December 27, 1881; all in box 222; Sidney Webster to BFB, September 3, 1881; Frank Blair to BFB, October 12, 1881; James Parton to BFB, September 8, 1881; Sidney DeKay to BFB, September 15, 1881, all in folder 3, box 126; all in BP-LC; Ames, *Chronicles from the Nineteenth Century*, 2:533.

64. BFB to John Russell Young, April 12, 1882, in box 223; BFB to Wendell Phillips, April 19, 1882, in folder 1, box 127; BFB to Frank H. Clarker, September 10, 1882, in box 223; all in BP-LC; Phoebe Couzins to BFB, September 21, 1882, BP-C.

65. BFB to J. D. Foster, October 16, 1882, and BFB to William B. Berry, September 26 and October 15, 1882; all in box 223, BP-LC.

66. *Massachusetts Spy*, November 8, 1882; BFB to Sisters of the Visitation of Georgetown, November 21, 1882; BFB to Frank Blair, September 24 and November 22, 1882; BFB to William H. Hunt, March 26, 1882; all in box 223, BP-LC.

CHAPTER 8

1. Butler, *Butler's Book*, 969; *Albany (N.Y.) Evening Post*, January 4, 1883; Roger A. Pryor to Benjamin Franklin Butler (hereafter BFB), January 5, 1883, in folder 2, box 127, Benjamin F. Butler Papers, Library of Congress, Washington, D.C. (hereafter BP-LC).

The governorship was a one-year term. Butler's term lasted from January 4, 1883, to January 3, 1884. The Massachusetts governor, Butler noted in his autobiography, "can nominate officers, but those officers cannot serve until the appointments are agreed to by an executive council of nine. . . . The governor cannot even pardon an innocent man out of the State prison except by the advice and consent of the council" (Butler, *Butler's Book*, 969).

2. *Massachusetts Spy*, January 30, 1883; Butler, *Argument before the Tewksbury Investigation Committee*, 3. Butler testified that "this tanning and use of human skins has come to be an industry," and sometimes involved the production of shoes and slippers for wealthy patrons. "What do you suppose people want of them?" Butler asked. "Well, there are old men and young men of jaded passions, worn out prematurely by their vices, and if they can put their feet in slippers made from

a woman's breast, perhaps they can feed their imaginations" (Butler, *Argument before the Tewksbury Investigation Committee*, 3).

3. Butler, *Argument before the Tewksbury Investigation Committee*, 21, 41; Blanche Butler Ames (hereafter BBA) to BFB, May 4, 1883, and N. W. Packard to BFB, April 10, 1883, both in folder 5, box 127, BP-LC. Among Tewksbury's most famous residents was Anne Sullivan, who lived there from 1876 to 1880 and later went on to become Helen Keller's teacher.

4. Butler, *Argument before the Tewksbury Investigation Committee*, 41, 42; Leonard, *The Present Condition of Tewksbury*, 5–14.

5. Butler, *Butler's Book*, 976; D. C. G. Field to Benjamin F. Butler, July 5, 1883, in folder 1, box 128, BP-LC; *Springfield (Mass.) Daily Republican*, June 1 and 2, 1883.

6. Butler, *Butler's Book*, 976; Edward Page to BFB, June 4, 1883; Thomas A. Pearson to BFB, June 28, 1883; and BFB to BBA, June 29, 1883; all in folder 7, box 127, BP-LC; Ames, *Chronicles from the Nineteenth Century*, 2:541.

7. In his autobiography, Butler noted that early in his tenure as governor, he did succeed in appointing the first Irish Catholic judge to the bench in Massachusetts, M. J. McCafferty (Butler, *Butler's Book*, 975; *New York Times*, January 18, 1883).

8. Frederick Douglass to George L. Ruffin, November 27, 1883, in folder 3, box 1; speech of George W. Williams, November 21, 1883, quoted in undated article from the *Boston Transcript*, in folder 3, box 3; both in the Heslip-Ruffin Family Papers. Descriptive material in Heslip-Ruffin Family Papers indicates that Ruffin was the descendant of slaves. But other material in the collection, including an excerpt from *Men of Mark*, says that he was "born of free parents." Of course, both things may be true, if his parents became free before he was born. Ruffin's wife was the great antislavery, civil rights, and women's rights activist and journalist, Josephine St. Pierre Ruffin.

9. Kantrowitz, *More than Freedom*, 405–6; Butler, *Butler's Book*, 974; excerpt from Simmons and Turner, *Men of Mark*, in folder 1, box 1; clipping from the *Hampton Institute Alumni Magazine*, January 1884, in folder 3, box 3; "Judge of the Charlestown District Court," unidentified newspaper clipping, November 23, 1886, in folder 10, box 1; all in Heslip-Ruffin Family Papers.

10. Butler, *Butler's Book*, 981; undated clipping from the *Essex Statesman* (Salem, Mass.), folder 5; and J. Edwards Brooks to BFB, October 4, 1883, in folder 4; both in box 128, BP-LC.

11. Butler, *Butler's Book*, 981; undated clipping from the *Essex Statesman*, folder 5; Franklin B. Parse to BFB, September 13, 1883, in folder 3; and D. E. Potter to BFB, December 31, 1883, in folder 5; all in box 128, BP-LC.

12. R. H. Shadrick to BFB, April 27, 1884; J. F. Thompson to BFB, May 8, 1884; John W. Seymour to BFB, May 29, 1884, all in Benjamin F. Butler Papers, Archives and Special Collections, Colby College, Waterville, Maine (hereafter BP-C); W. W. Servos to BFB, January 30, 1883, in folder 2, box 127; Phoebe Couzins to BFB, November 22, 1883, in folder 5, box 128; Susan B. Anthony to BFB, January 28, 1884, in folder 6, box 129; all in BP-LC.

"In Boston, where I resided until 1855," wrote Seymour, "I was a Free-Soil Whig, and ever since, a Republican. Then, you were a pro-slavery Democrat, and I hated you . . . but from the hour you initiated the magic word 'Contraband!' you became my hero. When you commanded in New Orleans, I was still further delighted. But, also, when in 1864 *your mere presence* in New York subdued the Copperheads and gave us the most peaceable election ever held in this city, I was enthralled" (John W. Seymour to BFB, May 29, 1884, in BP-C).

13. *Puck*, May 9, July 18, August 1, October 3, and December 26, 1883; Leonard, *Yankee Women.*

14. BFB to Seldon Fish, May 17, 1883, in Benjamin F. Butler Letters, Boston Public Library; BFB to Albert H. Donnell, January 25, 1884, in box 225; clipping from *American Sentry*, January 17, 1884, in folder 5, box 129; both in BP-LC; A. P. Elder to BFB, February 20, 1884; Frank M. Shoukwiler to BFB, April 17, 1884; J. F. Thompson to BFB, May 8, 1884; Patrick Elliott to BFB, May 14, 1884; Annie M. Upton to BFB, January 13, 1884; David Victor to BFB, March 16, 1884; Richard Tharp to BFB, June 16, 1884; Fred Tower to BFB, August 13, 1884; all in BP-C.

15. Walter Shupe to BFB, January 6, 1884; and Patrick H. Coney to BFB, January 9, 1884; both in folder 2, box 129, BP-LC.

In mid-February 1884 a supporter in New York City declared that the two major parties had become "very much like old 'buck and berry,' two old oxen that I used to drive when a boy." Buck and Berry, C. H. Pollock continued, "instead of pulling together and going straight forward, were either pulling or pushing each other all over the road," with the result that they had to travel "twice as many miles to reach a given point as they would have done if they had each pulled straight ahead," and also ended up being exhausted long before they reached their destination. "You," Pollock insisted, "are the only man that can drive our modern 'buck and berry' team," because Butler was virtually independent of either party and could instead bring together "the best men of both parties and draft us a platform that all can unite on" (C. H. Pollock to BFB, February 18, 1884, in folder 4, box 130, BP-LC).

16. W. J. S. Bowe to BFB, February 3, 1884, in folder 1; Robert J. Smith to BFB, February 14, 1884, in folder 3; both in box 130; BFB to John W. Seymour, June 5, 1884; and BFB to John W. A. Shaw, June 7, 1884; both in box 225; all in BP-LC.

17. Frederic Egner to BFB, July 8, 1884, in BP-C; BFB to C. H. Hanson, January 29, 1884, and BFB to P. M. Clark, January 29, 1884, in box 225, BP-LC. Butler added in his letter to Clark, "Having lived for nearly a quarter of a century under the microscopic investigation of bitter enemies of every act of mine, public and private, I am yet permitted to walk the streets without any molestation save the senseless clamor of the Satanic portions of the newspaper press which, seeing my opportunities for wrong-doing, and knowing that they could not have resisted the temptation to do wrong if they had been in my place, they naturally believe that I did as they would have done. Scales can only weigh to the extent to which they are adapted, and you can't weigh a load of hay on a fishmonger's scales."

18. J. R. Dodds to BFB, February 5, 1884, in folder 1, box 130; BFB to B. F. Shively, March 12, 1884; BFB to Frank H. Rose, March 25, 1884; and BFB to James Lewis, March 14, 1884; all in box 225; all in BP-LC.

19. BFB to P. M. Clark, January 29, 1884, and BFB to William D. Fuller, March 12, 1884, in box 225, BP-LC.

20. George Hewston to BFB, May 15, 1884, in folder 2, box 133; BFB to P. S. Dorney and W. H. Gagan, June 12, 1884, in box 225; both in BP-LC.

21. Clipping from *The Sun*, May 30, 1884, in folder 4, box 133, BP-LC; John R. Winston to BFB, June 11, 1884; Francis Smith to BFB, June 19, 1884; Mrs. A. Elmare to BFB, June 23, 1884; all in BP-C; M. J. Garrett to BFB, May 12, 1884, in folder 2, box 133, BP-LC.

22. Edward Ewald to BFB, July 4, 1884, in BP-C.

23. J. W. Elder to BFB, June 13, 1884; undated letter to the editor of the *Boston Globe* from H. Parks; both in BP-C.

24. T. W. Bartley to BFB, May 2, 1884, in folder 4, box 132, BP-LC; Arthur Vinette to BFB, July 3, 1884, in BP-C; *Dover (N.H.) Daily Republican*, July 3, 1884. No fan of Butler's, the paper predicted that Butler would deploy "his vast knowledge of political chicanery," his "utmost unscrupulousness," and his "enthusiastic and devoted followers" to bring the Democratic Party down.

25. *Detroit Evening Journal*, May 19, 1884; T. W. Bartley to BFB, May 15, 1884, and L. Curtis to BFB, May 13, 1884, both in folder 2, box 133; BFB to Henry Barnard, July 21, 1884; and undated statement of BFB on Cleveland, early August 1884; both in box 225; all in BP-LC. Butler, *Butler's Book*, 981–82.

26. BFB to Henry Barnard, July 21, 1884; undated statement of BFB on Cleveland, early August 1884; BFB to Nathaniel Hinckley, November 24, 1884; BFB to Thomas Y. Berry, July 22, 1884; all in box 225, BP-LC.

27. BFB to Charles A. Dana, August 6, 1884; BFB to John E. Barrett, August 31, 1884; BFB to E. V. Clements, August 23, 1884; and BFB to John F. Wallis, August 27, 1884; all in box 225, BP-LC. James S. H. Umsted to BFB, August 24, 1884; Thomas E. Thompson to BFB, July 14, 1884; Charles R. Everson to BFB, July 15, 1884; Frederick William Schwarz to BFB, July 18, 1884; Sam R. Tilton to BFB, July 28, 1883; and B. F. Schmeckpeper to BFB, undated; all in BP-C. Butler, *Butler's Book*, 982–83. In his letter to Butler, Schmeckpeper noted that he was seventeen years old.

28. BFB to Charles E. Buell, August 25, 1884, and BFB to Thomas Gonley, April 21, 1884, both in box 225, BP-LC.

29. S. M. Surrette to BFB, September 30, 1884, in BP-C; Ames, *Chronicles from the Nineteenth Century*, 2:544–45.

30. *Boston Globe*, January 17, 1883.

31. *National Review*, November 8, 1884; *Puck*, August 12, 1884; Norgren, *Belva Lockwood*, 140; Butler, *Butler's Book*, 983–84.

32. "An Independent Republican" to BFB, November 10, 1884, in folder 2, and Ira E. Perkins to BFB, November 6, 1884, in folder 1; both in box 142; BFB to Ira E. Perkins, November 24, 1884, in box 225; all in BP-LC.

33. B. W. Goodhue to BFB, November 5, 1884, in folder 1; B. F. Schmeckpeper to BFB, November 10, 1884, in folder 2; F. O. Willey to W. A. Fowler, November 7, 1884, in folder 1; all in box 142, BP-LC; BBA to BFB, November 10, 1884, in BP-C.

34. Cary, "A Dozen Ben Butler Letters," 494; Butler, *Butler's Book*, 983–84; L. G.

McDonald to BFB, November 5, 1884; Theodore Bourne to BFB, November 5, 1884; and John C. Risteen to BFB, November 5, 1884; all in folder 1, box 142, BP-LC; H. W. Eaton to BFB, November 22, 1884, in BP-C; BFB to William M. Green, November 24, 1884, in box 225, BP-LC.

35. BFB to W. H. P. Wright, August 12, 1886, in box 235; Stephen M. Allen to BFB, May 30, 1887, in folder 1, box 155; Frank Lanning to BFB, November 1, 1888, in folder 3, box 155; BFB to Thomas L. Bond, May 22, 1891, in box 251; all in BP-LC.

36. Susan B. Anthony to BFB, December 14, 1882, and Phoebe Couzins to BFB, December 22, 1882, both in folder 1, box 127; Susan B. Anthony to BFB, January 7, 1889, in folder 1, box 156; all in BP-LC.

37. BFB to P. Henry Dugro, June 23, 1885, in box 230, BP-LC; Henry C. Baldwin to BFB, April 20, 1885, in BP-C; clipping from unidentified newspaper, September 1, 1888, in folder 3, box 155; Mary Ann Riley to BFB, January 4, 1889, in folder 1, box 156; Bernard O'Kane to BFB, February 3, 1892, in folder 4, box 164; BFB to T. C. Quinn, May 26, 1890, in box 248; all in BP-LC.

38. M. A. Sawtelle to BFB, March 26, 1884, and April 15, 1885; and BFB to A. Baldwin, June 25, 1885; all in BP-C; Ames, *Chronicles from the Nineteenth Century*, 2:576, 580; Ysuff Mirza Khan to BFB, November 7, 1884, in BP-C; BFB to H. C. Gardiner, April 21, 1884, in box 225; BFB to William Walcott Astor, April 2, 1887, and BFB to William Walcott Astor, April 2, 1887; BFB to Henry A. Hills, April 25, 1887; and BFB to Merrill R. Erskine, May 13, 1887; all in box 239, in BP-LC; BFB to Charles A. Dana, April 13, 1887, in BP-C; BFB to Whitelaw Reid, January 11, 1888, in *Bound Correspondence*, vol. 2, BP-C; BFB to L. F. Parker, August 25, 1884, in box 225, BP-LC; James H. Young to BFB, January 5 and 8, 1884, in BP-C; BFB to F. N. Oxley, May 17, 1886, in box 234, BP-LC.

39. BFB to O. P. G. Clarke, February 19, 1885, in box 227, BP-LC; Mrs. R. L. Bennett to BFB, February 2, 1885; Charles L. Stewart to BFB, February 21, 1885; Anna Maria Sprague to BFB, March 25, 1885; Louis M. Braunlich to BFB, April 22, 1885; Harriet E. Snow to BFB, April 22, 1885; Rev. F. G. Bingley to BFB, April 24, 1885; all BP-C; BFB to Hugh L. Bond, June 25, 1887, in box 240; BFB to Agnes Van Zandt, January 27, 1887, in box 237; both in BP-LC.

40. C. Watson to BFB, November 23, 1887, in folder 1, box 155; BFB to Roger A. Pryor, October 13, 1887; BFB to Agnes Van Zandt, October 13, 1887; BFB to George A. Schilling, October 13, 1887; BFB to W. P. Black, November 3, 1887; BFB to J. C. Bancroft Davis, November 4, 1887; and BFB to George A. Schilling, December 19, 1887; all in box 241, BP-LC.

41. BFB to E. H. Den Kyne, March 1, 1890; BFB to New York City editor of a newspaper known as *The Voice*, March 26, 1890; BFB to W. M. Evans, May 20, 1890; BFB to Mrs. J. Reynolds, April 17, 1890; all in box 248; BFB to F. A. Strong, March 8, 1892, in box 253; all in BP-LC; *Puck*, August 27, 1890.

42. BFB to Charlotte Stevens, December 19, 1887, in box 241; BFB to Harriet H. H. Dunn, July 27, 1887, in box 240; BFB to Harriet H. H. Dunn, July 17, 1885, in box 230; Charlotte Stevens to BFB, May 3, 1891, in folder 1, box 160; Betsey Stevens to BFB, January 22, 1884, in folder 5, box 129; Betsey Stevens to BFB, March 23, 1884,

in folder 3, box 131; BFB to Betsey Stevens, February 27, 1887, in box 238; BFB to Betsey M. Stevens, February [date unknown], 1885, in box 227; BFB to Betsey M. Stevens, February 19, 1892, in box 253; Thomas Stevens to BFB, January 8, 1892, in folder 1, box 164; BFB to Charlotte Stevens, January 7, 1892, in box 253; BFB to Betsey Stevens, February 2, 1892, in box 253; BFB to Harriet H. H. Dunn, July 27, 1887, in box 240; all in BP-LC.

43. BFB to John Cassels, May 20, 1883, in Benjamin F. Butler Letters, Boston Public Library; BFB to George H. Butler (hereafter GHB), June 3, 1884, in box 225; BFB to T. I. Creamer, September 1, 1885, in box 231; BFB to Joanna L. Butler, November 12, 1885, in box 232; all in BP-LC; Joanna Butler to BFB, January 9, March 6, May 14, August 5, 1885; BFB to Joanna Butler, August 15, 1885; all in BP-C; BFB to GHB, February 8, 1886; and BFB to Joanna L. Butler, April 5, 1886; both in box 233; BFB to GHB, May 3, 1886; BFB to Joanna L. Butler, May 12 and 16, 1886; and BFB to J. H. Alexander, May 21, 1886; all in box 234, BP-LC.

44. BBA to BFB, March 4, November 6, December 9 and 31, 1888, in folder 3, box 155; BBA to BFB, May 4, 1883, in folder 5, box 127; BBA to BFB, June 29, 1888, in folder 2, box 155; BFB to BBA, August 15, 1887, in box 240; BBA to BFB, January [date unknown] and February 6, 1888, in folder 3, box 155; BBA to BFB, August 7, 1887, in folder 1, box 155; Butler Ames to BFB, September 14 and 26, 1888, in folder 3, box 155; all in BP-LC; BFB to Peter S. Michie, July 10, 1889, in BP-C; Ames, *Chronicles from the Nineteenth Century*, 2:561, 584.

Butler's affection for Blanche and her family at one point even led him to inquire whether he should use whatever political influence remained to him to try and procure for them a diplomatic post abroad where their younger children could also benefit, as he believed Bennie and Paul had done by studying in Germany decades earlier (Ames, *Chronicles from the Nineteenth Century*, 2:577).

45. Ames, *Chronicles from the Nineteenth Century*, 2:584; BFB to Hattie H. H. Dunn, July 17, 1885, in box 230; BFB to A. Thorndike Rice, August 19, 1885, in box 231; BFB to Charlotte B. Stevens, August 12, 1892, in box 254; BFB to BBA August 15, 1887, in box 240; BBA to BFB, August 7, 1887, in folder 1, box 155; all in BP-LC; Chester, *Embattled Maiden*, 232–33, 235–37; Gallman, *America's Joan of Arc*, 169, 173, 177, 184, 189–90; Susan E. Dickinson to BFB, January 12, 1891, in folder 4, box 160, BP-LC.

46. *Colby Echo*, February 8 and June 14, 1889; Mrs. J. B. Foster to BFB, December 9, 1889, in folder 5, box 156, BP-LC; Butler, *Dissertation Delivered before the Alumni of Colby University*.

47. *Boston Globe*, January 11, 1893; BFB to Charles A. Dana, August 7, 1885, in box 231; George W. Arnold to BFB, November 10, 1884, in folder 2, box 142; BFB to R. E. Bartlett, April 25, 1887, in box 239; Luther Stephenson to BFB, May 7, 1891, in folder 1, box 160; Willard H. Mallalieu to BFB, January 5, 1892, in folder 1, box 164; BFB to Willard F. Mallalieu, January 13, 1892, in box 253; all in BP-LC.

48. Janney, *Remembering the Civil War*, 175; Porter, *Incidents and Anecdotes of the Civil War*, 71–73, 262, 269, 273; George H. Bethard to BFB, March 11, 1885, in BP-C; *Cleveland Plain Dealer*, May 7, 1889; *Wheeling (W.Va.) Register*, May 13, 1889.

49. H. S. Brooks to BFB, March 17, 1885, in BP-C; BFB to J. P. Etheridge, September 2, 1885, in box 231, BP-LC.

50. BFB to Misses Emma L. Hays and May Thompson, November 16, 1885, in box 232, BP-LC.

51. BFB to Marion Twiggs Myers, September 21, 1886, in box 235; BFB to Lanier Dunn, June 24, 1887, in box 240; BFB to W. J. Wilbur, January 2, 1886, in box 232; all in BP-LC; BBA to BFB, November 16, 1888, in folder 3, box 155; BFB to William J. Betts, January 1, 1884, in box 225; all in BP-LC; Joseph A. Titus to BFB, June 23, 1884, in BP-C; Butler, *Butler's Book*, 985.

To the question about how much he slept each night, Butler replied, "About seven hours. Besides, the moment I am relieved from business or occupation I go to sleep and sleep an hour or more as the case may be. I ride from my house to the office, about twenty-five miles, three quarters of an hour, and I sleep more than one-half of the time in the car. That is true when I travel far. . . . I have no regularity in taking noon naps, although I sleep in the day time when I have nothing else to do. . . . I never took a sleeping draught in my life. I go to bed and if I am not asleep in five minutes I take a book and read, and then I am asleep in 99 cases in 100 in ten minutes. I then sleep about five to five and a half hours, it makes but little difference what time I go to bed. I then wake up, turn out, take a turn or two about my room, usually look out of the window to see what the wind and weather is, get a fair air bath, and then turn in and go to sleep again in five minutes, and usually sleep two hours. Then I wake up and read an hour or two or whatever time I have before I want to get up. . . . If I dine at six and go to bed at half past ten I want nothing more in my stomach. If I dine at six and go to bed at twelve I want a light supper. A full stomach keeps me partially awake, so that I dream. . . . I sleep everywhere, and have slept on horseback. . . . I take exercise when I conveniently can and go without it when I can't" (BFB to W. J. Wilbur, January 2, 1886, in box 232, BP-LC). One almost wonders if he was making fun of the inquirer!

52. BFB to John C. Rand, May 29, 1890, in box 248, BP-LC; Butler, *Butler's Book*, 985; Ames, *Chronicles from the Nineteenth Century*, 2:588; BFB to Herbert P. Jefferson, January 1, 1892; BFB to A. E. Pillsbury, February 13, 1892; BFB to Betsey Stevens, February 2, 1892; BFB to Frank H. Clark, March 10, 1892; "A Critic of Butler's Book Criticized"; all in box 253, BP-LC.

For contemporary reviews of the book, see, for example, *Daily Inter Ocean* (Chicago), January 30, 1892; *St. Louis Republic*, January 31, 1892; and *Oregonian*, February 7, 1892.

53. BFB to Blanton Duncan, June 27, 1892; BFB to William Mahone, May 21, 1892; both in box 254, BP-LC; *Harper's Weekly*, January 21, 1893; *Philadelphia Inquirer*, September 20, 1892; *Boston Daily Journal*, September 21, 1892.

In the spring of 1892, likely in response to the recent passage of the Geary Act, which had extended the Chinese Exclusion Act, Butler did evince a lingering interest in questions pertaining to US-China relations. "I agree with you that China has been used by us most shamefully," he wrote to John Russell Young in May, "and she is entitled to make such retaliation as will bring us to our senses and will be adequate to the vindication of her own honor without being acts of war on her part." Butler conceded that China had the right to "exclude all Americans from her borders, sending them away in good order and condition, and especially those who are seeking to establish religions inconsistent with that of the Empire" (BFB to John Russell Young, May 18, 1892, in box 254, BP-LC).

54. BFB to Joanna L. Butler, February 27, 1887; BFB to Betsey Stevens, February 27, 1887; BFB to O. D. Barrett, March 3, 1887; all in box 238, BP-LC; BFB to O. D. Barrett, February 26, 1887, and BFB to "My dear Bate," February 26, 1887, in *Bound Correspondence,* vol. 2, BP-C; Phoebe Couzins to BFB, February 28, 1887; John L. Greene to Mrs. H. A. R. Faye, February 1, 1888, in *Bound Correspondence,* vol. 2, BP-C; Phoebe Couzins to BFB, February 23, 1890; BFB to Phoebe Couzins, March 1 and May 5, 1890, in box 248, BP-LC; Ames, *Chronicles from the Nineteenth Century,* 2:583.

Couzins, a Republican, continued to hope that Butler would return to the party someday (Phoebe Couzins to BFB, March 11, 1889, in BP-C). Couzins also sought Butler out in connection with her appointment (later revoked because she was too outspoken) as one of the "lady managers" for the 1893 Chicago World's Fair Commission (Phoebe Couzins to BFB, October 25 and December 26, 1890, in BP-C; *New York Times,* April 16, 1891).

55. C. B. Dubois to BFB, January 1, 1893, in folder 1, box 163; BFB to Charlotte B. Stevens, January 3, 1893; BFB to Messrs. Galvin Brothers, January 3, 1893; BFB to Betsey Stevens, January 4, 1893; BFB to Paul Butler (hereafter PB), January 7, 1893; all in box 254, BP-LC.

56. *Washington Star,* January 12, 1893; "General Butler Dead," unidentified newspaper clipping, January 11, 1893, in BP-C; *Boston Globe,* January 11 and 17, 1893; *Boston Globe,* January 17, 1893.

57. W. H. Chase to Adelbert Ames, January 11, 1893, in folder 4, box 2, BP-LC; *Boston Globe,* January 11 and 17, 1893; *Boston Journal,* January 11, 1893; Lanier Dunn to PB, January 11, 1893, box 172, in BP-LC.

58. *Boston Globe,* January 11, 1893; *Daily Inter Ocean* (Chicago), January 11, 1893; *Boise Statesman,* January 11, 1893; *Boston Daily Journal,* January 11, 1893; *Jackson (Mich.) Daily Citizen,* January 11, 1893; *Aberdeen (S.D.) Daily News,* January 11, 1893; *Kansas City Star,* January 11, 1893.

59. *Indianapolis Freeman,* January 21, 1893; *Detroit Plaindealer,* January 20 and 27, 1893; *Parsons (Kans.) Weekly Blade,* January 21, 1893; *Washington Bee,* January 28, 1893. The *Torchlight* quote appears in the January 20 *Detroit Plaindealer* article.

60. *Sacramento Record-Union,* January 11, 1893; *Boston Globe,* January 11 and 14, 1893; *Washington Star,* January 14, 1893.

61. Formal announcement by Colonel Charles A. R. Dimon, GAR Post #42, January 12, 1893, in folder 4, box 2, BP-LC; *Washington Star,* January 12, 1893; *Washington Star,* January 13, 1893; *Boston Journal,* January 17, 1893; *Boston Globe,* January 11, 1893.

62. *Washington Star,* January 13, 1893; Massachusetts, State and Federal Naturalization Records, 1798–1950, for Edward H. Gannon.

63. *Boston Globe*, January 14 and 16, 1893; *Boston Journal*, January 16 and 17, 1893; *Washington Star*, January 14, 1893.

64. Edward Everett Brown to Colonel Charles A. R. Dimon, January 13, 1893; "Colored Citizens" of Newport, Rhode Island, to the Butler family, January 24, 1893; document listing the carriages for the burial escort; all in folder 4, box 2, BP-LC; *Boston Journal*, January 17, 1893.

West remained in Lowell for decades after Butler's death. Lowell City Directories and census records indicate that he stayed on with the family as a coachman and valet. The 1934 City Directory citation for Albert West in Lowell says he died on March 4, 1933.

65. *A Memorial of Benjamin F. Butler*, 21, 26, 29, 30, 43, 44, 46.

Bibliography

ARCHIVAL MATERIALS

Ames/Butler/Plimpton Families Collection, Ames Mansion, North Easton, Massachusetts

Ames Family Papers. Sophia Smith Collection. Smith College, Northampton, Massachusetts

Clara Barton Papers, Library of Congress, Washington, D.C.

Benjamin F. Butler Collection, Lowell Historical Society, Center for Lowell History, Lowell, Massachusetts

Benjamin F. Butler Papers, Archives and Special Collections, Colby College, Waterville, Maine

Benjamin F. Butler Papers, Boston Public Library, Boston, Massachusetts

Benjamin F. Butler Papers, Library of Congress, Washington, D.C.

Civil War Collection (MSS #20), Rose Library Archival Materials, Emory University, Atlanta, Georgia

Civil War Collection (Coll. #524), Howard Tilton Library Special Collections. Tulane University, New Orleans, Louisiana

Dodd Family Papers (Coll. #123), Amistad Research Center. Tulane University, New Orleans, Louisiana

Blake Goodrich Reminiscences, Robert Woodruff Library. Emory University, Atlanta, Georgia

Charles L. Harrod Journal (M-923), Howard Tilton Library Special Collections. Tulane University, New Orleans, Louisiana

Heslip-Ruffin Family Papers (Coll. #179), Amistad Research Center. Tulane University, New Orleans, Louisiana

Alfred A. Parmenter Papers (Coll. #690), Howard Tilton Library Special Collections. Tulane University, New Orleans, Louisiana

B. B. Smith Diary (M 1123), Howard Tilton Library Special Collections. Tulane University, New Orleans, Louisiana

Edwin M. Stanton Papers, Library of Congress, Washington, D.C.

DATABASES
Via Ancestry.com

Harvard College Class of 1875 Secretary's Report, no. 8, 1875–1905
Massachusetts Death Records, 1841–1915
Massachusetts Marriages, 1633–1850
Massachusetts Mason Membership Cards, 1733–1990
Massachusetts State and Federal Naturalization Records, 1798–1950
Massachusetts Town Birth Records, 1620–1850
Massachusetts Town and Vital Records, 1620–1988
Missouri Marriages, 1766–1983
Missouri Marriage Records, 1805–2002
New Hampshire Birth Index, 1659–1900
New Hampshire Births and Christenings Index, 1714–1904
New Hampshire Marriage Records Index, 1637–1947
New Hampshire Wills and Probate Records, 1643–1982
US Census Records
US City Directories, 1822–1995
US Civil War Draft Registration Records, 1863–65
US High School Student Lists, 1821–1923

Via Fold3.com

Letters Received by the Adjutant General, 1805–1821

PUBLISHED PRIMARY SOURCES
Newspapers and Magazines

Aberdeen (S.D.) Daily News
Albany Journal
American Advocate (Hallowell, Me.)
American Sentry
Army and Navy Journal
Augusta (Ga.) Chronicle
Augusta (Ga.) Daily Constitutionalist
Baltimore Exchange
Barre (Mass.) Gazette
Berkshire County Whig
Boise Statesman
Boston Commercial Gazette
Boston Courier
Boston Daily Advertiser
Boston Daily Atlas

Boston Daily Evening Transcript
Boston Daily Journal
Boston Globe
Boston Herald
Boston Journal
Boston Post
Boston Press and Post
Boston Recorder
Boston Semi-weekly Courier
Boston Star
Boston Sunday Herald
Boston Transcript
Centinel of Freedom (Newark, N.J.)
Charleston (S.C.) Courier
Charleston (S.C.) Mercury

Cincinnati Daily Gazette

Cleveland Plain Dealer

Colby Echo

Constitution (Washington, D.C.)

Council Bluffs (Iowa) Bugle

Daily Constitutional Union (Washington, D.C.)

Daily Critic (Washington, D.C.)

Daily Inter Ocean (Chicago)

Daily National Intelligencer (Washington, D.C.)

Daily Ohio Statesman

Detroit Evening Journal

Detroit Plaindealer

Dover (N.H.) Daily Republican

Emancipator & Republican (Boston)

Essex Register (Salem, Mass.)

Essex Statesman (Salem, Mass.)

Farmer's Cabinet (Amherst, N.H.)

Flake's Bulletin (Galveston, Tex.)

Frederick Douglass's Paper

Harper's Weekly

Hartford Daily Courant

Indianapolis Freeman

Jackson (Mich.) Daily Citizen

Kansas City Star

The Liberator

Literary Digest

Lowell (Mass.) Daily Citizen and News

Maine Cultivator and Hallowell Gazette

Massachusetts Spy (Worcester)

Michigan Weekly Citizen (Jackson, Mich.)

National Aegis (Worcester, Mass.)

National Review

New Albany (Ind.) Daily Ledger

New England Torchlight

New Hampshire Patriot and State Gazette

New Haven (Conn.) Columbian Register

New London Daily Chronicle

New York Arcadian

New York Commercial Advertiser

New York Daily Tribune

New York Evening Journal (Albany, N.Y.)

New York Evening Post

New York Herald

New York Times

New York Times Book Review

Oregonian

Parsons (Kans.) Weekly Blade

Philadelphia Inquirer

Pittsfield (Mass.) Sun

Portland (Me.) Daily Eastern Argus

Portland Weekly Advertiser

Portsmouth Oracle

Puck

Register (Sandusky, Ohio)

Repository and Observer (Concord, N.H.)

Rhode Island Evening Press

Richmond Whig

Sacramento Record-Union

Salem (Mass.) Observer

Salem (Mass.) Register

San Francisco Daily Evening Bulletin

Springfield (Mass.) Republican

St. Louis Republic

The Sun

Voice of Industry

Washington Bee

Washington Star

Wheeling (W.Va.) Register

Books and Articles

Ames, Blanche Butler. *Chronicles from the Nineteenth Century: Family Letters of Blanche Butler and Adelbert Ames*. 2 vols. Privately published, 1957.

Bland, T. A. *Life of Benjamin Butler*. Boston: Lee & Shepard, 1879.

Butler, Benjamin F. *Argument of Benjamin F. Butler before the Committee on Commerce of the House of Representatives for an Investigation of the Monopolies of the Standard Oil Company and Its Confederates*. Washington, D.C.: Gibson Brothers, 1880.

———. *Argument before the Tewksbury Investigation Committee by Governor Benjamin F. Butler upon the Fact Disclosed during the Recent Investigation, July 15, 1883.* N.p., 1883.

———. *Butler's Book: Autobiography and Personal Reminiscences of Major-General Benjamin F. Butler.* Boston: A. M. Thayer, 1892.

———. *Character and Results of the War: How to Prosecute and How to End It.* Philadelphia: Privately printed, 1863.

———. *Civil Rights: Speech of Hon. Benjamin F. Butler, Delivered before the House of Representatives, January 7, 1874.* Washington, D.C.: Government Printing Office, 1874.

———. *Dissertation Delivered before the Alumni of Colby University, July 2, 1889.* N.p., 1889.

———. *Honors Due the Private Soldier.* Washington, D.C.: J. G. White, Job and Book, 1878.

———. *Independence of Cuba: Speech of Hon. Benjamin F. Butler of Massachusetts.* Washington, D.C.: F. & J. Rives and Geo. A. Bailey, 1870.

———. *Ku-Klux Outrages in the South.* Washington, D.C.: M'Gill and Witherow, 1871.

———. *Letter of General Benj. F. Butler to Hon. E. R. Hoar.* Privately printed, 1876.

———. *Private and Official Correspondence of Gen. Benjamin F. Butler during the Period of the Civil War.* 5 vols. Norwood, Mass.: Plimpton, 1917.

———. *Reconstruction of Georgia.* Washington, D.C.: F. & J. Rives and Geo. A. Bailey, 1869.

———. *Remarks of the Honorable Benjamin F. Butler upon the Payment of Southern War Claims for Damages Done by the Army.* Washington, D.C.: n.p., 1879.

———. *Speech of Maj.-Gen. Benj. F. Butler upon the Campaign before Richmond, 1864.* Boston: Wright & Potter, 1865.

———. *Suggestions of the Effect of an Imported Laboring Class upon American Institutions.* Washington, D.C.: M'Gill and Witherow, 1870.

——— et al. *Remarks of Hons. G. S. Boutwell, B. F. Butler, and Thomas Williams on the President's Veto of the Reconstruction Bill; Delivered in the House of Representatives, July 19, 1867.* Washington, D.C.: Congressional Globe Office, 1867.

Catalogue of the Officers and Students of Dartmouth College: October, 1834. Newport, N.H.: Simon Brown, Printer, 1834.

A Chaplain's Campaign with Gen. Butler. New York: Printed for the author, 1865.

Coburn, Frederick W. *History of Lowell and Its People.* 2 vols. New York: Lewis Historical, 1920.

Cogswell, Elliot C. *History of Nottingham, Deerfield, and Northwood.* Manchester, N.H.: John B. Clarke, 1878.

Dickens, Charles. *American Notes for General Circulation.* London: Chapman and Hall, 1842.

Flipper, Henry Ossian. *The Colored Cadet at West Point.* Lincoln: University of Nebraska Press, 1998.

Foner, Philip S., ed. *The Life and Writings of Frederick Douglass.* 5 vols. New York: International, 1952.

General Catalogue of the Officers, Graduates and Former Students of Colby College. Waterville, Me.: Published by the College, 1920.

Gienapp, William E. *The Civil War and Reconstruction: A Documentary Collection*. New York: W. W. Norton, 2001.

Grant, Ulysses S. *Personal Memoirs*. New York: Penguin, 1999.

Hale, Edward Everett. *The Story of the States: The Story of Massachusetts*. Boston: D. Lothrop, 1891.

Impeachment: Selected Materials. Committee on the Judiciary, House of Representatives, 93rd Cong., 1st sess. Washington, D.C.: U.S. Government Printing Office, 1973.

Larcom, Lucy. *A New England Girlhood: Outlined from Memory*. Boston: Northeastern University Press, 1986.

Leonard, Clara T. *The Present Condition of Tewksbury*. Boston: Franklin, 1883.

Lossing, Benson J. *Pictorial History of the Civil War in the United States of America*. Vol. 1. Philadelphia: George W. Childs, 1866.

Lowell: A City of Spindles. Lowell, Mass.: Trades and Labor Council, 1900.

A Memorial of Benjamin F. Butler from the City of Boston. Boston: City Council, 1893.

Parton, James. *General Butler in New Orleans*. New York: Mason Brothers, 1864.

Pierce, Frederick Clifton. *Batchelder, Batcheller Genealogy: Descendants of Rev. Stephen Bachiler, of England*. Chicago: W. B. Conkey, 1898.

Pomeroy, Mark M. *Life and Public Services of Benjamin F. Butler*. New York: N.p., 1868.

Porter, David D. *Incidents and Anecdotes of the Civil War*. New York: D. Appleton, 1885.

Proceedings in the City of Lowell at the Semi-centennial Celebration. Lowell, Mass.: Pen Hallow, 1876.

Proceedings in Massachusetts and New Hampshire on the Death of the Hon. Jeremiah Mason. Boston: J. Wilson, 1849.

Reade, Philip Hildreth. *Origin and Genealogy of the Hildreth Family of Lowell, Mass*. Lowell, Mass.: Privately published, 1892.

Rice, Allen Thorndike, ed. *Reminiscences of Abraham Lincoln by Distinguished Men of His Time*. New York: North American Review, 1888.

Robinson, William S. *The Salary Grab*. Boston: Lee & Shepard, 1873.

Russell, William Howard. *My Diary: North and South*. Boston: T. O. H. P. Burnham, 1863.

Senate Report 108, part 3, *Report of the Joint Committee, 1863*, 37th Cong., 3rd Sess.

Sherman, William Tecumseh. *Memoirs*. New York: Penguin, 2000.

War of the Rebellion: A Compilation of the Official Records of the Union and Confederate Armies. Washington, D.C.: Government Printing Office, 1880–1901.

SECONDARY SOURCES
Newspapers and Magazines

Colby Echo
Colby Library Quarterly

Books and Articles

Abbott, Richard H. *For Free Press and Equal Rights: Republican Newspapers in the Reconstruction South*. Athens: University of Georgia Press, 2004.

Axelrod, Alan. *The Horrid Pit: The Battle of the Crater, the Civil War's Cruelest Mission*. New York: Carroll & Graf, 2007.

Belz, Herman. *Abraham Lincoln, Constitutionalism, and Equal Rights in the Civil War Era*. New York: Fordham University Press, 1998.

Bergeron, Paul H. *Andrew Johnson's Civil War and Reconstruction*. Knoxville: University of Tennessee Press, 2011.

Beringer, Richard E., et al. *Why the South Lost the Civil War*. Athens: University of Georgia Press, 1986.

Bernstein, Iver. *The New York City Draft Riots: Their Significance for American Society and Politics in the Age of the Civil War*. New York: Oxford University Press, 1990.

Borritt, Gabor S., ed. *Why the Confederacy Lost*. New York: Oxford University Press, 1992.

Brands, H. W. *The Man Who Saved the Union: Ulysses Grant in War and Peace*. New York: Doubleday, 2012.

Brown, D. Alexander. *The Galvanized Yankees*. Urbana: University of Illinois Press, 1963.

Brown, Thomas J. *The Public Art of Civil War Commemoration: A Brief History with Documents*. Boston: Bedford/St. Martin's, 2004.

Buell, Thomas B. *The Warrior Generals: Combat Leadership in the Civil War*. New York: Three Rivers, 1997.

Bunting, Josiah, III. *Ulysses S. Grant*. New York: Times Books, 2004.

Burkhardt, George S. *Confederate Rage, Yankee Wrath: No Quarter in the Civil War*. Carbondale: Southern Illinois University Press, 2007.

Campbell, Jacqueline. "The Unmeaning Twaddle about Order 28: Benjamin Butler and Confederate Women in New Orleans, 1862." *Journal of the Civil War Era* 2 (March 2012): 11–30.

Carnahan, Burrus M. *Act of Justice: Lincoln's Emancipation Proclamation and the Law of War*. Lexington: University Press of Kentucky, 2007.

Cary, Richard. "A Dozen Ben Butler Letters." *Colby Quarterly* 6 (September 1964): 486–97.

Case, Lynn M., and Warren F. Spencer. *The United States and France: Civil War Diplomacy*. Philadelphia: University of Pennsylvania Press, 1970.

Cecelski, David S. *The Fire of Freedom: Abraham Galloway & the Slaves' Civil War*. Chapel Hill: University of North Carolina Press, 2012.

Chester, Giraud. *Embattled Maiden: The Life of Anna Dickinson.* New York: G. P. Putnam's Sons, 1951.

Cisco, Walter. *War Crimes against Southern Civilians.* Gretna, La.: Pelican, 2007.

Coolidge, John. *Mill and Mansion: A Study of the Architecture and Society in Lowell, Massachusetts, 1820–1865.* Amherst: University of Massachusetts Press, 1993.

Cornish, Dudley Taylor. *The Sable Arm: Black Troops in the Union Army, 1861–1865.* Lawrence: University Press of Kansas, 1987.

Curran, Thomas F. *Soldiers of Peace: Civil War Pacifism and the Postwar Radical Peace Movement.* New York: Fordham University Press, 2003.

Dirck, Brian R. *Abraham Lincoln and White America.* Lawrence: University Press of Kansas, 2012.

———. *Lincoln and the Constitution.* Carbondale: Southern Illinois University Press, 2012.

———, ed. *Lincoln Emancipated: The President and the Politics of Race.* Carbondale: Southern Illinois University Press, 2007.

Downing, David C. *A South Divided: Portraits of Dissent in the Confederacy.* Nashville, Tenn.: Cumberland House, 2007.

Downs, Jim. *Sick from Freedom: African-American Illness and Suffering during the Civil War and Reconstruction.* New York: Oxford University Press, 2012.

Dublin, Thomas. *Women at Work: The Transformation of Work and Community in Lowell, Massachusetts, 1826–1860.* New York: Columbia University Press, 1993.

Duerk, John A. "Elijah P. Lovejoy: Anti-Catholic Abolitionist." *Journal of the Illinois State Historical Society* 108 (Summer 2015): 103–21.

Egnal, Marc. *Clash of Extremes: The Economic Origins of the Civil War.* New York: Hill and Wang, 2009.

Einolf, Christopher. *George Thomas: Virginian for the Union.* Norman: University of Oklahoma Press, 2007.

Escott, Paul D. *"What Shall We Do with the Negro?": Lincoln, White Racism, and Civil War America.* Charlottesville: University of Virginia Press, 2009.

Flesche, Andre. *The Revolution of 1861: The American Civil War in the Age of Nationalist Conflict.* Chapel Hill: University of North Carolina Press, 2012.

Foner, Eric. *Reconstruction: America's Unfinished Revolution, 1863–1877.* New York: Harper & Row, 1988.

Foote, Shelby. *The Civil War, a Narrative: Red River to Appomattox.* New York: Random House, 1974.

Foreman, Amanda. *A World on Fire: Britain's Crucial Role in the American Civil War.* New York: Random House, 2010.

Frassanito, William A. *Grant and Lee: The Virginia Campaigns, 1864–1865.* New York: Charles Scribner's Sons, 1983.

Frazier, Donald S. *Fire in the Cane Field: The Federal Invasion of Louisiana and Texas, January 1861–January 1863.* Buffalo Gap, Tex.: State House, 2009.

Freehling, William W. *The South vs. the South: How Anti-Confederate Southerners Shaped the Course of the Civil War.* New York: Oxford University Press, 2001.

Gallman, J. Matthew. *America's Joan of Arc: The Life of Anna Elizabeth Dickinson*. New York: Oxford University Press, 2006.

Glatthaar, Joseph T. *Forged in Battle: The Civil War Alliance of Black Soldiers and White Officers*. New York: Meridian, 1990.

Goldsmith, Barbara. *Other Powers: The Age of Suffrage, Spiritualism, and the Scandalous Victoria Woodhull*. New York: Alfred A. Knopf, 1998.

Grimsley, Mark. *The Hard Hand of War: Union Military Policy toward Southern Civilians, 1861–1865*. New York: Cambridge University Press, 1995.

Groom, Winston. *Vicksburg, 1863*. New York: Alfred A. Knopf, 2009.

Hamilton, Daniel W. *The Limits of Sovereignty: Property Confiscation in the Union and the Confederacy during the Civil War*. Chicago: University of Chicago Press, 2007.

Harris, William C. *Lincoln and the Union Governors*. Carbondale: Southern Illinois University Press, 2013.

Hearn, Chester G. *When the Devil Came Down to Dixie: Ben Butler in New Orleans*. Baton Rouge: Louisiana State University Press, 2000.

Heidler, David S., and Jeanne T. Heidler, eds. *Encyclopedia of the American Civil War*. Vol. 1. Santa Barbara, Calif.: ABC-CLIO, 2000.

Hess, Earl J. *The Civil War in the West: Victory and Defeat from the Appalachians to the Mississippi*. Chapel Hill: University of North Carolina Press, 2012.

———, *Trench Warfare under Grant & Lee: Field Fortifications in the Overland Campaign*. Chapel Hill: University of North Carolina Press, 2007.

Hollandsworth, James G., Jr. *The Louisiana Native Guards: The Black Military Experience during the Civil War*. Baton Rouge: Louisiana State University Press, 1995.

Holzman, Robert S. *Stormy Ben Butler*. New York: Macmillan, 1954.

Jackson, L. P. "The Origin of Hampton Institute." *Journal of Negro History* 10 (April 1925): 131–49.

Janney, Caroline E. *Remembering the Civil War: Reunion and the Limits of Reconciliation*. Chapel Hill: University of North Carolina Press, 2013.

Joiner, Gary D., ed. *Little to Eat and Thin Mud to Drink: Letters, Diaries, and Memoirs from the Red River Campaigns, 1863–1864*. Knoxville: University of Tennessee Press, 2007.

Josephy, Alvin M., Jr. *The Civil War in the American West*. New York: Vintage, 1991.

Kantrowitz, Stephen. *More than Freedom: Fighting for Black Citizenship in a White Republic, 1829–1889*. New York: Penguin, 2012.

Kendi, Ibram X. *How to Be an Antiracist*. New York: One World, 2019.

Lankford, Nelson D. *Cry Havoc! The Crooked Road to Civil War, 1861*. New York: Viking, 2007.

Lazerow, Jama. "Religion and the New England Mill Girl: A New Perspective on an Old Theme." *New England Quarterly* 60 (September 1987): 429–58.

Leonard, Elizabeth D. *Lincoln's Avengers: Justice, Revenge, and Reunion after the Civil War*. New York: W. W. Norton, 2004.

———. *Lincoln's Forgotten Ally: Judge Advocate General Joseph Holt of Kentucky*. Chapel Hill: University of North Carolina Press, 2011.

———. *Men of Color to Arms! Black Soldiers, Indian Wars, and the Quest for Equality.* New York: W. W. Norton, 2010.

———. *Slaves, Slaveholders, and a Kentucky Community's Struggle toward Freedom.* Lexington: University Press of Kentucky, 2019.

———. *Yankee Women: Gender Battles in the Civil War.* New York: W. W. Norton, 1994.

Logue, Larry M., and Michael Barton. *The Civil War Veteran: A Historical Reader.* New York: New York University Press, 2007.

Manning, Chandra. *What This Cruel War Is Over: Soldiers, Slavery, and the Civil War.* New York: Alfred A. Knopf, 2007.

Marriner, Ernest C. "Ben Butler at Colby College." *Colby Quarterly* 11 (September 1964): 479–85.

———. *The History of Colby College.* Waterville, Me.: Colby College Press, 1963.

Marten, James, and A. Kristen Foster. *More Than a Contest between Armies: Essays on the Civil War Era.* Kent, Ohio: Kent State University Press, 2008.

Marvel, William. *Tarnished Victory: Finishing Lincoln's War.* Boston: Houghton Mifflin Harcourt, 2011.

Masur, Louis P. *Lincoln's Hundred Days: The Emancipation Proclamation and the War for the Union.* Cambridge, Mass.: Belknap, 2012.

McFeely, William S. *Grant: A Biography.* New York: W. W. Norton, 1981.

McGinty, Brian. *The Body of John Merryman: Abraham Lincoln and the Suspension of Habeas Corpus.* Cambridge, Mass.: Harvard University Press, 2011.

McPherson, James M. *Ordeal by Fire: The Civil War and Reconstruction.* 3rd ed. Boston: McGraw Hill, 2001.

———. *War on the Waters: The Union & Confederate Navies, 1861–1865.* Chapel Hill: University of North Carolina Press, 2012.

McWhirter, Christian. *Battle Hymns: The Power and Popularity of Music in the Civil War.* Chapel Hill: University of North Carolina Press, 2012.

Mitgang, Herbert. *Abraham Lincoln: A Press Portrait.* New York: Fordham University Press, 2000.

Mountcastle, Clay. *Punitive War: Confederate Guerrillas and Union Reprisals.* Lawrence: University Press of Kansas, 2009.

Myers, Barton A. *Executing Daniel Bright: Race, Loyalty, and Guerrilla Violence in a Coastal Carolina Community, 1861–1865.* Baton Rouge: Louisiana State University Press, 2009.

Nash, Howard P., Jr. *Stormy Petrel: The Life and Times of General Benjamin F. Butler, 1818–1893.* Teaneck, N.J.: Fairleigh Dickinson University Press, 1969.

Nelson, Megan Kate. *Ruin Nation: Destruction and the American Civil War.* Athens: University of Georgia Press, 2012.

Nelson, Scott, and Carol Sheriff. *A People at War: Civilians and Soldiers in America's Civil War.* New York: Oxford University Press, 2007.

Nevins, Allan. *Ordeal of the Union: Fruits of Manifest Destiny, 1847–1852.* New York: Charles Scribner's Sons, 1947.

————. *Ordeal of the Union: A House Dividing, 1852–1857*. New York: Charles Scribner's Sons, 1947.

————. *The Emergence of Lincoln: Prologue to Civil War, 1859–1861*. New York: Charles Scribner's Sons, 1950.

————. *The War for the Union: The Improvised War, 1861–1862*. New York: Charles Scribner's Sons, 1959.

————. *The War for the Union: The Organized War, 1863–1864*. New York: Charles Scribner's Sons, 1971.

————. *The War for the Union: The Organized War to Victory, 1864–1865*. New York: Charles Scribner's Sons, 1971.

————. *The War for the Union: War Becomes Revolution, 1862–1863*. New York: Charles Scribner's Sons, 1960.

Nolan, Dick. *Benjamin Franklin Butler: The Damnedest Yankee*. New York: Presidio, 1991.

Norgren, Jill. *Belva Lockwood: The Woman Who Would Be President*. New York: NYU Press, 2007.

Oakes, James. *Freedom National: The Destruction of Slavery in the United States, 1861–1865*. New York: W. W. Norton, 2013.

Perret, Geoffrey. *Ulysses Grant: Soldier & President*. New York: Random House, 1997.

Pickenpaugh, Roger. *Captives in Gray: The Civil War Prisons of the Union*. Tuscaloosa: University of Alabama Press, 2009.

Rael, Patrick. *Eighty-Eight Years: The Long Death of Slavery in the United States, 1777–1865*. Athens: University of Georgia Press, 2015.

Raymond, Harold B. "The 'Beast' at the Top of the Stairs." *Colby Echo*, April 21, 1977.

————. "Ben Butler: A Reappraisal." *Colby Library Quarterly* 11 (September 1964): 445–79.

Reardon, Carol. *With a Sword in One Hand & Jomini in the Other: The Problem of Military Thought in the Civil War North*. Chapel Hill: University of North Carolina Press, 2012.

Richardson, Heather Cox. *West from Appomattox: The Reconstruction of America after the Civil War*. New Haven, Conn.: Yale University Press, 2007.

Rodrigue, John C. *Lincoln and Reconstruction*. Carbondale: Southern Illinois University Press, 2013.

Rogers, D. Laurence. *Apostles of Equality: The Birneys, the Republicans, and the Civil War*. East Lansing: Michigan State University Press, 2011.

Samito, Christian G. *Becoming American under Fire: Irish Americans, African Americans, and the Politics of Citizenship during the Civil War Era*. Ithaca, N.Y.: Cornell University Press, 2009.

Shaffer, Donald R. *After the Glory: The Struggles of Black Civil War Veterans*. Lawrence: University Press of Kansas, 2004.

Shugerman, Jed Handelsman. "The Creation of the Department of Justice: Professionalization without Civil Rights or Civil Service." *Stanford Law Review* 66 (January 2014): 121–72.

Simon, John Y. *The Union Forever: Lincoln, Grant, and the Civil War.* Lexington: University Press of Kentucky, 2012.

Simpson, Brooks D. *Let Us Have Peace: Ulysses S. Grant and the Politics of War & Reconstruction, 1861–1868.* Chapel Hill: University of North Carolina Press, 1991.

———. *Ulysses S. Grant: Triumph over Adversity, 1822–1865.* Boston: Houghton Mifflin, 2000.

Smith, Earl H. *Mayflower Hill: A History of Colby College.* Hanover, N.H.: University Press of New England, 2006.

Smith, Jean Edward. *Grant.* New York: Simon & Schuster, 2001.

Smith, John David. *Lincoln and the U.S. Colored Troops.* Carbondale: Southern Illinois University Press, 2013.

Stahr, Walter. *Seward: Lincoln's Indispensable Man.* New York: Simon and Schuster, 2012.

Tomblin, Barbara Brooks. *Bluejackets and Contrabands: African Americans and the Union Navy.* Lexington: University Press of Kentucky, 2009.

Trefousse, Hans L. *Ben Butler: The South Called Him Beast!* New York: Twayne, 1957.

———. *Impeachment of a President: Andrew Johnson, the Blacks, and Reconstruction.* New York: Fordham University Press, 1999.

Underhill, Lois Beachy. *The Woman Who Ran for President: The Many Lives of Victoria Woodhull.* Bridgehampton, N.Y.: Bridge Works, 1995.

Varon, Elizabeth R. *Southern Lady, Yankee Spy: The True Story of Elizabeth Van Lew, a Union Agent in the Heart of the Confederacy.* New York: Oxford University Press, 2003.

Von Drehle, David. *Rise to Greatness: Abraham Lincoln and America's Most Perilous Year.* New York: Henry Holt, 2012.

Vorenberg, Michael. *The Emancipation Proclamation: A Brief History with Documents.* Boston: Bedford/St. Martin's, 2010.

Warner, Ezra J. *Generals in Blue: Lives of the Union Commanders.* Baton Rouge: Louisiana State University Press, 1964.

Werlich, Robert. *"Beast" Butler: The Incredible Career of Major-General Benjamin Franklin Butler.* Washington, D.C.: Quaker, 1962.

West, Richard S., Jr. *Lincoln's Scapegoat General: A Life of Benjamin F. Butler, 1818–1893.* Boston: Houghton Mifflin, 1965.

White, Jonathan W. *Abraham Lincoln and Treason in the Civil War: The Trials of John Merryman.* Baton Rouge: Louisiana State University Press, 2011.

Whites, LeAnn, and Alecia P. Long, eds. *Occupied Women: Gender, Military Occupation, and the American Civil War.* Baton Rouge: Louisiana University Press, 2009.

Whittemore, Edwin Carey. *Colby College, 1820–1925.* Waterville, Me.: Trustees of Colby College, 1927.

Witt, John Fabian. *Lincoln's Code: The Laws of War in American History.* New York: Free Press, 2012.

Wongsrichanalai, Kanisorn. *Northern Character: College-Educated New Englanders, Honor, Nationalism, and Leadership in the Civil War Era.* New York: Fordham University Press, 2016.

Work, David. *Lincoln's Political Generals.* Urbana: University of Illinois Press. 2009.

Index

The abbreviation BFB refers to Benjamin Franklin Butler.

Antrobus, John, xvi, 155, 268, 310n56

Army and Navy Union, 161

Army of the James, BFB as commander of, xiv, 138–40, 144–48, 150, 158–59, 162, 164, 174, 213, 308n27

Arthur, Chester, 234

Ashley, James, 172–73, 179

Babcock, Rufus, 13, 285n21, 286n22

Bachelder, Elizabeth Barber Stevens (niece), 275

Bachelder, John B., 275

Bagley, Sarah, 29–30

Baker, Frank, 66–68

Balch, T. E., 327n60

Baltimore, Maryland: attack on Massachusetts Volunteer Militia in, 57–58, 63, 295–96n13; BFB's occupation of Federal Hill, 63–64, 65, 70, 126, 298n35, 300n46; secession activists in, 62–63

Banks, Nathaniel Prentiss: as commander of Department of the Gulf, 119, 120, 123, 124–26, 155, 306n66; as commander of Fort Monroe, 71–72; as governor of Massachusetts, 39, 43, 49; and Louisiana Native Guard, 125; as major general of US volunteers, 64; Maryland command of, 75; as speaker of Massachusetts legislature, 33, 39; as US Congressman, 171

Barney, Hiram, 157–58

Barrett, O. D., 273, 275

Barton, Clara, 164, 241

Bates College, 281n7

Baton Rouge, Battle of, 95, 105

Battle of the Wilderness, 140, 141

Beach, Erasmus, 41, 293n32

Beauregard, P. G. T., 93, 142, 144

Beecher, Catharine, 210

Beecher, Henry Ward, 210

Bell, John, 49

Bell, Joseph M., 119

Belle Isle prison, Richmond, 135

Berry, William B., 238

Big Bethel, Battle of, 72–73, 77, 93, 127, 152, 298n38, 299n39, 300n46

Bingham, John A., 176

Birney, David, 147

Bishop, Robert R., 239

Black, Jeremiah, 166

Black Americans: appreciation for BFB, xiii–xiv, 70, 85, 158–59, 188–89, 197, 202, 216, 220, 223, 238, 250–51, 268, 274, 277, 279, 317n51; Nathaniel Prentiss Banks on military service of, 125; BFB on Black southerners' self-defense, 207; BFB on capacity for military service, 104–8, 128, 196, 223, 303–4n31, 304n34, 306n66; BFB on civil and political rights of, xviii, xix, 132, 157–59, 161–64, 169–70, 171, 174–75, 186, 189, 196–97, 201, 202–3, 221, 222, 228, 238–39, 245, 251, 313–14n29, 315–16n48, 326n55; BFB on employment of Black civilians, 132, 135, 136; and BFB's death, 274; BFB's framework for "free labor" system, 109; BFB's recruitment of Black soldiers, 130–32, 136; disenfranchisement in South, 206; federal policies toward troops, 131–32, 307n12, 307n14; Ku Klux Klan targeting, 179–80; militia units of, 206–7, 208, 228; in New Orleans, 89, 94; and New York City draft riots, 128; Republican Party support for, 179–80, 182, 201, 314n36; self-segregation of, 223; West Point opened to, 171, 175, 182–83. *See also* enslaved Blacks; freedpeople

Black male suffrage, 163, 167–68, 170, 172, 179–80, 183, 312n9

Blackwell, Henry, 219–20

Blaine, James G., xii, 254, 258–59

Blair, Frank, Jr., 236, 239

Blair, Montgomery, 68–69, 71, 73, 78, 97, 298n37

Bland-Allison Coinage Act, 227

Bleeding Kansas, 37, 40

Bonney, Arthur P., 41

Booth, John Wilkes, 173, 313n25

Boston, Massachusetts, xiv, 2, 28, 37

Bosworth, George Whitefield, 17

Boutwell, George S., 33

Bowdoin College, 49, 281n7

Bowe, W. J. S., 251

Breckinridge, John C., 40, 48–49, 95

255; and ten-hour workday, 29–30, 33, 34, 35, 41, 171; US House of Representative election of 1858, 41

—AS US CONGRESSMAN: Appropriations Committee assignment, 172–73; and Black Americans' rights, 174–75, 186, 315–16n48; candidacies for, 35, 169–71, 172, 199, 215–20; as chair of committee investigating assassination of Abraham Lincoln, 174; currency and national finance questions, 172–73, 175, 181, 183–84, 197–98, 218–19, 224, 226–29, 233; dispute over doorkeeper of House, 229–30; electoral loss in 1874, 199–200, 201, 202; and freedpeople, 175, 187; house in Washington, DC, 179, 187; as House manager of impeachment of Andrew Johnson, 176–77; Ku Klux Klan threats to, 178; and patronage seekers, 178, 180–81, 224; policies of, xviii; political isolation of, 187; and Reconstruction, 171, 172, 180; reelection campaign, 178–79; speeches of, 173, 174–75, 176, 177, 178, 181–82, 184, 187, 188, 196–97, 201, 230, 233, 315n44; terms in House, 171–72, 189, 197, 199, 220–21, 223, 224, 226–30, 233, 250

—WORKS OF: "The Abolitionists" college essay, 286n24; *Private and Official Correspondence*, xii, 296n18; "The Private Soldiers in the War of the Rebellion," 230. See also *Butler's Book* (BFB)

Butler, Charlie (nephew), 17, 289n7

Butler, Charlotte Ellison (mother): and BFB's education, 10–11; BFB's relationship with, 5, 13, 18, 27, 193, 283n7, 283n8, 289n7; in BFB's will, 32; birth of, 1, 282n1; as boardinghouse keeper, 6, 7, 9, 25, 28, 290n12; burial of, 275; Calvinist faith of, 1, 5, 11, 12; death of, 193; family background of, 282n3; financial insecurity of, 4–5, 6, 16, 21, 185; marriage of, 1, 2–4, 282n2; as mother and stepmother, 1–6, 283n8; property of, 51; in Sonoma, California, 287n30, 289n7

Butler, George H. (nephew): alcohol problems of, 194, 205, 226, 235, 236, 264,

318n59; BFB's financial support of, 66, 137, 205, 264, 297n28; birth of, 17; burial of, 264, 275; and Sarah Butler's death, 211, 212; at Fort Monroe, 65–66

Butler, Joanna L. (sister-in-law), 17, 26, 137, 194, 226, 236, 264, 287n30, 289n7

Butler, John (father), 1–4, 18, 21, 32, 275, 282n2, 283n7

Butler, Paul (1st son), 27, 31, 275

Butler, Paul (2nd son): Blanche Butler Ames's correspondence with, 205; on Blanche Butler Ames's marriage, 193; in Annapolis, 65; BFB's correspondence with, 110, 190; and BFB's death, 273; and BFB's funeral, 275; BFB's relationship with, 212, 235–36, 266, 273; in BFB's will, 32; birth of, 31; Sarah Butler's correspondence with, 190, 192; and Civil War preparations, 62; education of, 52, 189–91, 205, 212, 242, 333n44; at Fort Monroe, 71, 130, 136, 141, 148; in Lowell, 75, 80, 110, 126, 145, 146; marriage of, 321n7; and United States Cartridge Company, 205, 225–26, 233, 266, 321n7

Butler, Sarah Batchelder, 2

Butler, Sarah Jones Hildreth (wife): as actress, 22, 26, 39; on Adelbert Ames, 192; Blanche Butler Ames's correspondence with, 79, 82, 116–18, 126, 128, 136, 139–41, 143, 187, 198, 205–6, 208–10, 298n36; in Annapolis, 65; BFB's correspondence with, 41, 44, 59, 61–62, 75–77, 95, 104, 105, 110–12, 113, 115, 118, 141–42, 145–48, 151, 153, 167, 190–91, 198, 293n36, 310n48, 319n61; BFB's meeting of, 22, 26; in BFB's will, 32; on BFB's work habits, 162; birth date of, 288–89n6; burial of, 274–75; on Andrew Jackson Butler, 115, 116–17, 136, 305n59; children of, 27, 31, 38, 52, 54; on children's education, 190; and Civil War preparations, 62; death of, 211–12, 231; dowry of, 291n23; at Fort Monroe, 65, 71, 129, 136, 139–43, 148; funeral of, 211, 212; health of, 110, 118, 205, 209–11, 290n16, 305n59; and Mary Todd Lincoln, 130; in Lowell, 75–76, 95, 110–11, 117–18,

labor movement: BFB's support for, 185, 186, 189, 218, 219, 224, 228, 229, 232, 233–34, 246, 247, 250, 253–57, 259, 316–17n51; BFB's support of ten-hour workday, 29–30, 33, 34, 35, 41, 171; and changing Lowell workforce, 290n12; and Chinese immigration, 184–85, 232, 237; Great Railroad Strike, 226–27, 325–26n46; Whig Party's opposition to, 33

La Mountain, John, 74–75

land reform, 158, 185, 219

Larcom, Lucy, 7

Lee, Robert E., 141, 143, 150, 159

Lefferts, Marshall, 58

Liberia, 223

Lincoln, Abraham: admission to US Supreme Court bar, 288n1; assassination of, 159, 173, 174, 313n25; and BFB as commander of Army of the James, 138, 139, 146; and BFB as commander of Department of Virginia and North Carolina, 129, 154, 159; BFB on "soft war" approach of, 59, 60, 100; on BFB's accomplishments, 124–25, 146; on BFB's contraband policy, 68–69; BFB sending David E. Twiggs's swords to, 113; and BFB's occupation of New Orleans, 97, 109; and BFB's recruiting expedition, 75–76, 77, 79; BFB's removal from command in Department of the Gulf, 119–20, 124; BFB's request for commission in regular army, 142; BFB's Ship Island assignment, 79; Sarah Butler's visit with, 130; cabinet of, 9, 111, 159, 161; call for troops in Civil War, 55–56, 61; debates with Stephen Douglas, 45; on emancipation, 100, 254; government officials appointed by, 172; inauguration of, 55; in Lowell, 31, 290n14; on Maryland, 62; and New Orleans economic activity, 112–13; policies toward Black troops, 307n12; political generals of, 295n6; as president, 54; presidential election of 1860, 48, 49; presidential election of 1864, 145, 147, 148–49, 150, 153, 309n39; promotion of BFB as major general of US volunteers, 64, 119; on provisions for runaway enslaved Blacks, 101–2; and George F. Shepley, 96; in Springfield, 17; staying of executions in Department of Virginia and North Carolina, 134

Lincoln, Mary Todd, 130, 190

Lincoln, Tad, 190

Lind, A. B., 228

Lockwood, Belva, 227

Long, John Davis, xiii, 234

Longstreet, James, 313n26

Lorimer, George C., 277

Lorimer, George Horace, 277

Lost Cause apologists, xiii, xv, 85, 221, 235, 269

Louisiana: Battle of Baton Rouge, 95, 105; secession of, 89. *See also* New Orleans, Louisiana

Louisiana Native Guard, 105, 106–9, 120, 125, 131, 306n66

Lovejoy, Elijah Parish, xvi–xvii, 14, 286n24

Lowell, Francis Cabot, 7

Lowell, Massachusetts: antislavery sentiments in, 14, 286n23; BFB joining Freemason's Pentucket Lodge in, 27–28, 29, 289n8; BFB's address at semicentennial celebration, 210; and BFB's death, 274–75; BFB's family in, 6–9, 65, 71, 75–76, 80, 95, 110–11, 117–18, 126, 128, 145–46, 284n12; BFB's law studies in, 18–20, 287–88n33; "Museum Building" of, 24, 51; political environment of, 21, 34; Republican caucus in, 162; Sanitary Commission fair in, 126; textile mills of, 6, 7, 9, 14, 21, 24–25, 28–30, 40, 210, 257, 286n23, 288n4, 291n22; tributes to BFB in, xiv; Whig capitalists of, 28–29

Lowell City Guard, 22

Lowell Female Labor Reform Association (LFLRA), 29, 30

Lowell High School, 9, 10, 11, 16, 284–85n15

lynchings, 128, 134

McClellan, George B.: and Battle of Philippi, 72; on BFB's Gulf of Mexico expedition, 79–80; Sarah Butler on, 111; death of, 268; Harrison's Landing letter, 69, 100;

relief, 86, 88–89, 121, 122; punishment of
Confederates, 91–93; quarantine regulations, 88, 227; sanitation infrastructure
of, 81, 88, 89, 122; social and political
difficulties of, 85; Special Orders No. 441,
109; supplying federal soldiers, 86–87, 88;
taxation of wealthy Confederate leaders,
89, 91, 121, 122; treatment of citizens in,
xv; troops needed for, 105–6, 125; yellow
fever epidemic prevention, 87–88, 89,
110, 118
New York City draft riots, 128, 149
North: indifference to South, 206; prejudice
against Blacks in, 69; reconciliationist
sentiment in, 181, 233; views on slavery
and emancipation in, 105
North Atlantic Blockading Squadron, 129,
144

O'Berne, James, 220–21
O'Brien, James, 244
Olcott, H. S., 132
Opdyke, George, 126
Ord, E. O. C., 147, 154
Ould, Robert, 135, 138, 153
Owen, Robert Dale, 132

Panic of 1819, 4
Panic of 1873, 171, 195, 198
Parton, James, 124, 143–44, 155, 222, 270,
301n1, 306n2, 310n51
Peake, Mary, 70
Peirce, Ebenezer W., 72–73
Pemberton Mill collapse, Lawrence, Massa-
chusetts, 43
People's Party, 256, 257
Phelps, Aurora H. C., 185
Phelps, John W., 79, 99–105
Philippi, Battle of, 72
Phillips, Eugenia Levy, 91
Phillips, Wendell, 170
Phillips Exeter Academy, 6, 7–8, 9
Pickett, George E., 133
Pierce, Edward L., 68, 73, 123–24, 128
Pierce, Franklin, 46
Plaisted, Harris Merrill, 164

Polk, James, 25
Pollock, C. H., 330n15
Pomeroy, Mark, 283–84n10
popular sovereignty, 37, 40, 41, 42, 45
Porter, David Dixon, 83, 150–52, 269,
301–2n2, 310n48
Port Hudson, 108, 306n66
Posse Comitatus Act, 227
Pryor, Roger A., 209, 234, 240, 321–22n15
Pullman Company, 316n48
Putnam, George W., 218

Quinby, Joseph B., 94

race relations: BFB's speeches on, 161–63,
174–75; and Lost Cause apologists, 221
racial justice: BFB's changing racist biases,
107; and BFB's law practice, 49–50; BFB's
leadership on, xviii–xix, 132, 135, 183,
202, 229
racism: BFB's reflection on, 196; of Chinese
Exclusion Act, 237; Ibram X. Kendi on
policies of, xviii–xix; at West Point, 183
Raymond, Harold B.: on BFB's administration of New Orleans, 121–22; at Colby
College, xv, 281n6; on oil portrait of BFB,
xvii, 282n10; reappraisal of BFB, xv, xvii,
xix
Reade, Philip Hildreth, 289n8, 291n20
Reconstruction: BFB on military governors
for former Confederate states, 161; BFB's
influence as US Congressman, 171, 172,
180; BFB's proposals for, 160–64, 167–69;
BFB's speeches on, 161–63, 169–70, 178;
Black American civil rights during, xviii;
and Bureau of Refugees, Freedmen, and
Abandoned Lands, 160; challenges of,
179; Ulysses S. Grant on, 177, 314n32;
Andrew Johnson's policies on, 160, 162,
167–69, 171–73; in wartime, 100
Reconstruction Acts, 172, 174
Republican National Convention (1860), 47
Republican Party: and Adelbert Ames,
206–9; antislavery agenda of, 39, 40, 43;
BFB's electoral loss in 1874, 199–200, 201,
202; and BFB's gubernatorial candidacy,

Soulé, Pierre, 92–93

South: BFB on economic and agricultural policies for, 160; BFB on freedpeople remaining in, 187, 311n2; BFB on social and racial transformation of, 169; BFB on treatment of Black Americans in, 162, 181–82, 197; Camilla Riot of 1868, 181; disenfranchised Black Americans of, 206; Federal troops in, 221, 222; neo-Confederate political power in, 180, 181, 216; John W. Phelps on collapse of society, 103, 105; Radical Republicans on social and racial transformation of, 159; Edwin M. Stanton on, 172; war claims of, 233; white supremacist terrorism in, 163, 171, 179–80, 183, 186–88, 197, 206–9, 219, 226, 228. *See also* Confederacy and Confederates

Southern Loyalists' Convention, 169

Specie Resumption Act, 233

Speed, James, 166

Stafford, Spencer H., 108, 120

Stanbery, Henry, 166

Standard Oil, 235

Stanton, Edwin M.: Nathaniel Prentiss Banks as rival of, 124; and BFB as commander of Department of Virginia and North Carolina, 129, 130, 135, 148; on BFB in City Point campaign, 141; BFB on advance on Richmond, 137; BFB on Black soldiers' conduct, 133–34; BFB on prisoner exchange, 135; BFB on recruitment of Black soldiers, 131; on BFB's argument in impeachment case, 176; BFB's communications with, 79, 82, 86, 92, 94, 96–97, 101–3, 105–6, 112–13, 301–2n2; on BFB's performance, 145–46; and BFB's Richmond advances, 138; and Andrew Johnson, 172, 175–76; and Abraham Lincoln's assassination, 173; and Abraham Lincoln's proposal for assignment of BFB, 124–25, 128; on military governors for former Confederate states, 161

Stanton, Elizabeth Cady, 181, 186

state's rights, 40, 294n38

Stevens, Betsey (half-sister), 2–5, 26, 211, 263–64, 272, 283n7

Stevens, Charlotte (niece), 263–64, 272–73, 275

Stevens, Daniel Barber, 5

Stevens, Thaddeus, 127, 161, 169, 170, 179, 232

Stevens, Thomas, 264

Stone, Lucy, 220

Stowe, Harriet Beecher, 35, 210

sugar plantations, cultivation with free labor, 109, 117, 160

Sumner, Charles: assault on, 40, 45; on BFB as commander of Department of the Gulf, 120, 124; civil rights bill sponsored with BFB, 196, 202; death of, 197; as namesake, 183; as US senator, 33, 40; and William B. Washburn, 189

Surratt, John, 173–74

Talbot, Thomas, 232–33

Tandy, C. H., 202

Tappan, Lewis, 299n41

Tarbox, John K., 216, 234

Taylor, Zachary, 30–31

telephone industry, 262

Ten Hour Movement, 30

Tenure of Office Act, 172, 175–76

Terry, Alfred H., 152

Tewksbury Almshouse, 241–42, 328–29n2, 329n3

Thirteenth Amendment, 158, 165, 202, 251

Thomas, George H., 151

Thomas, Lorenzo, 305n54

Thomas, William H., xiii

Tilden, Samuel, 221–22

Tilton, Elizabeth, 210

Tilton, Theodore, 210

Togus Veterans Administration Medical Center, 167

Townsend, James, 66–68

Train, Charles R., 41

transcontinental railroad, 171

Turner, Henry McNeal, 158–59, 179–80, 244, 314n36

Twiggs, David E., 53, 113, 270